LYNN RIGGS:
THE INDIGENOUS PLAYS

broadview editions
series editor: Martin R. Boyne

LYNN RIGGS:
THE INDIGENOUS PLAYS

edited by James H. Cox and Alexander Pettit

Preface by Daniel Heath Justice

broadview editions

BROADVIEW PRESS
Peterborough, Ontario, Canada

Founded in 1985, Broadview Press remains a wholly independent publishing house. Broadview's focus is on academic publishing; our titles are accessible to university and college students as well as scholars and general readers. With over 800 titles in print, Broadview has become a leading international publisher in the humanities, with world-wide distribution. Broadview is committed to environmentally responsible publishing and fair business practices.

© 2024 James H. Cox and Alexander Pettit

Library and Archives Canada Cataloguing in Publication

Title: Lynn Riggs : the Indigenous plays / edited by James H. Cox and Alexander Pettit ; preface by Daniel Heath Justice.
Names: Riggs, Lynn, 1899-1954, author. | Cox, James H. (James Howard), 1968- editor. | Pettit, Alexander, 1958- editor. | Justice, Daniel Heath, writer of preface.
Series: Broadview editions.
Description: Series statement: Broadview editions | Includes bibliographical references and index.
Identifiers: Canadiana (print) 20240303326 | Canadiana (ebook) 20240304055 | ISBN 9781554815913 (softcover) | ISBN 9781770489202 (PDF) | ISBN 9781460408513 (EPUB)
Subjects: LCSH: Riggs, Lynn, 1899-1954—Criticism and interpretation. | LCSH: American drama—20th century—History and criticism. | LCSH: American drama—Indian authors—History and criticism. | LCGFT: Drama.
Classification: LCC PS3535.I645 L96 2024 | DDC 812/.52—dc23

Broadview Editions
The Broadview Editions series is an effort to represent the ever-evolving canon of texts in the disciplines of literary studies, history, philosophy, and political theory. A distinguishing feature of the series is the inclusion of primary source documents contemporaneous with the work.

Advisory editor for this volume: Colleen Humbert

Broadview Press handles its own distribution in Canada and the United States:
PO Box 1243, Peterborough, Ontario K9J 7H5, Canada
555 Riverwalk Parkway, Tonawanda, NY 14150, USA
Tel: (705) 482-5915
email: customerservice@broadviewpress.com

For all territories outside of Canada and the United States, distribution is handled by Eurospan Group.

Broadview Press acknowledges the financial support of the Government of Canada for our publishing activities.

Canadä

Typesetting: George Kirkpatrick
Cover Design: Lisa Brawn

Broadview Press® is the registered trademark of Broadview Press Inc.

PRINTED IN CANADA

For Domino and Jacque and Ewan James and Claire

Contents

Contents

Acknowledgements

Many generous people helped us prepare this edition. We offer special thanks to Andy Couch and Brice Ezell. Andy, thank you for sharing, at all hours of the day or night, your knowledge of Riggs and his archives. Brice, we are grateful for your editorial skills, patience, and professionalism, all of which helped to keep chaos at bay. Hearty thanks are due as well to Twila Barnes, Martin Boyne, Kirby Brown, Charlotte Canning, Sarah Harris, Colleen Humbert, Jenna Hunnef, Daniel Heath Justice, George Kirkpatrick, Marjorie Mather, Cecelia Moore, Tere Mullin, Claire Vanhoutte Pettit, Michel Pharand, Chris Teuton, and Tara Trueman. For assistance with assembling archival sources, we thank Helen Conger, Jocelyn Clemings, and Bill Lubinger (Case Western Reserve University); I. Marc Carlson and Abigail Dairaghi (McFarlin Library, University of Tulsa); Paul Civitelli and Matthew Rowe (Beinecke Rare Book and Manuscript Library, Yale University); Katie Fortier and J.C. Johnson (Howard Gotlieb Archival Research Center, Boston University Libraries); Tyler Franklin (Western History Collections, University of Oklahoma Libraries); Kim Hazlett and Eileen Karsten (Donnelley and Lee Library, Lake Forest College); Kenneth Johnson and Chamisa Redmond Sr. (Library of Congress); Mariah Leavitt (Amherst College Library); Tom Lisanti (New York Public Library); John Martin (University of North Texas); Jason Nargis (McCormick Special Collections and Archives, Northwestern University); Mindy C. Pugh (Paul V. Galvin Library, Illinois Institute of Technology); Steve Robinson (Claremore Museum of History); and Brad Verter (Carpe Librum Rare Books, Manuscripts, and Archives). For funding and other forms of support, we thank the College of Liberal Arts, University of Texas at Austin, and UT's Department of English, especially the chair, Martin Kevorkian. Further assistance was provided by Vivienne Benesch (PlayMakers Repertory Company); Kristy Ironside; William Davies King; and Abbie Van Nostrand (Concord Theatricals). Primary material by Riggs, published and unpublished, appears courtesy of the Riggs family and their representative, Barbara Hogenson, Barbara Hogenson Agency (New York). This edition would not have been possible without their generosity and cooperation.

Figure 1: Allotments in the Cherokee Nation. Lynn Riggs's allotments are outlined in black. Image courtesy of the Oklahoma Historical Society.

Preface

Before His Time, Beyond His Place: Literary Legacies of Lynn Riggs

By Daniel Heath Justice (citizen, Cherokee Nation)

If you want to locate Lynn Riggs's allotments on a Cherokee Nation plat map from the early 1900s, both are to be found in Township 21 North, Range 15 East in what is now Oklahoma, just southwest of greater Claremore (see Figure 1). The larger allotment is in section 13, the second, smaller one in section 26. Even in these largely featureless beige charts covered with a patchwork of irregular dividing lines, it's easy to see that Riggs's two allotments are prime real estate within the capitalist values undergirding the US government's forced privatization of Cherokee lands.

Both allotments were near the fertile banks of the Verdigris River and on the edge of what would be the bustling community of Claremore, with its popular sulphur springs and profitable farms and ranches. Both allotments would have benefited from the river's proximity and had rich soil good for farming or for livestock pasturage. Waterways are among the very few identifiable geographic features to consistently appear on allotment maps, and the Verdigris meanders from top to bottom of this map in dynamic contrast to the rigidly artificial boundaries of squared-off plots with names and numbers. Like the horned snake Uk'tena of Cherokee tradition, a dangerous but powerfully anomalous creature associated with the chaotic watery underworld, the river is a disruptive force in the map's two-dimensional logic of order and arrangement, a great serpent's sinuous body stretching across the land, its antlered head and rattle-scaled tail vanishing somewhere off the map's horizons. The map's erratic grid structure presumes fixity, but the river's presence reminds us that these boundaries are an artificial imposition, that there's far more than what can be seen, a continuity and uncontainability beyond the conceptual limitations of the settler imaginary. The meaningful undercurrents that shape, inspire, and often even disfigure self, family, community, and history are a constant in Riggs's work; what isn't seen is often far more important than what's revealed.

But it wasn't just the economy or ecology of the region that would inform Riggs's early life and his later art. If you follow the

Verdigris fewer than 10 miles northward you find Claremore Mound, where pre-Trail of Tears Cherokee emigrants and a group of armed allies ambushed and slaughtered around eighty Osage women, children, and elders while Chief Gra-Mo'n (Claremont, or Claremore) and his warriors were on a buffalo hunt. This trauma-haunted site would be the primary geographic feature of Riggs's 1932 play, *The Cherokee Night*, and stands as a kind of symbolic epicenter for the complicated and morally contested Cherokee world into which Riggs was born and to which he would remain connected throughout his career.

Presence and absence, depths of shadow and light, history as liberation and binding alike, the weight of memory and tangled legacies of love and violence: for readers new to the work of Rollie Lynn Riggs, this volume is a welcome introduction to the key contexts, issues, and concerns of his writing, especially his most overtly Indigenous plays, with *The Cherokee Night* foremost among them. For those who are more familiar with his corpus, this volume is also most welcome, as it brings these creative texts into generative conversation with the last two decades of Riggs scholarship and the complexities of his life and artistry, while adding extensive new research and incisive analysis to that archive. Drawing on a wealth of primary texts and secondary scholarship, James Cox and Alexander Pettit provide a deep dive into Riggs's artistic significance; his complicated but compelling engagements of race, sexuality, class, and the politics of his time and, analogically, in ours; and his struggles to give dignified voice to the inhabitants of his two embraided worlds: the Indian Territory of his childhood, and the Oklahoma of his adulthood. Even Riggs's works ostensibly set far from the red soil of his imagination are rooted in those contexts, and this volume helps us understand both the how and the why of them. This is an exceptional scholarly contribution.

This gathering of Riggs's plays is also the first of its kind to fully address his sexuality as a vital aspect of his literary legacy, extending his critical contribution beyond Cherokee contexts. While Craig Womack dedicated an entire chapter of his landmark 1999 *Red on Red: Native American Literary Separatism* to a "Queer Oklahomo Theory" reading of Riggs's work, and although I and others have discussed these matters in the years since, the last collection to bring some of these plays together in 2003 couldn't fully address this issue. Thanks in part to a lessening of these restrictions by Riggs's current estate representatives, Cox and Pettit have addressed Riggs's life as a gay Cherokee artist with respect and fairness, and our understanding of his work is infinitely richer and more challenging as a result. As much as he was a queer Cherokee ancestor deserving of recognition, he was also a complicated one; his fetishizing of Brown and Black bodies is often quite disturbing, as is the physical and symbolic violence to which those bodies are subjected in his plays. Riggs was a light-skinned mixedblood Cherokee Nation citizen who chafed against anti-Native racism but nevertheless accepted some essentialist ideas about race, Indigeneity, modernity, and progress; he was also a passionate gay man who was drawn to what was often almost literally unspeakable in his era. To write openly and thoughtfully of these matters as Cox and Pettit have done means that we can better grapple with their implications on his life and his work, both the admirable and the painful.

While it's a firm cliché to say that an artist is "before their time," it certainly feels at least partially applicable to Riggs, whose subject matter and frank explorations of the shadow-side of humanity frequently scandalized his more conservative audiences while being hailed as revolutionary by his admirers. For all his undeniable artistic achievements, his contemporaries—audiences and critics alike—were not always kind to his work and often failed to understand its immersion in the particular histories and struggles of the region and its peoples. And as is made clear in the extensive editorial notes throughout, Riggs was not one to bend his vision to moral convention or crass commerce, so he struggled with economic insecurity throughout his life and suffered emotionally (and sometimes artistically) as a result. I suspect he would be both surprised and pleased to see the high regard with which his work is now held in multiple academic fields, with Indigenous literary studies foremost among them.

While he may well have been before his time as a playwright, he was, more importantly, *beyond his place*—that is, the Indian Territory of his birth, the land that would become Oklahoma but remained firmly distinct in life, memory, imagination, and law (as the US Supreme Court would affirm in its landmark 2020 decision, *McGirt v. Oklahoma*). There's a kind of double vision at work here, with two worlds and two temporalities interpenetrating one another, neither fully present but both existing simultaneously, with the cruel mundanity of settler Oklahoma always threatening but never quite displacing Indian Territory.

In considering this volume in that context, I can't help but consider the fate of the aborted State of Sequoyah. When the tribal leaders of Indian Territory finally accepted the inevitability of statehood, most came together in a movement to create a Native-majority state alongside the looming reality of settler-dominated Oklahoma. Named for the great statesman and inventor of the famed Cherokee syllabary, the State of Sequoyah would have maintained some measure of self-determination for the Five Tribes of Indian Territory; proponents even met in a constitutional convention in 1905 to draft the details and submit a proposal to Washington, DC. But President Theodore Roosevelt was wary of undermining Republican control in Congress, and Sequoyah would almost certainly have skewed Democrat, so the proposal was rejected and a single (Republican) State of Oklahoma moved forward. Native advocates didn't disappear, however; some would go on to contribute to the Oklahoma constitutional convention, so the State of Sequoyah lived on, at least in part. But Oklahoma would never realize the State of Sequoyah's promise for Native peoples, nor stand anywhere close alongside what Indian Territory actually had been for the Five Tribes.

It is surely no coincidence that Riggs wrote his Cherokee plays far from the everyday reality of Oklahoma, where the fallout of allotment and the subjugation of tribal sovereignty to settler possession were so cruel, callous, and omnipresent. Riggs was a man who had a deep nostalgic streak coupled with a healthy scepticism of that very impulse, and I'm not quite sure what he would have made of Highway 66 cutting through the Cherokee Nation of his childhood, or the ticky-tacky big box stores within minutes of his long-treasured main allotment. I suspect that, given his disdain for rank commercialism, he would have found them grotesque, but undoubtedly he would have also found some poetry in there somewhere.

Riggs's imaginative kinscape was, like the thwarted State of Sequoyah, far more expansive than the settler Oklahoma that rose around them, the Sooner State never quite able to supplant the Indian Territory over which it presumed uncontestable authority. Yet Riggs was beyond his place as a gay Cherokee man, too, in a time and country when both were often despised and could get you hurt, institutionalized, or even killed depending on circumstances. He championed art that spoke to the disenfranchised, the despised, the dispossessed, and he paid a heavy price for it among his peers and paying audiences in Hollywood and Broadway, and among his kin back home. Those who might have understood the beating red heart of his work the most were also some of those who understood him least, and that disconnect informs so much of what he produced.

As the editors of this long-awaited and impressively researched volume so ably demonstrate, Lynn Riggs was complicated, as are his legacies. He and his work continue to intrigue and challenge the field of Indigenous literary studies, and he is eminently deserving of more attention. He wasn't just a playwright—he was also a skilled poet, an essayist, and a hopeful novelist; there is far more published and unpublished work to consider. With *Lynn Riggs: The Indigenous Plays*, Cox and Pettit have ensured that some of his most powerful and provocative works are more widely available to a more diverse range of readers, and my hope is that this volume will inspire further critical consideration of Lynn Riggs, his art, his life, and his worlds.

Introduction

Rollie Lynn Riggs (1899–1954) was the first professional Native American dramatist and the only Native American writer of his generation devoted to the theatre. He offers in many of his plays an intimate view of the precarious lives of people in the Cherokee Nation, Indian Territory, and northeastern Oklahoma during a turbulent turn-of-the-century era in the region. As a gay man born a citizen of the Cherokee Nation, Riggs also brought his vision of socially transformative drama to plays set in Santa Fe, Yucatán, Mexico City, Cape Cod, and elsewhere.

During the period between the two world wars, Riggs exemplified Philip J. Deloria's "Indian in unexpected places": the Riggs of the 1920s and 1930s was a playwright, director, visiting university instructor, scriptwriter for Hollywood studios, and in-demand collaborator with some of the era's most respected artists and entertainers.[1] Non-Native writers, including ones Riggs deeply admired (Eugene O'Neill [1888–1953]) and ones with whom he became close friends (Paul Green [1894–1981] and George O'Neil [1896–1940]), had defined and continued to control how Indigeneity appeared on stage.[2] The three plays in this collection represent Riggs's most explicit efforts to dramatize new, unexpected expressions of Indigeneity, specifically the ongoing impact of a traumatic history on Indigenous families. They exemplify the timeliness, lyricism, and formal sophistication characteristic of Riggs's best work.

---

1 See Deloria. Deloria is a citizen of the Standing Rock Sioux Tribe. We draw on the work of other Indigenous scholars throughout this introduction but list their tribal nation identification or citizenship here: Craig Womack (Muscogee Creek-Cherokee), Daniel Heath Justice (Cherokee Nation), Gertrude Bonnin (Yankton Dakota), Ella Deloria (Yankton Dakota), Charles Alexander Eastman (Santee Dakota), John Joseph Mathews (Osage), John Milton Oskison (Cherokee Nation), Will Rogers (Cherokee Nation), Julie Little Thunder (Creek descent), Kirby Brown (Cherokee Nation), and Chadwick Allen (Chickasaw ancestry).

2 For Riggs and O'Neill, see Cox, "Saw" 1–5.

The Cherokee Dramatist

Riggs was born several miles from Claremore in the Coo-weẹ-scoo-wee district of the Cherokee Nation in Indian Territory, on 30 August 1899. After Rose Ella (Buster) Riggs, his Cherokee mother, died of typhoid fever during Riggs's infancy, his father married another Cherokee woman, Juliette Scrimsher Chambers.[1] Like the other Indigenous people of the region that eventually became the state of Oklahoma, the Riggs family experienced the division of tribally held land into individually owned allotments, the rapid dispossession caused by land runs, and the upheaval of statehood in 1907, with its attendant dissolution of Native governments.[2] Riggs spent five years, 1912 to 1917, at Eastern University Preparatory School in Claremore, after which he worked a variety of jobs in Chicago, New York, Tulsa, and Hollywood. He returned from California and matriculated in 1920 at the University of Oklahoma, having mortgaged his allotment to help support himself.[3]

At OU, Riggs began to see a future for himself as a writer and started to build the extensive network of scholars and authors that would sustain him personally and professionally throughout his life. He joined the editorial board of the *University of Oklahoma Magazine* in November 1921; submitted poems to local and national publications; and had his first play, *Cuckoo*, produced in May 1922. By then, he had published "Song" and "I Was a King," two of his eight poems that would appear that year in H.L. Mencken and George Jean Nathan's trendy magazine, *The Smart Set*. The publication of the first dyad earned Riggs a laudatory essay, "Proof That Persistence Wins," on the editorial page of the February 1922 issue of *University of Oklahoma Magazine*. Riggs's poem "To Vachel Lindsay," celebrating a poet then at the height of his fame, appeared on the cover.

Another poet had a more enduring impact on Riggs. Like

---

1 Rose lost her first husband; her legal name at the time of her marriage to William Riggs was Rose Ella Gillis. See Braunlich, *Haunted* 22–23.

2 See Denson, especially Chapter 7, on the late-nineteenth-century history of the Cherokee Nation in Indian Territory. The federal government made land formerly held by Indigenous people available to settlers, leading to land runs, or land rushes, between 1889 and 1895, during which those settlers claimed millions of acres of land.

3 See Braunlich, *Haunted* 37. Braunlich searched the Land Records at the Rogers County Courthouse in Claremore and learned that Riggs later sold his allotment (24).

Lindsay (1879–1931), Witter "Hal" Bynner (1881–1968) met Riggs when he lectured at Oklahoma in 1921. Bynner had moved to Santa Fe in February 1922 and spent time there recovering from illness at the Sunmount Sanatorium. Riggs had established a correspondence with Bynner at least by December 1922, when he wrote to his new friend from Norman, Oklahoma. In January 1923, he expressed a desire to move to Santa Fe, apparently at Bynner's suggestion or invitation: "Of course, you'd know I'd like nothing better than to come to Santa Fe. But how the deuce could I? You forget I'm a vassal of the state—have to teach freshmen how to write descriptions, and narratives, and one-act plays, etc." The rest of the paragraph contains various complaints about the university: Riggs calls it "tawdry" and the students "common-place and narrow," while noting the faculty fail to inspire him. He shifts to a more pleasant topic by informing Bynner that *Poetry* had accepted his poem "Rhythm of Rain."[1] It appeared in the August 1923 issue, which included poems by Lindsay and Bynner as well as Amy Lowell (1874–1925), Robert Frost (1874–1963), and Edgar Lee Masters (1868–1950).

Riggs eventually fulfilled his wish: after writing to Bynner in October 1923 to say he found himself in "terrible straits," he left the University of Oklahoma and moved to Santa Fe. In the same letter, he told Bynner he had submitted a collection of poems, *Rhythm of Rain*, to the Yale Series of Younger Poets contest.[2] By early December, his outlook had changed dramatically: "Hal— you saved my life you know—to Humanity the burden."[3] Within two months of his arrival, he had a rosier view of at least one of his mentors at Oklahoma. In January 1924, he sent a copy of *Rhythm of Rain* to "the ideal family": his friend and English instructor Walter Stanley Campbell; his wife, Isabel Jones Campbell; and their two young daughters.[4] Riggs completed his second play around this time. He set *Knives from Syria* in the "present" at an "Oklahoma Farm" (1927, p. 192). As in many of his plays, the place-names mark the setting as the post-statehood Cherokee Nation. The central family's surname—Buster—derives from his mother's genealogy.

Riggs entered a vibrant artistic and literary community in Santa Fe that included Ida Rauh (1877–1970), a writer, artist,

---

1   24 January 1923, Bynner Papers (restricted).
2   14 October 1923, Bynner Papers.
3   3 December 1923, Bynner Papers.
4   Enclosure, 19 January 1924, Campbell Papers, box 56, folder 3.

and feminist activist and an early contributor to the Provincetown Players. Rauh directed *Knives from Syria* at the Rialto Theater; Riggs told Barrett H. Clark (1890–1953), soon to be his agent and editor at Samuel French, that the play "was given four performances by the Santa Fe Players" and that he himself had acted the part of the "farm hand," Charley.[1] The full-length *Sump'n Like Wings*, written in the summer of 1925, is the second and last of Riggs's Santa Fe plays of this period.

Over the next fifteen years, Riggs would live months at a time away from his home base in Santa Fe. He spent the fall of 1925 in Chicago, where he wrote *Big Lake*. The next spring, he wrote *A Lantern to See By* in New York. *Big Lake*, a "folk tragedy of the western country," as Burns Mantle called it in his *Daily News* review, ran briefly at New York's American Laboratory Theatre in 1927. That critic declared the play "one of those simple, direct, bitingly true extracts from life cut out, set down and touched eloquently by the beauty of an imaginative writer's recital." Like two of the scenes in *The Cherokee Night* and the entirety of *The Cream in the Well* in the present volume, *Big Lake* is set in the Cherokee Nation in Indian Territory. Riggs does not identify his characters as Cherokee or Indigenous in *Big Lake*, which nonetheless establishes violent death as a central feature of Riggs's dramatizations of his homeland.[2] Riggs had stopped short of staging murder in *Knives from Syria*, but *Big Lake* features three deaths: a murder, a sheriff's fatal shooting of the wrong suspect, and a suicide by drowning. The threat or actuality of violent death characterizes many of Riggs's later plays, including the three in this volume and *Green Grow the Lilacs*.

By the end of the decade, Riggs had proven himself a prolific and well-respected playwright. Mainstream commercial success eluded him, however. Producers liked *The Lonesome West*, which Riggs had begun writing at Yaddo in Saratoga Springs, New York, in the summer of 1927, but the play was not staged until 1936 and has never been published. *Rancor*, also known as *Rancour*, followed that fall. Due partly to its prominence in the repertory of Jasper Deeter's Hedgerow Theatre, *Rancor* would be among Riggs's most frequently staged plays of the 1930s and 1940s. But productions at little theatres, community theatres, and college theatres generate

---

1 21 July 1927, Clark Papers, YCAL MSS 569, box 5.
2 *Big Lake* and *The Cream in the Well* are both set on or near the shores of Big Lake, where Riggs had played as a child (see Braunlich, *Haunted* 29).

more publicity than income. *Rancor* never played in a major market. It, too, remains unpublished.[1] *The Domino Parlor*, completed in April 1928, was quickly optioned by the powerful Shubert Organization. Clark would later recall that the production had been "badly miscast," in spite of a substantial overhaul of the cast during the rehearsal process.[2] When a June tryout in Newark drew the attention of local law enforcement, the Shuberts, who had already forced rewrites that Riggs had "disavowed," demanded further alterations. Riggs refused, prey here as elsewhere to an obstinance at odds with his commercial aspirations.[3] *The Domino Parlor* would ultimately be staged in 1940 and published in 1948, after extensive revision, as *Hang On to Love*. *A Lantern to See By* and *Sump'n Like Wings* were both optioned for Broadway but opened instead in 1930 and 1931, respectively, at the Detroit Playhouse, with which Clark had established a working relationship.[4]

Reckless, another Yaddo play from 1927, has fared best among Riggs's work from this period. Published in an anthology in 1928 and later copyrighted as *Roadside*, it became in September 1930 the first of Riggs's six plays to open on Broadway. The run was not successful, no doubt to the disappointment of Samuel French, whose November publication of the script suggests that they had counted on a buzz that never materialized. *Roadside*, however, would be among the plays that established Riggs as exceptionally popular in little theatres and on college campuses (see Appendix B).

Riggs went to France in July 1928 on a Guggenheim Fellowship and there wrote his best-known and most successful play, *Green Grow the Lilacs*, also set in the Cherokee Nation in Indian Territory. Clark regarded an early 1929 draft as sufficiently "saleable" to justify simultaneous pitches in or around April of that year to the Theatre Guild, Arthur Hopkins (1878–1950),

---

1 See a 26 June 1931 letter to Clark, in which Riggs indicated that he had "more or less promised" the University of Oklahoma Press that they could publish the play but floated a one-dollar Samuel French edition as an alternative.

2 Clark, *Hour* 153; the cast lists published in early- and mid-June newspapers differ substantially.

3 See Braunlich, *Haunted* 61; *Brooklyn Daily Eagle*, 24 June 1928. Braunlich (61) continues the quotation from Clark noted above: "because Riggs refused to let the manuscript be tinkered with, nothing more was done about it" (Clark, *Hour* 153).

4 For Clark and the Detroit Playhouse, see Weitzencamp 111–12. For the Broadway options, see Erhard 10–11. Erhard, who does not document his claim, asserts that *Sump'n Like Wings* was optioned thrice for possible Broadway productions (10).

Winthrop Ames (1870–1937), and unspecified other producers.[1] By mid-July, the Guild had optioned the play,[2] which would premiere at their Broadway theatre on 26 January 1931, with Franchot Tone (1905–68) as Curly, Helen Westley (1875–1942) as Aunt Eller, June Walker (1900–66) as Laurey, and Lee Strasberg (1901–82) as the Syrian peddler, a character revived from *Knives from Syria*.

The *New York Times* celebrated the premiere with a headline reading "And Now Lynn Riggs: After Several Ventures in the Theatre, He Arrives With 'Green Grow the Lilacs.'" A short personal and professional biography included the observation, subsequently repeated by biographers Charles Aughtry, Phyllis Braunlich, and Thomas Erhard, that as a child Riggs enjoyed reading "trash": Western pulp fiction or, in Erhard's phrasing, "dime novels."[3] Though the *Times* claims with evident relief that "between trashy books and living poetry, it was natural that [Riggs], upon discreet examination, should choose the latter," the author rightly acknowledges the continued influence on Riggs of the popular fiction available to him during his childhood. They do not remark, however, upon an equally important source of Riggs's representations of Indian Territory and Oklahoma: the long history of violence experienced by the Cherokees, also present, though not explicitly, in *Green Grow the Lilacs*.

Its sixty-four performances make *Green Grow the Lilacs* the second-most successful of Riggs's Broadway plays after *Russet Mantle*, which he started writing in 1934 and had completed by the first week of 1935. A satire of affluent Santa Fe residents, *Russet Mantle* ran for 117 performances at Theatre Masque in 1936. But *Green Grow the Lilacs* would prove the greater success. The Theatre Guild acknowledged the play's popular appeal by including it in its 1931 touring season, a highly publicized two-month junket through Cleveland, Pittsburgh, St. Louis, Milwaukee, Minneapolis, Chicago, and Detroit (see Appendix B). Twelve years later, first-time collaborators Rodgers and Hammerstein brought their adaptation of *Green Grow the Lilacs* to Broadway. *Oklahoma!* ran for a stunning 2,212 performances and revived the sagging fortunes of the Theatre Guild. Hammerstein insisted that audiences recognize the talented author of the source

---

1   Clark to Riggs, 6 April 1929, Riggs Papers, Beinecke, box 1, folder 15.
2   Clark to Riggs, 15 July 1929, Riggs Papers, Beinecke, box 1, folder 15.
3   "And Now Lynn Riggs"; see Aughtry 1; Braunlich, *Haunted* 63; and Erhard 4.

play. On 5 September 1943, the *New York Times* published a letter from him to the drama editor: "Mr. Riggs' play is the wellspring of almost all that is good in 'Oklahoma!' I kept many of the lines of the original play without making any changes in them at all for the simple reason that they could not be improved on—at any rate, not by me." To this day, by contract, Riggs and *Lilacs* are credited on programs and most publicity materials for all revivals of *Oklahoma!* The royalties from *Oklahoma!* gave Riggs the financial stability that had been elusive for most of his career.

Riggs also started writing *The Cherokee Night* during his fellowship year, although that play would reach stageable form only in 1932, after additional work in Santa Fe. *The Cherokee Night* dramatizes the lives of several generations of Cherokees in Indian Territory and Oklahoma. The other "Indigenous plays" of the present edition followed. Riggs produced a first draft of *The Year of Pilar* early in 1938 and had a version ready to share by September of that year, though a revised ending could have been written any time between 1938 and 1947. The play focuses on land redistribution from the *hacendados* (owners of large estates) to Mayans in Yucatán during the single term (1934–40) of reform-minded President Lázaro Cárdenas.[1] *The Cream in the Well*, written between November 1939 and August 1940, brings the audience into a Cherokee home on the eve of Oklahoma statehood. Samuel French would not publish *Pilar* and *Cream* until 1947, when they appeared in *Four Plays* with *A World Elsewhere* and *Dark Encounter*.[2]

With hindsight, the publication of *Four Plays* may seem to indicate that Riggs had remained a marketable playwright. It does not: although *Oklahoma!* increased Riggs's name-recognition, his period of commercial success ended in 1936 with *Russet Mantle*. By 1947, *The Year of Pilar*, *A World Elsewhere*, and *The Cream in the Well* had not succeeded commercially. *Pilar* had not been staged; *A World Elsewhere* had played at the Globe Theatre in San Diego for five nights in 1940; although *The Cream in the Well* reached Broadway in 1941, it closed after twenty-four performances. Riggs copyrighted *Dark Encounter* in 1944, but the play seems never to have received a full production.[3] *A Cow in a*

---

1 For land reform in *Yucatán*, see Fallaw.

2 For the compositional history of *Pilar*, see pp. 57–60.

3 *Dark Encounter* would be given a staged reading at the University of Iowa in 1948, at a festival that also included a staged reading of *Pilar* and a full production of *A World Elsewhere* (a one-act version of which had been published in 1940).

Trailer, a 1939 collaboration with the composer Jerome Moross and Ramón Naya, Riggs's partner and an aspirant playwright, exemplifies the period. The play was neither staged nor published; when it was presented on CBS radio in 1940, it was credited to Moross only.[1] The dilatory publication of *Four Plays* likely constituted Samuel French's attempt to profit from Riggs's association with *Oklahoma!* Insofar as his own career was concerned, Riggs had spoken presciently as well as truthfully in February 1940, when he complained that he had experienced "nothing but rotten luck" since Clark's 1936 departure from Samuel French to direct the newly formed Dramatists Play Service.[2]

The lament was personal as well as professional: Riggs and Clark had become close friends, and Riggs never established a rapport with Clark's successor, Garrett Leverton, a former academic who lacked Clark's bonhomie and capacious understanding of drama.[3] While working on the premiere of *A World Elsewhere*, Riggs informed Leverton that financial concerns necessitated the issuance of a new contract with French. But Riggs continued to seek professional advice from Clark, as he had been doing since the 1920s.[4] By 1940, Riggs was underfunded, even as *Roadside*, *Green Grow the Lilacs*, and *Russet Mantle* remained popular. *Roadside* continued to be revived throughout the 1940s, as, less frequently, were *Knives from Syria* and *Russet Mantle* (see Appendix B).

1 Riggs would read the play at a benefit for the New Mexico Association on Indian Affairs in May 1941.
2 Riggs to Clark, 7 February 1940, Riggs Papers, Beinecke, box 1, folder 19.
3 Leverton was a professor at Northwestern University and director of the university's theatre from 1928 to 1938. By 1941, he was serving as Riggs's agent. Although Riggs's obstinance sometimes served him poorly with both agents, an incident from 1941 suggests that Leverton represented his client injudiciously. After the University of Oklahoma Press expressed interest in an edition of Riggs's plays, most or all reprints, Leverton told Riggs he would prefer a complete two-volume set but would be willing to propose one volume comprising seven plays set in Oklahoma. That volume would include four unpublished plays: *The Lonesome West*, *The Cream in the Well*, *Rancor*, and *Hang On to Love*. Neither edition materialized. The financially straitened Riggs was at that time teaching in Waco, Texas.
4 See Riggs to Clark, 7 February 1940, Clark Papers. In response to Riggs's desire to go on a lecture tour, Clark proposed visiting college drama departments instead, which suggests his knowledge of Riggs's audience and his talent for identifying the best approach to reaching it. See Clark to Riggs, 19 February 1940, Riggs Papers, Beinecke, box 1, folder 19.

The Indigenous Plays

The plays in this collection foreground Indigenous history (*The Cherokee Night*), politics (*The Year of Pilar*), and families (*The Cream in the Well*) in ways that Riggs's other plays do not. Geography nonetheless binds *The Cherokee Night* and *The Cream in the Well* to *Big Lake*, *Roadside*, and *Out of Dust*.[1] In these plays, Indian Territory is coterminous with the Cherokee Nation. Characters in these plays live in, refer to, or visit Cherokee towns and move across a landscape marked with geographical features such as creeks, rivers, and towns within the nation's borders. *The Cherokee Night*, for example, includes references to Tahlequah, the capital of the Cherokee Nation, as well as to Bartlesville, Claremore, Dewey, Inola, Justus (Justice), Oolagah, Vinita, and Rogers County (and the Rogers County Jail). Cat Creek, the Verdigris River, and Spunky Creek are mentioned as well. Claremore Mound, the site of an 1817 battle between the Cherokees and the Osages and a nearly constant visual presence throughout *The Cherokee Night*, grounds the play in Cherokee, Osage, and Indian Territory history. When the characters travel to or from Sapulpa (Creek Nation) or Quapaw (Quapaw Nation), Riggs reminds the audience of the extent of the multi-national Indigenous geography of northeastern Oklahoma.

The history of this Indigenous geography weighs heavily upon the Cherokee individuals and families that Riggs depicts in *The Cherokee Night*. Riggs set Scenes 4 and 7 before Oklahoma statehood. The latter scene barely predates the Curtis Act (1898), the de facto extension of the Dawes Act (1887) that authorized both the division of land held tribally by the Cherokees, Chickasaws, Choctaws, Creeks, and Seminoles into fee-simple holdings and the creation of "Unassigned Lands" available for "white settlement" (Conley, *Cherokee Nation* 188). The other five scenes are set after Oklahoma statehood, when the federal government so severely constrained the sovereignty of Indigenous nations that Cherokee writer Robert J. Conley notes, "for all practical

---

1   Jace Weaver's pairing of *The Cherokee Night* and *Green Grow the Lilacs* is useful for its emphasis on the overlapping Indian Territory settings of *Green Grow the Lilacs* and *The Cherokee Night*. See Weaver, *That the People* 99–101. See also Weaver on *Lilacs* as in effect "*about*" the Native people that the play knowingly elides (Foreword xiii; emphasis in original). Plausibly, Weaver includes *Lilacs* and *Russet Mantle* in his accounting of Riggs's "'Native'-themed" plays (Foreword ix).

purposes, the Cherokee Nation had become dormant" (*Cherokee Nation* 202). Historian Andrew Denson holds a similar view:

> As most accounts of Cherokee history explain, the assault upon common land was the act that finally brought about the dissolution of the Cherokee Nation. With severalty came the end of independent tribal government, the extension of American law over Cherokees, the opening of the Indian country to American citizens, and eventually (early in the next century) the Cherokees' inclusion in the new state of Oklahoma. Allotment, in other words, initiated a thorough dismantling of the separate status that was the foundation of Cherokee autonomy. (202)

This tribal national history, this "thorough dismantling" of the Cherokee Nation's land base and institutions, informs the experimental structure of *The Cherokee Night* and the sometimes furious, sometimes quiet desperation with which Riggs's Cherokee characters seek understanding.

Riggs conceived of *The Cherokee Night* between July 1928 and April 1929, during his fellowship in France. In a 6 November 1928 letter to Clark, he includes the title in a list of one-act plays that he wanted to write.[1] Among other titles on the list are those that would designate Scenes 3 and 4 in the final version. By 10 March 1929, Riggs had seven scenes in mind, including five that would survive the revision process, one, "The Claw Hammer," with a new title, "The Hatchet."[2] Progress was slow, but by 20 October 1930, Riggs would proudly tell Clark that "the last scene of all concentrates a statement about and covers the entire field of Indian-White relationships in one dramatic incident such as I could never have foreseen. And it's not a protest—but a triumphant comprehension by an old Indian, a real nobleman, which makes the whole play dignified and austere beyond my first feeble calculations. I hope it will be my best play. It can be."[3] The play's unique popularity in Riggs's canon suggests the soundness of this observation.

Riggs read the play in April 1931 at the Playmakers Theatre of the University of North Carolina, where his close friend and advocate, the Pulitzer Prize–winning dramatist Paul Green, was

---

1 Clark Papers.
2 See Clark to Riggs, 10 March 1929, Clark Papers.
3 20 October 1930, Clark Papers.

on the faculty. In January 1932, he sent the finished script to Clark; the play premiered at Hedgerow on 18 June of that year. The *New York Times*'s Brooks Atkinson (1894–1984) hated it: "On Broadway ... 'The Cherokee Night' would seem like a pretentious piece of flummery. Even in Moylan-Rose Valley, amid the syca- mores and rambler roses, many soothsayers of the drama speak only ill of it." He was only getting started: "[Riggs] has written his play as badly as possible, substituting presumptuous artistic tenets for the virtue of a clear mind, which is a common failing of talented dramatists who refuse to learn their trade." Perhaps aware of Riggs's friendship with Green, Atkinson pauses to take a potshot at the latter's stylistically demanding *Potter's Field*.

Atkinson did not have the last or only word, however. *The Cherokee Night* was produced at the University of Iowa in 1932; the Little Theater of Public Hall in Cleveland, Ohio, in 1933; Syracuse University in 1934; and, in 1936, at the Provincetown Playhouse (New York), under the aegis of the Federal Theatre Project. The *Cleveland Plain Dealer*'s long-tenured theatre critic, William F. McDermott, found *The Cherokee Night* "stronger and more powerful" than *Green Grow the Lilacs* and *Roadside*. In *The Cherokee Night*, "[Riggs] deals with characters and scenes so authentically American as the Cherokee Indians and their descen- dants," he wrote; "Eugene O'Neill's plays might conceivably be written by a German or a Russian [but] Mr. Riggs' plays could not have been written by any but an American." McDermott rec- ognized the play's unconventional structure as "not coherent in the ordinary theatrical sense" but judged it "harmonious" and observed that "the separate scenes have an uncommon power to stir the imagination."

Riggs did not have the same confidence in *The Year of Pilar* that he had during his work on *The Cherokee Night*. He made early notes on a play called "Hacienda," among other proposed titles, from 26 February through late April 1938. He finished a penulti- mate version of the play under its final title in September of that year. Enrique Gasque-Molina (Ramón Naya), with whom Riggs had begun a romantic relationship by 1937, inspired the play. Naya summarized his family's history in Yucatán and New York in a letter dated December 1937, two months before Riggs began to write *Pilar*. Naya identified his father, Dr. Alonso Gasque Crespo; his mother, Doña Mercedes Molina de Gasque; his sisters, Flora Mercedes and Rosa María; and his brother, Alonso de Jesús. He explained, "My father practiced medicine as an assistant of Dr. [Frank] Albee in the French hospital in N.Y. (He also had his own practice but I doubt if that was O.K. with the U.S. Govt. because of the laws about foreign medicos)."[1] Riggs borrowed the first name "Alonso" and, evidently, the surname Crespo for *Pilar*, although it may be worth noting that a Pedro Crespo had gained fame as a heroic leader of the Mayans during the protracted Caste War that began in 1847. The Crespo family in *Pilar* includes two sisters (Chela and Pilar) and two brothers (Trino and Fernando). The patriarch in the play, Don Severo Crespo, has the same occupation—doctor—as Naya's father. One of the Crespo brothers, Trino, shares a talent for painting with Naya. Early in the drafting of the play, Riggs considered *The Year of the Crespos* as a title.

Although Riggs completed a full and nearly final draft of *The Year of Pilar* in the fall of 1938, Naya's letters the following year suggest Riggs's ongoing interest in his partner's childhood and perhaps touch on matters they had previously discussed. In a letter dated 4 July 1939, Naya describes the "black days" in New York following his family's flight from Yucatán in 1917, when political and social upheaval related to the Mexican Revolution delayed delivery of the income from the hacienda. He describes his father as a "brilliant young medico" who "had to go to work folding envelopes at twenty-five cents a thousand." Of his mother, he says: "she had had eight Indian criados[2] to jump at her command and now she had to get down on hands and knees to scrub floors.... Those days were pretty bleak. All the joy went out of them."[3] His parents regularly fought in front of Naya and his siblings and expressed regrets that they had chosen each other as spouses.

Riggs sets Scene 1 of his play in the Crespo family apartment on Riverside Drive in New York City. Doña Candita, Riggs's reimagining of Naya's mother, expresses a dismal view of the family's life in New York similar to the one Naya describes in his childhood home: it is a "cold, cold country," she says (p. 149). Don Severo, the patriarch inspired by Naya's father, "wants to be a great surgeon" but has fallen far short of this goal (p. 150). His daughter, Pilar, who experiences New York City in the same way as her mother, calls her father "a failure" (p. 155). Several younger members of the Crespo family have a happier life in New York City, but the "cold, cold" perspective prevails, and the family decides to return to Yucatán.

---

1   December 1937, Kroll Papers Relating to Lynn Riggs, Beinecke, file 2, box 5.

2   Spanish: servants.

3   4 July 1939, Kroll Papers, Beinecke.

They arrive at the family's henequen, or hemp, plantation near Mérida in Yucatán immediately prior to the institution of President Lázaro Cárdenas's land reform program. In a May 1939 letter from Mexico, Naya adopted a reportorial tone when he commented on the reforms that Riggs, in *The Year of Pilar*, presents as necessary and just:

> The injustices that are committed in the name of Socialism here are getting me down.... One fact stands out very clearly.... The Indian who earned fifteen and twenty pesos a week under Capital[ism] is now happy to get two pesos.... Hunger is everywhere. With the expropriation of the haciendas, almost all Mérida went off to Mexico City.... The people who are left are fighting over bones.... Some Indians have been going back to their primitive state, in the jungles, with their milpas [cleared fields] and the little they can hunt.[1]

Naya sounds as if he stands with the Indigenous peoples of Yucatán and protests the precarity of their lives, but he also implies that life under the hacienda system was better for them. Riggs conveys his own allegiances more clearly. As land reform proceeds in the region and the Crespos plan again to depart, Pilar finds herself the last member of the family willing to leave. Following a final argument with Cuco Saldívar, a neighbor to whom she is engaged, Pilar tells her Mayan half-brother, Beto, that she is prepared to die, prepared to sacrifice herself to hasten the end of colonial domination: "Not till I die—not till all such people as myself are dead—we, the ones who've lorded it over the weak and lowly—not till all of us are in the grave can a stricken people sing again, be free again!" (p. 210). The first ending that Riggs wrote for the play was radical. The second, reproduced in this edition, is shockingly so.

Riggs made notes toward an unrealized novel entitled "The Cream in the Well" in 1928. The title reappeared six years later, on 19 August 1934, on a list of short story titles that also includes "We Moved to Pomona," which would appear in the summer 1938 issue of *Laughing Horse*. Riggs did not write the play called *The Cream in the Well*, though, until the winter of 1939–40. He set it in a Cherokee-specific place at an anxious and uncertain time: on the shores of Big Lake in the Coo-wee-scoo-wee district of the

---

1   31 May 1939, Kroll Papers, Beinecke.

Cherokee Nation, Indian Territory, just southwest of Claremore in 1906, the eve of Oklahoma statehood. He had set one of his earliest plays, *Big Lake*, in the same place and time. The battle over ownership of the Big Lake district may have drawn Riggs's imagination back to the area. Lawyer and crime writer Albert Borowitz notes that the Cherokees and the Osages had "quarreled" over the lake and reports that "the Department of the Interior resolved the dispute by declaring the area Government property, and in the second decade of the twentieth century put the Big Lake district up for sale." Big Lake was then "privately developed as a gated community" (172).

The Sawters family's "big, tall-ceilinged, well-built house ... far from anything approaching civilization" (p. 219) sits on allotted land once shared with other Cherokees and soon to be encroached upon by the new state of Oklahoma. The Sawters struggle to maintain their holdings in the absence of a son who, in love with his sister, has left home and the "beautiful" but "shadowy" bedroom (p. 238) that had become his jail. Like Aeschylus' Orestes, Clabe Sawters returns with death in tow. Julie, Clabe's sister, leaves him in the familial home, departing as pointedly if less conclusively as Pilar does when she exits the Crespo's hacienda. Art Osburn provides another rough analogue in *The Cherokee Night*. Riggs's asynchronous sequencing allows us to see Art at a communal picnic in Scene 1, to imagine him exiting during an entr'acte, and then to encounter him moments later as a prisoner of the state, presumably, like Pilar and perhaps Julie, bound for death.

Again like the two earlier plays, *The Cream in the Well* uses geographical specificity to suggest an uneasy off-stage environment. Opal Dunham's mother is institutionalized at the Vinita Asylum, in the northeastern Cherokee Nation, and the rebuilt Cherokee National Female Seminary near Tahlequah that Julie had attended would, like Big Lake, soon pass out of tribal control. A lightly comic subplot gushes into prominence in the play's final moments, when the safely unimaginative Blocky and Bina assume A-couple status and promise a domestic stability that Julie and Clabe's conflict has deferred.

The Cream in the Well tried out briefly in Washington, DC, before premiering on Broadway on 20 January 1941. It earned neither commercial nor critical success. Braunlich (*Haunted* 162) notices the "scathing" reviews in New York, but some critics appreciated aspects of the play in production. Even the bilious Atkinson praised Riggs's writing of "individual scenes," although his general disdain elicited rebuttals from Ida Rauh and arts patron Ann Webster. The *Daily News* acknowledged "some fine performances" but regretted the play's "gloom"—a bizarre response to a tragedy but one reframed in Arthur Pollack's *Brooklyn Daily Eagle* declaration that the play was "almost comically glum." The befuddlement of these reviews—"Why?," Atkinson had begun and ended his review—suggests a play with artistic demands that the arch and critical vocabulary of the day could not easily accommodate and that, per Erhard, "never had a chance with the still hypocritically Puritan Broadway audience of 1941" (31). Rauh did well to generalize her objection to the *Times* review: Atkinson, she wrote, "seems to be reflecting the opinions of those who have learned all they know from some college course." Add some regional chauvinism, *et voilà*: Riggs is a hayseed and a mopus. Though gloomy, *The Cream in the Well* will reward less jaundiced analyses.

"We're Not All Anglo"

Riggs had a secure and, in the interwar years, well-respected position within various dramatic traditions. Rauh's life-long friendship and her influence on his career mark one of several links to the Provincetown Players and other affiliates of the Little Theatre movement, such as Deeter, the former Player and Riggs's avid supporter at Hedgerow. Riggs lived for several summers at Rauh's home in Provincetown, where he befriended the Players' co-founder Susan Glaspell (1876–1948). His letters record an enduring respect for O'Neill, who had been Rauh, Deeter, and Glaspell's colleague in that foundational company. As a playwright and a commentator on drama and the theatre, Riggs moved into and out of alignment with the American "folk drama" movement, rooted in Irish "peasant drama," often associated with the Little Theatre movement, and elsewhere exemplified by Green, Virgil Geddes (1897–1989), Josefina Niggli (1910–83), and O'Neill, among others (see Appendix A1). The Little Theatre movement emerged in the 1910s, theatre historian Dorothy Chansky notes, from "a spirit of anticommercialism" directed specifically against touring productions from New York. Inspired by European theatre, leaders of the movement committed considerable energy to creating local infrastructures for playwrights and playgoers (4).

Riggs was among the contributors to *Theatre Arts Magazine*, founded by Little Theatre advocate Shelden Cheney (1886–1980) to promote the movement nationally. Chansky argues for an enduring legacy of the movement: "Little Theatre rhetoric about the worthwhile nature of thoughtfully produced theatre came to infiltrate the thinking of educators, many audiences, cultural theorists, and funding sources nationwide. The rhetoric still serves American practitioners and educators who continue to fight battles about inclusivity, legibility, activism, social worth, and aesthetic innovation" (11). This reformist perspective on the cultural and social value of theatre influenced Riggs, as his commentary in *Theatre Arts* and elsewhere demonstrates. For example, in the 1939 "Vine Theatre Letter" (Appendix A4), Riggs dismisses contemporary theatre as a "racket," proposes an alternative that "maintain[s] a continuous alliance with life-giving forces," and admonishes his fellow-travelers "never [to] think of Broadway" (pp. 291, 298). These are familiar views in a manifesto-driven theatrical environment. More pertinently, they signal Riggs's sympathy with the ideals of the Provincetown Players; their more internationally minded predecessor, the Greenwich Village Players; and nearly contemporary companies from Rose Valley, Pennsylvania, to Pasadena, California.

Dramaturgically, too, Riggs takes the "little theatre" approach and disavows the Broadway "show-shop," as O'Neill often called it.[1] The older playwright's rare ability to toggle between downtown and uptown theatres helps account for the high esteem in which Riggs held him. O'Neill's *The Emperor Jones* (1920) and *The Hairy Ape* (1922) migrated efficiently from the Provincetown Playhouse to Broadway. But *The Cherokee Night*—affiliated with *Jones* in its resounding drumming and with both O'Neill plays in its reliance on short scenes—opened, and remained, out of town. Notable, too, is Riggs's distinctly "little theatre" contempt for the "star vehicle" manner of playwriting that O'Neill routinely criticized but only intermittently shunned. *The Cherokee Night* rejects this practice, and one must overlook a good bit of subplotting to consider Pilar and Julie as the "stars" of *The Year of Pilar* and *The Cream in the Well*, respectively. These are ensemble pieces—and, in the manner of Glaspell most notably, feminocentric ones.

Both *The Cherokee Night* and *The Cream in Well* qualify as folk drama, a flexible designation that Clark particularizes as the work of playwrights "intent upon depicting the lives of the people they know in the mountains and on the plains" ("Our New American" 762). Indeed, Clark makes Riggs the form's fullest practitioner when he asserts that "he writes as though the small world known to his characters were the only world in the universe" ("Our New

---

1   E.g., O'Neill, Letter to George Jean Nathan 73.

American" 766). Clark's perspective on Riggs points to the eccentricity of *Pilar*, in which the "known" people are those of the playwright's partner, not the playwright himself. In this respect, *Pilar* is unique in Riggs's oeuvre. *The Cream in the Well* is in this context, too, a return to Indian Territory after a detour through Riggs's upper-crust Santa Fe comedy, *Russet Mantle*, and the slightly later *Pilar*.

Clark was probably the first critic to consider Riggs and Paul Green fellow folk dramatists. Twelve years after Clark made this connection, Riggs solicited Green's cooperation in his "Vine Theatre Letter," written after *Pilar* and before *Cream* (Appendix A4). By 1939, Riggs saw both Green and himself as having been abandoned by the commercial theatre. "You yourself—your vigorous and lyric talent," he told Green, "have no continuous life in the theatre" (p. 289). However, although Riggs's career was not going well, Green's was. His North Carolinian pageant *The Lost Colony* (1937) had already ensured the continuity of his "life in the theatre" even as it highlighted his literal and figurative remoteness from Broadway. Ostensibly forward-looking, the Vine proposal is long on nostalgia, not only for the glory days of the foundational little theatres that Riggs just missed but also for a dramatic form that Green still inhabited but from which Riggs had moved away.[1] Clark recognized that Green was "unhampered by the demands of Broadway" and "uncontaminated by Times Square" ("Our New American" 769). But the remoteness of folk drama from commercial theatre that Green celebrated, Riggs endured. Riggs's criticism of Broadway circa 1939 is both an indictment of commercialized art and an anxious reaction to its author's commercial eclipse. As far as we know, Green did not respond to the Vine letter.

Nonetheless, it is as a regionalist and a folk dramatist that Riggs received much of his contemporary recognition. In his *Guide to Life and Literature of the Southwest*, the nationally known writer on Texas and Southwest folklore and literature J. Frank Dobie (1888–1964) calls Riggs "the most successful dramatist" in the Southwest (103).[2] In a 1929 *Southwest Review* article, Campbell (1887–1957), writing as Stanley Vestal, observes, "It is said that all good literature—which may be interpreted to include literary drama—is in the best sense provincial. Certainly the dramas of Lynn Riggs smack of the soil where he was born and bred

---

1 A 1942 reappraisal of the state of folk drama dwells on Green but mentions Riggs once and in passing; see Peery 156.
2 The statement is retained in the 1952 revised edition (186).

with an intimacy and intensity which might do credit to Thomas Hardy or some other literary lover of an English village" (64). Campbell also included Riggs in his *The Book Lover's Southwest: A Guide to Good Reading*, published in 1955. Fifteen years later, the Southwest Writers Series, published in Austin, Texas, issued the biography by Erhard, a dramatist and English professor at New Mexico State University. Erhard calls Riggs both "*the* Southwestern playwright" (2; emphasis in original) and "the nation's greatest playwright of folk life in the Southwest" (25). He favorably compares the regional speech of Riggs's characters to the Irish dialect in John Millington Synge's (1871–1909) plays—a remarkable yet credible claim.

Riggs was drawn to Hollywood as well as Broadway, despite his frequent complaints about both, and he would earn praise from the West Coast contingent long after he had fallen out of favor on Broadway. An initial trip to Hollywood in 1919 allowed him to try his hand at acting and screenwriting (Braunlich, *Haunted* 33). He returned in 1930 and wrote irregularly until 1943 for Pathé, MGM, RKO, Universal, Paramount, and Selznick International. In Santa Fe, he made his own film, *A Day in Santa Fe*, an earnest and whimsical celebration of the artists, writers, musicians, and laborers of his adopted hometown and the people of the nearby Santa Clara Pueblo. The film premiered in January 1932 at La Fonda Hotel in Santa Fe. While at Santa Clara, Riggs shot scenes of the harvest dance that remain today an important record of the continuity of this ceremony. Riggs also added three intertitles from his poem "Santo Domingo Corn Dance," testifying thereby to his durable interest in incorporating poetry into other artistic forms (see Appendix A3).

Legendary Hollywood producers and directors praised Riggs and sought to collaborate with him. David O. Selznick (1902–65) told the US Coast Guard Auxiliary that "Lynn Riggs worked under my supervision as a scenario writer. I found him to be the possessor of an extraordinary and very sensitive talent. I also found him to be extremely conscientious, hard-working and in every way of admirable character."[1] On several occasions around this time, 20th Century Fox sought Riggs's assistance, for example on a script for a film by two-time Academy Award nominee Otto Preminger (1905–86).[2] In the early 1950s, future Academy Award nominee Sidney Lumet (1924–2011) wrote to Riggs to ask

---

1 3 August 1942, Riggs Papers, Beinecke, box 5, folder 116.
2 F.D. Langton to Riggs, 8 December 1944, Riggs Papers, Beinecke, box

him to help adapt Katherine Anne Porter's (1890–1980) "Noon Wine" for a three-part film that also included adaptations of short stories by Ambrose Bierce (1842–c. 1914) and Willa Cather (1873–1947). Lumet's pitch blended sincerity and seduction. "The screenplay on it has to be done sensitively, lovingly, & poetically," he wrote, "while still retaining its earth. You're the best person to do it."[1]

Riggs collaborated with other luminaries in the performing arts. He worked with the composer George Gershwin (1898–1937) on a project that Riggs's friend, the opera singer and University of Oklahoma faculty member Joe Benton (aka Guiseppe Bentonelli, 1898–1975), called an "opera."[2] It was unfinished when Gershwin began to suffer in early 1937 from symptoms caused by the brain tumor that killed him later that year. A few years later, Edward Choate of Select Theatres Corporation asked Riggs to help a young Horton Foote (1916–2009) revise his play *Texas Town*. As part of his effort at recruitment, Choate assured Riggs that "it was agreed that no one could bring more to this particular script than you, and if after reading it you feel you can give it your attention, you will have our complete confidence in whatever you decide should be done."[3] By April 1945, Riggs and the composer Aaron Copland (1900–90) were well into an adaptation of Erskine Caldwell's 1944 novel *Tragic Ground* (Braunlich, *Haunted* 169). Riggs sent Copland thirteen pages of the script, a musical comedy, later that month.[4] The composer encouraged Riggs in his response on 21 April 1945 but had turned doubtful by early July.[5] Late that month, Copland responded to his receipt of a full draft by observing that although a "good show" might come of the musical, "it will be difficult to sell it to Broadway audiences who know a good leg-show when they see one."[6] This project, too, never came to fruition.[7]

6, folder 123. While no evidence exists in Beinecke's archives, it appears that Riggs declined to meet with Preminger.

1   11 June 1952, Riggs Papers, Beinecke, box 4, folder 79.
2   Benton to Riggs, 9 October 1936, Riggs Papers, Beinecke, box 1, folder 7.
3   Choate to Riggs, 30 June 1941, Foote Papers, box 138, folder 15.
4   19 April 1945, Riggs Papers, Beinecke, box 1, folder 21.
5   Riggs Papers, Beinecke, box 1, folder 21.
6   9 July 1945, Riggs Papers, Beinecke, box 1, folder 21.
7   "In 1946, Riggs worked on a Georgia play that was an adaptation of Erskine Caldwell's novel *Tragic Ground*. It was to have had music by Copland, dances by De Mille, and sets by Oliver Smith" (*continued*)

This sequence of unrealized collaborations must have frustrated Riggs. He fared better during his stint in the Army. In 1943, Riggs and the celebrated dancer José Limón (1908–72) were stationed in Virginia. Together, they mounted "We Speak for Ourselves" (Appendix A8), which Riggs describes in his headnote as "a dance poem conceived by soldiers ... danced by soldiers, and *for* them" (p. 317; italics in original). But Riggs never achieved the same level of fame as Gershwin, Copland, or Limón, nor would his work in Hollywood earn him renown. But the admiration of accomplished contemporaries in various media demonstrates a regard unmatched by any other Indigenous artist of the period, with the exception of fellow Cherokee Will Rogers.

Like Gershwin and the other collaborators, Riggs positions himself within long, celebrated artistic traditions. He conveys his appreciation of Shakespeare in the titles of *Russet Mantle* (from *Hamlet*) and *A World Elsewhere* (from *Coriolanus*), as well as in the undertones of *King Lear* and *Julius Caesar* that, in *Out of Dust*, augment the louder notes of O'Neill's *Desire Under the Elms*. In a 1924 letter, he praised "the enormous gusto and delight of the Elizabethans."[1] The typed catalogue of his library includes titles by Beaumont and Fletcher, Chekhov, Corneille, Ibsen, Lope de Vega, Marlowe, Molière, Pushkin, Racine, Shakespeare, and Sheridan. Numerous anthologies of drama appear therein, with the previous generation of dramatists represented by Pirandello, Shaw, Strindberg, Wedekind, Wilde and his nearer contemporaries by Maxwell Anderson, O'Neill, and Thornton Wilder, among others.[2] Theatre historian Brice Ezell, who helped us assemble this volume for publication, finds compelling evidence of Riggs's indebtedness to Oscar Wilde (1854–1900) in his writings for the theatre. The Greeks appear in Riggs's library, too, and were amply represented in his drama course at Baylor University in the fall of 1941. His teaching notes mention Aeschylus, Aristophanes, Euripides, and Sophocles, the more compellingly given the proximity of his tenure at Baylor to his work on *The Cream in the Well*, Riggs's most studious tragedy.

As we have noted, Riggs also aligned himself with Green and other contemporary regionalists, as well as with the globalist

---

(Braunlich, *Haunted* 169). This "Georgia play" appears to be the same project on which Riggs worked in 1945.

1 Riggs to Betty Kirk, 24 July 1924, Kirk Collection, box 1, folder 6.

2 "Bibliography of Lynn Riggs' library" (1936–41), Riggs Papers, Beinecke, box 25, folder 428.

O'Neill. He intersects with and diverges from other prominent American playwrights of the post-war period. His eroticized emotionalism anticipates Tennessee Williams (1911–83), whose breakout play, *The Glass Menagerie*, he admired (see Carroll). With William Inge (1913–73), Riggs shared an interest in the wounding interplay of suppression and excess. But Riggs's is a more learned and exacting dramaturgy than Williams's or Inge's, more deeply rooted and more broadly allusive. Like, for example, *The Cream in the Well*, Arthur Miller's (1915–2005) early tragedies draw self-consciously on Greek drama. But nemesis—the fatal comeuppance of classical tragedy—becomes in Miller's *All My Sons* and *Death of a Salesman* a function of ideology. Capitalism crushes Joe Miller in the former play and Willie Loman in the latter. The forces that conspire against Riggs's Clabe Sawters are murkier and multitudinous: sexual, familial, racial, and, to glance at Sophocles, often horrible for being difficult to comprehend. Riggs asks more of us than Miller does.

But like these three playwrights—and like O'Neill, who died before his remarkable "late plays" were known—Riggs was not well regarded toward the end of his career. Clark liked *Verdigris Primitive*,[1] but it died after summer 1948 tryouts in Connecticut and New Jersey. His departure from Leverton and Samuel French in 1949 extended his commercial decline. Two plays that Riggs sent to his new agent, Lucy Kroll, fared poorly. The Theatre Guild optioned *Out of Dust* and, as late as May 1949, considered bringing it to Broadway; but they lost interest after a tryout three months later. A musical entitled *The Boy with Tyford Fever* (1949) would be retitled *Some Sweet Day*; in 1953, Riggs was still seeking a composer. *Verdigris Primitive* has never been published; the underrated *Out of Dust* resurfaced in 1959 as a television adaptation featuring Uta Hagen but would not be published until 2003. *Toward the Western Sky* (1951), Riggs's last play, was a pageant commissioned by Western Reserve University (later Case Western Reserve University) to celebrate the university's 125th anniversary.

Riggs combated adversity with activity in his last decade of life, much as Williams would do for the long final slog of his career. After his hitch in the military, and during a period that included teaching, traveling, screenwriting, and adapting the work of others, Riggs wrote all or part of eight plays and revised

---

1   Clark to Riggs, 26 February 1948, Riggs Papers, Beinecke, box 1, folder 19.

two more. None fared well.[1] Although Sam Wanamaker's revival of the *Reckless/Roadside* remake *Borned in Texas* (1941) reached Broadway in 1950, even a cast that featured Marsha Hunt (1917–2022) and the up-and-comer Anthony Quinn (1915–2001) could not sustain the run beyond eight performances. A 1952 collection of verse, *Hamlet Not the Only*, was rejected by the University of North Carolina Press, notwithstanding Paul Green's presentation of the manuscript to them. He completed neither a novel entitled *The Affair at Easter* nor a one-hour show for Philco-Goodyear Television Playhouse on which he worked in 1953. Riggs's only published work of prose during this period was a short story entitled "Eben, the Hound and the Hare," which appeared in the Summer 1953 issue of *Gentry* magazine.

Hints toward a legacy, however, are ascertainable even in this trying time. *The Year of Pilar* was finally staged in 1951, at a small theatre in Greenwich Village. Riggs must have been gratified by his discussions the next year with Roberto Rodriguez Suarez, a graduate of the University of Puerto Rico and a language teacher, about translating *Pilar* for Spanish-speaking audiences in New York.[2] *Toward the Western Sky* prompted Riggs's receipt of an honorary doctorate from Case Western Reserve. Harper included *Roadside*—so often reworked and retitled—in *Twenty-Five Modern Plays* (1953), along with entries by Ibsen, Strindberg, Wilde, Gorky, Chekhov, Synge, O'Casey, O'Neill, Williams, Arthur Miller, and others. In 1954, the University of Oklahoma Press honored a distinguished alumnus by publishing a limited edition of *Green Grow the Lilacs*, illustrated by the famous painter and printmaker Thomas Hart Benton (1889–1975). Around this time, Riggs told his old friend Spud Johnson (1897–1968) that he had been invited to write a piece for the Ford Foundation's television series, *Omnibus*.[3] As admirers of Riggs's work, we imagine Riggs at this time headed for broader recognition and perhaps a career writing for television.

As scholars, however, we do not need to imagine what happened to Riggs's reputation following his death in 1954: it

---

1 The eight plays are *The Cream in the Well, Dark Encounter, Verdigris Primitive, Laughter from a Cloud, Out of Dust, The Boy with Tyford Fever, The Hunger I Got*, and *Toward the Western Sky*. He revised *The Domino Parlor* as *Hang On to Love* and *Verdigris Primitive* as *All the Way Home*.

2 Suarez to Riggs, 27 November 1951, Riggs Papers, Beinecke, box 5, folder 107.

3 Riggs to Johnson, 12 August 1953, Spud Johnson Collection, Harry Ransom Center, box 10, folder 2.

solidified haltingly but discernibly. A 1965 induction into the National Cowboy and Western Heritage Museum's Hall of Great Westerners testifies to Riggs's success in chronicling the lives of Indigenes and others in Indian Territory and Oklahoma. The first published biography, by Thomas Erhard, appeared five years later in Steck-Vaughn's Southwest Writers Series. It superseded a 1959 biographical dissertation by Charles Aughtry and would be the standard life until the 1988 publication of Braunlich's *Haunted by Home*. Braunlich collected the sonnets meant for *Hamlet Not the Only* with other poems in *This Book, This Hill, These People*, published as part of Oklahoma's Diamond Jubilee celebration in 1982. Much later, in 2004, the Oklahoma Center for the Book posthumously bestowed on Riggs the Ralph Ellison Award for contributions to Oklahoma literature; in 2017, the Lynn Riggs Black Box Theatre opened in Tulsa in the Dennis R. Neill Equality Center. OU's awarding of an honorary degree in 2022 was a welcome if belated gesture; more substantially, that year saw the opening of the Lynn Riggs Art Gallery in the Claremore Museum of History, dedicated to Riggs's library and art collection. Due especially to the efforts of founding executive director and former curator Andy Couch, the Claremore Museum of History has created a permanent Riggs exhibit and assembled a stunning collection of materials related to Riggs's personal and professional life. These plaudits, Braunlich's book included, confirmed Riggs's status as a regionalist, as does his authorship of the source-text of *Oklahoma!* So, too, do the acknowledgments in various reputable histories of American drama, although a more detailed engagement in J. Frank Dobie's *Guide to Life and Literature of the Southwest* constitutes a welcome exception.

The Indigenous Plays assists in the ongoing scholarly contextualization and appreciation of Riggs's talents. Scholars of Indigenous literature including Jace Weaver, Craig Womack, and Daniel Heath Justice began paying closer attention to Riggs, especially to *The Cherokee Night*, in the 1990s and 2000s. They view Riggs as an important contemporary of Gertrude Bonnin (1876–1938), Ella Deloria (1889–1971), Charles Alexander Eastman (1858–1939), John Joseph Mathews (1895–1979), John Milton Oskison (1874–1947), Will Rogers (1879–1935), and other Native writers and, as such, a significant precursor to the Renaissance generation of writers that emerged in the late 1960s and early 1970s. The anti-Black racism and Cherokee "blood politics" in *The Cherokee Night*, however, have come more sharply into relief, thanks prominently to Julie Little Thunder and to Weaver, Womack, Justice, and others.[1] Participants in this debate should benefit from Riggs's commentary on the theatre (see Appendix A), in which he considers, among other topics, the theatre's role in promoting social justice. This section, we hope, will more closely bind Riggs to Native writers of the civil-rights era.

Kirby Brown, Chad Allen, and Jenna Hunnef, among others, have more recently pondered the influence of Riggs's Cherokee Nation homeland on his plays and the significance of his career to Indigenous drama and literature. Additional work on Riggs's position in Indigenous and non-Indigenous dramatic traditions awaits the wider circulation of his writing and the more frequent performance of his plays. As we cycle through the centenaries of his more than twenty-five plays, the time has come to accord Riggs the respect received by his more acclaimed peers and to promote his plays to new audiences. Riggs was like most serious theatre-goers today in recognizing the limitations of the conventional dramatic canon, his enthusiasm for many of its practitioners notwithstanding. Lest the students at Baylor make assumptions about his identity, Riggs reminded himself to share with them the following perspective on the "The Anglo Tradition": "Is it? We're not all Anglo. I certainly am not."[2] He did not record if he told his students that he was Cherokee.

---

1 See Little Thunder 355–65; see Sturm, a study of the cultural, social, and political role of race and blood, including blood quantum, in Cherokee history.
2 Baylor University teaching notes (1941), Riggs Papers, Beinecke, box 9, folder 169.

Lynn Riggs: A Brief Chronology

Information in this chronology has been drawn from Aughtry; Erhard; Braunlich, *Haunted*; the US *Catalog of Copyright Entries*; newspaper articles and notices, often via newspapers.com; and letters and other materials held in the archives listed in the bibliography. For Riggs's published plays, see the bibliography, below; for performances, see Appendix B, below.

1899   31 August: Born on a farm outside of Claremore in the Cherokee Nation, Indian Territory, to the former Rose "Rosie" Ella Buster, a Cherokee also born in Indian Territory, and William "Bill" Grant Riggs, whose family had moved to Indian Territory from Missouri in 1878.

1900   27 October: Bill applies for Cherokee Nation allotments for himself, Rosie, and their children, including the thirteen-month old Lynn. He sits for an interview about the application with the Commission to the Five Civilized Tribes.

1901   November: Rosie dies of typhoid at the age of 33. Her death makes her ineligible for an allotment.

1902   22 June: Bill Riggs marries Juliette Scrimsher Chambers, a Cherokee born in Indian Territory.
6 October: The Commission, which approves the allotments for the three Riggs children, interviews Bill a second time about his application for citizenship by intermarriage in the Cherokee Nation.

1905   The Riggs family moves to Claremore.

1907   10 January: The Commission informs Bill that his application to enroll as a citizen by intermarriage has been rejected.
17 September: Oklahoma statehood.

1910   Appears on stage, presumably in a student or community production, in *The Miller's Daughter*, possibly an abridgment of Steele MacKaye's *Hazel Kirke*.

1912   Begins attending Eastern University Preparatory School in Claremore.

1917   Graduates from Eastern University Prep; travels to Chicago and New York, where he attends plays, works as a proofreader for the *Wall Street Journal*, and, he later tells Barrett H. Clark, "play[s] extras in western movies made in Astoria and the Bronx."[1]

1919	Returns to Claremore and begins writing poetry; in Hollywood, again acts as an extra in films; writes a screenplay that he destroys after Goldwyn rejects it; works as a proofreader for the *Los Angeles Times*, which publishes his first poem.
1920	Again returns to his hometown; matriculates at the University of Oklahoma and begins writing and publishing poetry under the pseudonym Wallace Duncan.
1921	November: Listed for the first time as an editorial assistant for *University of Oklahoma Magazine*; begins contributing to *Oklahoma Whirlwind* and *Oklahoma Daily*. December: Starts writing his first play, the short farce *Cuckoo* (unpublished), while in Norman over the winter break.
1922	April: Publishes the first two of an eventual eight poems in H.L. Mencken and George Jean Nathan's *The Smart Set*. Summer: Travels the Chautauqua circuit through the Midwest with the Southern Minstrels, led by Joe Benton, a music teacher at the University of Oklahoma, future opera star, and lifelong friend. December: Earliest extant correspondence with the poet Witter Bynner.
1923	August: "Rhythm of Rain" appears in *Poetry*. November: Experiences a personal crisis; goes to Santa Fe and enters Sunmount Sanatorium.
1924	19 January: Writes to Campbell and his wife, Isabel Jones Campbell, from Sunmount. He tells his friends that he is feeling better and shares gossip about famous locals.
1925	6 January: Tells Betty Kirk that he has discovered an unfinished musical comedy, *Play the Game*, and asks if she will inquire about producing it at the University of Oklahoma. In the same letter, he says that he has a one-act play called *Knives from Syria* that "only needs dialogue."[2] *Knives from Syria* reaches the stage in Santa Fe in the spring.

---

1 Riggs to Barrett H. Clark, 28 June 1928, Clark Papers.
2 Riggs to Betty Kirk, 6 January 1925, Riggs Collection, box R-43, folder 5.

February–April: Writes *The Primitives*, his first full-length play, which he destroys.

June–August: Writes *Sump'n Like Wings*.

c. September: Teaches at the Lewis Institute in Chicago, later the Illinois Institute of Technology.

November–December: Writes *Big Lake*.

1926   14 April: Poem "Santo Domingo Corn Dance" appears in *The Nation*.

May–June: Writes *A Lantern to See By* in New York.

Summer: Writes *The High Mountain* while living at and working on playwright Hatcher Hughes's farm in Cornwall, Connecticut. He will destroy the script but recycle the title for Scene 5 of *The Cherokee Night*.

1927   April: *Big Lake* plays at American Laboratory Theatre (Broadway).

Summer: Goes to the Yaddo retreat for artists in Saratoga Springs, New York; begins *The Lonesome West* and *Borned in Texas*, later entitled *Reckless* and *Roadside*.

c. September: Completes *The Lonesome West* (unpublished).

October: Applies for a Guggenheim Foundation fellowship in October.

November: Begins *Rancor* (unpublished; spells the title *Rancour* in numerous letters to Clark and elsewhere) in New York.

1928   January: In Oklahoma for a reading and speaking tour. On 10 January, he reads *A Lantern to See By* at a meeting of the Authors' League in Oklahoma City. He attends, as a distinguished guest, the Tulsa Shakespeare Club's annual tea on 27 January and reads *Rancor* to the club.

February–April: Writes *The Domino Parlor*, later revised, performed, and published as *Hang On to Love*.

13 March: The Guggenheim Foundation writes to Riggs to inform him that he has been awarded a fellowship.

July: Sails for France to begin his Guggenheim.

Fall–winter: Writes and destroys *On a Siding*, a one-act play.

November: Tells Clark that he is writing *Green Grow the Lilacs* and conceptualizing *The Cherokee Night* as a series of short plays. He will later tell the *New York World-Telegram* that he started *Green Grow the Lilacs* at Café Les Deux Magots in Paris.

December: Tells Clark that he is thinking about a play called *More Sky* (unpublished). In a request for an extension of his Guggenheim, Riggs says he would use the additional time to work on *The Cherokee Night* and a stage adaptation, unpublished, of James Gould Cozzens's 1929 novel *The Son of Perdition*.

1929   30 January: Posts the first three scenes of *Green Grow the Lilacs* to Clark.

March: In a letter to Clark, Riggs outlines the structure of *The Cherokee Night* and asks Clark to pitch *Green Grow the Lilacs* to the Theatre Guild.

April: Having completed his fellowship, Riggs sails for New York, where he faces financial hardship.

c. June: Moves temporarily to Provincetown, MA; stays with Ida Rauh.

July: Clark discusses *Green Grow the Lilacs* with the Theatre Guild.

27 July: Updates Paul Green on *Green Grow the Lilacs* and *Sump'n Like Wings*; says he is writing *Roadside* and plans to move forward with *The Cherokee Night* and *More Sky*.

August: Works on *The Cherokee Night* and *Roadside*; completes the latter by 26 August.

29 August: Clark responds very favorably to a partial reading of *Roadside* and tells Riggs that Kenneth Macgowan is interested in producing *The Domino Parlor*, pending some changes to the script.

1930   January: Travels to Hollywood to work on a film for Pathé Studios; contributes to John S. Robertson's *Beyond Victory* and *Siren Song*.

March: Mentions a plan to resume working later in the year on *The Son of Perdition*.

23 June: Tells Clark that he has seen Susan Glaspell and read her new play, *Alison's House*, which will win the Pulitzer Prize for drama in 1931.

September: Publishes *The Iron Dish* (Doubleday, Doran), a collection of poems.

26 September–4 October: *Roadside* plays at Longacre Theatre (Broadway).

October: Learns that the Theatre Guild will produce

Green Grow the Lilacs; continues work on *The Cherokee Night* in Provincetown.

1931   26 January: *Green Grow the Lilacs*, Riggs's most commercially successful play, debuts at Broadway's Guild Theatre. The play will run for sixty-four performances prior to a Midwestern tour.

1 February: Reads *Green Grow the Lilacs* at Playmakers Theatre, University of North Carolina in Chapel Hill; in North Carolina, works on a production of *The Cherokee Night* with Paul Green.

April: Reads *The Cherokee Night* at Playmakers Theatre.

May: Travels to Tulsa for a production of *Green Grow the Lilacs*; reads from *Roadside* at a lunch hosted by the Claremore Chamber of Commerce.

c. June: Publishes essay "When People Say 'Folk Drama'" in the journal *Carolina Playbook*.

August: In Santa Fe, films *A Day in Santa Fe* with his friend Jim Hughes; finishes *The Son of Perdition*.

13 October: The *New York Herald Tribune* publishes six sonnets by Riggs.

6–7 November: Riggs and Mrs. Howard Huey (Anna V. Huey) direct George S. Kaufman and Edna Ferber's *The Royal Family* at the Seth Hall auditorium in Santa Fe for the New Mexico Educational Association.

16 December: *The Nation* publishes his review of *Singing Cowboy: A Book of Western Songs*, collected and edited by Margaret Larkin.

1932   Samuel French publishes *Cowboy Songs, Folk Songs and Ballads from Green Grow the Lilacs*.

January: Publishes "A Day in Santa Fe," an article about his film, in *The Cine-Kodak News*.

6 January: *A Day in Santa Fe* premieres at La Fonda in Santa Fe.

12 January: Finishes *The Cherokee Night*, which he will lightly revise in 1935.

February: Clark talks with Cheryl Crawford about a Theatre Guild production of *The Cherokee Night*.

March: Attends performances of *A Lantern to See By* and *Roadside* at the Hedgerow.

April: More than three years after conceiving it, begins writing *More Sky* in Provincetown.

June: Directs *Green Grow the Lilacs* at Northwestern University with the support of Garrett Leverton, professor of dramatic production and director of the Northwestern University Theatre from 1928 to 1938.

18 June: *The Cherokee Night* premieres at the Hedgerow.

27 October: Writes to Clark from Iowa City, where he plans to direct *The Cherokee Night*.

16 November: Delivers talk entitled "Poetry—And Poetry in the Theatre" on WSUI radio, Iowa City.

7 December: Directs *The Cherokee Night* in the Auditorium of the University of Iowa's Hall of Natural Science.

1933   28 January: Sends the completed *More Sky* to Clark.

c. May: In Hollywood, works on W.S. Van Dyke's *Laughing Boy*, from the 1929 novel by Oliver La Farge, and William Wellman's *Stingaree*.

September: Harry "Ward" Ritchie privately publishes fifty copies of *Listen, Mind*, comprising six sonnets previously published in the *New York Herald Tribune*.

30 October: Tells Spud Johnson that he has purchased a lot in Santa Fe and plans to build a house on it.

1934   c. January: Works on screenplays, including *Family Man* (released as *His Greatest Gamble* without a writing credit for Riggs), for various Hollywood studios.

March: Negotiates successfully with Leverton to schedule a production of *More Sky* at Northwestern.

May: Still in Hollywood, works on *A Wicked Woman* for MGM; begins writing *Russet Mantle*.

July: Directs *More Sky* at Northwestern University.

October: Flies to Hollywood to work on *Broken Soil* for Samuel Goldwyn. Warner Brothers expresses interest in the movie rights for *Green Grow the Lilacs*. Riggs is skeptical; the play will never be filmed.

1935   7 January: Informs Clark that he has finished *Russet Mantle*.

February: Goes to Hollywood to work on *Delay in the Sun*, from the 1934 novel by Anthony Thorne. The film seems not to have been made.

May: *Green Grow the Lilacs* performed at the Festival of Southwestern Plays at Southern Methodist University, Dallas, with Riggs in attendance.

December: Requests a loan of $2,500 from Joan

Crawford to help finance *Russet Mantle*. Crawford promptly acquiesces; Riggs will settle the debt by October 1936.

1936   16 January: *Russet Mantle*, directed by Alexander Dean, opens at Broadway's Theatre Masque (now John Golden Theatre). Riggs gives his ticket to Rauh; it runs for 117 performances.

February: Talks about the success of *Russet Mantle* with the *Santa Fe New Mexican* and says that he has conceived of *A World Elsewhere*.

1 June: Tells Kirk that he has just returned to Santa Fe after working on *The Garden of Allah*, starring Marlene Dietrich and Charles Boyer. He adds that George Gershwin has approached him about collaborating on an opera.

c. July: Back in Hollywood, Riggs contributes to the script of *The Plainsman*, starring Gary Cooper and Jean Arthur, after which he returns to Santa Fe.

20 July: Clark attends a performance of *The Cherokee Night* produced by Works Progress Administration (WPA) drama teachers at Provincetown Playhouse.

23 July: Riggs reads the first act of *Russet Mantle* in Rodey Hall at the University of New Mexico in Albuquerque.

October: Works on *A World Elsewhere* in Santa Fe; plans the ultimately unrealized opera with Gershwin.

1937   April–May: In Mexico, with Spud Johnson and Betty Kirk; continues to work on *A World Elsewhere*.

c. June: Enrique Gasque-Molina (Ramón Naya) is living with Riggs in Santa Fe.

8 September: Writes to Campbell from Hollywood that he has run out of money.

1938   February: Has finished the one-act version of *A World Elsewhere*.

26 February: Makes notes toward *The Year of Pilar*, a fragmentary draft of which he will complete in April.

June: Publishes short story "We Moved to Pomona" in Summer 1938 issue of *Laughing Horse*.

1939   March: Returns to Santa Fe. In a letter to Green, Riggs proposes a project called the Vine Theatre.

By late March or early April, Riggs had returned to Mexico, where he and Naya continue work on their play, *A Cow in a Trailer*, with music by Jerome Moross.

11 June: Back in Santa Fe, Riggs and Naya complete *A Cow in a Trailer*.

November: Begins taking notes toward *The Cream in the Well*.

1940   19 February: Delivers talk entitled "Some Notes on the Theatre" at the Globe Theatre (aka The Old Globe), San Diego. In February 1941, *Theatre Arts* will publish "A Credo for the Tributary Theatre," a condensed version of the talk.

March: Begins rehearsing *A World Elsewhere* at the Globe Theatre.

27 March: Delivers talk in San Diego entitled "What the Theatre Can Mean to All of Us."

April: Sells his house in Santa Fe in which he had lived off and on for six years. He will periodically return to Santa Fe and stay with friends.

14 April: CBS radio presents *A Cow in a Trailer*, credited to Moross.

August: Completes *The Cream in the Well* but leaves open the possibility of revision.

1941   20 January–8 February: *The Cream in the Well* plays at Booth Theatre (Broadway).

26 January: Outlines the dire state of his finances in a letter to Frank J. Sheil at Samuel French.

7 February: Reports discussions with Leverton about proposing a collection of his plays to Random House. Riggs wants to include *The Cream in the Well*, *The Year of Pilar*, *More Sky*, *The Lonesome West*, *The Son of Perdition*, and *Hang On to Love*. Nothing will come of the project.

20 February: Reads *The Cream in the Well* to friends in Santa Fe. A representative of the group subsequently sends a letter defending the play to the *New York Times*.

23 May: Reads *A Cow in a Trailer* at a New Mexico Association on Indian Affairs benefit.

September: Begins teaching at Baylor University in Waco, Texas.

9 October: B. Iden Payne reportedly expresses interest in producing *The Cream in the Well* but says the war makes a production impracticable.

24 October: Gives a lecture to the Texas Institute of Letters after an introduction by Dallas playwright John William Rogers.

| | 13 November: Assists in a successful production of *Macbeth*, the first performance at Baylor's new theatre. |
| 1942 | 14 February: Registers for the draft. |

March–April: Works on screenplays for *Destination Unknown* (1942), *Sherlock Holmes and the Voice of Terror* (1942), and *Madam Spy* (1942).

June: Co-authors a draft of a screenplay with Bertram Millhauser for *Sherlock Holmes in Washington* (1943).

July: Drafted into the Army.

September: Theresa Helburn of the Theatre Guild updates Riggs on the status of Rodgers and Hammerstein's adaptation of *Green Grow the Lilacs*. Riggs is stationed in Fort Ord, CA.

23 November: Assigned to the 846 Signal Service Photo Battalion, Wright Field, Dayton, Ohio, along with the Pulitzer Prize–winning playwright William Saroyan.

1943 March: After a trial run in New Haven under the title *Away We Go*, *Oklahoma!* opens 31 March at Broadway's St. James Theatre with Riggs in attendance. The Theatre Guild's production will run through May 1948, comprising 2,212 performances, and will give Riggs some financial stability.

2 June: After his discharge from the Army, Riggs takes a position with the Office of War Information.

5 September: "We Speak for Ourselves," a "dance poem" written by Riggs and choreographed by José Limón, is performed by soldiers from Camp Lee at the Mosque Theater in Richmond, Virginia, on the campus of Virginia Commonwealth University. The miscellaneous program raised almost $250,000 for the war effort.

November: *The Dance Observer* publishes Riggs's commentary on "We Speak for Ourselves."

December: *Theatre Arts* publishes "We Speak for Ourselves"; writes *The Valley*, a three-act comedy (unpublished).

1944 June: Tells Kirk that he has started a new play, presumably *Dark Encounter*, which he will finish within the year.

1945 March–July: Works with Aaron Copland on an adaptation of Erskine Caldwell's 1944 novel, *Tragic Ground* (unpublished).

1946	Works on *Verdigris Primitive*, later revised as *All the Way Home* (unpublished).
	15 February: Completes draft of *Laughter from a Cloud* (unpublished).
	21 May: Sends Copland a letter with an updated script of their collaboration.
	June–August: Continues work on the adaptation of *Tragic Ground*.
1947	Works on *Out of Dust* and *The Boy with Tyford Fever*, which he renames *Some Sweet Day* (unpublished). Riggs produces many drafts of *Some Sweet Day* until completing the "last version" in 1954.
	20 May: Reports that he has purchased a home on Shelter Island with Gui Machado, a dancer working with Limón, casts *Laughter from a Cloud*, and waits for word from the Theatre Guild about *Verdigris Primitive*.
1948	16 November: Inducted into the Oklahoma Hall of Fame at a banquet at the Biltmore Hotel in Oklahoma City.
1949	29 March: Informs Leverton that he has ended his business relationship with Samuel French. He adds that he will send two plays—*Out of Dust* and *All the Way Home*—to Lucy Kroll, who will evidently be his agent henceforth.
1950	Invited by Western Reserve University (now Case Western Reserve University) to write a pageant, ultimately called *Toward the Western Sky*.
	February and March: Riggs produces new drafts of *Out of Dust*.
	21–26 August: *Borned in Texas* plays at Fulton Theatre (Broadway).
1951	March: In Chapel Hill completing *Toward the Western Sky*; reads the nearly finished play with playwright Josefina Niggli at Green's home on 11 March. He makes his final visit to Oklahoma this month.
	April: Finishes *Toward the Western Sky*.
	11 June: Western Reserve University awards Riggs the honorary degree Doctor of Letters (Litt.D.). On the same day, *Toward the Western Sky* was staged in Cleveland Heights, Ohio, at Cain Park Theatre. The Press of Western Reserve University publishes the play later in the year.
	24 July: Attends the 500th performance of Green's

historical pageant *The Lost Colony* on Roanoke Island, Virginia.

6 September: Bill Riggs dies at the age of 82; Lynn does not attend the funeral.

1952   Late January: Arrives in Chapel Hill, where he will stay until July.

19 March: Attends a public reading and lecture by Robert Frost in the Hill Hall Auditorium at the University of North Carolina.

August: Sends a collection of poems, *Hamlet Not the Only*, to Green, who would submit it to the University of North Carolina Press. The press rejects it.

1953   March–April: Works on a novel, *The Affair at Easter*, at his home in Shelter Island.

May: Publishes the short story "Eben, the Hound and the Hare" in *Gentry* (Summer 1953).

August: Tells Spud Johnson that he has been asked to write a piece for the Ford Foundation's television series *Omnibus*.

November: Still at his Shelter Island home, Riggs shifts focus from the novel to a one-hour show for Philco-Goodyear Television Playhouse.

12 December: Hospitalized in New York for a stomach hemorrhage. Four days later, he will inform his friends Jacques Hardré and Bill Baskin III of his illness and convalescence.

1954   28 January: Tells Spud Johnson about his emergency visit to the hospital in December.

c. February: Visits friends in Chapel Hill; has an operation at Duke University Hospital for a stomach ulcer.

June: Hospitalized with throat, lung, and stomach cancer at Memorial Hospital, in New York. His sister, Mattie Riggs Cundiff, comes to New York and stays at his bedside in the hospital.

30 June: Dies at the age of 54 following a visit from Spud Johnson.

6 July: Interred at Woodlawn Cemetery in Claremore after a funeral service at the First Methodist Church.

A Note on the Texts

Texts of the three plays in this volume are based on first editions published by Samuel French: *The Cherokee Night* from *"The Cherokee Night" and "Russet Mantle"* (1936), and *The Year of Pilar* and *The Cream in the Well* from *Four Plays* (1947). Only *The Cherokee Night* among this triad has been republished in print; indeed, almost all of Riggs's plays remain either out of print or unpublished. Jace Weaver's 2003 edition of *The Cherokee Night* is a valuable contribution to Riggs studies but does not include a statement of textual principles or offer insights into Riggs's professional life beyond what we know from Phyllis Cole Braunlich's carefully researched 1988 biography.[1] Therefore, it has not influenced our editorial work. Neither have the online texts marketed by Alexander Street, which are compromised by errors of transcription or conversion.

The French editions of all three plays—our copy-texts—retain the orthographical "inconsistencies" that Riggs acknowledged in his work. The published texts of *The Cherokee Night* and *The Cream in the Well* are scrupulous, too, in their respect for the idiomatic speech that Riggs described as "backwoods" but "rich, flavorous, lustrous, and wise."[2] The high quality of these texts has allowed us to follow an expedient method: we have identified instances of evident, presumed, or possible errors in the copy-texts; collated these passages against Riggs's typescripts; emended our base-text accordingly; and tabulated our findings.

The sequencing of early states has been essential to our work: to what state or states, and according to what hierarchy, does one turn when a copy-text presents erroneous or dubious readings? Happily, stemmata, or textual histories, of these three plays may be reconstructed with reasonable accuracy. Except in several instances, duly noted in the textual apparatus below, we have applied a hierarchy that privileges stemmatic proximity to the copy-text.

The lack of page proofs of these plays, marked or unmarked, has sometimes forced us to rely on inference, for example in our

---

1 The edition also includes *Green Grow the Lilacs* and the previously unpublished *Out of Dust*. Weaver draws the chronology, headnotes, and bibliography from Braunlich.

2 Riggs to Henry Moe, 28 December 1928 (copy), Clark Papers, box 5.

attempts to distinguish instances in which Riggs expected French to impose a house style onto texts from instances in which he preferred to retain authority over them.[1] But every serious editorial project involves challenges of this sort, and every serious editor is obliged to specify the actions they have taken to meet them. The following comments will allow readers to understand our work; the tables and notes in the textual apparatus will allow them to judge it.

With few exceptions, we have retained non-idiomatic departures from conventional orthography that recur in Riggs's typescripts and migrate into the first edition. For example, "drumbeat" and "drum beat" both appear in the typescripts of *The Year of Pilar*, and the erroneous "grainary" appears consistently in typescripts of *The Cream in the Well*. Riggs's occasional Anglicisms (e.g., "wilful") remain. French accepted these and many analogous readings, and we find no basis for dissent. We have, however, favored readings from earlier typescripts when misspellings originate in last-known states and recur in copy-texts. For example, the possessive "Mr. Sawters'," from an earlier typescript of *The Cream in the Well*, corrects the erroneous "Mr. Sawter's," common to a later typescript and the first edition that was evidently set from it. Riggs's and French's use of the n-word remains in *The Cherokee Night* and *The Cream in the Well*, albeit unpleasantly.

French faithfully replicated Riggs's expressive punctuation; his medial and terminal truncations (e.g., "sump'n" and "leavin'"); and his often irregular but rhythmically suggestive use of ellipsis points. We have done so as well, except when collation has suggested error in the copy-texts. We have regularized the setting of stage directions according to stylings favored but not uniformly practiced in *Four Plays*. The spacing of dashes in stage directions and dialogue also follows the general practice observed in that collection.

A handful of obvious errors of house-styling have been silently corrected: unique parentheses in a stage direction are set as square brackets, a single letter set roman in an italic sequence is regularized, a dropped period is restored, and so forth. Speech

---

1 Riggs rarely mentions proofs in his letters. On 13 July 1927, he told his agent, Barrett H. Clark, that he had "sent ... proofs [of *Knives from Syria*] yesterday," presumably to French, marked (Clark Papers, box 5). A cover letter to Clark dated 19 February 1936 and beginning "here are the proofs" indicates that Riggs returned proofs of *"Russet Mantle" and "The Cherokee Night"* (Riggs Papers, Beinecke, box 1, folder 18).

prefixes and names in stage directions are set in small caps with an initial majuscule, as they are, generally, in *Four Plays*. We have silently rectified several errors of scaling. For example, in *The Cherokee Night*, we have corrected the copy-text's speech prefix "Hutch and Gar" to "HUTCH AND GAR," and, twice, have converted the charactonym "Man" to "MAN," per other instances in the copy-text. The casts of characters, the synopses of scenes, and the intertextual act/scene designations generally follow the format of *Four Plays* but, conventionally, are regularized for consistency.

Although Riggs would claim to have begun thinking about *The Cherokee Night* "in March & April, 1929," his earliest thoughts on its form date to November 1928, when he considered working on several of the short plays that he would later fold into the longer offering.[1] By March 1929, he had committed to constructing his "curious, most novel long play" from an overlapping list of shorter works.[2] The project was "fermenting rapidly" by April but soon stalled as Riggs attended to *Green Grow the Lilacs* and other matters.[3] In October 1930, Riggs declared that *The Cherokee Night* "begins to look very exciting."[4]

Riggs "finished" *The Cherokee Night* twice. According to a notation on his desk calendar, he did so initially on 12 January 1932, a comfortable five months before the play premiered at Jasper Deeter's Hedgerow Theater in Rose Valley, Pennsylvania.[5] More

---

1 Riggs to Clark, 20 October 1930, Clark Papers, box 5; see Riggs to Clark, [6 November] 1928, Clark Papers, box 5. On 2 February 1928, Riggs had included "The Place Where the N[*****] Was Found" in notes toward the novel entitled *The Cream in the Well*. See Riggs Papers, Beinecke, box 10, folder 185.

2 Riggs to Clark, March 1929, Clark Papers. Braunlich references a letter from Riggs to the Guggenheim Foundation's Henry Moe on "[a play] I have contemplated for some time, a dramatic study of the descendants of the Cherokee Indians in Oklahoma, to be called The Cherokee Night" (*Haunted* 77). Her source is the Guggenheim Foundation's "Riggs File"; she implies, but does not say, that the letter was dated 28 December 1928 (*Haunted* 77, 213n7). The passage does not appear in the Beinecke's copy of Riggs to Moe referenced above or in a second 28 December letter to Moe, also held as a copy at the Beinecke (Clark Papers, box 5).

3 Riggs to Clark, 7 April 1929, Clark Papers, box 5.

4 Riggs to Clark, 20 October 1930, Clark Papers, box 5.

5 "Finished 'The Cherokee Night'" (finding aid, Riggs Papers, McFarlin Library, University of Tulsa, 1920s–1990s [2021], entry for box 11, folder 1). All finding aids referenced herein are available via institutional websites. The play opened on 18 June 1932.

than three years later, on 4 June 1935, he wrote "Final Draft" on the front of a binder containing a lightly revised version.[1] Both pronouncements are accurate in their own ways. Conventionally, Riggs completed, and filed with his publisher, a first "final" version of his script meant for production and copyright but not necessarily for publication. (Then as now, French licensed plays as well as published them.) Again conventionally, he submitted two copies, one a carbon of the other. Riggs marked each text lightly for corrections and addenda. The markings in the two states are almost identical with respect to wording, but the carbon adds cues for the sound designer in another hand, perhaps Deeter's. These non-authorial and production-specific cues suggest that French retained the original typescript and forwarded the carbon either to the Hedgerow or the University of Iowa, which would mount a production later in 1932.[2] The omission in later states of a passage marked for deletion on the carbon, but not on the original, suggests the carbon's supersession of the original. We have thus selected the carbon for our collations. It is identified by the siglum *CN-TS1* in our textual apparatus.[3]

The second "finished" version—the 1935 "Final Draft"—is either the state Riggs submitted for publication or a near predecessor of it. Designated *CN-TS2* in our textual apparatus, it is the most authoritative typescript of *The Cherokee Night*.[4] *CN-TS2* incorporates all the changes that Riggs marked in *CN-TS1*, the most notable of which is Bee Newcomb's revelation to Art Osburn in Scene 2 that she and Gar Breeden "had the same

---

1 Lynn Riggs, autograph note, binder cover, *The Cherokee Night*, Performing Arts Research Collection, New York Public Library, LCOF+ Riggs, L. Cherokee night.

2 For the Iowa production, see Riggs to Clark, 27 October 1932 (Clark Papers, box 5); see also Braunlich, *Haunted* 120.

3 *CN-TS1* is held in the Riggs Papers, University of Tulsa, box 1, folder 9; this text is misleadingly identified in Tulsa's finding aid as "another version [of *The Cherokee Night*]." The marked passage appears on Scene 5, page 17 of that text. For the original, see Riggs Papers, University of Tulsa, box 1, folder 8, erroneously catalogued as a "third version," i.e., as subsequent to the "second draft," discussed below (p. 57).

4 *CN-TS2* is held in the Performing Arts Research Collection, New York Public Library, LCOF+ Riggs, L. Cherokee night. Riggs Papers, University of Tulsa, box 1, folder 7, is a carbon of the NYPL text. Bibliographical descriptions suggest that the text held by the Institute of American Indian Arts, Santa Fe, is another copy. WorldCat lists the NYPL and IAIA texts jointly.

daddy," Edgar Spench.[1] Most of these changes would, in turn, be incorporated into the copy-text (*CN-SF*), along with several autograph corrections that Riggs made to *CN-TS2*.[2] Samuel French copyrighted the play in March 1936, two months after Riggs had signed the contract for its publication.[3]

Late in 1937, Riggs's partner, Enrique Gasque-Molina (Ramón Naya), shared with Riggs an account of his family's life in Yucatán and New York City. Naya's letter provided the impetus and background for *The Year of Pilar*, on which Riggs began work early the next year.[4] An autograph manuscript written from 26 February to 1 March 1938 chronicles the development of a play, initially entitled *Hacienda*, "showing the debacle of a Mexican family—conditioned by its inheritance, by New York, by a return to Yucatàn [*sic*]." On 27 February, Riggs settled on the final title and was evidently content to regard these notes as a first "draft."[5] A later manuscript indicates that he returned to *Pilar* on 4 March and then worked on it intermittently through most of that month and almost daily from 28 March to 20 April. An autograph addendum on a separate sheet, dated 21 April, reads, "The second draft completed—here attached."[6] Another note on the same sheet—"the play is now finished"—cannot apply to a fragmentary text that is far less coherent than, for example, the first "finished" state of *The Cherokee Night*. Riggs might nonetheless have written these lines in late April, intending something like "I have fully conceptualized this play"; or he may have added the sheet later, saying, in effect, "the play drafted herein has since been completed."[7]

---

1 See *CN-TS1*, Scene 2, p. 8; and *CN-TS2*, Scene 2, p. 9. Riggs may have wanted to maximize expository effect: his "people" lists in *CN-TS2* and *CN-SF* identify Spench only as "Gar's father."
2 Riggs's ad hoc longhand instructions in *CN-TS2* about blocking and furniture placement are not represented in the copy-text.
3 Copyright information herein is from the *Catalog of Copyright Entries*. Barbara Hogenson (Barbara Hogenson Agency, New York) generously shared information on contracts.
4 December 1937, Riggs Papers, Beinecke, box 4, folder 89. See also Introduction, p. 23.
5 See Riggs, "Hacienda," Riggs Papers, University of Tulsa, box 5, folder 7 (catalogued as "Hascienda").
6 See Riggs Papers, University of Tulsa, box 5, folder 8.
7 An autograph entry on the last page of the first known typescript supports the latter conjecture: "2nd Draft Finished | April 21, 1938" (Riggs Papers, University of Tulsa, box 5, folder 9). The typescript is otherwise undated but, as the seriatim dates in Riggs's "second draft" (*continued*)

In any case, he would produce or cause to be produced at least four distinct typescripts after the March–April manuscript. On 19 September 1938, he would tell his friend and fellow playwright Paul Green that "I have a new play, The Year of Pilar."[1]

Braunlich, taking Riggs at his word, declares that the playwright "completed" *Pilar* in September 1938.[2] This is not inaccurate, but it is misleading. As in the case of *The Cherokee Night*, Riggs seems to have "finished" *Pilar* more than once—a common practice, as playwrights respond to producers, directors, audiences, actors, and censors, as well as to their own second thoughts. Understandably, given the state of the Riggs archives in the 1980s, Braunlich did not notice that Riggs wrote two endings for *Pilar*.[3] Complete typescripts fall into two categories: early texts that conclude with the guilt-addled Pilar Crespo intending to "drag out [her] bitter years alone," in atonement for the sins of colonialism and settler colonialism; and later states in which she wanders out of her family's hacienda, "straight to her fate, her immolation," signaled by "a wild and terrible cry [that] bursts from the Indians, menacing and terrifying."[4] The only states that include the latter ending are the last known typescript (*YP-TS4*) and the published edition. Braunlich, familiar with the letter to Green but not with

---

prove, must postdate 21 April. This state is designated *YP-TS1* in our textual apparatus; its primacy is established by autograph addenda that Riggs incorporated into later states.

1 19 September 1938, Green Papers, University of North Carolina at Chapel Hill, 3693.

2 See Braunlich, *Haunted* 152. Braunlich must have based her claim on the 16 September letter, but she references only a 6 September 1938 telegram from Riggs to Green (Green Papers, 3693) that says nothing about *Pilar*.

3 Braunlich does not reference three of the archives that hold typescripts of *Pilar*. The Beinecke Riggs Papers were donated in 1984 and perhaps were inaccessible during her research; the Lake Forest Leverton Papers may have escaped notice in a pre-electronic age; and acquisition data suggest that the Lucy Kroll Papers at the Library of Congress were being assembled well after the publication of Braunlich's book. The Beinecke and LoC Kroll finding aids were created in 1993 and 2002, respectively. Braunlich was among the bequeathers of University of Tulsa's Riggs Papers and presumably encountered typescripts that she deemed irrelevant to her work.

4 See Kroll Papers, Library of Congress, box 575, folder 4, designated *YP-TS4* in our textual apparatus; the Samuel French edition is *YP-SF*. Riggs Papers, Beinecke, box 21, folder 337 is a mimeograph of the Kroll text; the original is not identified in the Beinecke's finding aid.

the play's textual history, assumed that the published text was established by September 1938, "immolation" ending and all.

This is unlikely. In a 26 October 1938 follow-up letter to Green, Riggs registered Green's interest in "trying out the play"— surely *Pilar* and surely in Chapel Hill, North Carolina, home to Green and the Playmakers Theatre, with whom he was affiliated.[1] Green must have read a script before making this gesture and may have been prompted to request one by Riggs's 19 September letter: "God alone knows who would do [*Pilar*]. I'm afraid to offer it." He read the earlier ending: both of the complete, presentable early typescripts, *YP-TS2* and *YP-TS3*, end with Pilar's decision to live on as the representative of "the wrong and the viciousness and the tyranny" from which her family has profited.[2]

The neatness of these two states suggests that Riggs intended them for circulation, and their similarity affirms proximity in a textual lineage. *YP-TS2* is a carbon (original unidentified) with one autograph correction and one autograph addendum, both in Riggs's hand and neither extant in *YP-TS3*. The precise routing of *YP-TS2* and its carbon is impossible to determine, obscured for example by Riggs's move from Hollywood to New York during the gap between his letters to Green and by the installation of a new literary editor at Samuel French: Barrett H. Clark's replacement, Garrett Leverton, who would also become Riggs's agent.[3] That Leverton retained *YP-TS3* we know from its preservation in his papers at Lake Forest College.[4] But this is irrelevant to a discussion of content, per se; and it remains inconceivable that, in a matter of a month or so, Riggs completed, distributed, and added a shockingly radical ending to a play that he was already "afraid to

1 26 October 1938, Green Papers, 3693. Braunlich discusses only the part of the letter concerned with the Vine Theatre (see *Haunted* 154–56). Riggs, who had just received Green's "much forwarded and re-forwarded letter of Oct. 12," was noncommittal about the "tryout": "I might easily like to do that—if I don't get too tied down [in New York]."

2 *YP-TS2* is held in the Riggs Papers, Beinecke, box 21, folder 336; *YP-TS3* is held in the Leverton Theatre Collection Series, box 2, folder 39.

3 Leverton was working full-time at French by October (see "Rialto Rambling"), after what various newspaper accounts suggest was a gradual transition from his professorship at Northwestern University.

4 *YP-TS2* and *YP-TS3* are closely related; our sequencing is supported, but not proven, by the evidently professional preparation of *YP-TS3*, in which stage directions, act/scene designations, and paratext are typed in red—uniquely, in our documentary investigations.

offer." His interests were elsewhere, as we know from his March 1939 apology to Green, referencing the "many complications" that had prevented him from "com[ing] down and help[ing] with the production of The Year of Pilar."[1]

The "immolation" ending may date to the period shortly before the publication of *Four Plays* in 1947. A mimeograph of *YP-TS4* is preserved in a William Morris Agency folder, and it is difficult to imagine that glitzy outfit gambling on Riggs before the 1943 opening of *Oklahoma!*, Richard Rodgers and Oscar Hammerstein II's hugely successful adaptation of *Green Grow the Lilacs*.[2] The likeliest time for later composition is the span from 16 September 1946, when Riggs signed the contract for *Four Plays*, and mid-1947, when he must have submitted his manuscript to the press. *Oklahoma!* was drawing throngs throughout this period, and Riggs's name was on the programs and the publicity materials.[3]

The play's performance history is also blurry. Braunlich assumes that Green and Riggs did in fact work together on a Chapel Hill tryout (*Haunted* 151). However, no corroborative evidence suggests that such a tryout ever took place. An exhaustive search of documentary materials has not discovered any record of a performance or reading of *Pilar*, or any record of Riggs, in or around Chapel Hill at that time; nor is Green anywhere associated with an actual performance or reading of that play.[4] Neither the Green-Riggs papers nor Green's published letters record any correspondence between the two playwrights from October 1938 to March 1939.[5] A 1959 dissertation by Charles Aughtry reproduces a passage from a Samuel French memorandum declaring that "no record of production of any sort [has] been given" (62n15). Braunlich, who references Aughtry in other contexts, seems to have come around to his perspective: in an appendix presumably written late in her work, she enters "none" for *Pilar* under "Play

---

1 5 March 1939, Green Papers, 3693.
2 For the mimeograph, and the William Morris folder, see Riggs Papers, Beinecke, box 21, folder 337.
3 *Oklahoma!* ran from March 1943 to May 1948. The inclusion of Riggs's name was stipulated by contract.
4 We thank Cecelia Moore, former university historian at the University of North Carolina at Chapel Hill, for her investigation of this matter.
5 Riggs visited Chapel Hill on other occasions and had at least twice considered but decided against making the trip; see Green 171. Riggs's financial difficulties in the late 1930s might help account for a cooling of his interest in *Pilar*.

Production" (*Haunted* 204). Riggs seems to have apologized to Green for missing an event that never occurred.

It is easy to imagine Green or his colleagues getting cold feet, given the play's subject matter. An analogous fate would be visited on the play a decade later: in 1948, a planned production at the University of Iowa was demoted to a reading by the author, perhaps, the local columnist Jack O'Brien opined, owing to the play's "hint of homosexuality" and its representation of "illegitimacy, prostitution ... and both the lethargizing effect of religion and the stimulating effect of cocaine."[1] The Amato Opera House in Greenwich Village staged the play in 1952, perhaps without authorization, French's memo to Aughtry suggests; and Andrius Jilinsky of Tamara Daykarhanova's School for the Stage (New York) considered staging *Pilar* with Mary Hunter Wolf's American Acting Company in May 1939.[2]

The Year of Pilar has posed editorial challenges unique in the "Indigenous plays." Riggs included Spanish words but was not in the habit of typing diacritical marks. Specifically, he declined the cumbersome backspacing and overstriking required to create an accent from an apostrophe; and of course his typewriter would not have had keys for the Spanish *eñe* or the tilde that would have allowed him to mimic it. He typed "Yucatán" as "Yucatan," "Señora" as "Senora," and so forth. In these cases, he conventionally ceded authority to the compositors, whom he assumed would supply the diacritical marks. We have met these expectations. Our examination of autograph manuscripts of *Pilar* indicate that French sometimes did, and sometimes did not, do so. French's solecistic "Chichen Itzá" exemplifies both categories. We have deferred to the autograph manuscripts in making our determinations; so, for example, we have restored "Chichén Itzá," the correct form and the one that Riggs preferred when he was drafting in longhand.[3] Senora becomes "Señora," and so on, per Riggs's autograph states.

---

1 O'Brien references Riggs's *A World Elsewhere*, which replaced *Pilar* in the season (but never opened on Broadway). O'Brien's reference to cocaine perhaps indicates an ad hoc substitution in the reading for Pilar's reference to heroin use (see p. 154). O'Brien added that Riggs "has come to campus to witness the production [of *A World Elsewhere*]," one of the three full productions of his plays Iowa had scheduled "as a sort of one-man play festival." Riggs's reading took place on 23 April.

2 See Shanley; see also Jilinsky to Riggs, 14 May 1939, Riggs Papers, Beinecke, box 3, folder 62.

3 See Riggs Papers, University of Tulsa, box 5, folder 7, p. R (autograph pagination); and, less clearly, box 5, folder 8, p. 4.

Our blanket emendation of "Pilár" to "Pilar" demands particular mention. Riggs used only the common unaccented form in his autograph manuscripts and in the hand-drawn cover sheets that he affixed to three early states. Two Samuel French folders containing typescripts read "Pilar," as do the William Morris folder, the 1948 and 1952 reviews, Eloise Wilson's 1957 dissertation, and Braunlich's later biography.[1] And so do the authors or typists of several in-house memoranda by the press, privately held. We have found the accented form only in Aughtry's 1959 dissertation and in the entries for the play itself and for *Four Plays* in the US copyright register—a source that reproduces the press's spelling. In the absence of marked proofs and any record of Riggs's correspondence with French about this play, we conclude that French added the accent without warrant.

French's compositors did not consistently follow the playwright's cues for italicizing non-English words. For example, Riggs underlined forms of "señor" and "señora" only once each and perhaps then to indicate the need for emphatic speech. French, however, consistently set these words in italics.[2] This class of alteration strikes us as a legitimate exercise of compositorial prerogative, implicitly authorized by Riggs but distinct from the misspelled place-names as constituting common value-free house-stylings rather than plain errors. We have respected the press's authority in these instances. We have, however, rejected French's unprompted addition of emphases to several English words, which, without contrary information from marked proofs or correspondence, can claim no sanction.

On 7 February 1940, Riggs told Barrett Clark, by then with Dramatists Play Service, that he was working on a "new play" that "looks promising."[3] The play was *The Cream in the Well*, extensive notes toward which Riggs compiled from late November 1939 through early August of the next year. An autograph note dated 3 August 1940 declares the play "finished"; Riggs added, "I think

---

1 For Riggs's longhand spelling "Pilar," see Riggs Papers, University of Tulsa, box 5, folders 8, 9, and 10; all three states include cover-sheet drawings by Riggs with the spelling "Pilar." For the Samuel French folders, see *YP-TS2* and *YP-TS3*; for the William Morris folder, see Riggs Papers, Beinecke, box 21, folder 337.
2 See the play's final lines, spoken by the Radio Voice, presumably with brio: "<u>Buenos noches, senoras y senores</u>" (*YP-TS1–4*); "*Buenos noches, señoras y señores*" (*YP-SF*).
3 7 February 1940, Clark Papers.

it will all stand up pretty well," although "I shall probably do little things to the 4th scene."[1] Riggs copyrighted the script that month, prior to a mid-January tryout at the National Theater in Washington, DC, and an unsuccessful run at Broadway's Booth Theatre later that month and in early February (Braunlich, *Haunted* 162).[2]

A typescript of *The Cream in the Well* held by the Library of Congress (*CW-TS3*) is the most proximate predecessor of our copy-text (*CW-SF*).[3] These states are sufficiently similar to suggest that the edition was set from the typescript.[4] *CW-TS2* joins *CW-TS3* as the only typescripts to present the five-scene form in which, we know from the playbill, the play premiered: three scenes in the first act, two in the second, with Act 1, Scenes 2 and 3 set in Clabe's bedroom, in the morning and night, respectively.[5] The presence in *CW-TS2* of numerous autograph revisions that appear intratextually in *CW-TS3* establishes the sequence of those texts. *CW-TS1* is the latest of the earlier, four-act typescripts that mark the transition to morning with a quick curtain in Act 1, Scene 2.[6]

The four-act structure survived nearly to the Broadway opening. A folder housing a carbon of *CW-TS1* records a completion date of 10 December 1940, a mere five weeks before the originally scheduled opening at the Booth Theatre on 15 January 1941 and thus close to or during the rehearsal period.[7] A prompt copy based

---

1 Riggs Papers, Beinecke, box 12, folder 214, p. 215. In 1928, Riggs compiled notes toward a novel entitled *The Cream in the Well*; see Riggs Papers, Beinecke, box 10, folder 185. Riggs considered another title: an autograph notation above the familiar title on an undated typescript reads "Julie Sawters (?)" (Riggs Papers, Beinecke, box 13, folder 216).
2 "Preliminary performances" were originally planned for Baltimore (see "News of the Stage").
3 *CW-TS3* is held in the Kroll Papers, Library of Congress, box 572, folder 7.
4 Kroll replaced Leverton as Riggs's agent in or around March 1949; see Riggs to Leverton, 29 March 1949, Riggs Papers, Beinecke, box 3, folder 75.
5 *CW-TS2* is held in the Riggs Papers, Beinecke box 12, folder 215; the playbill is accessible via playbill.com.
6 *CW-TS1* is held in the Riggs Papers, University of Tulsa, box 2, folder 4.
7 The opening was delayed until 20 January (see "News of the Stage"). For the carbon, see Riggs Papers, Beinecke, box 13, folder 217; the date appears on a bifolium coversheet. This text comprises carbon pages of *CW-TS1*, some with unique autograph corrections or minor revisions, some with minor autograph corrections or revisions recreated from marked passages in *CW-TS1*. Sheets with typed notes and (*continued*)

on *CW-TS1* and held by the New York Public Library also lacks a scene-break. The extensive longhand cues and notes added to it—presumably by the director, Martin Gabel (aka Martin Gable), or the stage manager, Charles Alan—could only have been written during or right before the start of rehearsals.[1] The "five-scene" texts *CW-TS2* and *CW-TS3*, then, must have been prepared after 10 December 1940 but are more likely to have been prepared in January 1941. And, as in the case of *The Year of Pilar*, they may have been prepared as late as 1947, when *Four Plays* went into production.

Riggs did not retain any of the ad hoc cuts and revisions from the prompt copy of *The Cream in the Well*. These must have been meant either to clarify passages that might otherwise have been unclear in performance or to cater to the presumed sensitivities of the audience. Several excisions attenuate Julie's cruelty and her passion for her brother, Gard. Quaintly, one effaces Mrs. Sawters's declaration in Act 2, Scene 1, that she will kiss her husband, unbidden.

One editorial challenge merits special mention: the intratextual presence in *CW-TS1* of two readings that reappear, longhand, in the margins of *CW-TS3* but are not present in *CW-TS2* or *CW-SF*. Explanations come readily to mind but resist proof. Perhaps, for example, Riggs briefly considered restoring text that he had once rejected. Lacking a fuller textual record, we are content to observe the tenuous status of these passages in *CW-TS3*, to note the absence of these passages from the copy-text, and to assert the near-certainty that marked proofs would be consistent with the copy-text.

In our preparation of texts for Appendix A ("Lynn Riggs on the Performing Arts"), we have silently corrected unambiguous errors of spelling and typography and silently supplied dropped terminal punctuation. Passages that Riggs marked for deletion have been expunged; his corrections, typed and autograph, have been silently entered. We have regularized the texts of the previously

---

revisions are interfoliated as well. Stab marks indicate that the carbon pages were once bound with the originals; the imprimatur of the professional typist on the Beinecke coversheet must of course refer to the original (*CW-TS1*), not to the copy from which it was evidently separated. The stemmatic relationship of this text to *CW-TS1* is thus horizontal, not vertical. The Beinecke text has not proven useful in our collation.

1 See New York Public Library, Performing Arts Research Collection, LCOF+ Riggs, L. Cream in the well.

published documents. In new texts set from typescripts, we have endeavored to reconcile Riggs's typographical and formatting choices with the layout of the Broadview edition generally. Several corrections appear within square brackets.

Only "What the Theatre Can Mean to All of Us" from this group has required us to decide between copy-texts. A folder at the Beinecke holds two states of that speech: a typescript and a carbon.[1] A comparison of autograph corrections and addenda on the two texts suggests that Riggs delivered his address from the carbon. The typescript, with a corrected date and an after-the-fact remark on the event, is evidently the state that Riggs filed for safekeeping. The carbon is therefore our copy-text. Differences between the two states are few and minor.

1 See Riggs Papers, Beinecke, box 23, folder 382.

THE HISTORIC "CLAREMORE MOUND" 6 MILES NORTHWEST OF CLAREMORE, OKLA

WHERE THE LAST BATTLE WAS FOUGHT BETWEEN THE FAMOUS CHEROKEE AND OSAGE INDIAN TRIBES

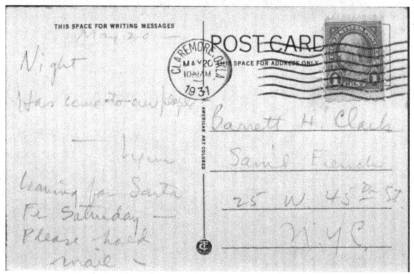

Claremore Mound (Rogers County, Oklahoma) was the site of a bloody 1817 battle between the Cherokee and the Osage. It is a nearly constant visual presence in *The Cherokee Night*. Riggs, writing to his friend and agent Barrett H. Clark from Claremore in May 1931, reproduces the last two lines of his epigraph for the play.

THE CHEROKEE NIGHT

The grass is withered,
Where the river was is red sand,
Fire eats the timber.
Night
Has come to our people. . . .[1]

1 Riggs records these lines in a 10 March 1929 letter to his agent, Barrett
   H. Clark, and identifies them as "from the Cherokee" (Clark Papers,
   box 5).

People

VINEY JONES
AUDEAL COOMBS
BEE NEWCOMB
HUTCH MOREE
ART OSBURN
GAR BREEDEN
OLD MAN TALBERT
SHERIFF
GUARD
DEPUTY
SARAH PICKARD, VINEY'S *sister*
MAISIE PICKARD
HUTCH ⎫
ART   ⎬ *as boys*
GAR   ⎭
A NEGRO
A CHEROKEE
HENRY
RUFE
ABNER
LIZE
ANNIE
AILSEY
JONAS
KATE WHITETURKEY
GEORGE MOREE, HUTCH'S *brother*
CLABE WHITETURKEY
JOHN GRAY-WOLF
SONNY
EDGAR BREEDEN (SPENCH), GAR'S *father*
TINSLEY
MARTHY BREEDEN, GAR'S *mother*
FLOREY NEWCOMB, BEE'S *mother*
TOWNSPEOPLE
OTHER MEMBERS OF THE "LOST TRIBE"
CHEROKEE SINGERS

Scenes

SCENE 1. Sixty-seven Arrowheads
Claremore Mound. Dusk, summer.
SCENE 2. The Hatchet
Rogers County jail. A spring night.
SCENE 3. Liniment
A room. A winter morning.
SCENE 4. The Place Where the Nigger[1] Was Found
The woods near Claremore. A summer afternoon.

INTERMISSION

SCENE 5. The High Mountain
A church near Tahlequah. Noon, summer.
SCENE 6. The White Turkey
A farmhouse. An autumn morning.
SCENE 7. The Cherokee Night
A log cabin. A winter night.

The action of the play takes place in various parts of Oklahoma; and in Indian Territory before statehood.[2] The time sequence is not chronological.

---

1 A deeply offensive, racist slur used in various ways but primarily, then and now, to demean and dehumanize people of the African diaspora in the United States. Jace Weaver, Craig Womack, Daniel Heath Justice, and Julie Little Thunder have expressed concerns about racism in the play. For "racism against African-Americans" in this scene specifically, see Little Thunder 364.
2 Indian Territory in this play refers to the land west of the state of Arkansas and east of Oklahoma Territory. The state of Oklahoma, established in 1907, encompasses both territories. For Oklahoma statehood, see Preface, pp. 13–14, Introduction, p. 18.

Scene One

From a place of darkness a gigantic teepee thrusts itself up into the light—white and glistening. Its skeleton poles cross each other at the towering summit. Its flaps are drawn down across the opening and tied. The shining buffalo skin sides, once stretched and taut, shedding both rain and sun, lie slack on the poles as if the inner structure had withdrawn a little, had crept inward toward a center, inching along the earth.

In pictographs all over the teepee's front is the story of a man's life: the first deer he killed stumbles to crooked knees, a feathered arrow in its heart; three buffaloes charge his pony; he stands before a mountain with a summit of flame; a woman lifts her hand out of nowhere; a road branches out in seven ways, and on the seventh—and widest—coils a rattlesnake; before a waterfall is a willow tree; across a deep chasm a warrior leaps, and in his hands are curious fetishes carved from granite.

No smoke rises from this ghostly habitation. But somewhere inside is the muffled thud of a drum and the sound of deep voices.

The teepee vanishes. The drum, the voices are silent. The land, a flinty and shaly slope near the top of Claremore Mound, appears.[1] *It is twilight of a summer day in 1915. A shale cliff capped with limestone and about six feet high, runs across the back, uneroded by the years. Behind it, the hill mounts steadily to the summit covered with scrub oak and hickory, rocks, small brush, etc. At the left, a fissure like a trench, very narrow and as tall as a man, is gashed into the cliff by eroding elements which have profited by a curious displacement of the protecting lime-stone. It is as if a roofless corridor went a little way into the hill. A gnarled cedar tree clings to the edge a little distance back, and sways against the still sky. From its high stance it looks two ways—forward down the flinty slope, and backward down another cliff and the unseen river bed hundreds of feet below. Many stars have come out in the darkening sky.*

At the right, and forward, a fire burns. Three couples—boys and girls—sit about it, eating their picnic supper. They are all part Cherokee Indian, some a quarter, some a sixteenth or a thirty-second; one of them is a half-breed.[2] *The fire crackles, its light playing over them*

---

1 Claremore Mound, the site of an 1817 battle between Cherokees and Osages, is 7 miles north-northwest of Claremore, thus roughly 36 miles northeast of Tulsa.

2 A racist term for people with one Indigenous parent and one European parent, though it was often used to describe anyone with both Indigenous and European heritage. For a study of Native American identity, including the calculation of fractions of Indigenous heritage (blood quantum), see Garroutte.

mysteriously. VINEY JONES, *a talkative, brown-haired country-school teacher, is in the middle of a story.*

VINEY. Yep! It's the truth. The first job of teaching school I ever
    had. Out here to Justus.[1] Hutch here was one of my scholars.
[*She indicates* HUTCH MOREE, *a blond, hefty, rather dumb oil-field
teamster.*[2]]
HUTCH. [*Stuttering.*] Sh-she—she's a-tellin' the tru-tru-truth.
VINEY. 'Way back, five years ago—nineteen ten it was. Hutch
    hadn't started in to teaming in the oil-fields then. He was
    gettin' *educated.* I'll never forget the day I told him he had to
    stay in after school. The big goof! He come rearin' up to me
    the minute I'd let the rest of school out, and says, "Whu—
    whut's the idy—" He stuttered then, too. "Whu-whu-whut's
    the idy—" he says, "keepin' me in af-af-after sch-school
    this-a-way?" "'Cause you don't work your 'rithmetic," I told
    him. "'Cause you spit on the floor, and 'cause your overalls
    is filthy dirty, and your neck is not clean. *And*—'cause you
    stutter!"
[AUDEAL COOMBS *hoots unbelievingly. She is a marcelled*[3] *young
blonde, who runs a beauty parlor in Claremore.*]
AUDEAL. Hoo, I *bet* you did! Hutch ud a-turned you over his knee
    and spanked yer tail.
VINEY. Didn't I, Hutch? Didn't I tell you that?
HUTCH. [*After a moment, dropping his eyes.*] Y-ye-yeah, I reckon you
    did.
VINEY. See there!
[ART OSBURN, *a dark, scowling young man, looks sharply up at*
VINEY.]
ART. When he was a boy he didn't stutter. I knowed him when he
    didn't. Wasn't none of your business, anyhow! Why didn't
    you sock her one, Hutch? She's jist a smart-alec schoolmarm,
    thinks she knows it all.
HUTCH. [*Puzzled.*] I b-b-been a-tryin' to figger out fer five year
    why I didn't—why I didn't hit her.
ART. [*Scowling.*] *I'd* a-socked her.

---

1 Small town a few miles southeast of Claremore.
2 Riggs might have been imagining Hutch working in the rich Osage oil
    fields, which made national news in the 1920s when the FBI investi-
    gated numerous murders of Osages. The murders were part of a scheme
    by outsiders to the Osage Nation to gain access to Osage oil wealth.
3 Hair waved with hot tongs, a popular hairstyle in the 1920s.

VINEY. [*Contemptuously.*] Yes, you would, Art Osburn. [*She gets up, crosses to* ART, *bends over, facing him contemptuously.*] Sock me now, why don't you?

ART. How's that?

VINEY. [*Defiantly.*] Sock me! Show everybody how you'd a-done it!

[*He looks at her darkly, suddenly reaches out and slaps her face, almost upsetting her.*]

AUDEAL. Art!

[BEE NEWCOMB, *a dark, vivid, strange-looking girl, grins with delight.*]

BEE. For God's sake!

VINEY. [*Astonished and livid.*] I'll get even with you, Art Osburn, if it's the last thing I do! Better not let Jack Clepper get a sight of you, he'll take your stinkin' hide off 'th a blacksnake whip! Strikin' a woman!

[*She crosses, fuming, to the left, and stands.*]

AUDEAL. [*Placatingly.*] Aw, Viney—he didn't mean nothin'.

VINEY. [*Turning to* HUTCH.] Jack Clepper's a man. *He* wouldn't let no one slap me like that.

BEE. [*Amused, and contemptuous of* VINEY.] All in fun! All in fun, Viney! Set that hot behind of your'n on a piece of limestone, cain't you?

HUTCH. [*To* ART.] Whu-whu-whut in hell'd you go and do *that* fer, Art?

ART. [*In dark bewilderment, hesitating.*] I—I don't know. Set down, Viney. I didn't aim to.

VINEY. [*Unappeased.*] Didn't *aim!* If you *had* aimed you'd a-jarred all my teeth loose. [*Severely, didactic, sitting again.*] You're too *broody*, Art Osburn, that's what's the matter 'th you. Just like all you Osburns. No one can tell about you—you're too blame quick on the trigger. Everybody that trades horses with that Pap of yours says all you Osburns ought to be shot. Some day you'll *get* shot, too, or my name isn't Jones.

BEE. Aw, have a pork chop and shet up! [*She hands one to* VINEY. VINEY *glares at* BEE *resentfully, snatches the chop. To* ART, *with a sidelong look.*] If I come over there and kissed you, what would you think?

ART. What'd you reckon I'd think?

BEE. [*Looking away again, quietly.*] I won't do it then. [*There is a moment of silence, each one absorbed in eating, or in his own feelings. Bee looks round at* GAR BREEDEN, *who is sitting quietly,*

not eating. He is twenty-one, lithe and dark, a half-breed.] Look
at old Tight-Mouth! Heap Big Chief! Hey, Gar, wake up!

AUDEAL. [*Derisively.*] Cat's got his tongue.

HUTCH. He's thinkin'.

BEE. Two or three year ago he talked as much as anyone. *Now*
look at him! Him don't eat, him don't talk. Him think. Him
name Chief Squat-in-the-Grass.

AUDEAL. [*Tittering.*] Chief Squat-in-the—
[*She giggles.*]

HUTCH. [*Curious.*] Whu—whutta you—whutta you thinkin'
about, Gar?

[GAR *looks at them a moment, speculatively, then looks away.*]

GAR. Do you know whur we are?

ART. [*Scornfully.*] Shore I know whur we are. In jail.

AUDEAL. I bite. Whur are we?

ART. [*To* GAR.] We're at Claremore Mound, you damn fool!

GAR. [*Strangely.*] You said it.

ART. [*With puzzled annoyance.*] Whut the hell's *eatin'* him, anyway!

AUDEAL. Aw, let him alone. He's crazy.

BEE. [*Pointedly.*] No crazier'n *some* I could name—a dizzy blonde,
for instance, that cuts dirty finger nails in a barber shop.

HUTCH. [*Snuggling up to her.*] C-c-calm down, Bee! C-c-come out
in the bresh with me, why don't you? I'll calm you down.

BEE. [*With contempt.*] Yer brother ud beat you up 'f he could hear
you.

HUTCH. N-n-naw, he wouldn't. G-g-George wouldn't keer.

BEE. Is this a offer?

HUTCH. A good un.

BEE. I charge high, Big Boy.

VINEY. [*Severely.*] That's not a very nice way to talk, Bee.

BEE. [*Unruffled.*] I never said it was nice.

VINEY. If he laid his hands on *me*, I'd slap his face.

BEE. I reckon you would. That's what's the matter 'th you.

VINEY. [*Hotly.*] Everybody knows what *you* are.

BEE. [*Eyeing her.*] I'm a waitress in the Sequoyah Restaurant at
Claremore[1] and don't you forget it!

VINEY. Waitress, hunh? I wouldn't *say* the word *you* are.

BEE. [*With asperity.*] How come you're out in sich bad comp'ny,

---

1   It is unclear if Riggs has a specific restaurant in mind, though there was
a Sequoyah Hotel in Claremore. It opened in 1902 and was torn down
in 1961. Sequoyah (George Guess, c. 1775–1843) created the Cherokee
syllabary.

then? Whyn't you go home to yer teachin'? Go on, git in yer old rattle-trap Ford and step on it. Go and see that dumb-bell farmer, Jack Clepper, why don't you? He appreciates you. Beat it!

VINEY. [*Complacently.*] Hutch'll go with me, if I go home.

BEE. [*Contemptuously.*] Oh, he will, will he? He always has *some*body to tell him what to do. Too bad he ain't got no one better'n you to tell him.

VINEY. He'll take me home, just the same.

BEE. He's your'n, Miss Jones. 'F you c'n git him—which I doubt. You been tryin' fer five years. [*She turns back to* GAR, *sharply.*] For God's sake, Gar, come and talk to me! You brung me here. [*Then, noticing his absorption, her manner changes abruptly.*] Whut is it you're so wrapped up in? Anything special?

GAR. [*Turning round.*] Bee.

BEE. Well.

GAR. How much Cherokee are you?

BEE. You know damn well how much I am. A quarter.

GAR. [*Strangely.*] Do you feel anything?

[*He lifts a hand. She looks round at the night.*]

BEE. No. Why?

GAR. [*Retreating into himself again.*] Oh—I don't know.

ART. [*Bursting out angrily, to* GAR.] Will you quit actin' so goddamned funny?

[*Somewhere back of them a rock overturns as if dislodged by a foot, and a little clatter of sliding pebbles can be heard distinctly. They all look round quickly.*]

AUDEAL. Whut was that!

ART. Be still!

[*They wait, breathless. There is no further sound.*]

HUTCH. Wu-wu-wasn't nothin' a-tall. Was it?

VINEY. Just an old possum out looking for grub, I bet.

ART. Maybe a skunk.

HUTCH. Maybe a c-c—maybe a coyote.

BEE. [*Shortly.*] Maybe a elephant.

[*They laugh.*]

GAR. [*When they are still again, quietly.*] Er maybe a dead Indian—a ha'nt of a dead Indian.

AUDEAL. Gar!

GAR. [*With some fire.*] Well, you're all of you part-Cherokee, like me! [*Lapsing again into quietness, looking away.*] We're settin' on the graves of a lot of dead ones—in case you've forgot.

BEE. [*Softly.*] Here?

GAR. Here.

[*They are silent for a moment, awed a little, something forgotten coming to life in them.*]

VINEY. [*Breaking the spell.*] Oh, *now* I know what he's talking about! You mean *here*—Claremore Mound. [*Didactically, getting up, circling slowly in back to center.*] Oh, sure! Where the Osages and the Cherokees fought their last big battle. That was 'way back in eighteen hundred and sump'n. The killing was godawful. And only one woman of the Osage camp got away. Clumb down yand' side the Mound, swum the river and was never heard of again. *I* ought to know. I *teach* it! Why, old Claremont,[1] Chief of the Osages, is buried around here some'eres.

GAR. [*Pointing.*] In that ditch—jist below that cedar tree. [*The others look round.*] He's buried. In all his war paint. They say he is.

VINEY. [*Not much interested.*] Yes, sir. They's *some* old Indian's grave there. [*Kneeling close to* HUTCH.] Look around, kids, you might find some arrowheads. You *can,* sometimes, if you—

BEE. [*Sharply.*] Hush up, Viney! Gar was gonna say sump'n. What was it, Gar?

GAR. [*Relapsing into his customary uncommunicativeness.*] Nothin'.

VINEY. [*Glibly.*] A year ago this summer—I found three arrowheads all the same day. Two of 'em was flint, the other one was made out of some funny-looking kind of—

[*The rattling sliding noise is heard again, followed by a swish as of something brushing against twigs, and a dull repeated thud.*]

AUDEAL. [*Frightened.*] Art, now that *is* sump'n!

VINEY. [*Standing.*] I b'lieve it is! Sump'n a-moving!

ART. [*Getting up, disgusted.*] God's sake! A bunch of 'fraid-cats! Gimme that flash. [HUTCH *hands him a flashlight.*] I'll go and skeer that ha'nt to death. [*He starts out, stops, picks up a rock.*] I'll ram this rock down his th'oat.

[*He goes deliberately toward the fissure in the cliff, the others watching him tensely. He pauses a moment at the dark entrance, throws a beam*

---

1 According to Osage historian John Joseph Mathews, Gra-Mo'n (Arrow-Going-Home) or Ghleh-Mo'n (Arrow) was an Osage leader called Claremont, Glamore, or Claremore by French and English speakers. His village was "close to the spot on which the modern town of Claremore, Oklahoma was later built" (418). Gra-Mo'n was not present at the Battle of Claremore Mound.

of light into it, and disappears. AUDEAL *gets up, involuntarily, takes a step toward him.*]

HUTCH. [*Pulling at her skirt.*] He's all right, Audeal. 'Tain't nuthin' but a little r-ra-ra-rabbit, or sump'n like that.

VINEY. [*Venomously.*] If it's a rattlesnake, I hope to God he steps on it.

[*She sits again.*]

HUTCH. Viney!

VINEY. Slappin' *my* face.

HUTCH. Don't listen at her, Audeal. 'Tain't nuthin' but some little n-n-night varmint, like a bat or a weasel.

BEE. Or a *jy*-raffe.

[AUDEAL *laughs, her fear vanishing a little. She comes and sits, but still faces toward the fissure anxiously.*]

VINEY. [*Resentfully.*] You had a lot to do, Gar Breeden, scarin' us that-a-way. Ha'nt, yer foot! [*Knowing the answer.*] Why didn't you stay at the Agriculture College[1]—where you was? You and your ha'nts!

HUTCH. He—he—he got kicked out, didn't you, Gar?

VINEY. [*With satisfaction.*] I'll say he did.

BEE. He made the freshman team, anyway, smarties! And tuck all the honors in track.

VINEY. "Heap big Injun athulete!" [*To* BEE, *slyly.*] You take up for him like he was your own kinfolks—your own brother or sump'n.

BEE. [*Quickly.*] I'd shet my mouth, Viney, 'f I was you. And keep it shet!

VINEY. They tell me you had the same pappy. Edgar Spench, the desperado.

BEE. You got one slap tonight!

VINEY. [*Ignoring the threat.*] Course it's just talk. But I don't think I'd try to get so thick with someone that might turn out to be my own brother.

BEE. [*Contemptuously.*] I reckon not. If you was married, you wouldn't git thick with yer own husband.

AUDEAL. [*Who has been looking back all this time, anxiously.*] I wonder whut's happened to—

---

1 Oklahoma Agricultural and Mechanical College in Stillwater was founded in 1890; in 1957, it became Oklahoma State University for Agriculture and Applied Science, familiarly known as Oklahoma State University.

VINEY. Rattlesnake bit him.

BEE. [*Rising, walking left in an impatient half-circle.*] Aw, he's probably lit out fer home to git away from sich a goddamned picnic! Ain't that the Ford I hear a-startin' up? [*She listens, with mock intensity, her hand at her ear.*] I wouldn't blame him.

AUDEAL. Be still, Bee. [*With relief, as* ART *appears out of the dark fissure.*] Here he is!

[ART *comes forward. Half-way to them, he stops and looks round anxiously, as if followed. The rock is still in one hand, the flash in the other.*]

HUTCH. G-G-God, you look funny, Art!

AUDEAL. Whut's happened?

[*She stands up, quickly, almost hysterically.*]

ART. Nuthin'. Le's git goin'.

AUDEAL. Art, whut is it?

[*The others look round, a little fearfully.*]

ART. [*Strangely, venomously.*] Ain't you all finished eatin' yit? Fool around all night.

AUDEAL. You seen sump'n. Whut was it?

ART. [*Harshly.*] For God's sake, cain't you keep still?

BEE. Let him alone, Audeal.

VINEY. [*Exasperated.*] A rattlesnake bit him.

ART. [*In a low voice.*] You know that old Indian—kinda crazy— lives down here at the foot of the Mound?

AUDEAL. Old Man Talbert?

ART. [*Nodding.*] Yeah, him. [*Indicating.*] He—he's in *there.*

AUDEAL. [*Looking round.*] In there?

HUTCH. [*Curious.*] Whu-whu-whut of it, Art? He won't bite you.

BEE. Whut's he doin' in there?

ART. Diggin'.

HUTCH. [*Getting up.*] Diggin'?

ART. [*His voice betraying his strange fear.*] In the ditch there—right below that gnarly cedar tree! Grubbin' around with a pick-ax!

[*They are a little alarmed and stirred, in spite of themselves.*]

VINEY. [*In a hushed voice.*] Where old Claremont's supposed to be buried?

ART. [*Nods.*] I turned the flash on him—and seen him. Plain.

VINEY. [*Standing up, abruptly.*] Come on, le's go home!

[*A dark shape appears suddenly at the fissure's mouth. The group turns quickly, facing it.* AUDEAL *gives a startled cry, runs to* VINEY. ART *follows, but wheels, facing the intruder and throws the flashlight full on him—an old man in rough clothes, with long hair and strange, startled eyes.*]

ART. [*Hoarsely.*] Whutta you want? Whutta you doin' here? [*The old man comes forward swiftly, his eyes fixed on* ART.]

OLD MAN TALBERT. [*Intensely.*] You didn't see me! I didn't do nuthin'! [*As if reminded, he looks down involuntarily.* ART *shifts the flash downward. In the old man's hand, grasped firmly, tensely, is a pick-ax. His voice roars out.*] Spyin' on me, you sneakin' bastard! I'll kill you all, I'll kill you!

[*He steps forward, terribly.*]

ART. [*His voice suddenly brassy, savage.*] Stand whur you are, old man! Drop that pick!

[*The old man stares a moment. He drops the pick. A crafty look comes into his eyes.*]

OLD MAN TALBERT. You wouldn't hurt a ole man, would you?

ART. [*Grimly.*] You damn right! Kick that pick outa yer reach. [*The old man hesitates, stoops, starts to reach for the instrument.*] Kick it, I said!

[*The old man complies. The heavy tool clangs forward at* ART'S *feet.* HUTCH *picks it up.*]

TALBERT. [*With hypnotic fervor.*] You didn't see nuthin'. I wasn't robbin' the grave. Not *me!* It's ghouls does that. *Ghouls!* And white trash[1] and black niggers. Not me! [*He looks at the group, staring at him, fascinated, silent.*] Who are you, anyway! Whut're you doin' around here? [*With wild anger, raising a hand in denunciation.*] Gadabouts! Snakes! Squirmin' and crawlin'! Git out! Git on away from here!

ART. [*Fiercely.*] Shet up yer yellin'! We got a right here, same as you. You don't own this hill.

AUDEAL. [*Nervously.*] Le's go, Art. Ain't no tellin' whut he'll do.

ART. I'd like to see him start sump'n!

BEE. He don't know whut he's doin'. Pore old man. Crazy's a loon.

HUTCH. Not too crazy to—not too crazy to brain you 'f he tuck a notion.

[*He holds up the heavy pick.*]

ART. I ain't skeered of him. I'll crack his head open. [*As he sees the old man backing away craftily.*] Hey, whur you goin'? Stand whur you are! Whut you think you're up to?

[*He lifts the rock threateningly. The old man stops.*]

GAR. [*Interfering.*] Let him alone, Art. [*He turns to the old man.*] Mr. Talbert. Mr. Talbert, don't you know me?

TALBERT. [*Fiercely.*] Git on away from here!

---

1 Slur against poor white people that emerged in the 1820s.

GAR. I'm Gar Breeden. You ort to recollect me.

TALBERT. Never seen you before!

GAR. Why, I've come on picnics here at Claremore Mound ever since I was knee-high. Gar Breeden. You know *me*. Once I ask at yore house fer water, and you give me a drink from the well, years ago. And you give me sump'n else, too. [*He pauses, as if at a troubled ecstatic memory.*] You give me a eagle feather. Don't you remember?

TALBERT. Whut if I did! Whut about it!

GAR. I kep' it. And these here—they was all raised around here, same as me. This is Art Osburn, and that's Viney Jones over there and—

TALBERT. [*Suddenly crying out.*] I know you! I know you all! Everyone of you. Knowed you all yer lives, the whole goddamned crew of you! 'Cept that gal—in the red dress. I never seen her before. [*He indicates* BEE.] That don't matter. [*His voice harsh.*] I seen too much of you, anyway! Clutter up the world—all of you—that's whut you do! Good fer nuthin'. [*With strange quiet finality.*] You're no use to anybody. You're lost. You might as well be dead.

ART. [*Angrily.*] Is that so? And who're you to say who's any good and who ain't? [*Brutally, rapidly.*] Whut was you diggin' in there fer, you grave robber? Whut'd you expect to find but some rotten buckskin and the skull of a dead man! Answer me that, you loony old Indian, you half-witted old ghoul!

TALBERT. [*Fearfully.*] I wasn't doin' nuthin', didn't aim to take nuthin'—! [*Angrily.*] Ain't they land enough in Rogers County[1] fer you to travel over, and you have to spy on a ole man who don't mean no harm—? [*Mysterious, mad.*] I'll tell you whut I was up to. You'll wish I hadn't! You'll run from the sight of me, the sound of my voice! It'll burn yer ears, you'll stumble and fall down, the briars'll claw deep down into yer bones. [*His voice stranger, madder, possessed.*] And the sperrits—yeah, *them*. [*Softly, as if afraid of being overheard.*] Thick in the air over yer head. [*He looks up and around.*] Hear the whisper of rawhide? See the streaks of blood on their faces? Look! All over, all around you—!

ART. [*Sharply.*] That's enough, old man!

VINEY. [*Disturbed.*] Le's go—

---

1 The county, in the Cherokee Nation in northeastern Oklahoma, was named for Clement Vann Rogers (1839–1911), the father of Cherokee entertainer, actor, and writer Will Rogers (1879–1935).

BEE. Gether everything up—
AUDEAL. [*Shaken.*] He's crazy mad!
HUTCH. [*Starting.*] Come on, Viney!
TALBERT. You wanted to hear me. Now listen and be damned,
    then!
ART. Keep it to yerself!
[*He crosses to left, stops left of* VINEY, *his back to* TALBERT. BEE *moves
up toward* TALBERT, *drawn irresistibly. She is now between* GAR *and*
HUTCH.]
TALBERT. [*Unheeding.*] Never sleep again—like me! Never walk
    'thout sump'n creepin' at yer heels. Grub turned to pizen, the
    air crammed with sights to remind you, yer brain hammerin',
    hammerin'—! [*His convulsion passes. He looks around. Then he
    turns back in amazement, his voice low, full of wonder.*] I ain't
    follered. Nuthin' clost to me. I c'n tell you now and not be
    eavesdropped. [*The group stands, still afraid, but hypnotized,
    rooted, unable to move. A mysterious drum beat rises in the silence,
    growing slowly in volume through the rest of the scene. The old
    man goes on, softly, with mad clarity.*] Listen. Ten year ago this
    summer. A night jist like this. Stars. I come up here by myself
    to smoke and laze. I built a f'ar—jist like that. There I set. I
    looked off and seen the lights of my house winkin'. I heared
    crickets. A dog way off toward Oologah[1] barked and barked.
    [AUDEAL *sits involuntarily, listening, held.* HUTCH *does likewise.*]
    I remembered I hadn't turned the calf away from the cow
    after milkin'. I remembered the time I got a scar on my head
    from divin' in the Verdigree River.[2] I started in to think about
    when I was a boy and lived on the banks of Panther Crick.[3]
    I thought about it a lot. [*His excitement rising.*] *Then sump'n
    happened.* First, it was like a wind tetchin' the pine tops. Then
    it was a sound—slow and sneakin'—like feet all padded the
    way a cat's is—a-stealin' up the hill. I jumped up. Jist in time!
    [*Crying out.*] They'd a-walked on me like I wasn't there! Their
    feet in moccasins, feathers scrapin' together, light on the
    quivers a-showin' plain!
ART. [*Excitedly.*] Whut was it, whut'd you see?

---

1 Approximately 15 miles north-northwest of Claremore in Rogers
  County.
2 The Verdigris River, which flows generally south from Kansas through
  northeastern Oklahoma and west of Claremore before joining the
  Arkansas River at Muskogee, Oklahoma.
3 Panther Creek, which empties into the Verdigris south of Claremore.

TALBERT. You know, don't you? Cain't you guess! [*Deliberately, his teeth showing.*] Don't you know—whut I seen—on this hill—*this un!* The Cherokees! Painted for war! A-stealin' up on the Osages asleep up there by their camp-fires! [*Savagely, with frightful passion.*] Fall on 'em, cut their th'oats, bury yer tomahawks in their thick skulls, let yer muskets thunder! At every Cherokee belt a row of Osage scalps—with long black hair swishin' and drippin'! I seen it—all of it—*my people!* I heared the Osage groans!

ART. [*Almost hysterically.*] Stop it, you devil! You couldn't a-saw it, couldn't! Happened 'way back, a hundred years ago. Happened before you was born!

TALBERT. [*Unheeding.*] And *more*—they was *more* that happened! When it was all over, they seen me. They looked at me. They come toward me down the mountain. From 'way up there— the crest of the Mound—streamin' like a river! One of 'em— the biggest one—in his war bonnet, he stood right in front of me. He looked th'ough me like I wasn't there! He was turrible! He started in to speak. "Jim Talbert," he said— [*The old man straightens up, his eyes shut, seeing clearly, as if tranced. His voice becomes something like the voice of the Cherokee brave. His shoulders lift.*] "Now you've saw, you've been showed. Us—the Cherokees—in our full pride, our last glory! This is the way we are, the way we was meant to be."

[*With passionate fervor, the mysterious drum beat swelling up through his words.*]

"In the gray night we walked into ice-cold water,
Our drums had no tongues,
Seven sharp turkey bones cut our flesh.

The Shaman pressed three beads into the sand,
They leaped into his hand crying the names of the chosen.

We prayed to our brothers, the hawks,
'Brothers! Hawks!
Fall from the sky into the camp of the Osages,
Strike with your wings, beaks, talons the bodies of our enemies!'

The hawks, our brothers, came.
The Osages lie heaped on the mountain.

But this was moons ago;
We, too, are dead.
We have no bodies,
We are homeless ghosts,
We are made of air.

Who made us that, Jim Talbert? Our children—our children's
children! They've forgot who we was, who *they* are! You too,
Jim Talbert, like all the rest.

Are you sunk already to the white man's way—with your soft
   voice and your flabby arm?
Have you forgot the use of the tomahawk and the bow?

Not only in war—in quiet times—the way we lived:
Have you forgot the smoky fire, the well-filled bowl?
Do you speak with the River God, the Long Person no more—no
   more with the vast Horned-Snake, the giant Terrapin, with
   Nuta, the Sun?[1]
Are you a tree struck by lightnin'?[2]
Are you a deer with a wounded side?
All of you—all our people—have come to the same place!

The grass is withered.
Where the river was is red sand.
Fire eats the timber.
Night—*night*—has come to our people!"

[*He shrivels, cowers back, as if the spectre now stood before him.
   Then he recovers. He goes on.*] That was all. I never seen him
   again. That was ten years ago. I went down from here—but I
   remembered all I had saw and heared! [*Crazily, triumphant.*]
   And I knowed whut I had to do—I knowed how I could
   prove my right to be a Cherokee like my fathers before me!

---

1 Cherokee speakers refer to a river as *yvwi ganvhida*, translated as Long
   Person. Riggs appears to understand Long Person as a "River God."
   By horned-snake, Riggs means Uk'tan or Uk'tena, the Cherokee
   "winged serpent or flying dragon"; the literal translation is "shiny
   eye or shining eyes." Like Uk'tan, Terrapin (Daksi) is a figure in
   Cherokee storytelling traditions. Riggs translates Nuta (Nvdo) from
   the Cherokee for readers. Special thanks to Chris Teuton for the content of this annotation.
2 For Cherokee, the wood of a tree struck by lightning has special powers.

Even though I lived in a frame house, and paid taxes, and et my grub out of a tin can—I knowed whut I could do not to be lost. I found the way before too late. That's whut I was doin'—*there!*—when you saw me! When you snuck up on me and th'owed a lamp in my face! [*Madly, drawing something out of his pocket and holding it up.*] You didn't stop me, though! I found some. Two more to add to the pile of whut I got! See there! You cain't deny I got 'em!

VINEY. What is it?

ART. I cain't see.

TALBERT. [*Triumphantly.*] Arrowheads! Two more! That makes sixty-seven I got! Sixty-seven arrowheads! If I'd jist a-thought all these years to git me a pick and dig—I'd a-had hundreds by this time. The sperrits is pleased with me now, proud of me! Nobody cain't stop me now! I'll go on and on till I drop, I'll dig up the whole mountain, I'll find thousands and thousands! I'll give 'em to all the Cherokees. When they touch 'em, they'll remember. *The feel of flint in their hands!* Take 'em, you! Take 'em!

[*He moves toward them, circling in front,* HUTCH *jumps up.* AUDEAL, *frightened, clings to* VINEY. ART *steps forward menacingly.*]

ART. Git back there!

VINEY. [*Stepping back a step.*] Th'ow that rock at him!

[*All except* BEE *and* GAR *cry out simultaneously:* "Stand back, old man! Git him on away! Don't let him git any closer," *etc.*]

ART. Go away!

TALBERT. [*Angrily, circling back till he is at right.*] Anh, I mighta knowed! You—all of you! Muck and scum! Who are you, anyway! Dribbles of men and women! Whut do you do to show yer birthright? Nuthin'. You're dead, you ain't no good! Night's come on you. You there in the red dress—whut do you do? Whut're *you?* Answer me that!

BEE. [*Her eyes flashing, her voice dangerous. With one step forward.*] I'm a whore, old man! A whore—smellin' of Djer-Kiss![1]

GAR. Bee—for God's sake!

BEE. [*Brassily.*] Part-Cherokee, too! Have one on *me,* old man, for the sake of the tribe! It won't cost you a cent! Don't stand there like you was deef and dumb! You hear whut I'm sayin' to you— Oh! [*Her voice breaks. She drops to a rock, her head bowed.*] Go away, go away from here!

---

1 A French perfume, pronounced "dear kiss."

[*The old man's eyes have clouded. He has turned away, unheeding. His head bends, listening, forward. The drum beat is higher, tenser.*]

TALBERT. I hear 'em now. The whisper of rawhide! The whing of tomahawks! The groans of the dyin'! [*He turns, his head lifted toward the top of the Mound. He goes upstage toward it.*] Look! See the light on their painted arms! They've come back like before! See the hair shine! Come down, come down! Show yerselves! Yer people have forgot who you are. They're withered like leaves. Come down! [*The group stands, transfixed, rooted, afraid to move. Exultantly.*] You hear me! I see you. You're coming! I knowed you would! Light on yer war bonnets! Yer feet step soft. Yer teeth glitter. *This* way! *This* way!

[*The lights have begun to go down, all except a glow on the summit of the hill. It begins to move slowly downward. The stars have gone out. The glow creeps down the hillside strangely. The throbbing drum goes on into the darkness.*]

Scene Two

The sound of rain beating gustily on a sheet-iron roof insinuates itself into the insistent drum beat. The sound of the drum grows fainter, and dies away.

The rain swirls down, hammering at the roof. Then the lights come up slowly. Two tiny cells separated only by bars, and with a wall in back, appear from the darkness, under the sloping metal roof of the Rogers County Jail. From behind, Claremore Mound looms in the darkness, dim and silent, dwarfing the scene.

A GUARD, *a rough-looking, dull, young man, about thirty, and the* SHERIFF, *a rather gruff older man, appear from the left, hatted and dripping, and pass along the corridor in front of the two cells. The* GUARD, *jangling a bunch of keys, begins to unlock the barred doors.*

SHERIFF. [*Turning to someone out of sight along the corridor.*] Well, come on, cain't you?

VOICE. [*In the gloom, out of sight.*] What's yer hurry?

[*A girl enters. She is dark, strange, vivid. Her clothes are the clothes of 1927. She wears a dripping hat and a short coat. She looks sullen and reluctant. It is* BEE. *She stops at center.*]

SHERIFF. Well, what's the matter?

BEE. [*Shortly.*] I don't like it.

SHERIFF. Now looky here, you said you'd go ahead and—

BEE. I don't like it, I said.

SHERIFF. [*Protesting.*] We got it all planned. It's got to be someone he knows. You cain't go and back out on me—

BEE. Who the hell says I cain't?

SHERIFF. [*Sharply.*] Say, I give you ten dollars and the promise of fifteen more, and I be goddamned if you're gonna back out on me! Now cut it out and git in that cell!

[*He makes a move as if to force her. Without a word, she hands out a ten-dollar bill. He looks at it, astonished. He waves it away.*]

BEE. Take it.

SHERIFF. [*Changing his tactics.*] Aw listen, Bee. A good gal like you ort to— Say look, all you got to do is git him to talk. *He'll* talk. It won't hurt *you* none if he *tells* on hisself.

BEE. [*Quietly.*] Whut'll it do to him, though?

SHERIFF. What?

BEE. Whut'll it do to *him*?

SHERIFF. [*With relish.*] Hang him, by God, if we're lucky! Hang the hound dog!

BEE. [*Wryly.*] That'll be nice. They's nuthin' like hangin' a man to make you feel good. [*She starts toward the cell. Half to herself.*] I don't like him anyway. [*She bursts out quickly to the* SHERIFF, *silencing something in herself, seeing that the* GUARD *has banged one of the cell doors wide open.*] Well, for God's sake, do I have to get in a cell?

SHERIFF. [*His hand on her arm, urging her, reassuringly.*] That'll be all right.

BEE. And locked up, too! When do I get out?

SHERIFF. We'll let you out. He'll suspect sump'n if we don't have yer door locked like you was in fer sump'n. It's got to look real.

BEE. [*Acquiescing, contemptuously.*] Hmmm. What am I in fer, Mr. Sheriff? Waitin' on tables?

SHERIFF. Well, uh—how about fer bein' drunk?[1]

BEE. Fine. You got a drink on you?

SHERIFF. Here. [*He takes a flask from his hip pocket, removes the stopper, hands it to her. She takes a long drink, wipes her mouth, starts to take another.*] Here, go easy on that!

BEE. It's got to look real, ain't it? [*She drinks, pretends to blink dizzily.*] Whew! It'll be real, all right. I better keep this. I might need it. [*She puts it in her pocket, takes a step toward the*

---

1 Riggs sets this scene in 1927, during Prohibition: the Sheriff's flask contains bootleg liquor.

cell. Then she straightens up, and looks at him with a curious and acid stare, her brows narrowed.] Say, how did I get to be on your side, anyway?

SHERIFF. Because I'm givin' you twenty-five dollars.

BEE. Oh. So that's it, is it? [*Muttering.*] That ain't all of it, though. [*She turns away, toward the* GUARD.] Well, which is *my* bunk, Big Boy?

[*She begins to take off her hat and coat. Her dress is short and brightly orange. Her hair is closely bobbed.*[1]]

GUARD. [*Showing her the cell on the right.*] This un is your'n, Miss Newcomb.

BEE. [*Raising her eyebrows.*] *Miss Newcomb.* How are you, Count So and So? [*Looking at him.*] Ain't I saw you some'eres before?

GUARD. I've et a meal or two at the restaurant you work at.

BEE. My name's Bee to you, then.

GUARD. Howdy, Bee.

BEE. You married?

GUARD. No.

BEE. Come in and I'll give you a plank steak sometime.

GUARD. I'll do that.

[*She goes into the gloom of the cell, looks around, sits on the stool near the front bars, thrusts her face between two of them.*]

BEE. All right. Shoot, Sheriff.

[*The* GUARD *locks the door.*]

SHERIFF. You all ready?

[*He goes in the other cell to be nearer her.*]

BEE. Yeah.

SHERIFF. [*To the* GUARD.] Go and get him, Smiley. Frank's got him out there givin' him a little third degree. That'll help. [*The* GUARD *disappears along the corridor.*] I told you what to do now. We cain't git a confession out of him. Make him talk, that's all. Tell him no one cain't hear him. You can see yourself they ain't a place in this end of the jail for no one to hide at and listen. But *we'll* hear, all right, don't *you* worry.

BEE. How you gonna hear?

SHERIFF. Never mind how. And don't be surprised if you find a spotlight throwed on you both in a minute.

BEE. A spotlight? My God, am I gonna sing or sump'n?

SHERIFF. [*Starting toward the door of his cell.*] Go as fur as you like.

BEE. Say, Sheriff. Come 'ere. [*When he returns, she says soberly.*]

---

1 Bee has adopted the flapper aesthetic of the 1920s.

The papers said she got drownded. Did he kill her, do you think?

SHERIFF. *Course* he killed her. [*A door clangs.*] Here he comes. I don't want him to see me. [*He hurries off right. Another door clangs.*]

[*The sound of the rain increases for a moment. Then the* GUARD *brings in along the corridor a young man about 32, shaken and troubled. His hair is in his eyes. But in spite of his distress, his eyes burn with a fierce wild venomous glow. It is* ART OSBURN. *He strides into the cell quickly, turns like a caged panther and snarls at the* GUARD, *who is busy with the door.*]

ART. All right! Lock it, you bloody bastard!

GUARD. [*Pushing him into the cell.*] I'm lockin' it.

ART. That deputy son of a bitch! [*As the* GUARD *looks at him.*] Go on, go on, beat it! I ain't talkin' to you. [*The* GUARD *goes; the door clangs after him.*] Yanh! [*He turns away again, walks once swiftly around his cage. Suddenly he sees* BEE *on the stool in her cell. He takes a step backward, sharply.*] Who're you? What're you doin' here?

BEE. [*Shortly.*] I'm not gonna bite you, little boy.

ART. Christ. [*He turns away, muttering.*] Scared by a chippy.[1]

BEE. Who's a chippy?

ART. [*Impatiently.*] You, you!

BEE. Yeah? Well, you're a murderer.

ART. [*Fiercely, crazily, grabbing the bars between them.*] I didn't kill her, I didn't kill her! God's sake! I told you— I— [*His eyes fasten on the girl. His voice goes low.*] I know you. You're Bee. Bee Newcomb.

BEE. [*Levelly.*] I know you, too. Art Osburn.

[*His legs give way under him. He sinks to his stool, his arms sliding down wearily between the bars.*]

ART. Jesus! [*Weakly.*] They beat hell out of me.

[*She rises and for a moment makes as if to go toward him. Her impulse dies. She stares at him coolly.*]

BEE. I guess you had it comin' to you.

ART. [*Wearily.*] I reckon.

BEE. You orten't to a-killed that old Indian womern—

ART. I keep *tellin'* you—!

BEE. All right, all right. I don't keer whether you did or not. Kill a dozen, you cain't make *me* mad. Competition's fierce.

---

1 Slang for a promiscuous woman or a prostitute.

[*Looking at him.*] You look shot, all right. Crime don't pay, does it?

ART. [*Helplessly, fiercely.*] Cain't you let up on it, cain't you!

BEE. Sure. Sorry I mentioned it. I guess I better keep my mouth shut.

ART. You can talk if you want to.

BEE. I wouldn't know where to start at, I ain't saw you in so long. Us livin' in the same town, too. It's funny, ain't it?

ART. [*Strangely, in a dark absorption, his frenzy rising.*] How did I get here? What am I doin' here?

BEE. [*Disturbed.*] You got me there.

ART. [*Desperation and fear in his voice.*] What's the matter with me? [*Turning to stare at her, crazily, half-rising.*] What're they tryin' to do to me, what're they tryin'—!

BEE. [*Quickly, standing up, fiercely shouting.*] Shut up! You're crazy. You're talkin' crazy!

[*Her sharp strength overpowers him.*]

ART. [*Quieter.*] I feel that way. [*He sinks back.*]

BEE. [*Remembering her mission, sitting again.*] You can talk all you want to, crazy or not. Nobody'll hear you.

ART. I don't want to talk.

BEE. There ain't a soul in this end of the jail. Nobody—but us. You and me.

ART. What're *you* doin' here?

BEE. I was drunk.

ART. I wish to God I was!

BEE. [*Handing him the flask.*] Get tight. [*He takes a long drink, sets the flask on the floor.*] That'll cheer you up. [*Looking at him.*] We mighta been friends. [*With real feeling, real bitterness.*] I ain't got so many. You remember Gar Breeden? He won't look at me no more, won't give me a tumble. He ain't even *looked* at me for five year. D' you know why? We had the same daddy, and what'd you think of that? Purty mess, ain't it? [*He nods dully.*] Listen, whatever become of Audeal?

ART. Audeal?

BEE. *You* know. Audeal Coombs. The little fool. Bet you got good and t'ard of her. Somebody told me she run off to Springfield[1] with a drummer.[2] You musta h'ard him to take her off yer hands. [*A curious light comes into her eyes.*] You know—that time at Claremore Mound—you slapped Viney

---

1 Possibly Springfield, Missouri.
2 Traveling salesman.

Jones? She had it comin', that one did. I'd a-kissed you fer that 'f I hadn't a-been skeered you'd give *me* a whack. [*With quiet scorn.*] What I cain't understand—how a man like you could do that nen turn around and take up 'th that old witch of a Indian womern—Clara Leahy. Old enough to be yer own mammy! A lot of ready-made kids hangin' onto her. Nen to *marry* her! Bad enough to have her *keep* you's long's she did. [*As he does not answer.*] Shore treated you nice, too, didn't she? Appreciated you. Yeah! Onct last winter I seen her come in the picture show and climb all over everybody and drag you outside a-cussin' the livin' daylights out of you—and you never said *Boo.* [*Harshly.*] How much money'd she 'low you fer yer excitin' comp'ny, eh? Musta been a plenty to pay fer whut you tuck off of her! Yeah, but that's all over now, ain't it? You don't have to stand fer it now. [*Brassily, almost fiercely.*] She's dead—dead as a door nail—drownded in the Verdigree River, 's fur as anybody can make out— Drownded! Dead and gone. And you got her money! Ain't you lucky?

ART. [*With absorbed concentration, a fevered excitement underneath.*] Listen, I tell you— I ain't told nobody. When me and Clara got in the boat they was sump'n funny happened. That little girl of her'n come runnin' down to the river bank yellin', "Don't go, mammy! Don't go, mammy!" Musta felt sump'n was gonna happen. We was jist goin' acrost the river to see 'bout buyin' me a ridin' horse—that spotted cow pony of Bill Chambers'. We pushed out in the current 'th that kid standin' yellin' on the bank. We went upstream a ways till the kid was out of sight. I mean we had to go upstream, anyway. In clost to the bank, they was a lot of willer trees hangin' down. [*His eyes wide, seeing it, his hysteria growing, his speech rapid.*] I couldn't help it when Clara riz up in the boat like she'd went crazy, could I? I couldn't help it when she jumped in head first right in the shaller water the way she did! She musta went plumb crazy! She cut her head wide open, her body shot downstream 'fore I could stop it! I tried to! [*Fearfully, in a swift, clear rush.*] Her blood come up on the water the way oil does. She floated on down and drifted right in whur that kid was standin'! Her head was cut open from the rocks. The kid stopped cryin' long enough to yell at me 'at I killed her mammy! I *didn't* kill her! She *jumped* in! She hit her head on the rocks. I told the kid to shut up. I told her I'd kill her 'f she told anyone I killed her mammy! You *know* how sharp them rocks is! Boys is always cuttin' their heads on 'em, you know that yerself—swimmin'. They wouldn't take that kid's word fer it, would they? They couldn't hang me like they said they would? I never killed her! Why—I was married to her—I—

BEE. [*Scornfully, brassily, in sharp snarling accusation.*] Yeah, and *loved* her, I reckon? Swore to perfect and cherish her till death did you part, didn't you? Death parted you, all right. And you got her money, too, didn't you? Don't cry! Don't weep for her! She's dead. Put up a swell tombstone! A weepin' willer tree over her grave! Dike yerself up[1] in blue! Go callin' on the gals from here to Sapulpa![2] [*Snarling in loud disgust as she jumps to her feet.*] Anh—You killed her! You hit her with sump'n! You killed her for her money!

[*When* BEE *rises, a sharp flooding spotlight is turned on them quickly. He rises, one hand out as if suspended, breathless, his head turning from side to side, crazily.*]

ART. No! Sh! Don't say— I tell you—You won't tell on me— Don't tell on me! I— No one cain't hear me, can they? I hated her. Don't you know what it is to hate? [*In a rush.*] Her leathery old face, them eyes all bloodshot, her stringy hair, she hissed with her teeth when she talked, like a snake! You've saw her. I hated her. I wanted to kill her. I *always* wanted to kill her! [*Fiercely.*] See the blood spout from her ugly face, see her quiver and shake and fight to keep from dyin'! You're a girl, you don't know the way it got me. [*Softly, with mounting, horrible fervor.*] In the boat they was a hatchet—one of them little hatchets—sharp—sharp off the grindstone! I retch fer it. She grinned at me. I hit her and hit her, her grinnin' at me like a fool! Hit her seven or eight times, her clawin' to git away! Killed her, throwed her overboard! The blood come on the water like oil! Not fer her money, though, don't you think that! I wouldn't do that. I hated her, that's why, hated *her,* hated everybody—!

[*He is shouting now.*]

BEE. [*With savage joy, topping him in volume.*] Hate! Everybody! Me, too! Like me! [*Almost hysterically.*] I won't—that's all right—I'll never tell—I won't give you away—I thought it was money—I thought— [*Darkly, terribly.*] Anh, that's different!

1　To be dressed in one's best clothes. The phrase, originating in the US in the mid-nineteenth century, was used primarily to describe young men, as Bee does here.

2　Approximately 40 miles southwest of Claremore in Creek and Tulsa counties.

I never had the nerve! Listen, that's the way I feel— All the men I'd kill! I can see how you felt. [*Hypnotized.*] I can see her there in the boat—grinnin' up at you—her hair stringy, her eyes all bloodshot! Kill her! [*Startled.*] There! Look there! [*She is suddenly staring fearfully toward the back of his cell, her arm outstretched. On the wall past his shoulder something luminous is glowing in the darkness.*]

ART. Bee! What're you doin'? You're crazy—you're— [*He turns. The face of the dead woman grins down at him from the wall. His voice becomes a tense whisper.*] It's Clara! It's her! [*With fierce conviction.*] Anh, it cain't be! It's a trick. It's them! It's that deputy son of a bitch! [*He grabs the picture of the dead woman from the wall. He jumps on it, stamping it, his voice crazy and jubilant.*] You're dead, dead! I killed you! They thought they'd skeer me, did they, with a dead goddamned face on the wall— They thought they'd fool me—they—

BEE. [*Sharply, a horrible realization of something further in her.*] Art!

ART. Whutta they think I am, anyway? God, what a bunch of lousy hicks—a school kid wouldn't be took in by it—! Grin at me, will you— Grin in hell where you're burnin'!

[*He gives a final fierce stamp.*]

BEE. Art! [*Pointing.*] What's that?

[*In the spot of light on the wall is a small black oval box-like projection. He looks. He backs away slowly, his eyes on it. When he speaks again his voice is low, with a taut and fearful excitement thrumming underneath.*]

ART. [*Turning to her.*] Bee—What's that— D' you ever see a— They couldn't do that—Whut'd I say? I didn't say anything— It cain't be—! [*Sharply.*] It *is!* It's a dictaphone![1] [*He turns swiftly, clutching* BEE *through the bars. His face is livid, a cold sweat stands out on him; his voice is thick, his nostrils dilated.*] It's *you!* You knowed it! You was in on it!

BEE. Art! Art!

ART. You got me to tell on myself! [*His hands are on her throat, choking her.*] I'll kill you, I'll choke you till yer eyes come out of yer head! You've killed me—you hear?—you've murdered me the way I murdered her! Anh! Before I die—they'll be another dead 'un! What's another'n! What difference does it make now?

[*A door clangs as he speaks. Feet run hurriedly along the corridor. The*

---

1 A device for audio recording, specifically for dictation.

GUARD, *the* DEPUTY, *and the* SHERIFF *burst into sight. The* GUARD *quickly unlocks the door, fumbling at it.*]

SHERIFF. [*Cutting into* ART'S *speech.*] Open it! Open it! Don't let him—! Hurry up, there! [*The* GUARD *and the* DEPUTY *spring into the cell and drag him away from the girl. He cries out wildly as they jerk him along the corridor.* BEE *has sunk down against the bars.*] Are you hurt? Listen! [*He shakes the bars.*] Are you all right?

BEE. [*Wearily.*] Go away.

SHERIFF. Guard! Smiley! I cain't get in! Bring me the key! Dyke can handle him! Come on here!

[*The* GUARD *comes in, running, unlocks the cell and goes to the girl.*]

GUARD. Are you all right? D' he hurt you? Git up on yer feet. [*He lifts her up, holding her.*] We got here quick 's we could. Here, Miss.

BEE. [*Strangely, her eyes clouded.*] Leave me here. Go away.

SHERIFF. [*Going into* ART'S *cell.*] We didn't think he could git at you. I swear I thought you had sense enough to—You orten't to a-got so close up to him. You knowed he was dangerous— I told you what he—

GUARD. [*To* BEE, *who has said something to him.*] What? What's that, Miss?

BEE. [*Quietly.*] Leave me here. Slam the bolts to! What's the dif? I'm dead. Bury me.

SHERIFF. [*Softly, alarmed.*] Bring her on out here. [*The* GUARD *leads her out gently, her hat in his hand, her coat over his arm. The* SHERIFF *comes out.*] You'll be all right. I'm shore sorry he went and done that. Go to Dr. Bayes. Tell him I sent you. He'll fix you up, all right. Here. [*He hands her some money.*] Take it.

BEE. What is it?

SHERIFF. It's your'n, what I owe you. You shore earned it. Take it.

BEE. [*Wryly.*] Why not?

[*She takes it, puts it in her stocking.*]

SHERIFF. [*Delightedly.*] I shore am powerful indebted to you! He'll hang now! We got it all down—his own words. Why, his life ain't worth a damn! We'll rope that neck of his'n and jerk him so high he'll think a buzzard's got him. I shore do thank you!

BEE. [*Harshly.*] You're welcome. It's a pleasure! Don't git too clost to a rope yerself, Mr. Sheriff! It'd jerk that head of yours plumb off! Yer wife ud have a hard time with no one to call her "Honey"—somebody swell like you. [*Turning away, in disgust.*] Anh, Christ!

SHERIFF. [*Nonplussed.*] 'F I can ever help you, in any way—The county shore owes you a lot.

BEE. The county owes me a plenty.

SHERIFF. Well, good-bye, Miss Newcomb.

[*Puzzled, he goes out along the corridor. She grimaces, turns to* SMILEY, *remembering.*]

GUARD. [*Softly.*] Good-bye—Bee.

BEE. [*Smiling ruefully.*] Thanks.

GUARD. Say—

BEE. What is it?

GUARD. [*Awkwardly.*] Say—is that the truth 'bout you wantin' to kill everybody?

BEE. What!

GUARD. You know—what you said about all the men you'd kill—?

BEE. God, did that thing hear ever' word *I* said, *too?* [*With desperate irony, her voice harsh and troubled.*] It's a lie, Big Boy! I wouldn't hurt a fly! I go to church. I'm a good girl— I'm happy as hell. I love everybody. You'll see. You'll find out. When I was born, they wondered why I looked so sweet. Now they *know* why. I *am* sweet, that's the trouble with me. I cain't help it. I was born that way—

[*On part of the speech she crosses to him slowly, seductively, she puts up a hand on his shoulder.*]

[*The sound of an organ, wheezing and reluctant, pours down the corridor, drowning out the sound of her voice, and the sound of the rain on the roof. The jail fades quickly from sight.*]

Scene Three

The lights come up on a small room on the edge of Claremore, in the winter of 1931. It is a sordid, miserable, chill-looking room with a cold winter morning sun shining outside. A door is at the back. At the left is a window; another door at right goes to the rest of the shack. Claremore Mound is very dim, towering above.

The room is sparsely furnished—chairs, a small heating stove, etc.— the principal object being a wheezing organ at which sits MAISIE, *the child-wife of* ROLL HENLEY. *She is 17, pathetically thin and white, with stringy hair, and as she pumps she sings a hymn "My Faith Looks Up to Thee" in a flat tired voice. Her mother,* SARAH PICKARD, *a gaunt dark woman of 50, sits by the stove. Her features are pronounced and positive, her high cheek bones stand out in her leathery, proud face.*

MAISIE. [*Turning round, having finished the first verse.*] You want me to sing another'n, Maw?

SARAH. I wish you would, Maisie.

MAISIE. What one you want?

SARAH. Anything, Maisie.

[*She moves her legs, as if in pain.*]

MAISIE. What's the matter, Maw?

SARAH. Nothing. Is this all the wood they is left?

MAISIE. [*Soberly, looking down, shamefacedly.*] Yes. Less'n Roll gets some along Cat Crick[1] as he comes by. Here. [*She jumps up, picks up a rag rug off the floor and puts it around her mother's knees. Then she kneels by her.*] Is the pain mostly in your knees again?

SARAH. Oh, tain't much.

MAISIE. You'd ort to have some liniment[2] to rub on.

SARAH. I don't need it.

[MAISIE *suddenly bursts unaccountably into tears.*]

MAISIE. I don't see why— I don't see—!

SARAH. [*Compassionately.*] Maisie, honey—

MAISIE. My own maw down and ailin' with rheumatism and pains, and we ain't got enough money to do anything about it— Cain't even keep her warm enough!

SARAH. Now, Maisie—

MAISIE. It ain't fair, it ain't fair!

SARAH. Don't talk like that.

MAISIE. I don't keer, it ain't! [*She stands up, quieter.*] Maybe Roll'll get some money. [*Protectively.*] He tries, he works hard!

SARAH. Of course he does. He's a good man and a good husband to you. [*Soberly.*] Listen, Maisie—we've *all* done our best. It might not a-been right, but we done all we knowed how to do.

MAISIE. To think we used to own our own farm and here we air like this—

[*She crosses toward the organ stool.*]

SARAH. They's people worse off.

MAISIE. [*Turning toward the organ, dabbing her eyes.*] I'd like to know who?

SARAH. Plenty of folks.

MAISIE. [*Unappeased.*] I don't see how they live, then.

SARAH. [*Turning to look at her.*] Don't cry, Maisie. [*Her eyes stop at*

---

1 Cat Creek runs south of Claremore.
2 Pain-relieving lotion.

the window as she turns back.] Maisie, is that someone comin'
up the road?

MAISIE. [*Going to her side, looking.*] Yes.

SARAH. Who could it be?

MAISIE. She's all dressed up, whoever it is. I don't know.
[*Suddenly.*] Maw! Why, it looks like Aunt Viney.

SARAH. Viney?

MAISIE. Looks like her pictures.

SARAH. What on earth—? I ain't saw her fer ten years or more.
[*She stretches aside in the chair to see.*] It *is* Viney.

MAISIE. [*Eagerly.*] Maw— Maybe Aunt Viney'll help us. She's
doin' well, ever'body says, up at Quapaw—[1]

SARAH. Yes, maybe she will, Maisie, I never thought of— [*Then,
something strangely final coming into her voice.*] I couldn't ask
her— I—

MAISIE. But if we was to starve! If we could just get a little ahead
to see us through a few weeks, Maw. Roll'll get his money for
teamin' maybe pretty soon—

SARAH. [*Firmly.*] I wouldn't take help from Viney. Not after the
way she— Here. [*She takes the rug off her knees.*] Put this back
on the floor where it belongs. Straighten things up a little.
[MAISIE *obeys.*] Maisie—

MAISIE. Yes, Maw.

SARAH. I'd ask Viney to help if I could.

MAISIE. Why cain't you? It's just pride, Maw, and you know it!

SARAH. [*A flicker of amazing dignity and strength in her face.*] Pride?
Maybe. When you've got nothing left in the world but pride,
you're bad off.

MAISIE. You *will* ask her, then?

SARAH. Viney's my sister, Maisie—but I ain't got any claim on her.
She's left me alone for ten year. Even *one* year makes people
different. They go their own way, and it's fur apart. How do I
know she ain't a stranger walkin' into my house?

MAISIE. A stranger—your own sister, Maw?

SARAH. Viney and me was always kind of strangers to one another.

MAISIE. How?

[*There is a knock.*]

SARAH. Go to the door.

[MAISIE *opens the door.* VINEY CLEPPER *comes in. She is 41 now,
well-dressed in small-town taste,—she is unmistakably complacent,*

---

1 In northeastern Oklahoma (Ottawa County), approximately 70 miles
from Claremore.

righteous and patronizing. But she feels for a second the constraint of the meeting.]

VINEY. Hello, Sarah.

[*She crosses her, to* SARAH'S *right.*]

SARAH. Come in, Viney.

VINEY. Is this Maisie?

MAISIE. [*Coming up close to her mother.*] Yes. Howdy, Aunt Viney.

VINEY. I hear you're married now.

MAISIE. Yes'm. Roll Henley.

VINEY. Who's he?

MAISIE. Bob Henley's son. He's a teamster.

VINEY. Oh.

SARAH. Set down, Viney. What're you doin' in Claremore?

VINEY. [*Sitting down on the organ stool.*] Just came down with Jack—on business. Thought I'd run out and say Hello. How're you feeling, Sarah?

SARAH. Not very well.

VINEY. Rheumatism?

SARAH. Yes.

VINEY. [*In her old didactic manner.*] You ought to get some liniment. There's a good kind called Vamos.[1] Costs only fifty cents a bottle. You try it. Jack used one bottle and hasn't had an ache or a pain since.

SARAH. How *is* Jack?

VINEY. Oh, he's fine. You know, of course, he's got to be the mayor of Quapaw?

SARAH. I heard that, yes.

VINEY. We've sent Alma off this winter to a boarding school. That fine one in Kirksburg. She's a big girl now—fourteen.

SARAH. I wouldn't know her.

VINEY. I wouldn't have known Maisie, either. [*To* MAISIE.] So you're married, honey? Pretty early, isn't it?

MAISIE. I'm seventeen.

VINEY. 'Course our mother married when she was sixteen. But that was different—

SARAH. [*Quickly.*] Maisie, see about dinner, will you? Maybe Aunt Viney will stay.

MAISIE. Yes, Maw.

[*She goes out, right.*]

VINEY. So Maisie married a teamster, did she? Is he working?

SARAH. It's Sunday.

---

1 Riggs perhaps invented the name, which means "let's go!" in Spanish.

VINEY. Where'd he team yesterday?

SARAH. [*Coldly.*] It rained yesterday.

VINEY. Oh. I hope he gets enough work to take good care of you all. These hard times. Most people don't know where the next meal's coming from. I'm thankful to say that me and Jack are— Is it cold in here, Sarah?

SARAH. [*Looks at her sharply, then says simply.*] Yes, it *is* cold, Viney.

VINEY. [*Drawing her fur about her.*] You've used up your land allotment, have you, Sarah?

SARAH. The mortgage took it.

VINEY. How long since Ed died?

SARAH. Five years.

VINEY. Where've the boys got off to? I can't seem to keep up with you all.

SARAH. They're married and gone—long ago.

VINEY. Your oldest boy must have got Indian land, too, didn't he? He was born in 1898 about. What'd he do with it?

SARAH. He sold it when he was twenty-one.

VINEY. What was his name? I was trying to tell Jack. What was it?

SARAH. Who?

VINEY. Your oldest.

SARAH. [*Gravely.*] You named him, Viney. You named him after Paw.

VINEY. Oh, I'd forgotten. [*She looks about the bare and dismal room. At sight of the organ, she gets up, to get a look at it; she is downstage of organ.*] I see you still got Maw's old organ. I'd sell it and buy me a radio. [*Reaching in her pocketbook.*] Oh, I brought you something. [*She brings it out, goes over to* SARAH.] A picture of our place in Quapaw. That's me and Alma on the porch. Here's Jack over here by the garage. And look! The maid stuck her head out the window so as to be in the picture.

SARAH. It's very nice.

VINEY. They call it The Mansion.

[*She crosses, lays picture and bag on the upper end of organ, stands there.*]

SARAH. [*Gravely.*] You've done very well, Viney.

VINEY. Well—Jack was the main one, I guess.

SARAH. And Hutch—whatever became of him?

VINEY. [*Viciously.*] I don't know and I don't care. It was Hutch that came close to ruining my whole life. That dumb Indian, that's all he was! You never could tell about him, couldn't get on to what he was up to! [*Thoughtfully, half to herself.*] He didn't have any *change* in him, he was stuck someway. He was broody and sullen, he couldn't seem to get hold of himself, like a lot of part-Indians around here.[1]

SARAH. And what about you, Viney?

VINEY. What about me?

SARAH. You're more Cherokee than Hutch.

VINEY. Well, I'm thankful to say it doesn't show.

SARAH. [*Strangely.*] Every word you say shows. Everything you say shames you. You try too hard to deny what you are. It tells on you. [*Harshly.*] You say Hutch didn't have any *change* in him. They's nuthin' else in you *but* change. You've turned your back on what you ought to a-been proud of.

VINEY. [*Angrily.*] Being a part-Indian? What would it get me? Do you think I want to be ignorant and hungry and crazy in my head half the time like a lot of 'em around here? Do you think I want to be looked down on because I can't do anything, can't get along like other people? Do you think I want to make the kind of mess of my life *you* have—and live in a filthy hole like this the rest of my days—?

SARAH. You won't have to. The hole you live in is filthier, and it suits you down to the ground.

VINEY. [*Sitting down on the organ stool, fuming and disturbed.*] What do you mean?

[*The lights begin to go down strangely. A fantastic glow from the stove creeps into the room, blotting out its realistic outline, its encompassing walls, throwing* SARAH'S *shadow, huge and dark, on the wall.*]

SARAH. [*Fiercely, growing in strangeness, like an oracle.*] Mean? Listen to me. You're not my sister. Your blood ain't mine and never was! Change, change till doomsday—one thing'll stay! Your heart's as black as ever and hard as flint. Be mean and cunning and full of hate, like the Indian. Be greedy and selfish the way the white man is. None of what's good—let the good things be! You're past 'em! Use the most shameful things you got in you to get ahead. *You'll get ahead, all right!* [*Seeing it darkly, slowly facing front.*]

You'll come to a close tight place in the hills, between rocks. The rocks'll get closer together! They'll squeeze you dry. Your flesh'll fall from you like feathers,

---

1 A person with Indigenous and other ancestry. Unlike "half-breed," above, it is not necessarily offensive.

Your bones'll crumble!

You can't turn back:
You'll *want* to turn back!

You walkin', turrible, dried-up thing, you'll be crushed to a gray
    powder!
Your cupful of ashes'll scatter on the wind!

One thing you can't do, you with your table full of meat and furs
    around your neck:
You can't take a path you ain't meant to.
It'll take you to the jaws of wild animals,
It'll guide you west, to the rivers of quicksand,
It'll take you to jagged cliffs,
It'll lead you to death!

VINEY. [*Jumping up, crying out, with febrile anger.*] Yanh, I'm to stay
    here and rot then! I'm not to be smart enough to keep meat
    on the table and the cold wind outside! Oh no! It isn't decent,
    it's not the way to be! [*Her anger has carried her above the
    organ, facing front.*]
SARAH. No. It's not the way to be. [*She has gone inward.*] The
    way to be is to be humble, and remember the life that's in
    you. Our Maw told us once the way we was meant to live.
    "Remember it," she said. "Remember it and your days'll
    be food and drink. They'll be a river in the desert, they'll be
    waving grass and deer feeding." [*Quietly, like a prayer.*]

"The man'll plow the ground," Maw said.
"And he'll plant and cultivate.
The woman'll have her garden and her house.

There'll be pork and corn dodgers,[1] molasses from the cane
    patch, beans on the vine.
There'll be berries and fruit—blackberries, strawberries, plums.
The woods'll be thick with squirrels.
The woman'll go down to the branch with her apron full of corn
    and a pan of ashes to make hominy.[2]

---

1 A cornmeal cake similar to corn pone or corn bread.
2 Dehulled kernels of corn used in stews and other dishes, including
    posole.

The nights'll come.
Children'll be born.
The gods of the earth things—the gods of the stone and the tree
    and all natural things
Will live by their side.
And the God of the Christians, too,
Will keep them from sin."
[*Crying out, as the vision and the memory have become slowly too
powerful, too painful.*]
Maw! Maw! Where are you?
Where has the good life gone to?
It's got fur away and dim. It's not plain any more.
I can't follow.
I tried! I tried—!

[*She relaxes weakly, miserably, her hand at her face.*]
VINEY. [*Taking a step nearer.*] Sarah, what is it?
SARAH. [*From her dark.*] I failed.
VINEY. You mustn't go on like that.
SARAH. [*Lifting her head.*] I'm a failure, too—like you. We're both
    failures. But I tried, and you didn't. I wouldn't trade places
    with you.
VINEY. [*Bridling.*] Well! You wouldn't? It's lucky you feel that
    way, because I feel the same way about it. And let me tell
    you something, Sarah. As long as I've got money and a good
    home, and am living right, I don't call myself a failure. And
    neither does anyone else, but you. If you haven't anything
    better to say to me after ten years, I'm going. [*She gets her bag
    from the organ. Turning slyly, cruelly.*] Oh! If your rheumatism
    doesn't get any better, you'd better get that liniment I told you
    about. Vamos, it's called. Here's fifty cents. [*She holds it out.*]
SARAH. [*Fiercely.*] Get out!
VINEY. [*Coolly, going to her.*] I'm giving you a little present.
SARAH. [*Dangerously.*] Get out, Viney!
VINEY. [*A cruel delight coming into her face. She goes to door, turns,
    her back almost to audience.*] I'll go, Sarah. I may never see you
    again. And all the same, you may need fifty cents. [*She tosses it
    into the middle of the room and goes out, quickly.*]
[*Hearing the door close,* MAISIE *comes in.*]
MAISIE. Aunt Viney gone? I thought she'd stay for dinner! [*Seeing
    the money on the floor.*] Why Maw, here's fifty cents on the
    floor!
[*She starts to stoop for it.*]

SARAH. [*Fiercely.*] Leave it alone, leave it alone!
MAISIE. [*Astonished.*] Whut! Why, Maw! [SARAH *bursts into tears.*]
    What is it, Maw?
SARAH. [*Wiping her tears away, wryly.*] Nuthin'.
MAISIE. Where'd this fifty cents come from?
SARAH. [*With quiet despair at her dead pride.*] You musta dropped
    it, Maisie. Or maybe Aunt Viney did. Pick it up. We'll need it.
[MAISIE *picks it up, crying out joyously.*]
MAISIE. I don't know how it got there, and I don't care! Look,
    Maw, it'll buy you some of that liniment Aunt Viney told you
    about, that's whut it'll do! It sure will!
[*She flies to the organ, and starts pumping gaily, and singing again, the
last verse of "My Faith Looks Up to Thee."*]
[*The Scene begins to fade.*]

Scene Four

The organ wheezes out its bass notes, its tremolo shrill and harsh.
MAISIE *lifts her voice in nasal joy. Far away a mockingbird sings in
a wood, dizzy with summer. The organ gives way, retreats, its pedals
creaking. The girl's voice grows faint. The tawdry room disappears. The
outline of Claremore Mound becomes sharper in the distance.*
    *Into a tight hot cleared basin in the woods, the summer sun pours
down. The shadows of leaves dapple the ground. In front of the golden
pool is a dark gloomy place, thick with heaped dead leaves and tangled
brush. The trees meet overhead, roofing out the sun. Briary thick
underbrush, the trunks and branches of oaks and hickory stand out
blackly against the brilliance. The trees move, sighing. The sound of
feathery movement, the swift sharp clash of wings comes down.*
    *Stalking carefully through the woods and into the bright circle of
sun, three boys, about ten or twelve years old, come into sight. They are
bent and tense, far apart, watchful—as if they expected to come upon
some astonishing and fearsome thing. One of the boys is lithe and very
dark; another is heavy-limbed and tow-headed; the third is sharp, with
a scowling intense face.*
    They are GAR, HUTCH *and* ART. *It is 1906.*
    ART *is first. He motions to the others.* GAR *comes next, then* HUTCH.
When he comes up to GAR, *they both stoop down, looking at the
ground.*

ART. [*With suppressed excitement.*] Wait—!
HUTCH. [*Getting up.*] Whut is it?

ART. Be still! [*He strains forward, tensely, alert, immobile.*] This is it. [*He comes forward a step or two, looking at the ground. He straightens up.*] Hutch—

HUTCH. Whut?

ART. [*Pointing.*] D'you see anything there?

HUTCH. Leaves.

ART. [*Contemptuously.*] Leaves!

HUTCH. Tracks.

ART. [*Nodding, with conviction.*] Umm. This is the place he was found at.

HUTCH. Anybody could make tracks, Art.

ART. [*Firmly.*] This is the place.

HUTCH. I don't see. 'S jist a track.

[GAR, *who has been standing very still, not looking at the two, absorbed, now speaks.*]

GAR. This is it.

[*He comes forward, the other side of* HUTCH *so that* HUTCH *is in the middle.*]

HUTCH. Aw, you two gimme the belly-ache! You don't know half's much's you think you— My brother told me and he ort to—

[GAR *shoots out a hand in a curious motion, as if pushing the words back at him, silencing him strangely. It is curiously like the motion we have seen him make in Scene One.*]

[HUTCH'S *voice flounders, stops.*]

GAR. [*When it is still again.*] Art told you.

ART. [*Quietly.*] The dead nigger was found here.

HUTCH. Was not!

ART. I can tell.

HUTCH. Aw, it was down fu'ther—clost to the railroad track! They was playin' cards—last night—four of 'em, niggers—when it happened. One nigger beat the other'n's head in. They was camped. They was playin' High, Low, Jack and the Game.[1] George told me. It was fu'ther down.

ART. The camp was here. See that burnt wood?

HUTCH. [*Looking at the ground, reluctantly.*] Somebody was camped here.

GAR. *They* was. My pappy told me.

HUTCH. [*Closer to* GAR.] Pappy! You ain't got a pappy. Yore pappy died. A way back. They shot him. Yer mammy died, too. Both of 'em's dead.

---

1 A card game, also called High Low Jack or Pitch. It derives from the English card game All Fours.

GAR. My guardeen[1] told me.

HUTCH. A guardeen ain't a pappy.

GAR. Mr. Ferber is same as my blood kin.

HUTCH. He *ain't* blood kin. He's a Dutchman. A furriner like him!

GAR. [*Quietly.*] He's a German. He's smarter'n anyone around here, Mr. Ferber is. He's good as my pappy was— [*Thoughtfully*] —better'n my pappy. [*Inside, to himself, turning, facing front.*] He wants me to be smart.

HUTCH. Why *don't* you be, then?

GAR. I'm gonna be.

HUTCH. [*With loud contempt.*] Hoo! [*He turns from him.*]

GAR. [*Turning on him fiercely, forcing him to face his anger.*] You think I ain't?

HUTCH. [*Retreating.*] How—how'd *I* know whut you're gonna do?

GAR. [*Quietly again.*] The nigger was kilt here. Mr. Ferber told me. [*He turns his back on them both, solid and final.*]

ART. [*Interrupting.*] Tom Bussey told *me*. He ort to know.

HUTCH. [*Crossing to him.*] Runs the Dirty Dozen, Tom Bussey does. They stole all the washin' off Miz Anderson's line. And money!

ART. He's growed.

HUTCH. Humh! Fifteen.

ART. I *said* growed. He told me this was the place whur the nigger was kilt at—and it *is*. By that sycamore, he says, the path widens out. A stump sets out on the main road. We seen the stump—

[HUTCH *crosses downstage to right, in easy scorn.*]

HUTCH. Aw, George told me. He figgers things out. Told me it was fu'ther down—and it *is!*

GAR. [*Turning, facing the others.*] Shet up! [*Quietly.*] Listen, Hutch.

---

1 Riggs likely means a legal guardian, an adult serving in a parental role. However, in 1906, the year in which Riggs sets this scene, the US Congress passed the Burke Act, an amendment to the 1887 Dawes Act. The Burke Act kept allotted land in federal trust status for twenty-five years or until an allottee was deemed "competent and capable," at which time they were issued ownership in the form of a fee simple patent. Congress subsequently passed the Act of May 27, 1908, which transferred responsibility for the guardianship of allotees in the "Five Civilized Tribes" (Cherokees, Chickasaws, Choctaws, Creeks, and Seminoles) from the federal government to county courts. This guardianship system was deeply corrupt and allowed guardians to enrich themselves at the expense of allotees.

Use yer head. Be still. [*When they are still, he faces front, strangely gripped.*] Is this it—or ain't it?

HUTCH. [*Sniffing the air, his brow drawn together in concentration, moving slightly toward them.*] They's sump'n funny here—

GAR. Plain as day. 'F you'd listen to yerself a little, you'd know sump'n.

HUTCH. I listen to George. He's older'n me.

GAR. If tain't him, it's someone.

HUTCH. [*Going toward* ART.] Aw, but this don't have to be whur the nigger was kilt at! It could be a thousand places. [*He kicks viciously at the heaped leaves.*] George said the way it'd be. You'd see signs of they bein' a fight er sump'n. The leaves ud be tore up 'stid of all smooth. You might' nigh could tell the minute you—

[*He is staring with wide-open eyes at the ground in front of him. The others watch. He falls to his knees, downstage center, picks up something from among the leaves, his eyes fastened on it.* ART *runs and kneels also.* GAR *follows, on* ART'S *left.*]

ART. [*His eyes glittering, snatching the card.*] Playin' card!

HUTCH. [*Hoarsely, half rising.*] Ace of spades.

ART. Tore on one corner!

HUTCH. It was here! [*A bird squawks and flaps somewhere overhead and forward. The faces of the three boys turn upward swiftly, their bodies rigid, their eyes following the flight across from left to right.*] Crow!

GAR. Hawk!

ART. [*With abnormal intensity, looking straight forward.*] Buzzard!
[*The two turn toward him quickly.*]

GAR. Whut?

ART. [*His gaze riveting to the bunched leaves at their feet.*] Buzzard!

GAR. [*Sharply.*] Was *not* a buzzard! [*He looks above and right— swiftly.*] See there! Yander he sails. Chicken hawk!

HUTCH. [*In crazy, almost hysterical triumph, jumping clear up, running down right, pointing.*] Chicken hawk, chicken hawk! See him flyin' there, Art? You don't know's much's you think you do! Chicken hawk, chicken hawk!

ART. [*Holding up his hands, tensely.*] Sh! Be still! [*To* HUTCH, *with quiet scorn, after a moment, getting up.*] They ain't nuthin' to be skeered of.

HUTCH. [*Quickly, in a rush, crossing back to* ART.] I ain't skeered— Who's skeered?— I ain't skeered!

ART. Jabberin' at a chicken hawk.

HUTCH. I *ain't* skeered! Gimme that card back! It's mine! I found it!

[ART *hands it back.*]

GAR. [*Quietly, getting up.*] You can trade it.

HUTCH. I'm gonna keep it. I found it. I bet that nigger had it in his hand before he was kilt! I'm gonna give it to—I'm gonna give it to someone.

[*All three walk around stage, looking for things among leaves. Silence for a moment. All at once* ART *stops suddenly. They both look at him where he stands up center.* HUTCH *is right of* ART, GAR *left.*]

ART. [*Absorbed.*] What if he'd come back?

HUTCH. Who?

ART. The nigger that done the killin'. [*He looks round tensely.*] What if he'd be hidin'—here in the bresh some'eres—lookin' at us—right now! What if he'd grab us?

HUTCH. Art!

ART. He *might*. He might kill us!

HUTCH. [*Quickly.*] No, now Art! A man seen him up by Quapaw. The Sheriff's went up there to hunt fer him. Anyway—he'd be skeered to come here—whur—whur that—

[*He looks at the heaped leaves.*]

ART. No, he wouldn't. It wouldn't skeer him. Niggers is funny. They got a funny way. When the niggers was run out of Claremore,[1] Pap said a funny thing. When a nigger would git shot, he wouldn't know it. He'd keep on runnin'.

HUTCH. Couldn't he feel it?

ART. [*With curious tensity, crossing way down left on speech.*] I'd a-shot him till he felt it. They was one all covered 'th blood run plumb to Inola.[2] When he got there, he fell over dead.

HUTCH. [*Kneeling, hunting in leaves.*] Somebody told me them old Creek Indians married niggers. Us Cherokees wouldn't do that.[3]

[*He has found nothing. He gets up.*]

ART. [*With contempt, facing him.*] You ain't a Cherokee.

---

1 Riggs appears to have invented this episode, though he draws it from a history of anti-Black racism in the Cherokee Nation and Oklahoma, most infamously the 1921 attack on the Black neighborhood of Greenwood in Tulsa. See Sturm, especially Chapter 7, on the Cherokee Freedmen; and Miles.

2 Approximately 15 miles south-southeast of Claremore in Rogers County.

3 Notwithstanding Hutch's assertion, Cherokees did marry African Americans.

HUTCH. I am! I'm a sixteenth. I got land, I guess.

ART. [*Absorbed.*] Niggers'll *kill*—and not keer! It don't bother 'em none! 'F I kilt a nigger, I wouldn't keer! I'd kick him, I'd tromp on him after I kilt him!

[*He is parting the leaves with his hands, stooping down. He sinks to his knees, continues his search.* GAR *looks away to the center; his eyes gleam. He walks swiftly, lithely, over the spangled earth, the others arrested by his concentration.* GAR *picks up a tin cup. The others come over quickly.*]

HUTCH. Tin cup!

[*They look at each other in awe, finger the cup, striking it till it rings. They turn and stare back at the place.*]

ART. They was drinkin' coffee.

HUTCH. [*Dips his finger in the cup, tastes it.*] Whiskey.

[*He looks over to right for an instant, showing his awed feeling for the place.*]

ART. [*In a vibrant, hushed voice, as if talking in the night.*] D' you hear how he was kilt?

HUTCH. Umh. My brother told me.

ART. George don't know.

HUTCH. He does, too! He knows a lot. He told me. They set here—four of 'em—four niggers—drinkin'— [*With a look out of the corner of his eye at the cup*] —out of a tin cup—and playin' cards. It was night. They had a f'ar. This nigger was losin' money. They played fer pennies—

ART. Pennies!

[*He looks down at his feet, as if he expected to see some.*]

GAR. They wouldn't leave no pennies.

HUTCH. All of a sudden this nigger riz up—

ART. Whut nigger?

HUTCH. [*Excitedly, enacting it, crossing a little toward down left.*] The dead nigger! He riz up and grabbed the pennies out of a pile in the middle. Nen they was a fight. One nigger retch out his hand fer a big piece of arn a-layin' there—

ART. [*With savage intensity.*] A axe! It was a axe!

HUTCH. No! Piece of arn!

ART. [*As before.*] Axe! A sharp axe. A big axe fer choppin' down trees. He hit him in the head. They was blood all over everything—over the nigger's clothes, all over the ground! His blood gushed out of him—he turned purt' nigh white the way the blood spouted from him! I seen him—layin' on the slab—

HUTCH. You didn't!

ART. [*Fiercely, ecstatically.*] Sneaked in and seen him—layin'
on the slab! The axe slashed his head open—it hacked off
one ear—it split his jawbone! He had a gold tooth, I seen
it shinin'! Hack him! Hack him! [*He starts to run, in a wide
circle, hypnotized, around the central pile of leaves, scooped up
like the mound of a grave. As he runs, he stoops quickly, picking
up a heavy short club. He cries out in a kind of fierce, jubilant
incantation.*]
'F *I* seen a nigger, I'd hack him!
'F *I* seen a nigger, I'd hack him!
'F *I* seen a nigger, I'd hack him! Hack him!
[*The other two boys, carried away, swoop into the circle.* GAR *has his
tin cup in one hand;* HUTCH *clutches his crumpled card. They begin
slapping rapidly their own open mouths, from which pours the high
queer interrupted conventionalized Indian cry, fearful and disturbing
in the shaken gloom.* ART'S *savage cry goes on and on. At the top of
Claremore Mound a drum begins. Suddenly, as if by plan, the running
figures stop dead still, close together, holding out their trophies, as if
acting out a ritual. The drum rises and reverberates in the silence, like a
great and quickened heartbeat.* ART *looks at the tin cup, at the playing
card, drops his club, goes on his knees, feverishly tearing the leaves
apart with his hands. He leans forward, then back quickly, rises, his
hands out in front of him, turned down. He turns them over. The palms
are streaked with blood.*]
HUTCH. [*Left of* ART, *down beside him.*] Whut is it?
[GAR *drops down too.*]
ART. [*In quick horror.*] Blood! [*He jumps up.*]
HUTCH AND GAR. Blood! [*They jump up, staring in horror.*]
ART. [*In ecstasy and horror.*] Got blood on my hands!
[*The three back away, side by side, in a line, staring fearfully at the
place, stepping together with the beat of the drum.* ART'S *hands run
once convulsively down his legs, to rid them of the blood. The three
continue to back away. Halfway across the open ground, they stop, turn
quickly and flee into the woods off right.*]
[*The drum stops, cut off short. Silence. The sun becomes brighter, more
dazzling, behind the pool of close shadow. The trees move, swaying in
the sunlight. A bird calls briefly. Then slowly, rising from the warmed
and fertile earth, a giant* NEGRO, *naked to the waist, lifts himself into
the sun from behind the thick underbrush. His black body glistens. He
stares off toward the fleeing boys, stretches himself, comes forward a step
from sun into shadow, in a movement real and ghostly, as if he were
two presences: the murderer undismayed by his crime, and the very
emanation of the dead man himself. He stands a moment in the gloom,*

*his dark hulk tremendous against the sun. His eyes follow the boys; one
hand moves itself forward to a blackberry spray, in an uncalculated
reflex, gathers two berries and lifts them idly to his mouth. Then he
yawns. Then the sun dies. All below becomes dark.*]
[*A light goes up, glows on the summit of Claremore Mound. An Indian,
slim, aristocratic, minute in the distance, stands up against the sky. A
drum is beating—harsh and troubled. It is like a fevered and aching
disquiet at the pit of the world.*]

CURTAIN
INTERMISSION

Scene Five

*On Eagle Bluff, which overlooks the Illinois River and the town of
Tahlequah, seat of the Cherokee Nation,*[1] *a bell begins to toll. The lights
come up. Perched close to the perilous edge of the cliff is a primitive little
church, its forward side open, revealing the interior. In the right end is
the altar with a round window above it, and a tiny platform on which
is a chair and a reading stand. In the right wall, near the corner, is a
door into the study and farther along toward the left, in the back wall
(part of which is left out) is a large colored window. In the left end,
the main door to the outside, with two steps going down to the rocky
ground. Rough hand-hewn benches face right toward the altar. Two
steps lead front, to the ground, as if from a door in the forward sidewall
of the church. The whole structure is made of rude, unplaned slabs of
pine, somewhat in decay, and is surmounted by a bell-tower with a bell
in it. The rope is visible near the left door.*

*Outside the church, a gnarled and twisted tree is at the left, on the
very edge of the sheer cliff. At the right, and through the hole where part
of the back wall is left out, away off beyond and far below the sharp cliff
edge, the valley of the Illinois River, with its minute colored fields and
patches of wood, can be seen. A tall post stands just outside the place
where the wall is gone. On the distant horizon, small, indistinct against
the sky, is the shape of Claremore Mound.*

It is noon of a summer day in 1913. The hot sunlight pours down.

*Standing inside and near the left door of the church, an unshaven,
rough-looking man,* HENRY, *is pulling the bell-rope.*

ABNER *and* RUFE, *in coarse jackets and corduroys, appear,* ABNER

---

1 Approximately 60 miles southeast of Claremore.

from up center, RUFE *from the left.* HENRY *finishes ringing the bell and comes forward.*

HENRY. [*With a wave of his hand, as he comes down.*] Mornin', Abner. Mornin', Rufe. [*Softly.*] No sign of trouble?
[RUFE *has sat down on the fourth bench.*]
ABNER. [*Shortly, from a place near the pulpit.*] Ain't no trouble.
HENRY. [*Philosophically.*] Well, I jist ask.
[*He goes out of sight.*]
RUFE. Reckon anything'll happen?
ABNER. What would?
RUFE. Oh, I don't know. People git sick and t'ard of havin' things stole off of 'em.
ABNER. [*Going to second bench, putting his foot on it, leaning closer to* RUFE.] Look, Rufe. Down there in Tahlequah, the land's good for farmin', makin' a good livin'. Up here on the bluff—why, this ole bluff and table land does ever'thing it *can* to keep from raisin' a form thing. Well, it won't hurt 'em none down there to help God's Chosen People a little bit, will it? We got to eat *some*way, ain't we?
RUFE. You blame right.
ABNER. Ain't we one of the Lost Tribes of Israel?[1] Ain't we God's favorites? Them ole Cherokees ort to be proud to furnish God's People a cow or a sack of corn or half a hog onct in a while. Do 'em good. You heared what Jonas said this mornin' in meetin'—
RUFE. Yeah, I heared—
ABNER. Well, there you air.
RUFE. [*Getting up.*] Yeah, but—we had trouble *onct*—the time that Shuruff come up here from Tahlequah and—
ABNER. Shet up about it! We don't know nuthin' about that! Besides, it'd be purty hard to climb up the bluff, you know.
RUFE. They could go around—and come up the long way.
ABNER. [*Lifting his rifle.*] What'd you think these here things are fer?
[*People of the congregation—men, women and children—begin to come in from every opening, casually, laughing and talking. They are ragged and unkempt, the women in old dresses and mother hubbards,[2] some*

---

1 The Twelve Tribes of Israel descended from the twelve sons of Jacob. Ten of the tribes were lost to history in the eighth century BCE.
2 A loose-fitting dress intended for daily wear that emerged in the 1870s and 1880s.

wearing sun-bonnets. They begin to sit down, chatting. ABNER *and*
RUFE *disappear around the tabernacle.*]
PEOPLE. Was a-skeered to chop no furder 'th old Butch runnin'
    around in the bresh liable to git fell on.
How'd you find bee's honey—most a bucketful?
Frankie! Frankie!
I'm gonna set clost to the door so's to spit ef'n I want.
The wind was on the prairies! Clouds clumb nigh up here with
    lightnin' showin' forked in the folds! Wish't it had stormed!
Put up or shet up. If you had no more'n that, I'd be shamed to tell
    it!
Where's Jonas at?
Ain't come out of his study yit.
Le's git set down.
[LIZE *and* ANNIE, *two brown-faced, raw-boned women of the Tribe,*
greet each other down front. LIZE *is much amused at something. She*
has come in at center, with others, caught sight of ANNIE *who has*
entered left, and waved to her.]
LIZE. Listen, Annie. My man Luke went to the spring to git water.
    They was a big ole copperhead settin' there. [*She laughs.*]
    Luke come on back with the bucket empty.
ANNIE. Was he afeared of a ole copperhead snake?
LIZE. No, not a-tall, to hear him tell it. He says to me, "Lize," he
    says, "that snake's got as much right to git hisself a drink as *I*
    got." And he was right.
ANNIE. Pshaw! He was jist afeared.
LIZE. I 'spect he was, Annie. But he made out like he was jist bein'
    kind.
ANNIE. Men'll do that.
[*She sits in the fourth row.*]
LIZE. 'Cause he 'spected that was the way he'd orter feel—kind-
    like. Luke—he's awful silly, Luke is.
ANNIE. Women folks won't lie to *their*selves.
LIZE. Not even if Jonas tells 'em. Jonas'd jist laugh if he knowed
    what Luke'd done.
[*She starts to her seat in the second row.*]
ANNIE. [*Chortling.*] Wouldn't he jist laugh! [*Calling* LIZE *closer.*]
    Lize, come 'ere. [LIZE *does so.*] Sh! Jonas. He's ailin'.
LIZE. [*Soberly.*] I noticed this mornin' in meetin'.
ANNIE. If he died, I don't know who'd lead us.
LIZE. We'd git along, I guess.
ANNIE. We'd *have* to git.

[*A child,* AILSEY, *about seven years old, has run in from left, and run up to* LIZE.]

AILSEY. Maw! [*Eagerly.*] I seen a cotton-tail and a toad-frog.

LIZE. Whur at, Ailsey?

AILSEY. Out by them rocks other side of the tabernacle.

LIZE. Shore 'nough, Ailsey?

AILSEY. Uh-huh. Cotton-tail and a toad-frog. Jist a-playin' there like a pet calf. I looked at 'em, an' they looked at me.

LIZE. Lands alive! Well, go and set down now. Meetin's gonna start.

AILSEY. I don't keer. I got me a prayer all made up.

LIZE. You're too little to need any. Prayers is for big folks.

AILSEY. I ain't no littler'n Benny. Benny's made him two—one about milkin' the old red cow and one about pullin' grapes offen the grape-vine tree. Mine's about—sump'n. Don't you wish you knowed?

LIZE. [*Smiling.*] I c'n wait, I guess.

AILSEY. You *got* to! [*Starting.*] Guess I'll set up there clost to the altar.

LIZE. [*Following.*] Hain't you gonna set by me, Ailsey?

AILSEY. Nope. Gonna set whur I can see Jonas. [*She starts up the aisle.*]

LIZE. Well, go on, then.

[AILSEY *sticks out her tongue impudently, then runs back and kisses her mother.*]

AILSEY. That's for the rheumatiz.

LIZE. Ow! Ailsey, you got stains all over yer mouth.

AILSEY. [*Showing one hand, keeping the other behind her—proudly.*] All over my hands, too.

LIZE. What you been pickin'? 'Pears like blackberries.

AILSEY. Don't know as I'll tell you!

[*She runs up the aisle, and before anyone has noticed, she climbs up on the altar where she stands framed against the round window, her hands behind her back.* LIZE *has sat down.*]

PEOPLE. [*Excitedly.*] Ailsey! Get down from there! Standin' on the altar—my lands!

Lize, look at Ailsey—standin' on the altar!

LIZE. [*Jumping up.*] Ailsey! Get down from there! What you aimin' to do? Jonas'll see you—

AILSEY. I'm a-standin' on the Rock!

LIZE. [*Anxiously.*] Get down! Here Jonas comes. Get down now—'fore he ketches you! Land's sakes!

[*She sits.*]

[*But* JONAS *has already come in from his study. The* PEOPLE *sit up, watching him respectfully, reverently. He is dressed in rough shoes, baggy trousers, and a faded blue shirt. His white hair and beard give him an air of ascetic nobility. But his eyes are strange, fanatic.*]

AILSEY. [*Shouting to him.*] Jonas! Jonas! Look at me—I'm a-standin' on the Rock!

JONAS. [*Smiling, standing before the altar, facing her.*] You've taken my place, Ailsey.

AILSEY. I brung you sump'n, Jonas.

JONAS. What is it?

AILSEY. [*Holding out both hands.*] Blackberries! A whole handful. I found 'em in the side pasture.

JONAS. Thank you, Ailsey.

AILSEY. You got to eat, Jonas. Make you fat.

JONAS. [*Taking some and eating them.*] They're very good. You're a good little girl, Ailsey. [*He lifts her down. She runs toward a front bench, her face beaming.* LIZE *stands up and motions for her to sit. She does.* JONAS *goes up on the rostrum, turns and surveys his audience. The People lean forward expectantly.*] People of the Lost Tribe. God's Chosen! Let us begin—

JONAS AND PEOPLE. [*In full round tones, like an organ.*]
O Lord most high!

JONAS.
O Lord in the heavens, hear us in this hour!

PEOPLE.
O Lord most high!

JONAS.
The day is half gone. The sun has climbed to its peak in the sky.

PEOPLE.
You are the Sun, O Lord!

JONAS AND PEOPLE.
O Sun most high!

JONAS.
The clouds have scattered before you—
Sunlight descends.

JONAS AND PEOPLE.
You are the Sun, O Lord!
You are the rain and the snow!
You are the hail descending!
Hear us, be with us, O Lord!
[*Hands have begun to go up in ecstasy.*]

A WOMAN. [*With a rapt, ecstatic look, as if praying, jumping to her feet.*]

I went out this mornin' when the bees was about—
The bees was singin' where they flew about the flowers.
PEOPLE.
Hear us, O Lord!
A MAN. [*Jumping up.*]
The cows knowed thy presence—
The calves leaped up for joy.
PEOPLE.
Hear us, O Lord!
A WOMAN. [*Jumping up in front and turning back to the others.*]
The f'ar burned most of itself when I struck the flint;
The peas is gettin' ripe and fat in their pods.
PEOPLE.
Hear us, O Lord!
A MAN. [*Jumping up.*]
When I crossed the crick a-lookin' for my coon dog,
He come a-runnin' and a-lickin' my face like he was happy.
PEOPLE.
Hear us, O Lord!
A WOMAN. [*Jumping up.*]
My sister in Caroliny sent a bolt of blue calico—[1]
And I'm a-restin' easy where I been ailin' so long.
PEOPLE.
Hear us, O Lord!
[*Exclaiming, outside the litany rhythm.*] Hear us, O Lord! Praise
    Jesus! Bless his holy name!
Halleluia!
A MAN. [*Jumping up.*]
Water flowed uphill I swear to my time!—
For me to git a drink of where it hadn't got muddy.
PEOPLE.
Hear us, O Lord!
A BOY.
Grapes was so green they puckered up my mouth so I'd learn to
    whistle.
PEOPLE. [*Smiling.*]
Hear us, O Lord!
AILSEY.
Toad-frog a-settin' right there on a rock

---

1   A versatile, inexpensive cotton fabric, usually patterned, packaged in
    bolts (rolls). Lengths vary, but as the woman's remark suggests, the gift
    is generous.

Jist looked at me and grinned all over.

PEOPLE.
Hear us, O Lord!

A MAN.
A-hoein' the corn my hoe got sharp in the sand-stones,
Blackie treed a squirrel for my wife to cook.

PEOPLE.
Hear us, O Lord!

A MAN. [*Leaping to his feet, excitedly.*] When I was a boy back in the
Ozarks, I used to go a-barefoot. And I'd steal apples. And sass
my Paw. I'd beat the ole cow. I'd be mean to my little sisters
and brothers. I wouldn't be thankful jist to be a-livin'. I was
always wantin' sump'n. *And* a-gettin' nuthin'. *And* a-cussin'.
And a-swearin'. And a-gettin' next to all the girls like a wild
hoss. And I was a-gettin' wickeder and wickeder when Jonas
come along, praise the Lord! And I follered him, praise the
Lord! And I lissened and heared him, praise Jonas! And I'll
die happy like I'm a-livin', praise the Lord on high!

A WOMAN. [*Rising, ecstatic.*] My maw prayed for me to do better
but I wouldn't listen. I wouldn't churn or darn. Or sweep the
floor, and land knows it was always a-needin' it! I wouldn't
cook. I wouldn't mind no one. I was wild and crazy-like. And
a-feared of the dark. One day I heared Jonas a-callin' me.
And I left off my sinful ways. And I begin to do whut was
right. Never a-complainin', never a-sighin'. Always a-singin'
like I'm singin' now, praise the Lord!

PEOPLE. [*Shouting.*]
Praise Jesus!
Glory be to God!
Took away our sins, washed us clean!
Bless his holy name!

A MAN. I was a hoss thief and a mule stealer. And a wife beater.
And mean to my kids. And the stock and the houn' dogs. But
no more. Now I walk where the sun's at. And I praise the
Lord!

PEOPLE. [*Beginning the litany rhythm again.*]
O Lord most high!

JONAS.
O Lord in the heavens, hear our testimony!

PEOPLE.
O Lord most high!

JONAS.
The day is half gone. The sun is resting on its peak in the sky—

JONAS AND PEOPLE.
You are the sun, O Lord!
O Sun most high!
JONAS.
The clouds have scattered before you—
Sunlight descends.
JONAS AND PEOPLE.
You are the sun, O Lord!
You are the rain—
[*There is the sudden sound of a rifle shot. The* PEOPLE *stop their chant raggedly, some continuing.* JONAS *stops a moment too, then begins again.*]
JONAS.
The clouds have scattered before you.
Sunlight descends.
JONAS AND PEOPLE.
You are the sun, O Lord!
You are the rain and the snow!
You are the hail—
[ABNER, *rifle in hand, bursts in up center.*]
ABNER. [*Shouting.*] 'D he come in here? A man! I think I got him—climbin' up the cliff— I thought he run this a-way!
JONAS. No one's been here, Abner.
ABNER. [*Circling in front of people and going out up left as he speaks.*] He must be hidin' in the bushes back of the tabernacle! I'll git him! Once I git a fair shot—
[*He disappears.*]
[*The* PEOPLE *murmur among themselves uneasily.* JONAS *lifts his hand.*]
JONAS. Here! Is this going to interrupt your worship? God is our protection— [*With a smile*] —and we've got plenty of guns, you know.
A MAN. But it might be the law, Jonas!
JONAS. [*Fixing on him a sharp hard stare.*] The law? Who is the law of this mountain?
A MAN. [*Grudgingly.*] Well, God's the law,—I guess.
JONAS. God is the law of this mountain. God is the ruler, the preserver. On Him the burden of our safety and peace lies easily. Nothing can disturb His calm: let nothing dismay His people. Peace be to you as to Him!— [*There is another shot back of the tabernacle and* GAR BREEDEN *stumbles in from the study door, closing it after him. His shirt and trousers are dirty and torn. His hair is awry, his face streaked with blood where the briars*

have scratched him. Instantly, there is a wild confusion. Most of the PEOPLE *scramble back, but some advance threateningly. There are screams of dismay.*] Wait! Stand back! [*They stand back a little.*] Who are you? What do you want here?
[GAR *looks from the* PEOPLE *to* JONAS *and back.*]
GAR. Don't let him shoot me!
PEOPLE. [*Muttering.*]
What's he doin' here—bustin' in?
Come breakin' in the tabernacle this-a-way—
Spyin' on us, I reckon!
Shoot him, that's what we'd orter do with him!
JONAS. Stop it! Luke! Charley! Hear what he's got to say. [*To* GAR.] What is it?
GAR. I climbed up the cliff here— I—I'll go.
[*He turns as if to go out the back.*]
[ABNER *bursts in quickly at the left, running right to about third row and down front.*]
ABNER. There he is! I thought I'd run him—!
[*He puts his gun to his shoulder as if to fire.*]
GAR. [*To* JONAS.] For God's sake! Give me a chance, can't you?
JONAS. Go away, Abner! Put your gun up.
ABNER. Stand back, Jonas! I'll shoot him—the skunk!
JONAS. [*Going toward him.*] Do as I tell you! You've done enough shooting. [ABNER *relaxes, rebelliously.* Turning to GAR, *who is now at his right.*] Now, tell me what this—Wait a minute. Are you hurt?
GAR. No. He missed me.
JONAS. [*Puzzled.*] Missed you? Abner did?
GAR. Twice.
JONAS. I don't understand that. [*Smiling.*] Abner, you'd better go and sit down.
ABNER. [*Muttering.*] If I'd a-had fair shot—
[*He sits down, disgruntled, on the fourth row.*]
JONAS. Abner's the best shot on the mountain.
GAR. He hasn't any business shootin' at me.
JONAS. You haven't any business on the mountain.
GAR. [*Hotly.*] This is a free country, ain't it? You don't own this mountain, do you? What right has he got to shoot at me for climbin' up the cliff?
[ABNER *jumps up. Several men rush threateningly toward* GAR.]
PEOPLE. [*Angrily.*]
Why, the young snappin' turtle!
He cain't talk that-a-way to Jonas. By God, I'll—

Shet up yer talk, you!

Abner'd orter shot him in the back.

Give *me* a chanst, and he won't git away!

JONAS. [*Silencing them.*] Here! I'll attend to this. [*To* GAR.]
    Where'd you come from?

GAR. Down below here.

JONAS. From Tahlequah?

GAR. Yes, Tahlequah.

[*Something in the question and answer reminds him of a forgotten
distress. His present anger dies. He speaks as if far away, lost in his
isolated despair.*]

JONAS. Came up to spy on us, eh?

GAR. No.

JONAS. What's your reason, then?

GAR. [*After a moment of hesitation.*] No reason.

JONAS. Oh, you just came to look at us, is that it? [*Scornfully.*]
    Heard we were a strange lot of religious fanatics, didn't you?

GAR. Yes.

JONAS. [*Scornfully.*] So you came to look us over, so you could
    go back and boast how you'd been here and seen terrible
    goings-on, and come away unharmed—though you were shot
    at by the crack marksman of the Tribe? Is that it?

GAR. No.

JONAS. No? Do I look especially stupid or ignorant?

GAR. [*With a little surprise.*] No.

JONAS. Then perhaps I might understand.

[GAR, *suddenly, unaccountably, puts a hand to his forehead, in violent
and unbearable agony. He slumps. His voice becomes choked, his words
almost indistinguishable, as he cries out against an inner desperation.*]

GAR. Christ! Where—where—?

JONAS. [*Quickly.*] Abner, Annie—all of you. Go outside. Wait there.

ABNER. Now, Jonas—

JONAS. You hear me. Outside, go on!

ABNER. What're you gonna do?

JONAS. Never mind. Do as I tell you. Abner—keep your ears open.
    Is Rufe on the bluff?

ABNER. Yes.

JONAS. Keep your rifles ready.

[*The* PEOPLE *file out, puzzled and grumbling.* JONAS *crosses a little to
left and upstage of benches, as if to be sure everyone is out. Then he
turns back to* GAR, *his face full of concern and cunning. He comes
down.*] Now, then. What's troubling you, son? You can talk to
me if you want to. What is it?

GAR. [*His voice agonized.*] Why should I talk to you? Anyone!

JONAS. It'll help.

GAR. [*Lifting his head, violently.*] Listen! It's all shut up in me, it's drivin' me crazy!

JONAS. Talk.

GAR. Knowed they wasn't no use comin' to Tahlequah— No use anywhere!

JONAS. Try to be calm.

GAR. [*Intensely.*] Let me out of here. Let me go!

JONAS. Quiet—take it easy—

GAR. Old men, settin' in the square!

JONAS. Here, sit down.

[*He leads him forward, puts a stool in the clear place between benches and rostrum.*]

GAR. [*Drooping, sitting.*] I'm t'ard.

JONAS. [*Still left of him.*] You'll be all right.

GAR. [*With more composure.*] Sorry to bust in— I—little crazy.

JONAS. If you'd like to tell me—

GAR. [*Darkly.*] Why not? [*His head droops. He stares at the floor.*] I'm not from Tahlequah. I just came down from Claremore. Run away.

JONAS. Why?

GAR. Had to do sump'n. Listen, you're a good man, ain't you? They say down below here you're all crazy, 't you steal and are no-'count. You don't look crazy. I come up to see. I come up to find out.

JONAS. To find out what?

GAR. [*In a jumbled rush.*] They's no place for me anywhere, see! Mr. Ferber wanted me to be educated, like him. He's my guardeen. He sent me to A. and M.[1] I played football, made the track team. Didn't study. Didn't want to study. I got kicked out. I didn't belong there. Don't belong in Claremore. No place for me anywhere! Come down to Tahlequah yesterday to see if—to see—I thought this bein' the head of— Listen, I'm half Cherokee. I thought they could help me out here, I thought they— Old men sittin' in the square! No Tribe to go to, no Council to help me out of the kind of trouble I'm in.[2] Nuthin' to count on—!

---

1 Oklahoma Agricultural and Mechanical College.

2 Oklahoma statehood led to the dissolution of tribal nation governments; see Introduction, pp. 18, 25–26. Gar has no tribe or tribal council from which to seek aid.

JONAS. [*A gleam in his eye.*] You're just a kid. Seventeen or
eighteen at most. You need guidance, guidance of the spirit.
This Mr. Ferber you speak of—

GAR. He's my guardeen. My pappy's dead. He was Edgar Spench.
They killed him down on Spunky Creek—a year after I was
born.

JONAS. And your mother?

GAR. She's dead, too.

JONAS. [*A fanatic intensity growing in him.*] You're alone, then.
Lost! No one to help. What your guardian wants you to do
is not for you. You tried it, didn't you? There's no help from
the Cherokees. They're dying out. They're hardly a Tribe
any more. They have no order of life you could live. Their
ways are going. Their customs change. That part of you can
never be fulfilled. What's left? You must look to heaven! Like
us! [*A terrific intensity and power, almost hypnotic, has gathered
in his voice. The lights everywhere begin to go down, except a
concentrated glow on* GAR *and the fanatic old man.* GAR *begins
to feel the strangeness. The valley and the colored fields have
disappeared. Claremore Mound's faint outline no longer stands up
on the horizon. Somewhere in the speech,* JONAS *crosses, mounts the
rostrum, hypnotic, queer, powerful.*] Our eyes on the hereafter!
Our feet in the Now! We walk here on the mountain-top away
from the world and its wickedness. We lay up treasures in
heaven. Listen to me! After I worked my way through college,
I went up in the Ozarks all alone. I worked out a way of life all
by myself, far from civilization. It had work in it, and prayer,
and simple delights. Others joined me—men and women sick
of the life they had known. Mostly ignorant people. We built
us a church. But civilization crept up on us, forced us out.
Back in the 90's we moved to Oklahoma. But not to the towns.
We had seen the ways men called Christian. And that is why
we preferred the peace of this high mountain. [*Rapt, quietly
ecstatic.*] We rise before the sun rises. In the hushed hour, all
is gray and quiet. We touch the rocks. We lift a hand as a tree
lifts its branches. We are a part of wild, growing things. The
sun rises. We are exalted and stirred. We work, struggle, sweat
at our daily toil. But there is no strife and no anger. For the
peace of the morning goes with us—till the sun is gone, and
we sleep again. Or perhaps there is storm. Lightning cracks
across the sky. The heavens open. The voice of God speaks to
us from the tempest. We lift up our heads to hear His words.
We lift up our hands to receive the power He looses above us.

GAR. [*His eyes on the old man.*] Let me go!

JONAS. [*Coming down, touching his shoulder.*] Listen to me. I'm getting old. Year by year I can feel death creeping up on me. And in all the Tribe there's no one to take my place. I've tried to train men—Abner, Rufe—many others. They're not good enough. They're not only ignorant, they are crude souls, who understand only the simplest things. [*He goes left toward benches, crossing in front of* GAR, *in his anguish.*] I can't go away and leave these people without a leader, surely you see that! They're children who must be watched and guided. Through all the years, there has been only one hope I clung to: someone must come—*from outside*—someone who had courage and insight. What if I offered you this? You could join the Tribe. You could work to become worthy. In time you'd become worthy—

[*He has gone toward* GAR, *rapt, mad.*]

GAR. [*Getting up.*] Let me go.

JONAS. [*Back a step, brought back to reality.*] Go?

GAR. [*Watching the old man, in alarm.*] You've never seen me before. You'll never see me again! Let me go!

[*He goes upstage, harassed, turns back.*]

JONAS. [*Cunningly.*] You want to go? Go, then.

GAR. They'll shoot me.

JONAS. Are you so afraid of bullets? Are you such a coward?

GAR. [*Intensely, unable to endure the strangeness, as if stating a creed.*] Listen! I don't want to die with a bullet in my back! I'm lost, yes! *We're all lost.* We don't know where we are. We've never even lived. But if *I* have to die, I want to face the direction death's coming from, do you hear me! I want to see what he looks like! I want to find out why we're afraid of him. In that moment, I'll be alive, alive!—no longer afraid of death, do you understand! Call off your men. Let me out of here!

JONAS. [*With a dangerous smile.*] I said you could go.

GAR. And get shot in the back!

JONAS. Suppose you stay, then. Of your own free will. This is God's house. It's safe here.

[*He holds up his arms, as if benignly.*]

GAR. [*Fiercely.*] God's house! Den of cow-thieves and madmen. What you offer me is crazy! They were right about you down below. You touch the rocks, yes! You are exalted and stirred, O God yes! Let me go!

JONAS. [*His voice sharp with anger and hate.*] You scorn our religion! You mock our way of life! You refuse bread offered you when you're starving. All right! You're not the first. Look! Do you see that post? [*He indicates the post, standing in the clear space in the back.*] Once a scoffer stood there, too. Chained to that post. [*With a vicious smile.*] Would you like to know who it was? Sheriff Johnson.

GAR. [*His voice low.*] You killed him.

JONAS. [*With mad delight.*] Oh, no, I wouldn't say that. He came up here, as you did. I talked to him as I talked to you. I thought he'd been sent by the Almighty to take my place. He grew violent. We chained him there. He sprang at me, tried to kill me. Abner shot him—to save my life. It was God's will. We wouldn't want God to kill you, too—you *so young*—!

[*There is a loud hammering at the left door, and* ABNER *bursts in, crosses in front of benches to center.*]

ABNER. Jonas! They's a whole crowd a-horseback comin' to the foot of the cliff!

JONAS. A crowd?

ABNER. Ten or more—headin' straight this way!

JONAS. [*To* GAR, *angrily.*] It's a trick. You've been lying!

GAR. I don't know what you—I don't know what you're talking about.

JONAS. Listen! Some things were stolen at Tahlequah last night. Don't tell me you didn't know it! They sent you up here to spy on us! I might have known!

GAR. I don't know anything about it!

JONAS. Now a posse is coming. Let 'em come! If they fire on us, it'll be too bad for you! Abner—

ABNER. We'll sneak down and open f'ar on 'em, Jonas!

JONAS. No, wait. They won't come up the cliff.

[RUFE *and* HENRY *burst in, left.* HENRY *stops back of seats.* RUFE *runs to upstage of benches.*]

RUFE. Jonas! They're turned! They're goin' plumb round the mountain to come up on the other side!

JONAS. I thought so. It'll take several hours to get here. In the meantime we'll—

ABNER. You want us to go and meet 'em, Jonas? You better let us! They'll shoot up the place.

JONAS. No. But keep an eye out for 'em.

ABNER. [*Protesting.*] Jonas.

JONAS. Watch them—some of you. But don't shoot—unless I tell you.

ABNER. [*In consternation.*] They'll come up here—plumb up here, Jonas!

JONAS. Warn everyone to stay in the enclosure. Bar the gates, Rufe.

RUFE. Well, it 'pears to me—

JONAS. [*With violent command.*] Bar the gates!

RUFE. But if *he* gits away and tells—nuthin'll stop 'em! They'll f'ar on us! They'll burn us out! They'll be hell to pay!

JONAS. I'll take care of that. Go on! [*He crosses to the platform. RUFE goes out.*] Abner—in the study there—you'll find hanging on a nail, by the door—

ABNER. [*Grinning.*] I know, Jonas.

[*He goes swiftly in.*]

JONAS. Henry, call everybody in.

[HENRY *begins to toll the bell in the corner.*]

ABNER. [*Entering with lock and chain.*] Here y'air, Jonas.

JONAS. All right—over there—

ABNER. [*With relish.*] I know what to do, all right, all right! [*He starts putting the chains on* GAR'S *wrists.*]

GAR. You can't do this.

ABNER. [*Gloating.*] Oh, we're jist a-treatin' you *nice.* Wait'll you find out what's a-goin' to happen to you!

JONAS. Abner, stop that talk! Put the lock on. [ABNER *does, and ties* GAR *to the ring in the post.* JONAS *has gone to the pulpit; the* PEOPLE *come in and take seats. The bell-tolling stops. The* PEOPLE *mutter about* GAR, *excited, whispering, gesturing.* JONAS *lifts his hand for silence. The excitements of the morning seem to have left him unmoved. Majestically.*] Let us begin—

LIZE. Where you left off, Jonas?

JONAS. Let us begin at the beginning—

JONAS AND PEOPLE.

O Lord most high!

JONAS.

O Lord in the heavens, hear us in this hour!

PEOPLE.

O Lord most high!

JONAS.

The day is half gone. The sun has climbed to its peak in the sky.

JONAS AND PEOPLE.

You are the sun, O Lord!

[GAR *breaks out suddenly with decisive and loud anger, while the chant goes on.*]

JONAS AND PEOPLE.
O Sun most high!
JONAS.
The clouds have scattered
   before you.
Sunlight descends.
JONAS AND PEOPLE.
You are the sun, O Lord!
You are the rain and the snow!
You are the hail descending!
Hear us, be with us, O Lord!

GAR. I won't die this way! I'm
tied up here, yes. But some
day I'll get loose. You won't
kill me! You won't kill me.
You can't kill me! I'm going to
live. Live! And I'll burn your
God damned tabernacle to the
ground! Do you hear me?
Your God damned tabernacle
to the ground!

[*The voices go on into the darkness. The angry repeated sound of a
motor Klaxon*[1] *thrusts itself sharply into the litany.*]

Scene Six

*The lights slowly reveal the Whiteturkey home on the outskirts of
Bartlesville.*[2] *It is a ramshackle old farmhouse, up right, once painted,
but now gray and weather-beaten. There is a front door, with windows
on either side of it. A bright canvas chair is standing left; an old bench
is up center with an Indian blanket over it. It is a fall day; the trees
are leafless, the grasses in the front yard dry and gray, a profusion of
Jimson weeds everywhere. Claremore Mound is a thin far silhouette
against the sky.*

   *Near the corner of the house, left, and facing forward in all this
drabness, the front end of a Stutz Bear-Cat,*[3] *1919 model, of a startling
red color. The motor is running and* KATE WHITETURKEY, *an Osage
Indian girl about eighteen, is at the wheel. She can not be seen yet but
she sounds the motor horn loudly several times. Away off in the house, a
voice is heard replying:*

VOICE. [*Inside.*] Oh, all right!
KATE'S VOICE. Hurry up!
[KATE *gives one more impatient push on the horn, turns off the motor,
jumps out of the car and comes in. She is dark, petulant, and arresting.*]

---

1 A loud, electrical horn.
2 In Washington County, approximately 50 miles north-northwest of
   Claremore.
3 An expensive roadster produced from 1912 into the early 1920s. Kate
   Whiteturkey has Osage oil money.

KATE. [*Impatiently.*] Hutch!

HUTCH. [*Inside.*] Yeah!

KATE. [*Crossing to center.*] For God's sake! Ain't you dressed yet? I been ready for half an hour!

HUTCH. [*Inside.*] Comin', honey. Whur'd you put my socks?

KATE. In the bureau drawer, in the bureau drawer. Whur'd you think I put 'em?

[*She turns away.*]

HUTCH. [*With rough affection.*] Sweetheart! I'd like to break your neck!

KATE. What?

HUTCH. You heard me!

KATE. [*Smiling.*] You big bum! Now hurry up, will you?

[A YOUNG MAN, *about thirty, rather well-dressed, has come into sight from the left. He is blond, a little complacent, certain of himself and of most things.*]

YOUNG MAN. I beg your pardon, Miss.

KATE. [*Wheeling like a shot at the sound. Then coldly:*] Who're you?

YOUNG MAN. [*Crossing to left of center.*] Is this the Whiteturkey place?

KATE. [*Hostile.*] Yes, what of it?

YOUNG MAN. Do you live here?

KATE. [*Impatiently.*] Yes, I live here, what about it?

YOUNG MAN. Are you Kate Whiteturkey, by any chance?

KATE. [*She looks at him sharply, her eyes narrowing.*] What if I am?

YOUNG MAN. I'm George Moree.

KATE. [*Surprised.*] George Moree!

GEORGE. Hutch's brother.

KATE. [*Looking him over, contemptuously.*] Oh! So you're the one?

GEORGE. The one what?

KATE. "George says this and George says that!" I made him stop that, you bet your life! Well, what'd you want with him? He'll be out in a minute.

GEORGE. He's here, then.

KATE. Well, of course he's here. He lives here.

GEORGE. Oh! You and Hutch aren't married, are you?

KATE. [*Turning a little away, toward front.*] Who said we was? Whose business is it?

GEORGE. I just asked. You're Osage, aren't you?

KATE. [*Quickly, furious at being questioned, turning back to him.*] Yes, and rich. I got three Stutzes, and I'm gonna have an airplane next month. So don't you try to buy Hutch away from me! You ain't got money enough, you hear!

GEORGE. [*Astonished, but unperturbed at her outburst.*] I haven't got the slightest intention of buying him away from you.

KATE. Well, you *couldn't*, you hear! He's crazy about me! He can't *live* without me.

[*She faces him, arrogantly, going toward him, conscious of her strength.*]

And let me tell you sump'n, Mr. George Moree. Your family don't like me, I know that. Just the same, when I met Hutch he didn't have a clean handkerchief to his name. Now he's got ten silk shirts, and I bought 'em for him!

GEORGE. [*Whistles softly. Then satirically, turning forward a little.*] How many pairs of shoes has he got?

KATE. [*Literally, hostile.*] Six, if you want to know!

GEORGE. That's a lot of shoes.

KATE. It's just his hard luck to be born part-Cherokee instead of full-blood Osage. [*As she crosses farther to right.*] He might just as well be white trash for all the good bein' Indian does him.

GEORGE. [*Following a little.*] He's got eighty acres of land, his allotment, in Rogers County. Good land, too.

KATE. [*With supreme contempt.*] Who wants to farm?

GEORGE. [*Slyly.*] When your father was alive, *he* farmed, didn't he?

KATE. Yeah, but he's dead. And I'm rich.

GEORGE. [*Smiling.*] So you said. Look here, Miss Whiteturkey, you've got me all wrong. I'm not here to make trouble. I just came over to see the rodeo at Dewey.[1]

KATE. [*Shortly.*] I guess you mean the rode-eo. You don't need to be so damned hifalutin' just because you been to college.

GEORGE. Well, the rode-eo. I haven't seen Hutch in years. I've been away a lot. I heard he was living here with an Osage girl named Whiteturkey, so I thought I'd look him up.

KATE. [*She looks at him a moment, her brows drawn, measuring the depth of his intent. Evenly:*] He'll be out in a minute, I said.

[*She crosses him, goes left.*]

GEORGE. I'll just wait here, then.

[*He starts right.*]

KATE. You can set down there, if you want to.

[*She indicates the bench.*]

GEORGE. Thanks.

[*He goes toward it.*]

KATE. But I'll just tell you now—if you wasn't Hutch's brother

---

1 Approximately 5 miles north of Bartlesville in Washington County.

you could get the hell off the place, and get off quick!

GEORGE. [*Bowing.*] Thanks, Miss Whiteturkey. [*He sits.*] That's a nice name you've got—Whiteturkey.

KATE. [*Glowering.*] Are you tryin' to kid me?

GEORGE. Of course not.

KATE. I think it's a hell of a name!

GEORGE. Do you know where it came from?

KATE. It was my paw's name, of course. [*She sits, petulant and disdainful, in the chair at left.*] He used to go around in a blanket. *White* Turkey. He looked more like a thing out in front of a cigar store![1]

GEORGE. I mean originally. The name comes from an Osage legend. You know it, don't you? About the girl?

KATE. What girl?

GEORGE. This girl of the tribe. She was lying by a stream on a summer day, half-asleep. [*Softly, with an ironic smirk.*] Sure, you've heard this. [*He goes on.*] Suddenly she heard leaves crackling, and she looked up, and there a beautiful white turkey came through the sumac brush behind her. He stepped very softly and didn't say a word for a minute. Then he made that noise turkeys make in their throats and said: "Down the river and around that bend is a canoe painted crimson. Take that boat and paddle for three moons till you come to a place where the water starts to—"

KATE. Who said that?

GEORGE. The white turkey.

KATE. Of all the bunk! Turkeys don't talk.

GEORGE. [*Grimacing.*] No, you're probably right. All lies. [*Looking around.*] You don't farm here any more, do you?

KATE. Of course not. We don't have to.

GEORGE. Haven't you got a brother?

KATE. Yeah. Clabe. He's around somewhere.

GEORGE. Weren't Hutch and your brother in the war together?[2]

KATE. [*With an astonishing and deep sense of gratefulness and wonder.*] Hutch saved his life. [*She retreats into herself, remembering.*]

---

1 Long used to identify tobacconists' shops, carved, highly stylized "cigar store Indians" are now widely regarded as offensive.

2 Approximately ten to twelve thousand Native Americans fought in World War I. Their involvement in the war became an important part of the argument for US citizenship, which came for many Native Americans with the passage of the Indian Citizenship Act (1924).

GEORGE. What does your brother do now?

KATE. Hunh? [*Her absorption broken.*] Oh, Clabe. Doesn't do anything. Hunts a little. [*She is a little friendlier now.*]

GEORGE. [*His eyes on the vivid motor.*] Drives a Stutz too, I guess.

KATE. He's too lazy to learn.

GEORGE. But you drive quite a bit, eh?

KATE. From mornin' till night.

GEORGE. Where do you go?

KATE. I been lots of places. Kansas City, Nevada, California, Colorado—

GEORGE. Pike's Peak?

KATE. Last summer! Drove to the top in high.

GEORGE. Is that so? What's it like? [*She pushes her hair back from her forehead, staring at him, amazed at his ignorance.*]

KATE. It's just a peak. Ain't you ever saw it?

GEORGE. No.

KATE. I picked up a rock on the top of it. [*She gets up, crosses toward* GEORGE.] I got it in there on the library table. You want to see it?

GEORGE. N-no, I don't think so.

KATE. I tell you how it is: You go places—and they're just like any other place. You can say you've saw 'em, and that's all they is to it.

GEORGE. Yes, I suppose that's what it all comes to, in the end. [HUTCH'S VOICE *calls from inside.*]

HUTCH. Kate! Who you talkin' to?

KATE. Come on out.

HUTCH. Who's out there?

KATE. Well, for God's sake, can't you come on out and—! [HUTCH *appears in the doorway. Seeing* GEORGE *he stops short, hostile, defensive.*]

HUTCH. What do you want?

GEORGE. Hello, Hutch.

HUTCH. Snoopin' around!

GEORGE. [*Easily.*] Who's snooping? I just came to see you.

KATE. [*Contemptuously.*] Came to see him! Yeah, sure you did.

HUTCH. [*Quickly, to* KATE.] What'd he say to you? [*Turning on* GEORGE *fiercely.*] You be careful what you say to Kate! I'll break you in pieces, you hear me! I don't want you around here. Why don't you leave me alone? [*He turns away from him.*]

GEORGE. [*Genuinely surprised.*] Hutch! What's the matter with you! You never talked like that to me in your life!

HUTCH. [*Shortly.*] I've started.

GEORGE. I don't know you. What's come over you? You don't even talk the way you used to.

KATE. [*Interrupting, quickly, scornfully, going closer to* GEORGE *on the bench.*] He don't stutter any more, if that's what you mean. I cured him of that. It's more'n you could do, for all your education! You not gonna get him back! I c'n tell you that, right now! You'd have him tied up in knots, you'd have him eatin' out of your hand, you'd—

GEORGE. [*Peremptorily, with sharp command, getting up.*] Now shut up, both of you! Of all the damned *manners* I ever saw! I won't stay here another minute!

[*He turns on his heel, crosses in front of* KATE *to left, turns slowly, his back almost to audience.*]

KATE. Beat it, then! See if anybody cares!

GEORGE. [*With a sly smile, going right toward* HUTCH.] All right, Hutch. *You're* not responsible, anyway. I won't hold it against you. Bad temper and bad manners are in the air, it looks like. I suppose you can catch them—just like smallpox.[1] [HUTCH *stares off right, not looking at him. A gun booms somewhere in the distance.*] I'd better go before I get shot at. [*With satiric amusement.*] I suppose that's the—the brother, whose life you thought was worth saving.

HUTCH. [*Sullenly.*] Get the hell out of here!

GEORGE. But first—I want to explain something—

HUTCH. I don't want to hear!

KATE. Don't waste your time on him!

HUTCH. [*Going farther right.*] Always talk me around, run my life for me. Always get your own way! Always had it over me 'cause you're smart!

GEORGE. Listen, Hutch. [*Amused at the idea.*] You seem to be afraid of me.

HUTCH. Afraid! If you wasn't my brother I'd mash your face in!

GEORGE. [*With guile.*] I seem to make you uneasy about something. What on earth is it? Why, you're happy, you're living here with your— [*With a sly look round at* KATE] with friends. You've got a nice Stutz to drive around, you've got ten silk shirts and six pairs of shoes—why, you're fixed!

---

1 Indigenous peoples in North and South America experienced devastating epidemics of smallpox, among other diseases.

Why do you let me upset you? You've got nothing to worry about—you're fixed! Lots of money and nothing to do. Why, it's as good as being an Osage! You could wrap yourself up in a blanket and nobody'd know the difference!

KATE. [*Outraged.*] Hutch!

HUTCH. Get out of here, get out!

GEORGE. [*His voice sharper with scorn.*] It used to be the Cherokees and Osages were enemies. Not any more! Great things have come to pass! They share the same food—the Osage furnishes it. Their roof is the same—built by Osage hands. Cherokee and Osage—the lion and the lamb lie down and sleep together![1]

[HUTCH'S *brooding wrath rises up in him. His face becomes mask-like, dangerous. He goes quickly toward* GEORGE *when there is the sound of running feet and crackling twigs off in the brush, and a man bursts into sight, left, a gun in one hand, a dead squirrel in the other. He is dark, an Indian, with a fierce lithe grace. He wears rough, ordinary farm clothes, but his feet are in beaded moccasins. His voice, when he speaks, is more the muttering inarticulate sound of anger than words. He goes right to* GEORGE, *his face dark, his body rigid. It is* CLABE WHITETURKEY. *The three are down center.*]

CLABE. Whatta you want—whatta you want around here—!

HUTCH. [*Sharply.*] Clabe!

CLABE. [*Dropping the squirrel at his feet.*] Get the hell outa here, go on!

HUTCH. Clabe! Let him alone, I tell you! It's my brother.

CLABE. [*Unheeding, his voice harsh and ominous.*] Sneakin' around whur you ain't wanted!

HUTCH. Do as I tell you! [*He crosses to him, puts a firm fierce hand on his shoulder.*] It's my brother!

[CLABE *turns to look at him, comprehending slowly. He relaxes a little, still dark and unrelenting. With quiet dignity, unapologetic, unmoved, he picks up the squirrel and walks into the house,* GEORGE *staring after him.* HUTCH *remains staring before him.*]

GEORGE. [*Breaking the silence.*] Pleased to meet you, Mr. Clabe Whiteturkey. Charming fellow.

[HUTCH, *disturbed and thoughtful,* GEORGE'S *eyes on him, goes upstage and drops to the bench. With an impatient movement, the girl goes across to the red Stutz.*]

---

1 A familiar, if misleading, condensation of Isaiah 11.6: "The wolf also shall dwell with the lamb, and the leopard shall lie down with the kid; and the calf and the young lion and the fatling together." George's "sleep together" conveys disgust.

KATE. Hutch! Let's get started. We can't sit around all mornin'.
[*She disappears. He sits, distressed, his ease shattered by something he can't understand.*] Hutch!
GEORGE. [*Sardonically.*] She's calling you. Never mind me. I'll go.
[*With soft persuasiveness, going up to him.*] Listen, I'm at the hotel till tomorrow. Come and see me. They're making that new road from Claremore north through Vinita[1] and on up to the Kansas line. It would be a good job for you, get you away from this—all this. Your teams are in the pasture, idle. They ought to be working. *You* ought to be working. If you have to have women, pick and choose, why don't you? You'll find plenty of them waiting for you, don't worry. Why don't you marry one, some decent woman? Don't you ever get tired just sleeping round with any woman you run across?
KATE'S VOICE. [*Sharply.*] Hutch, come on!
GEORGE. I'm going tomorrow. I'll be at the hotel.
[*He goes out left.*]
[KATE *sounds the horn sharply. Then she calls out, with sudden premonition.*]
KATE. Hutch! [*She gets out of the car swiftly, enters.*] Why're you sittin' there! [*Rushing toward him in angry alarm.*] Why don't you answer me!
HUTCH. [*Looking up, his brows drawn.*] Wha-wha-what am I g-g-gonna do?
[*She pushes her hair back in her characteristic way, and stands staring at him.*]
KATE. [*Desperately.*] Hutch! Hutch!
[*The Scene is blotted out quickly.*]

Scene Seven

In the darkness, a drum-beat rises, grows tremendous in volume, as if in a cramped enclosure its resonance filled all available space, thudding at the walls for more room. The tone dies down to a steady insistent beat.
Claremore Mound rises in a pale clear light under a wintry night sky, with only a few stars in it. Snow is over the slopes, is standing in the depressions and gullies, is thick on the black branches of trees and bushes, edging them with white. A bitter cold wind from the north pours over the Mound, raking the visible down-slope. Snow crystals whirl

---

1 Within the boundaries of the Cherokee Nation in Craig County, approximately 40 miles northeast of Claremore.

from limb and rock, glistening. Under the sharp sound of the wind the drum-beat goes on, low and regular. A deep male voice begins to sing a Cherokee song. The light on the Mound begins to die down, as if an unseen moon had gone behind a cloud.

Then a fire begins, first to glow, then to blaze, from the exact spot of the picnic fire of Scene One. Its wavering tongues of light are thrown down sharply across the smooth dirt floor of a log house. It becomes bright enough in the room to reveal an obtuse-angled corner of the cabin. The fire comes from in front as if from a rock fireplace. In one of the two sides visible are a small window and a heavy oaken door. Extending along one side is a rough straw cot covered with blankets and crazy quilts; in the corner is a waterbucket on a box, washpans, a tall shot-gun, cooking utensils, etc. Stools and chairs, primitively hacked out, are scattered about. Outside, the snow-covered Mound gleams whitely. The year is 1895.

Inside the cabin, at center, and touched by the firelight, JOHN GRAY-WOLF, *an Indian about fifty-five or sixty, sits on a low stool, beating a drum. He has just finished singing. His face is dark, prominent, his mouth firm; his long black hair is tied in a pigtail and drawn back from a brow of singular nobility. He sits quietly; great serenity and grace flow out of him.*

His little grandson, a boy about eight, with black, eager eyes, in a grave dark face, sits on the floor at his right watching excitedly. GRAY-WOLF *finishes, lets the drum rest again on the floor. He smiles at the little boy.*

GRAY-WOLF. You like that, hunh?

SONNY. What's it say, Grampaw?

GRAY-WOLF. It's about huntin', Sonny. It says:

Listen, let me shoot much game!

Let my appetite never be satisfied.

Let the mangled game hang thickly from my belt!

O Ancient White Fire, I offer you the clotted blood of the birds in
     payment!

SONNY. Couldn't the birds fly away, Grampaw?

GRAY-WOLF. The hunter is in a tree. He shoots them with arrows
     from his blow-gun.[1]

SONNY. [*Intensely.*] I'd fly away—clean acrost the river some'eres!

GRAY-WOLF. The birds don't know.

SONNY. I don't like it.

---

1   Cherokees, among other Indigenous peoples, used blowguns made from
    river cane.

GRAY-WOLF. You go to bed now.

SONNY. [*Shuddering.*] It's cold. They's ice in the water bucket.

GRAY-WOLF. You go to bed. [*He begins to beat the drum softly. He stops.*] Sonny—

SONNY. When you tell me about the Cherokee fighter.

GRAY-WOLF. Then you go?

SONNY. Yes, Grampaw.

GRAY-WOLF. The big fighter of the Cherokee Tribe, when he was in a battle didn't want to be killed. So he found out how he could put his life up in the top of a sycamore tree while his body went on fightin' in the front row of the battle. Then his enemies would shoot at his body but couldn't hurt him a-tall. His life was safe—way up high in the tree out of sight. Once his enemies found out about it. At the next battle, they quit shootin' at his body, and shot all their arrows up in the top of the sycamore. So the warrior fell down dead.

SONNY. Why did he have to die?

GRAY-WOLF. His life was killed.

SONNY. [*Soberly.*] I don't want-a die. I would run away! Fast!

GRAY-WOLF. [*Gravely.*] When Death wants you, it's better to sit and wait.

SONNY. I would run! I would run!

GRAY-WOLF. Take the Cherokees at Tahlequah. When one of 'em does sump'n bad, the law says: "You got to die. You're a bad Indian. We let you go now to your home. Tell your wife goodbye, tell your children. But on Saturday, come back and be punished." The Indian goes away home and says to his wife: "Goodbye, wife." He says to his children: "Be brave, children." Then he gets on his pony and rides in to Tahlequah. There they put a rope around his neck and hang him to a tree.

SONNY. I wouldn't go back and get hung.

GRAY-WOLF. He has to go.

SONNY. Why?

GRAY-WOLF. [*Slowly.*] Death—*wants* him.

[*Somewhere outside in the night, two pistol shots ring out, the first more muffled than the second.* GRAY-WOLF *and the boy turn quickly, stare back into the cabin toward the window and door. Another muffled shot. Then two more shots, in quick and angry succession, can be heard.* GRAY-WOLF *gets up, goes to the door and pushes down the heavy oaken bar, looks at* SONNY, *hardly breathing. Then, going rapidly to the window, he pulls aside the rough curtain and looks out. He comes down again, sits.*]

SONNY. [*In a whisper, rising to his knees.*] What is it, Grampaw?

GRAY-WOLF. [*In an absorbed tone, a dark memory rising in him.*] Death.

SONNY. [*Startled.*] What, Grampaw, what? [*He sits back.*]

GRAY-WOLF. [*Unheeding.*] When your pappy was killed it was a cold night just like this. His family was hungry. He took a side of beef from the smoke-house on Rucker's Ranch. To him it wasn't stealin'. To the Indian, food was sump'n to keep you and your family alive, sump'n you had a right to. Your father didn't know the word "Stealin'." But they caught him and killed him. A cold night, just like this— [*He shakes his head, comes back to the present, looking round.*] It's better not to get mixed up in things when they's shooting goin' on. Indian Territory is plumb full of men with six shooters now—cattle rustlers, desperadoes— [*Breaking off.*] The door's barred. You go to bed now, Sonny. [*He reaches for the drum, involuntarily, as if in song he found expression for a mood. There is a bang at the door, repeated and repeated, with the sound of a man's voice crying out desperately, the words thick and indistinct. GRAY-WOLF gets up quickly, faces the door from right stage.*] Who is it? What'd you want?

[SONNY *has gone to him.*]

VOICE. [*Muffled and angry.*] For God's sake! [*Then pleading.*] Hurry! Let me in!

GRAY-WOLF. Who is it? I can't let you in less'n you tell me—!

VOICE. [*Muttering darkly.*] You want me to break your door down! [*The unseen figure moves from the door, his heavy boots crunching the snow piled up around the cabin. Suddenly the glass of the window is smashed inward, and a hand, reaching in, rips off half the curtain. Another hand with a pistol is thrust through and pointed at* GRAY-WOLF. *A man's agonized and angry face can be made out dimly beyond the broken pane.*]

THE MAN. You goddamned Indian, open that door! Let me in, I say! [*A spasm of pain comes over his face.*] Hurry, let me in! I'm bleedin' to death! I'm dyin'— Jesus Christ—

[*He sways weakly, collapsing in the window, sinks to his knees out of sight. The pistol clatters to the floor inside, the hand which held it disappearing over the sharp broken glass of the pane.* GRAY-WOLF *goes swiftly to the door, draws up the bar and rushes out. Seeing his grandfather disappearing,* SONNY *cries out in fear.*]

SONNY. Grampaw! Where—! [*He runs to the window.* GRAY-WOLF *comes back into sight.*] Grampaw!

[GRAY-WOLF *comes in, half carrying a man, middle-aged, with a lean, hard and desperate face. One hand clutches his side frenziedly. His clothes are thick with fresh blood. His head rolls in pain; muffled groans come from his twisted mouth. Slipping out of* GRAY-WOLF'S *supporting arm, the* MAN *half falls onto the cot, right, doubled up in agony.*]
THE MAN. [*Piteously.*] Stop the blood— Stop the blood.
[GRAY-WOLF *goes quickly to the water bucket, jabs the dipper into it sharply to break the ice, pours some water in a pan, picks up a cloth and comes back, bending over the* MAN. *He begins to pull away the clotted clothes, trying with the cold water to stanch the wound. He kneels by the cot. The* MAN *groans.*]
GRAY-WOLF. Try to be still now. Sonny, put some more wood on the fire. [SONNY *obeys, struggling with a log.*] It's pretty bad. It'll stop bleedin' if you'll just lay still.
MAN. [*Weakly, assenting.*] Umm.
[*A single shot rings out sharply. The* MAN *struggles upward with a cry, feeling for his pistol.*]
GRAY-WOLF. [*Standing up.*] No, no, lay still! [*He bends to stop him.*]
MAN. It's them! Where's my pistol?
GRAY-WOLF. Lay down, I said! You'll bleed to death.
MAN. My pistol—! Where is it? God damn you, what've you done with it!
GRAY-WOLF. You dropped it over there—inside the window. Be quiet!
MAN. Get it, damn you!
GRAY-WOLF. You lay down.
MAN. Anh! [*With an animal-like snarl, he begins to crawl off the cot, clutching his side.*]
GRAY-WOLF. [*Stopping him.*] Here! Lay down! You'll start the blood again! [*The* MAN's *head droops down to the pillow weakly.*] I'll get your pistol.
[*He goes over and brings the pistol, starts to hand it to him.*]
MAN. [*Lifting his head.*] How many bullets I got left?
GRAY-WOLF. [*Looking.*] Two.
[*The* MAN'S *head falls back. His hand lifts.*]
MAN. Give it to me.
[*The* INDIAN *puts it into his hand.*]
GRAY-WOLF. Now you lay still.
[*He dabs carefully at the wound with the cold water.*]
MAN. [*Muttering feverishly, in pain.*] They won't get me!
GRAY-WOLF. Now, now—
MAN. I'll get away yet! I dropped my other pistol in the snow some'eres— I got two bullets left!

GRAY-WOLF. There, be quiet—

MAN. [*With terrible quietness, his voice dead.*] I wish I could sleep.

GRAY-WOLF. [*Compassionately.*] You rest. Take it easy.

[*There is a moment of silence.*]

MAN. [*Without feeling or intensity.*] I killed the bastard.

GRAY-WOLF. [*Softly.*] Who?

MAN. Irwin.

GRAY-WOLF. [*Drawing back, staring at him.*] Old Man Irwin?

MAN. Shot him twice, the dirty bastard.

[GRAY-WOLF *goes to the stool, sits.*]

GRAY-WOLF. [*In a hushed voice.*] He was a good old man.

MAN. He's dead.

GRAY-WOLF. [*Turning a little toward him.*] Why?

MAN. [*With difficulty.*] Wanted the money in his store. He
wouldn't tell me where it was. Shot through the lean-to door
at me. Got me—in the side. I kicked the door down. There he
was—on his knees. Begged me. "Don't kill me. For the sake
of my little girl—" [*Fiercely.*] I let him have it!

GRAY-WOLF. [*In a strange hollow voice.*] Shot him dead—

MAN. On his knees he was!

GRAY-WOLF. —In cold blood. [*He is absorbed, as in a dream.*
SONNY, *who has stood motionless by the window, runs to him.*]

SONNY. Grampaw!

[*Without being conscious of it,* GRAY-WOLF *puts his arm about the
child. Finally he speaks.*]

GRAY-WOLF. I know who you are now. You're Spench.

MAN. [*Weakly, but with some pride.*] Edgar Spench.

GRAY-WOLF. That ain't your right name, though.

SPENCH. No.

GRAY-WOLF. It's Breeden, Edgar Breeden.

SPENCH. Know ever'thing, don't you?

[GRAY-WOLF *stands up abruptly.*]

GRAY-WOLF. My little boy—he wants to go out.

[*The* MAN *rolls over, his face toward the* INDIAN, *the pistol in his
hand.*]

SPENCH. Stay here. Don't you move.

GRAY-WOLF. [*Firmly.*] My little boy.

[*They eye each other a tense second.*]

SPENCH. [*Dangerously.*] I got two bullets—one for you, one for the
kid.

GRAY-WOLF. He'll come right back.

SPENCH. [*After a moment.*] Let him go. You stay here.

[*The* INDIAN *takes the boy to the door.* SONNY *looks up at him questioningly. The* MAN *on the pallet watches.* GRAY-WOLF'S *face is inexpressive, mask-like.*]

GRAY-WOLF. [*Softly.*] Hurry back, Sonny.

[SONNY *goes out. Closing, but not barring the door,* GRAY-WOLF *turns, sits, faces the* MAN. *Their voices become muted, bell-like, as if their words had no meaning, or as if meant only for themselves.* SPENCH'S *voice is weak,* GRAY-WOLF'S *filled with a soft vehemence and a kind of wonder.*]

GRAY-WOLF. The wife you left, she's around some'eres.

SPENCH. Course.

GRAY-WOLF. Still talks about you. Thinks you're sump'n fine, 'stid of a killer.

SPENCH. Marthy.

GRAY-WOLF. Your boy's a year old now. Looks like you.

SPENCH. Named after me.

GRAY-WOLF. Maybe'll *take* after you. Maybe'll kill men in cold blood for a little money, a little filthy gold!

SPENCH. Maybe.

GRAY-WOLF. Florey Newcomb's with child, your child.

SPENCH. Yeow.

GRAY-WOLF. Carries it, tells ever'body she's carryin' a kid of Edgar Breeden's, proud of herself.

SPENCH. Florey.

GRAY-WOLF. Proud to have a kid by a desperado, a man that don't like no one's life but his own, a man that ain't got a heart in him no place, that was born with a gun by his side, that—!

SPENCH. [*Softly.*] The blood—

GRAY-WOLF. [*Gets up, goes to him.*] What is it?

SPENCH. Stop the blood.

[GRAY-WOLF *kneels down by* SPENCH'S *side. Outside, the wind lifts for a moment, sighing. The warm glow of the firelight flickers over the two figures.* GRAY-WOLF *puts the pan under the cot.*]

SPENCH. [*After a moment.*] I wish I could sleep.

GRAY-WOLF. You rest. You'll be all right.

SPENCH. Never be all right, never be—!

GRAY-WOLF. Here. Put your head on the pillow.

SPENCH. [*Turning to look at him, the wan beginnings of wonder in his eyes.*] Why're you good to me?

GRAY-WOLF. [*Standing up.*] Tain't nuthin'.

SPENCH. Me, Edgar Spench, wanted ever'whur, rewards out for me! I ain't worth it!

GRAY-WOLF. Lay still!

SPENCH. Robbery, arson—I'm guilty. Wife desertion, rape, murder!

GRAY-WOLF. Why'd you do all them things?

SPENCH. [*With almost a sob in his throat.*] I don't know—!

GRAY-WOLF. Nobody knows.

SPENCH. [*Weakly, feverishly, anguished.*] I tried ever'thing. Tried to farm. Too restless. Cattle herdin', ridin' fence. Sump'n always drove me on. The bosses! Burned down their barns, rustled their cattle, slept with their wives. Shot the bastards down—! Sump'n inside—no rest, I don't know— Bad blood. Too much Indian, they tell me.

GRAY-WOLF. [*The revelation growing in him from what SPENCH has said.*] Not enough Indian.

SPENCH. How—!

GRAY-WOLF. [*With troubled compassion.*] I'm full blood—Cherokee. I live peaceful. I ain't troubled. I remember the way my people lived in quiet times. Think of my ancestors. It keeps me safe. You though—like my boy. He's dead. He was half white, like you. They killed him, *had* to kill him! Not *enough* Indian. The mixture.

[*He sits on the stool again.*]

SPENCH. [*Softly.*] When I'm dead, will you bury me?

GRAY-WOLF. You're not dead.

SPENCH. By the Verdigree River. It's quiet there. I was born there. Bury me deep.

GRAY-WOLF. You're alive.

SPENCH. Lost so much blood. Feel my life runnin' out of me, slow. White blood, Indian—it don't matter. It spills out, runs out of me like water. Don't try to stop it anymore.

GRAY-WOLF. Don't talk.

SPENCH. Listen. I'll be better off dead. Caused trouble for ever'body. Myself, too. I'll be better off.

GRAY-WOLF. You got to fight.

SPENCH. Fight!

GRAY-WOLF. Fight to live!

SPENCH. [*Shakes his head.*] Not any more. [*With utter weariness, his voice flat, final, unemotional.*] No more fightin'. I've had enough.

[*A hand with a pistol is shoved through the window and aimed at SPENCH's head. A man and the moving bodies of many men and women can be seen through the window. A voice roars out.*]

TINSLEY. Get away, Gray-Wolf! Jump back!

[GRAY-WOLF *springs up and back into the corner.* SPENCH *sits*

up quickly. TINSLEY'S *pistol is fired twice in quick succession.*
SPENCH *falls back without a sound.*]

GRAY-WOLF. [*Crying out in horror.*] No, no! You can't do that, can't do it! In cold blood!

[*He turns away, leaning against the wall, bent over as if the pain were inside him.*]

[TINSLEY *and some men of the posse rush in.* TINSLEY *is tall, fair, righteous. He crosses to* SPENCH, *right.* GRAY-WOLF *edges downstage to left of door.*]

TINSLEY. Dead, all right. The dirty bastard!

[SONNY *comes running in, clings to his grandfather.*]

TINSLEY. [*Briskly, turning, facing nearly front.*] Gray-Wolf. My name's Tinsley. Your little grandson come and told the posse, but don't think that gives you a lien on the reward. I finished him, and I get the money, don't forget that. It's time someone killed him. A bad half-breed, that un. One of *your* tribe, Gray-Wolf. Let this be a lesson and a warnin'. Teach your grandson. Tell ever'body what it means to oppose the law. You Indians must think you own things out here. This is God's country out here—and God's a white man. Don't forget that.

[*Several women have come in at the door.*]

A MAN. [*By the door.*] Get back, you women. Mrs. Breeden, go on now.

[MARTHY BREEDEN, *a gaunt dark woman with a year-old baby in her arms, walks deliberately forward.* FLOREY *follows* MARTHY *in and stops by the door.*]

MARTHY. I got to see. [*They make way for her.* TINSLEY *crosses up to window. She stands above the dead man, bends over him.*] Edgar. Husband. They got you. We always knowed they would, didn't we? [*Her face is lined and strong. Her voice is unemotional, but full of a rich warm, earthy and compassionate power. The others watch her, compelled.*] What you done was what they call wrong. You couldn't help it, I know that. You tried to do right. It was too much. You was hounded day and night, inside and outside. By day, men. At night, your thoughts. Now it's over. Sleep. Rest now. [*She shifts the child in her arms, looks down at it.*] But here's your son. In him your trouble. It goes on. In him. It ain't finished. [*She turns, calls to a young woman, who is weeping quietly.* FLOREY *comes over to her.*] Florey. Here's Florey Newcomb, bearin' your child. You're at rest. Sleep. Your disgrace, your wickedness, your pain and trouble live on a while longer. In her child, in my child. In all people born now, about to be born. [*Her face becomes luminous, as her mind gropes toward an impersonal truth.*] Someday, the agony will end. Yours has. Ours will. Maybe not in the night of death, the cold dark night, without stars. Maybe in the sun. It's got to! It's what we live for.

FLOREY. [*Sobbing, crying out.*] He's dead! How can you stand there! Edgar's dead!

MARTHY. [*Compassionately, trying to comfort her.*] It's what he wanted. He'll rest now. Let him die.

FLOREY. But it goes on, it goes on!

MARTHY. In our children, yes. In our children's children, maybe no.

TINSLEY. [*Turning forward, to* GRAY-WOLF.] We'll take him away.

GRAY-WOLF. Leave us. It's *our* dead.

[TINSLEY *goes out. The* MEN *follow him, quiet and troubled.* GRAY-WOLF *turns round to the door, puts the bolt down. Then he crosses over to the bent figure of* FLOREY, *helps her down onto the stool. Now* MARTHY *crosses in front of* GRAY-WOLF, *stops by the door with her back to the audience. It is like a curious and solemn ritual. A drum has begun to beat, low and throbbing and final. Now* GRAY-WOLF *goes over to the cot and pulls a blanket up over the dead man. He stands up, turns slowly to face* MARTHY, *who turns to face him. A far-away look is in* GRAY-WOLF'S *eyes, a quality of magnificent dignity and despair as if he mourned for his own life, for the life of his son, for his grandson, for* SPENCH, *for the women, for a whole race gone down into darkness. The lights fade slowly. The fire flickers. Claremore Mound glitters in the night. A few stars are in the sky.*]

CURTAIN

THE END

THE YEAR OF PILAR

People

MARUCA
DOÑA CANDITA CRESPO
GRAZIELA (CHELA) CRESPO
TRINIDAD (TRINO) CRESPO
PILAR CRESPO
DON SEVERO CRESPO
FERNANDO CRESPO
CUCO SALDÍVAR
JOSEFA SALDÍVAR
BETO
CHATA
LUCIO
NINON LUJAN
CHUCHO
MAYAN INDIANS

Scenes

SCENE 1. Apartment of the Crespos on Riverside Drive, New York. Afternoon. January, 1937.
SCENE 2. *Corredor*[1] of Techoh,[2] the family *hacienda*,[3] Yucatán. A Sunday afternoon in February.
SCENE 3. Doña Candita's bedroom. Half an hour later.
SCENE 4. A hemp field,[4] by a Mayan ruin. An hour later.
SCENE 5. The hemp mill. That night.

INTERMISSION

SCENE 6. The *corredor* again, seven months later. October. Six o'clock in the morning.
SCENE 7. Inside Beto's *jacal*.[5] Noon, two months later. December.
SCENE 8. The bedroom again, that night.

---

1 Spanish: corridor.
2 Small town a few miles east of Mérida in the state of Yucatán. "Yucatán" also refers to the large peninsula that encompasses three Mexican states and parts of Belize and Guatemala.
3 Spanish: large estate.
4 Yucatán was known for its production of henequen (sisal fiber, sisal hemp), especially in the late nineteenth and early twentieth centuries.
5 Shelter made of poles, adobe, and grass.

Scene One

The small living room in the apartment of the Crespo family on Riverside Drive,[1] New York City, an afternoon in January, 1937. The room is crowded with evidences of Yucatán, messy but comfortable. On the walls are family pictures, especially one of Don Alonso Tuero. Outside, it is cold winter. Frost and sleet are at the windows, and the sky is dismal.

DOÑA CANDITA, *the sweet, birdlike mother of the family, sits listening raptly to the vespers music on the radio.*

MARUCA, *the old servant, comes in, having heard the music from the kitchen.*

MARUCA. [*With a happy, incredulous smile.*] Doña Candita!
DOÑA CANDITA. Sh, Maruca! It is from the Church of the Sorrows. The vespers music.
[*They speak English—but with an accent.*]
MARUCA. I could not believe! So beautiful!
[*They both listen. The music dims down as they talk.*]
DOÑA CANDITA. Yes, Maruca, it is beautiful. I was there—in that very church, the same one, this morning. But this is different, it seems to come from far away.
MARUCA. [*Protesting.*] Up the Riverside Drive, it is but a step, Señora. A few blocks only.
DOÑA CANDITA. Farther, farther! Not from New York, this cold, cold country—this, this— No, no, the music seems not from here.
MARUCA. It makes the Señora think of Yucatán.
DOÑA CANDITA. Yes, home. The Cathedral in the Plaza Grande[2] where we used to go. So long ago.
MARUCA. [*Comfortingly.*] Not so long.
DOÑA CANDITA. Too long.
MARUCA. Señora. Do not cry. New York is a fine city.
DOÑA CANDITA. Yes, it is fine.
MARUCA. Your dear husband, your children are here. This is home now.
DOÑA CANDITA. Home, yes. I am happy. It has happened like this. It must be the will of our dear Lord, of the Blessed Virgin. This morning on the Drive—at six—it was snowing— I gave

---

1 Running north and south for more than 6 miles on Manhattan's West Side, from 72nd Street to Dyckman Street.
2 The Mérida Cathedral, built in the sixteenth century.

the pigeons some scraps of bread from my pocket. They followed me. I am happy here. I am content. [*She breaks down.*] I will go to my room now.

[*She gets up.*]

MARUCA. [*Touched and distressed.*] Doña Candita. Do not be unhappy. You know we cannot go back to Yucatán. Mexico is in revolution.[1] We would all be murdered.

DOÑA CANDITA. [*Smiling, more cheerful.*] Maruca—how far behind you are! They say I am a child—even my children they laugh at me. I have borne four children, and they tell me I have a child's mind! But you—you are a little *niña* in the cradle, Maruca! The Revolution was over many, many years ago.

MARUCA. *Señora.*

DOÑA CANDITA. Twenty years ago. Even *I* know *that*. There is peace in Mexico.

MARUCA. Then why do we stay here?

DOÑA CANDITA. My husband, Don Severo, wants to stay. He wants to be a great surgeon.

MARUCA. Why?

DOÑA CANDITA. Why? Do not ask the ways of men. Men are very strange. In Yucatán, we could be so happy, so happy! And warm, Maruca. It is so warm there now—with flowers opening at night and miles of the green hemp! I will pray that we go back. I would never do it—but lately my husband seems to feel all is hopeless, so difficult.

MARUCA. I have notice' that.

DOÑA CANDITA. He used to walk with a springing step, and his eyes glittered and he was very proud and joyous. But lately . . . ! Oh, I think he would leave in a minute! I will pray now—this instant! [*She starts, remembers, draws out a little fancy bottle.*] Maruca—this morning at the church, I got this holy water. Just now I sprinkled some about the room here— and see! That is why the radio suddenly began to give us the vespers music! Jazz it was playing before—very sinful—swing, they call it! But a few drops only—like this—!

[*She sprinkles a little about.*]

MARUCA. *Verdad?*[2]

---

1   The Mexican Revolution (1910–20) began as opposition to the rule of Porfirio Díaz (1830–1915), Mexico's president from 1877 to 1880 and 1884 to 1911. Numerous factions vied for power before the election to the presidency of Álvaro Obregón (1880–1928) in 1920.

2   Spanish: "[Is that the] truth?"

DOÑA CANDITA. Oh yes, it is so, it is a miracle, Maruca! If I sprinkle now a little bit of the holy water in my husband's room—who knows? Perhaps his heart will be changed, and we can go back to the *hacienda*, back to beautiful Techoh. You think this is foolish, Maruca?

MARUCA. No, no, no, *Señora!* In that way I cured a toothache last week. And also a roast can be made to cook in an hour— I know this by experience. Of course I believe!

DOÑA CANDITA. Dear good Maruca—you are the only one who understands me. The others make such fun of me.

MARUCA. *Señorita* Pilar does not make fun of you.

DOÑA CANDITA. No. Pilar believes in the Church, as she was taught. But the others!

MARUCA. You must not mind the younger ones teasing you.

DOÑA CANDITA. I do not mind. I am only afraid for their souls, Maruca. My babies must not be lost. Oh, I must be a very sinful woman to have let my darling children become such mockers and scoffers!

MARUCA. *You* are not sinful.

DOÑA CANDITA. Yes—I will pray for them.

MARUCA. You needn't pray for *la niña Pilar*, Señora. *She* does not scoff.

DOÑA CANDITA. No. Pilar is a good girl. She will manage.

MARUCA. Her grandfather, Don Alonso Tuero, would be proud of her. Proud! [*She studies Don Alonso's portrait.*] The Tueros were a great, great family, *Señora!* It shows in the face.

DOÑA CANDITA. [*Coming over.*] Pilar is *like* her grandfather. Her mouth is the same.

MARUCA. Her will is the same.

DOÑA CANDITA. [*With a little laugh.*] And her temper! To think such a strong girl should come from such a weak vessel! Truly, it is miraculous, Maruca. I will never get over it.

MARUCA. You are laughing, *Señora.* How good it is to hear!

DOÑA CANDITA. [*Softly, happily.*] I am seeing such things! The flowers under the snow, I can smell them, Maruca! A ship blown into safe harbor, the harbor of Progreso.[1] Sunlight slants and falls—through clouds, through leaves, upon the floor of the Cathedral. It touches the face, the pitiful wounds, the body of joy! We must have something special, something Yucatecan for supper tonight!

---

1 City on the Gulf of Mexico directly north of Mérida.

MARUCA. *Sí, sí, Señora! Sí. Frijol con puerco.*[1]

DOÑA CANDITA. Yes! And the *papazul*[2] I was making for Sunday! I will go now—and sprinkle the holy water.

[GRAZIELA—CHELA—*comes in, flinging aside her coat. She is dark, young, lively. The radio switches, after a short muttered announcement, to a rumba.*]

CHELA. *Mamacita!* [*She kisses her rapturously.*] Little mother! Look at her, Maruca, she looks about ten—twelve at most. And the smile! Somebody's been giving her a new doll.

DOÑA CANDITA. Where have you been?

CHELA. [*Mockingly.*] "Where have I been?" Rehearsal, baby, rehearsal.

DOÑA CANDITA. What is rehearsal?

CHELA. It's a very naughty word—and you wouldn't understand. Oh, *mama*—it's wonderful! I have a dance number—and I'm to do a song all by myself—something like that one. Think of it!

[*She begins to hum and dance to the radio.*]

MARUCA. What's happened to the radio?

[DOÑA CANDITA *merely lifts her hands and eyes in resignation to the caprices of heaven, and starts to go.* MARUCA *goes out into the kitchen.*]

CHELA. *Mama,* imagine! I am just an amateur yet they give me a chance like this! Isn't it wonderful!

[TRINO *comes in, drawing materials and a canvas under his arm. He is dark and rather shy, a little somber. A sullen and searching fire is in him.*]

DOÑA CANDITA. If you are happy, it is wonderful.

[*She goes out.*]

TRINO. What's wonderful, Chela?

CHELA. [*Seizing him.*] Oh, Trino darling! Berman says I get the job! I'm going to sing, I'm going to dance!

TRINO. Chela! What do you know! Tell me all about it!

CHELA. At the audition I was scared wall-eyed, and my legs knocked. Whew! Just to think of it!

TRINO. I know.

CHELA. But it must have been all right, because Berman said,

---

1 Spanish: beans with pork, in this context a specially prepared Yucatecan dish.

2 Yucatecan specialty prepared from warmed corn tortillas flavored with pumpkin seed sauce and *epazote* and filled with hard-boiled eggs and tomato sauce.

"Honey, you get the job. Why, kid, you're a combination of Lupe Velez,[1] Libby Holman,[2] and somebody I met in a whore-house in Rio." Then he gave me a pat on the fanny and said, "Scram, beautiful. Come back tomorrow at ten—in shorts."

TRINO. Why shorts?

CHELA. I don't know. My legs, I guess.

TRINO. Sounds tough enough.

CHELA. Oh, it's tough, I guess, Trino. But you have to start somewhere. It's a job.

TRINO. Yes, honey, you did it. Now you're going to be famous! What did I tell you!

CHELA. Oh, I don't know, Trino. It takes a long time and I'm just starting and—What's that?

TRINO. Just a picture.

CHELA. Let's see.

TRINO. Flowers.

CHELA. Oh, it's beautiful!

TRINO. Pretty, I guess. But what of it?

CHELA. You're an artist, that's what of it!

TRINO. It doesn't seem to matter. With the horrible things going on in the world. [*Genuinely troubled.*] This morning—did you see the headlines? How can Spain go on—our own people, brothers almost—how can they have the heart to struggle on against such odds? The Fascist powers allied against them. Bombs from the air tearing them apart. It's sickening![3]

CHELA. Don't think of it, little brother. You can't do anything—so try to forget it. What does Locher say about you?

TRINO. [*Impatiently.*] Oh.

CHELA. Tell me.

TRINO. He says I have talent.

CHELA. Of course you have! Hang the picture up, *chiquito.*

TRINO. Where?

CHELA. [*Pointing to the space where the portraits hang.*] There. Where we can see it.

TRINO. [*Doubtfully.*] Should I?

---

1 Lupe Velez (1908–44) was a Mexican performer famous for her eight "Mexican Spitfire" films (1939–43).

2 Libby Holman (1904–71) was a Broadway actress and singer. Riggs was likely familiar with the scandals that plagued Holman's life.

3 The Spanish Civil War (1936–39), which brought Fascist dictator Francisco Franco (1892–1975) to power.

CHELA. But yes! That's the place for it.

[*He takes down the portrait of Don Alonso, and a picture of a wedding party, and hangs the flowers in the space.*]

CHELA. Oh, it's nice, honey. Did you make it up—or did they pose for you?

TRINO. They posed—till they wilted.

CHELA. [*Gaily.*] Oh, my brother is an artist, and I am an actress! You have talent, *I* have talent. We're the best of the Crespos— yes, even the Tueros, except *mama*—and she's a baby, she doesn't count!

[*She hums the rumba, seizes* TRINO, *and drags him into a few steps of the dance.* PILAR *comes in. She is a vibrant girl, with the cool aristocratic authority and pride of years of privilege. Her mind has the keenness and the violence of her Conqueror forefathers;*[1] *her emotions the fierce range that will devastate others—or herself. A bitter directness and a resolve to do a dangerous act possess her at the moment.* CHELA *and* TRINO *stop in their tracks. She just looks at them, turns to take off her heavy fur coat, sees the picture.*]

PILAR. Whose picture is that?

TRINO. Mine.

PILAR. Who took down the portraits?

TRINO. [*Sullenly.*] I did.

PILAR. [*Calmly.*] How dare you. [*She goes over, examines the picture.*] Hummmm. Flowers. [*She jerks it down, hands it to* TRINO. *He throws it into a corner savagely, face up.*] Put those portraits back.

[TRINO *moves to obey.* PILAR *goes over and snaps off the radio.* DOÑA CANDITA *comes in.*]

DOÑA CANDITA. Pilar.

PILAR. Where's father?

DOÑA CANDITA. He has not come home yet. [*Seeing the picture on the floor, picking it up—admiringly.*] Flowers! Trino!

[*She flashes a happy look at* TRINO, *takes the picture with her, out of the room.*]

CHELA. [*Sullenly.*] We were dancing.

PILAR. Yes, I saw that.

CHELA. You have no right to shut us up the way you do!

PILAR. I haven't said a word to you.

---

1 The conquistadors, Spanish and Portuguese colonizers such as Francisco Vázquez de Coronado (1510–54), Hernán Cortés (1485– 1547), Hernando de Soto (c. 1496–1542), and Juan Ponce de León (c. 1460–1521).

CHELA. You know what I mean!
PILAR. I have what rights I can get. So have you. Why don't you
get them? Because you're a weakling—you're both weaklings.
[*She hangs up her coat.*] I'm sorry if you hate me. But you'll
have to think of something better. I'm used to it—and it
makes very little impression on me. I have other things to
think about just now. Important things. [DOÑA CANDITA
comes back in.] Mother.
DOÑA CANDITA. Yes, Pilar.
PILAR. You want to go back to Yucatán, don't you, *mamacita?*
DOÑA CANDITA. Oh, but yes, *niña!* I pray for it night and day!
PILAR. We're going. I've had enough.
DOÑA CANDITA. Truly?
PILAR. Immediately.
DOÑA CANDITA. But your father—?
PILAR. He'll agree.
DOÑA CANDITA. Oh, I don't think he will.
PILAR. He'll have to.
DOÑA CANDITA. He thinks he must stay for a while longer in New
York.
PILAR. What do I care what he thinks!
DOÑA CANDITA. He's your father.
PILAR. "He's my father." Shall I tell you what he is? A failure—
that's what he is! I'll tell him so!
DOÑA CANDITA. [*Shocked.*] Pilar! You wouldn't!
PILAR. I would! I'm going to. Tonight I'll tell him.
DOÑA CANDITA. Please don't, Pilar! He'll be angry.
PILAR. What do I care for his anger? Is he God? I'm sick of the
whole mess. It's time something was done! Father won't
make decisions. *I* will.
DOÑA CANDITA. [*Distressed.*] Please, Pilar, baby. You're tired.
Don't do anything to upset him. He'd never forgive you. You
know the way he is.
PILAR. You can't stop me. The minute he comes in! I've seen too
much! It's time there was plain speaking in this house!
DOÑA CANDITA. Pilar!
[DON SEVERO CRESPO *comes in. Once very dashing, very
distinguished-looking, he seems tired and wan and gray. There is a
great silence. He merely looks at his family, without speaking, starts to
his room, is out of sight.*]
PILAR. Father.
[*No answer.*]
DOÑA CANDITA. [*Pleading.*] No, Pilar!

PILAR. Father!

DON SEVERO. [*In the door.*] Well?

PILAR. I—I want to talk to you.

DON SEVERO. Later.

PILAR. No, now!

DON SEVERO. Later.

PILAR. It's important. You've got to listen!

DON SEVERO. [*Coldly.*] Do I?

PILAR. Yes! [*Momentarily faltering.*] I mean it's this—we've got to go back to Yucatán.

DON SEVERO. We've got to? Who's giving orders?

PILAR. No one's giving orders. [*Gathering her courage.*] Oh, don't you see what's in front of your eyes? Everything's going to pieces here.

DON SEVERO. Be silent!

PILAR. Why do we have to be silent about it? Save your lies for the world. Let's have the truth here at home!

DON SEVERO. I don't care to hear this.

PILAR. Please, please listen to me. This afternoon I was at the del Hoyos. You should see what's happened to them! The great del Hoyos are trying to be New Yorkers. Their drawing room is full of drunken bums, cheap cafe society, maudlin, jittery imbeciles, just like the rest of New York! The girls drink like fish, Clotilda takes heroin. Grace is gone out of them completely, their manners are the manners of pigs, they stink with filth and decay. My God, is that what we're going to turn into? No, no! I won't have it! Look at us. Poor *mamacita*—her head buried in the Church—like an ostrich. Look at Trino, thinks he's an artist. Good God, who'd spit on an artist? Grandfather would roll in his grave. And Chela sucking around Broadway with her tongue out after lecherous Jews[1] who might give her a job.

CHELA. [*Interrupting defiantly.*] I've *got* a job. I've got it!

PILAR. Yes? In what? A lousy tenth-rate Hot-cha show.[2] And Fernando—hanging around with strikers—taxi-driving riffraff,[3] and little painted girls from the factories. What does he care about them, anyway? Just a girl to sleep with—and

---

1 A common, pernicious stereotype.

2 Review featuring the popular late-1920s dance. Florenz Ziegfeld's *Hot-Cha!* ran in 1932, with Lupe Vélez among the stars.

3 Violent taxi strike in New York City (1934), dramatized by Clifford Odets (1906–63) in his popular 1935 play, *Waiting for Lefty*.

you know it! A God-damned paternalistic condescending Communist the party wouldn't have for a million dollars! Our family—mother's family at least—used to amount to something. It can again. But not here. We're going back—where we came from—where our roots are, where there's something to live for, something to fulfill!

DON SEVERO. [*Troubled.*] We're staying here. We can't go back. You don't understand.

PILAR. Oh, I understand you very well, Father. You jumped at the chance to run away from Yucatán in the Revolution—not to save your life, or the lives of *mama* and Fernando and me—Oh no! You were jealous of the Tueros, *mama's* family, their money and power. You wanted to show them up. You'd get out of the country, you'd flee to New York, study, become a great surgeon, illustrious, world-famous! You'd go back and cut them dead—or if you spoke at all, you'd deign to bow to them only, with rude arrogance.

DON SEVERO. Pilar, I forbid you!

PILAR. [*Unheeding, full of smoldering violence, and finally a choked anger.*] I was there, don't forget. I was a child—but I remember—everything! I see every day, every night of that flight from *pueblo* to *pueblo* in the *bolan*[1]—Fernando, mother and me—tossed and pitched till we were black and blue, and dying for food. I see you, *papa,* very clearly—your frightened face—riding beside us—like something desperate and hunted. And at night—in the hot dark jungle peace—screwing whatever you could find! Passing on your sickness and incompetence to fill the world, to overwhelm the world and destroy it! For you *are* sick, and you *are* incompetent! Oh, I know, *mi papacito!* I've been to the hospital, I've talked with Dr. Easton, and I know. You'll never be a great surgeon. You won't even be passable. . . . You're a failure, a failure. We're all—all—failures! It's time we faced it! [*There is a horrible silence. After a moment,* PILAR *recovers enough to speak.*] I'm sorry. It was rotten of me.

DON SEVERO. [*After a moment—huskily.*] You've said everything.

PILAR. [*Brokenly.*] Father!

DON SEVERO. We'll go back. Maybe it's best. For all of us.

PILAR. Just for a year, Father! Let's try it, shall we? It'll be better. I know it will!

---

1 Spanish: village to village in the animal cart (i.e., *volán*).

DON SEVERO. I hope so. We'll go Tuesday—if we can get ready. There's a boat. The *Orizaba*.[1]

PILAR. [*Going to him, putting her arm on his shoulder.*] Forgive me.

DON SEVERO. [*Coldly—without emphasis.*] Don't touch me. [*He goes out.* PILAR *turns away from watching him, looks at her family. In her face is no arrogance, no triumph, only the spent, almost pleading, almost tearful look of the disciplined and the proud after a hard victory. She goes out of the room.*]

DOÑA CANDITA. Maruca! Maruca! [*Rushing to take* TRINO *and* CHELA *in her arms.*] Babies! My babies! [*She is beaming.*]

MARUCA. [*Coming in.*] Señora?

DOÑA CANDITA. Pack, pack! We're going home!

MARUCA. Oh, *Señora, Señora!* I cannot believe!

[FERNANDO *breezes in at the door.*]

FERNANDO. Hello!

DOÑA CANDITA. [*Going to him.*] Fernando baby!

CHELA. We're going to Yucatán.

FERNANDO. What!

CHELA. Tuesday.

FERNANDO. But I—I—there's a meeting next Thursday. I promised to speak.

CHELA. [*Bitterly.*] You won't be able to, *chiquito*. Things like that don't count. Pilar *wants* to go. Pilar!

FERNANDO. Oh.

DOÑA CANDITA. [*Blissfully, her face transfigured.*] You see, Maruca! What did I say? Only a little holy water—and a lot of faith!

CURTAIN

Scene Two

The corredor *of Techoh, the family* hacienda *near Mérida, Yucatán, Mexico, seen from the house. It is a comfortable place, with chairs, a new radio, a hammock, flowers, etc. Beyond the pillars and arches at the back, a windmill towers up out of sight covered with flowering vines. Farther still are the long green orderly rows of hemp receding to the*

---

1   The *SS Orizaba*, which the US Navy used to transport troops during the two world wars, carried passengers between New York, Cuba, and Mexico in the 1920s and 1930s.

horizon under the tropic sky. It is a far cry from wintry New York—and it is an afternoon in February.

A little band of Indians, with violins and brasses, is concluding the last phrase of some dance music. They conclude as soon as the curtain is well up, and begin to saw and toot, tuning up again.

CUCO SALDÍVAR, *immaculate in white—attractive, about thirty-one—holds up a hand for silence. He is usually good-humored, but now he has some worries.*

His sister, SEÑORITA JOSEFA SALDÍVAR, *rather hefty and absurd, but nasty—with the malice of the bored—lies in a magnificent Yucatecan hammock of yellow, white lace, and ropes of peacock blue, which is slung from one column to the wall of the house.*

CUCO. All right, now that's it. Mind you play it well. I wish somebody would dance, too. Beto, you know how to dance the *jarana,*[1] don't you?

BETO. [*A dark quietly arresting young Indian boy, about nineteen.*] Yes.

CUCO. That's fine. You and Chata, then. Chata?

CHATA. [*A young Mayan girl, giggling.*] Señor Saldívar! Me?

CUCO. Will you do it? [CHATA *nods bashfully, overcome.*] All right, Beto—there's your partner. Do you want to rehearse?

BETO. I won't dance.

CUCO. What!

BETO. No.

CUCO. Why not? [BETO *is silent.*] You're glad to see the Crespos, aren't you? [*No answer.*] Aren't you?

BETO. No. They are nothing to me.

JOSEFA. [*Sitting up.*] There! What did I tell you, Cuco?

CUCO. [*Severely.*] Señor Crespo is your *patron,* your master. The family owns you—all of you! In future, you'll take orders from them. But until they arrive, I'm still giving the orders, do you understand? So you'd better welcome them—as I tell you—or you'll have to suffer the consequences! Is that clear?

INDIANS. Yes, *Señor* Saldívar. Oh, we will bid them welcome, never fear! Trust us, *Señor.* Whatever you say, *Señor.*

CUCO. You refuse to dance, Beto?

BETO. Yes, *Señor.*

JOSEFA. [*Jumping up, angrily.*] See here, *mentecato!*[2] Don't you

---

1 Yucatecan dance for paired participants, in ¾ or ⅝ time.
2 Spanish: fool.

dare be insolent to my brother! You need a good beating to teach you some manners!

CUCO. Josefa, shut up! It's lucky you don't belong to me, Beto.

BETO. Yes.

CUCO. I'm going to report you to *el Señor* Crespo, you know that, don't you?

BETO. As you like.

CUCO. [*Furiously.*] Get out of here, all of you!

AN INDIAN. Are we not to play, *Señor?*

CUCO. Yes, of course you're to play! When you see them coming. Keep a sharp lookout, too. They'll be here any minute now.

INDIANS. *Sí, Señor.* We understand. Valdez, go and stand by the gate to warn us.

[*The Indians go out.*]

CUCO. Damned stupid insulting bastard!

JOSEFA. If you weren't such a softie, Cuco, you'd have taken a whip to him. [*With a knowing look.*] Bastard is right, you know that, don't you? Who do you think he looks like, eh, Cuco?

CUCO. What the hell do I care who he looks like?

JOSEFA. Let's see—Don Severo was a man in the old days, they tell me! 1917, 1937— Oh, yes, I see it all! *Madre de Dios!* That Beto! The Indians are getting so impudent it makes my blood boil! [*She is suddenly overcome with ridiculous fury.*] Where *is* that boy? I'll scratch his eyes out!

CUCO. [*Stopping her.*] Josefa!

JOSEFA. [*Struggling.*] I will! Let me go! I'll teach him to be rude to ladies. I'll teach him!

[CUCO *pushes her down into a chair roughly.*]

JOSEFA. [*In silly consternation.*] You pushed me! My own brother!

CUCO. Josefa—you're a mess.

JOSEFA. It's a man's world. You're all brutes. [*Cunningly and accusingly.*] I know what's got into *you,* though. You smell a woman coming. It's Pilar. *I* know.

CUCO. Listen, you idiot—I saw Pilar last when she was five years old, and scrawny as an ant-eater. She's probably buck-toothed, and ugly as you are, and I wouldn't spit on her for seaweed.

JOSEFA. [*Exasperatingly.*] All the same, you've gone to a lot of trouble.

CUCO. Look, Josefa—we're friends of the Crespo family, and always have been. The least we can do is try to welcome them home.

JOSEFA. You've run their *hacienda* for them for years—as if it were your own. Isn't that enough? No, it seems not! This past week you've practically done the house over for them. I never saw such scrubbing and digging and white-washing! Neglecting your business too—and for what?

CUCO. [*Absorbed.*] Josefa—do you see that crack in the plaster? A vine had grown up there and was tearing the house down— just the way they do at the ruins of Uxmal.[1] I had it cut down only last week—and look at it! Grown a foot already!

JOSEFA. Don't change the subject. I know what's on your mind. I always know what's on a man's mind. One thing. Just one. Well, thank God, the Crespos are a *good* family, anyway. There's Tuero blood in it. But I predict New York hasn't done them any good. I expect the worst—and don't say I didn't warn you.

[*The Indians hurry back in.*]

INDIANS. They're coming! They've just driven through the *portal grande!*

[*There are sounds of an automobile stopping, and the slamming of doors.*]

CUCO. Take your places. Now. Ready? Play.

[*They start to play an old melody. It is charming, but the violins whine, and the trumpet toots crazily.* CUCO *and* JOSEFA *hurry off. After a moment,* PILAR *comes in. She is radiant, but almost overcome with nostalgia. She stands for a moment taking in the familiar place. Then she goes to one of the columns, leans against it. She puts up both arms around it, kisses it, stands there, her cheek pressed close. She does not see for a moment some Indians hurry through with baggage. She does not heed, either, when* CHELA *comes in swiftly, before all the Indians have disappeared into the house. The music stops.*]

CHELA. Lucio! Don't take that bag in. Put it down—right there. And the little one Abram has.

LUCIO. *Sí, señorita.*

[*He does as directed. The other Indians vanish with the other baggage.*]

CHELA. Better still—put them back in the car.

[PILAR *becomes conscious of what is going on, turns to look.*]

LUCIO. Back?

CHELA. Yes, yes—do as I tell you. And tell the man to wait.

LUCIO. *Sí, señorita.*

---

1 Mayan city southwest of Mérida that features the Pyramid of the Magician.

[*He hurries out with them.* CHELA *nods to the players, then sees* PILAR.]

PILAR. [*Coming down.*] Chela, what is it?

CHELA. It's *my* business.

PILAR. But what are you doing?

CHELA. Don't mind me. You're home. Enjoy it!

[*The other* CRESPOS, *the* SALDÍVARS, *and* MARUCA *come in, calling to the players as they do so.*]

CRESPOS AND SALDÍVARS. *Gracias, gracias,* all! *Que bonito!* You play very well. That will do for the present. Later, you can play some more. Etc.[1]

DON SEVERO. [*When they are in.*] Cuco, I wouldn't have known you. You must have been about nine when I saw you last.

CUCO. Eleven, *Señor.*

DON SEVERO. A little boy. I needn't tell you how grateful I am for everything you've done.

[DOÑA CANDITA *goes to* PILAR, *hugs her ecstatically, beaming with childish happiness.*]

CUCO. I've served myself, too, Don Severo. An overseer's salary is something to have in these times.

DON SEVERO. Yes, I suppose so. You and your sister will stay for supper, of course.

JOSEFA. *Con mucho gusto,* Don Severo.

DON SEVERO. Sit down now, and we'll have a little talk.

CUCO. Yes, with pleasure. [*To the musicians.*] You can go now. [*Remembering.*] Oh! I may as well do this now as later. One of the boys—I've just had a little trouble with him. This one. He was insolent. [*The other Indians go out—all except* BETO.] I asked him to dance the *jarana* and he refused.

DON SEVERO. [*Gravely.*] Come here. [BETO *goes and stands before him.*] Is this true?

BETO. Yes.

DON SEVERO. [*Looking at him curiously.*] What's your name?

BETO. Beto.

DON SEVERO. Beto what?

BETO. [*After a moment.*] Beto, *Señor.*

DON SEVERO. [*Disturbed strangely, reluctant to go on, but feeling that he must.*] Where did you learn English?

BETO. I studied.

DON SEVERO. Is your family here?

BETO. My mother worked here on the *hacienda.*

---

1 The abbreviation authorizes actors to continue the passage as they will.

DON SEVERO. [*His voice low.*] Where is she now?

BETO. Dead, *Señor.*

DON SEVERO. [*Almost inaudible now.*] I see. [*He rouses himself to his duty.*] You can go now. In future, be careful to obey. This time I won't punish you.

[TRINO, *seeing the implications of the scene, goes over to* BETO, *holds out his hand.*]

TRINO. My name is Trino.

[BETO *looks, in quiet surprise. After a moment he takes the proffered hand.*]

BETO. *Gracias.*

[PILAR *gasps indignantly.* JOSEFA *looks angrily, but triumphantly at* CUCO. *In the shocked silence,* BETO *goes out.*]

PILAR. You don't have to give your hand to an Indian!

TRINO. [*With quiet significance.*] I think you do. I think so.

PILAR. Don't talk nonsense!

DOÑA CANDITA. In Mérida, as we came through—there was the Cathedral. [*They all look at her rapt expression.*] I had to stop and give thanks. And here—the way I have dreamed it. Flowers and music . . . the cattle at the drinking trough as before . . . the soft air . . . home . . . my family . . . God is good. . . .

[*Her eyes cloud with tears. She sits down.*]

PILAR. [*Going to her.*] Mother, dear.

DOÑA CANDITA. [*Ashamed.*] Don't mind me. I am happy. Maruca, go and see about— No— [*She gets up.*] I'll come with you.

DON SEVERO. Candita can't wait to get back to her kitchen.

DOÑA CANDITA. Charcoal is best for cooking. Uhhh! [*She shudders.*] The smell of gas—I can forget it now.

[*She and* MARUCA *start out.*]

CHELA. Mother, please. Just a—I have something to say.

[MARUCA *disappears.*]

FERNANDO. [*Half-derisively, but good-naturedly.*] Flowers, music, home!

CHELA. Be quiet, Fernando. This is hard for me to do, hard for me to speak. I ask you to forgive me beforehand if I hurt anybody.

DOÑA CANDITA. Why, child!

DON SEVERO. What is it, Chela?

CHELA. [*Troubled, but resolved.*] You know I had a job when we left New York so suddenly. I didn't want to come. I had to agree. There was nothing else for me to do, because somebody has always told me what to do, made up my mind for me. I knew there was nothing here for me, I'd never have a chance to make a life for myself. I was right. I don't like it here and I'm not going to stay!

DOÑA CANDITA. But Chelita, see, it is beautiful, you will come to love it.

CHELA. No, I won't. I hate it already. Something horrible hangs in the air! I'm afraid!

DON SEVERO. Make her lie down and rest. She's upset. Please excuse her, Cuco. You know how it is.

DOÑA CANDITA. You're tired, Chelita. The trip. Oh, that boat! I too can feel it still!

CHELA. [Febrile and tortured.] I'll never like it here. Hemp, hemp, nothing but hemp and horizon and sky! No hill to go over, no vista to hope for. It's so open, it shuts you in because no barrier is in sight. But the barriers are there, just the same! The miles that stretch out and out till your mind cracks to think of them! And if you escape the miles—the sea and the jungle. Restless and crawling and fetid and menacing. It's awful!

PILAR. Why do you want to escape? Everything is here—everything!

CHELA. If there's something inside you you like, you can bear it. I hate everything I am, every thought I ever conceived, everything I ever did. It's *myself* I want to get out of!

PILAR. You're sick.

CHELA. Yes, it's sickness, if you like. But I'll cure it—or die of it—in my own way. That way isn't to be found here.

PILAR. And where will you find it, do you think?

CHELA. Havana.

PILAR. Havana.

CHELA. [Defiantly.] Yes, Havana!

PILAR. [Outraged.] The sink of the world, for God's sake!

CHELA. I don't care.

PILAR. And what will you do in that pestilential sewer, tell me that?

CHELA. Work.

PILAR. Doing what?

CHELA. You all saw the man on the boat I talked to a great deal. I introduced him. Carlos Rivas.

PILAR. My God!

CHELA. Save your "My Gods," Pilar. He's as good family as you are, if that's what worries you.

PILAR. The Rivases don't even mention his name. Carlos! That slick, pomaded[1] little pimp!

CHELA. He offered me a job in Havana before he got off the boat. He begged me to get off the boat with him. He says I have talent.

PILAR. Talent! My God! Brainless innocence! Don't you know yet there are just two careers open to Latin women? Only two! Marriage or prostitution. Take your pick. I guess you've taken it. It can't be marriage our little perfumed friend offers you. He'll put you in a house—don't you know that? I hope it's a swell one—with a good bed, and a high-class trade. *Politicos* or nothing, put your foot down. It's important to be high-class!

CHELA. [*Furiously.*] I'll remember, Pilar! And perhaps someday I'll ask you to visit me in my red plush parlor, and offer you a shot of *tequila* and a reefer. [*Subsiding.*] It's not that kind of a job. I have a contract to sing in a cabaret. It's good any time for two weeks. . . . It's signed. [*She brings it out.* PILAR *takes it, tears it in two pieces, and throws it on the floor.* CHELA *picks it up.*] A torn contract is still a contract. You wouldn't know that.

DOÑA CANDITA. Chela, my little one. I was so happy.

CHELA. I'm sorry, *mamacita!*

DOÑA CANDITA. Once you had a baby brother. He was ill of pneumonia. He suffered so. You don't remember. At the ninth day they told me he would live. He smiled at me. Yes, he winked at me from his cradle! His dear bright eyes! Picture my joy. That night—he died. Picture my grief. On the heels of joy, death, dark wings.

CHELA. Mother, trust me!

DON SEVERO. I can't tell you not to go, Chela. I can't tell you not to break your mother's heart.

PILAR. I can tell her! She's not going. Cuco, please run and tell the man to take the bags out of the car again.

TRINO. Cuco, don't do it! You have no right to interfere!

PILAR. Neither do you. Oh, this is bad enough—and outsiders to see it! Can't you hold your tongue?

CUCO. I'm not an outsider, Pilar. Don't think of me that way.

PILAR. But the talk! The talk! This isn't New York.

CUCO. No one will talk. [*He looks sharply at his sister.*] No one.

PILAR. Thank you, Cuco. Give me a cigarette.

---

1 Rivas uses pomade, a hair-styling product, to sculpt his hair.

CUCO. [*Offering them.*] You're trembling.
[*He lights her cigarette.*]
DOÑA CANDITA. [*Not wanting to hear any more.*] I'll go now.
Supper must be—
PILAR. Wait, mother. Chela—once and for all—do you want to
disgrace us?
CHELA. Myself only.
PILAR. That's ridiculous and you know it! We'll be the joke of
Mérida! We still have to hold up our heads. Someone has to.
TRINO. You'll do that, Pilar. You—you only. For all of us! That's
the way it will end.
PILAR. [*Struck.*] No, no, I can't. Is everybody against me? You
can't do this to me!
TRINO. We'd all run if we had the courage. *I* would. Fernando
would, too.
FERNANDO. Leave me out of it! I'll do my own talking.
CHELA. [*Gently.*] Pilar, I'm sorry for you. It's the first time in my
life. I've always been afraid of you. Try to think as well of me
as you can.
PILAR. Well, go—if you're going. Why do you stand there?
CHELA. I'm not going at your orders, Pilar. I've *chosen* to go.
PILAR. Get it over with, then.
CHELA. [*Like a child.*] Yes. Will anyone see me off? Will anyone
wave to me from the *portal?*
TRINO. Yes, honey.
CHELA. [*Tears welling up in her eyes.*] Thank you.
[*She and* TRINO *go off. After a moment,* DON SEVERO *goes gravely
too. At this,* DOÑA CANDITA, *who has been afraid he won't, but who
hasn't dared to make the move, hurries off after him. Next* FERNANDO
goes. PILAR *turns to look.* CUCO *is watching her. Then she goes quietly,
firmly, into the house.* CUCO *stares after her, like a man struck dumb.*]
JOSEFA. Whew! [*She goes and throws herself, fat and ridiculous and
acid, into the hammock.*] A nest. Veritably a nest! Oh, the smell!
I'm ill! Wait till I tell this in Mérida.
CUCO. She's beautiful . . . and alone. My God, courage!
JOSEFA. A woman is supposed to keep her mouth shut, except to
say "Yes." [*Sitting up.*] Would you look at a girl who smokes
in public, swears in public, wears her hair like a harlot, and
doesn't know the way decent women are supposed to behave?
Would you? [*No answer from* CUCO.] They say such women
will do anything. [*In disgust.*] What is it about a man—*every*
man—? The minute they see a cheap woman—itch, itch,
itch!—all over the place!

CUCO. Be quiet, Josefa.

JOSEFA. I *won't* be quiet! Would you marry a girl whose brother shakes hands with Indians, and whose sister is a cabaret singer, or worse?

CUCO. Certainly. I intend to.

JOSEFA. You wouldn't dare.

[*She throws herself back in the hammock.*]

CUCO. [*He goes over, in a burst of high spirits.*] Wait—wait and see, Josefa!

[*He gives the hammock a terrific push.*]

JOSEFA. [*Swinging wildly, in consternation.*] Cuco! You're murdering me!

CURTAIN

Scene Three

DOÑA CANDITA'S *bedroom, half an hour later. It is a beautiful, high-ceilinged, quaintly personal room crowded with things—family pictures on the walls, a huge bed with its draped mosquito netting, a wardrobe, a tiny altar with candles lighted before the Virgin. There is also a small radio, which* DOÑA CANDITA *has brought from New York. Two windows look out onto the* corredor *and the hemp fields beyond.*

DOÑA CANDITA *has not yet unpacked. She is on her knees praying at the altar.*

The door to the corredor *opens softly and* PILAR *comes in. She is pale and quiet. She has changed her dress to something cool and summery.*

PILAR. I knew what you'd be doing.

DOÑA CANDITA. [*Rising.*] For little Chela. Out in the world alone.

PILAR. [*Gently.*] Yes, mother.

DOÑA CANDITA. She will be all right now. I have asked the dear Lord to guide her and keep her safe.

[*She sits down.*]

PILAR. And will He, *mama?*

DOÑA CANDITA. Of course! But look, I have not yet unpacked!

PILAR. *Mama.*

DOÑA CANDITA. Yes, Pilar, what is it?

PILAR. Pray sometime for me.

DOÑA CANDITA. But I do—all the time, Pilar. What is it?

PILAR. I feel very low and hateful.

[*She goes to her Mother for comfort, kneels down, her head in* DOÑA CANDITA'S *lap.*]

DOÑA CANDITA. You!

PILAR. Yes. I've driven Chela away.

DOÑA CANDITA. But no, that is nonsense. She wanted to go.

PILAR. I didn't even say "goodbye" to her.

DOÑA CANDITA. Never mind.

PILAR. It was despicable of me, and I feel sick about it. I only mean to do right for us all. And look at the way it makes me act. There must be something wrong with me.

DOÑA CANDITA. Nothing is wrong, Pilar. You are a Tuero—truly. You must do what has to be done.

PILAR. Yes, I forced us all to come back here. If I hadn't, we wouldn't have lost Chela like this. It's like a warning. I feel it.

DOÑA CANDITA. Now see, Pilar, that is all you know. It was the will of Heaven that sent us back. The Blessed Virgin was at work to do good to us. I know exactly how it happened.

[*She smiles at her secret.*]

PILAR. [*Getting up, still troubled.*] Was it a mistake, maybe, just the same?

DOÑA CANDITA. Oh no, Pilar. How could it be? God does not make mistakes.

PILAR. [*Trying to shake off her dark premonition.*] At any rate, *you* are glad to be here, aren't you, *mama?*

DOÑA CANDITA. Glad? It is Heaven almost.

PILAR. [*Grasping at every straw.*] And Father. He seems already ten years younger.

DOÑA CANDITA. Yes, he does! Have you notice'? In a week, you won't know him. He will be like the dashing young doctor I married. Such good food we will give him to eat!

PILAR. But Chela's gone.

DOÑA CANDITA. She'll come back.

PILAR. Changed, mother, don't you think?

DOÑA CANDITA. All is change. Except the true heart. Chela's heart is true and good.

PILAR. The boys don't like it here either. I feel it.

DOÑA CANDITA. It is strange to them now. But Fernando was born here, he will begin to remember things his baby eyes looked on. And Trino will come to love it, as we do. [*She goes to* PILAR.] Don't worry, Pilar. [*Chidingly.*] You are a little child to worry about such grown-up matters.

PILAR. [*Looking about.*] There they all are. Watching us.

DOÑA CANDITA. Yes. Just the same. When we fled—twenty years

ago—they were there—there was no time to pack them. And there they are still—to welcome us home.

PILAR. Do they believe in us, or are they waiting to see how puny the blood stream has become after all?

DOÑA CANDITA. Their eyes are on us with hope.

PILAR. They look a little grim to me just now.

DOÑA CANDITA. They never have before. You used to look at them by the hour. See, *chiquita,* there is your great uncle, José, smiling away with his young bride. Nothing is grim about that!

PILAR. No, Mother.

DOÑA CANDITA. And there is you, Pilar, with your curls. You were very pretty. Everybody adored you. I had a hard time keeping you, they all wanted you so! You were a Tuero from the first. You were such a little princess—with your imperious ways! What is that little girl in the wicked pictures that talk?

PILAR. Shirley Temple.[1]

DOÑA CANDITA. Yes. Oh, you were a little Shirley Temple—only an aristocrat! You were like the little Princess Elizabeth of England[2]—and you knew your place, too! Such a fuss we made over you! Such orders you gave . . . such storms of anger! It makes me laugh to think of! Once when you were little—not yet three—we let you take some flowers in to your grandfather, Alonso. He had company with him, if you please—the great Don Porfirio Díaz himself! They sent me a message, written out—"The little Pilar you will have all your life. Let us keep her for a week." And a big seal, with ribbons! What could I do? When you came home—it was in a cart with two tiny ponies. And you wore a little lace dress from Paris. There you are!

[*She studies the picture with pleasure.*]

PILAR. [*Quietly, absorbed, not looking.*] Why is this, *mama?* If you look about you closely—no matter who you are—what the circumstances of your life are—it makes you afraid. Only if you look back is the heart truly joyous. Where must one look, then?

DOÑA CANDITA. Joy and pain—in the past, are all one—and the color of delight. It is safe to rest the eyes there. But in the

---

1 Child actress (1928–2014) who gained international stardom in the 1930s.

2 Later Queen Elizabeth II (r. 1952–2022), the Princess turned twelve while Riggs was writing this play.

present—try to look only at pleasant things. If things are not pleasant, look to the Church. Time passes then, and the knife-cut in the bleeding flesh is only a slight scar, and the memory of life lived.

PILAR. [*Restlessly.*] It's the way of a child. It's *your* way, *mama*. I don't want to be a child.

DOÑA CANDITA. [*With secret guile.*] You depend on yourself too much.

PILAR. Grandfather did. On himself alone.

DOÑA CANDITA. But he was a man. You are a woman. The rules are different.

PILAR. Why should they be? Why?

DOÑA CANDITA. You trouble your head so!

PILAR. Someone has to!

DOÑA CANDITA. [*Driving toward her purpose.*] Then let the men do it. The men! Pilar. [*And her meaning is out.*] You should marry.

PILAR. Oh, mother.

DOÑA CANDITA. Yes. It would settle so many things for you.

PILAR. That's all very well—but who is there to marry?

DOÑA CANDITA. Oh, there are men enough!

PILAR. That man in New York, with the pilot's license?

DOÑA CANDITA. The aviator man? Flying about in that contraption of the devil? God forbid!

PILAR. Then who?

DOÑA CANDITA. Look about you.

PILAR. Cuco Saldívar?

DOÑA CANDITA. Oh, it is a match! I can see it!

PILAR. I've barely met the man.

DOÑA CANDITA. All the same, you've seen him. And he likes you. He has his own business, too—the cigar factory—money. And you know who the family is. It's enough.

PILAR. [*Thoughtfully.*] I could give myself to a man, I think. But I shouldn't care to marry one for life.

DOÑA CANDITA. Holy Mother of God—don't think such thoughts!

[*She snatches her little bottle of holy water, and sprinkles some about the room.*]

PILAR. I'm sorry. You're shocked.

DOÑA CANDITA. In my own bedroom, to hear such sentiments!

PILAR. [*Amused and charmed by her mother.*] Mother—you're like a little bird! [*She hugs her tenderly.*] How did you get to be so *good?*

DOÑA CANDITA. Oh, it is not so. I am a very wicked creature.

[PILAR *laughs*.]

PILAR. You're sweet. In this room—I am at home. Why is that? Is it you—or the room?

DOÑA CANDITA. You were born here.

PILAR. You were a bride here. Look—here you are dressed for your wedding—with that angel face.

DOÑA CANDITA. [*Looking—carried back*.] Severo was so handsome. And is still. The girls were all after him, I can tell you!

[*And then she sees what forbidden topics she has strayed into. Her eyes go down quickly*.]

PILAR. Yes, I know. [*She looks at her mother, who turns away*.] I—I didn't mean to remind you.

DOÑA CANDITA. [*Distressed and loyal*.] Please, Pilar! Severo has always been a good husband to me.

PILAR. Of course, mother. [*Looking now at the picture of herself in the pony cart . . . to drop the painful subject*.] Now would you believe it! Is *that* what I looked like in the pony cart?

DOÑA CANDITA. Exactly.

PILAR. I remember the ponies. One of them used to follow me for sugar. This one, I think. That's a cute little face—the Pilar that was—for heaven's sake. And look at me now!

DOÑA CANDITA. [*Gravely*.] I am looking at you, baby. I see our future in your face. You are strong—and your eyes have a light in them. [*Light again*.] Your own mother admires you—which in this day and age they tell me is a miracle.

PILAR. [*Touched and happy*.] Mother, you make me feel so good, so far from evil! I could conquer the world. I am happier than I've ever been—since I was a child. I won't fail you, *mamacita!*

[FERNANDO *bursts into the door, excited and jittery with pleasure about something*.]

FERNANDO. Mother!

DOÑA CANDITA. Yes, Fernando.

FERNANDO. Do you remember your old friend, Amira Lujan?

DOÑA CANDITA. Amira? Is she here?

FERNANDO. [*Stopping her*.] No, mother, listen. She's sent her daughter—with a message. She and the *nana* have just driven out.

DOÑA CANDITA. Amira's daughter—imagine! I'll come at once.

FERNANDO. Let her come here—the daughter.

DOÑA CANDITA. But my room—the mess! I've not unpacked.

FERNANDO. Please, *mamsie!*

DOÑA CANDITA. Why is this? Why?

FERNANDO. They're all there talking in the *corredor*. The Saldívars, too. She's shy with them. Let me bring her here, *mama*, please!

DOÑA CANDITA. Very well, then. Only—

FERNANDO. You blessed little thing! [*He kisses his mother ecstatically, and then in an excess of good spirits hugs* PILAR.] I'll get her!

[*He hurries out.*]

PILAR. [*Gaily.*] It's all working out! Mother, you were so right. Fernando's himself again.

[*She is hurrying out.*]

DOÑA CANDITA. Where are you going?

PILAR. There's something I must do. I've been spiteful and mean to Trino. I'll make it up with him. We're the same blood. He'll love me again, won't he, *mama?* I'll make him. I'm tired of discord. I'll humble myself if I have to. Then we'll all be together again!

[*She hurries out happily.* DOÑA CANDITA *straightens a few things quickly.* FERNANDO *brings in* NINON, *a pretty girl, but common, with extreme clothes and a petulant mouth—like a bitter little doll.*]

FERNANDO. Mother, this is Ninon.

DOÑA CANDITA. Ninon. [*She opens her arms.* NINON *goes to her.* DOÑA CANDITA *embraces her tenderly.*] My dear Amira's child. And how is your dear mother, Ninon?

NINON. Oh, mother's all right. She's always all right. You couldn't kill mother. She's a horse.

DOÑA CANDITA. [*Puzzled.*] Kill? A horse?

FERNANDO. She means her mother's fine, she's well, mother.

DOÑA CANDITA. Oh.

FERNANDO. Aren't you glad?

DOÑA CANDITA. Yes.

NINON. She sent you a message, Mrs. Crespo. "Tell Doña Candita," she said—"tell Doña Candita I wish her well—and joy of her homecoming. If she wants to see me—I can be found."

DOÑA CANDITA. [*Softly.*] Is that all?

NINON. Yes.

DOÑA CANDITA. And she didn't come to see me herself.

NINON. Mother's got her reasons.

DOÑA CANDITA. But we—we were friends from childhood. Inseparable. I don't understand.

NINON. [*Bursting out.*] You'll understand only too well after

you've been here twenty-four hours! Things aren't the same
as— [*Then, seeing* DOÑA CANDITA, *her old face, her gray hair.*]
You—you're older than I thought you'd be.
DOÑA CANDITA. The years leave their traces.
NINON. That used to be the rule, all right.
DOÑA CANDITA. Your mother is my age exactly.
NINON. Oh, but you'd never believe it! You wouldn't know
mother, if she stood right here in front of you. [*Bursting out
spitefully.*] She runs me a race, I can tell you! Practically
swipes the boys from under my nose. Her hair blackened and
red on her nails—even her toes—!
DOÑA CANDITA. Red on her toes?
NINON. And no stockings, just to show them off. You know—like
the girls in the technicolor pictures.
DOÑA CANDITA. The girls here in Mérida like that? I thought only
in New York . . . the big cities of the world.
NINON. Only mother is like that, Mrs. Crespo. My God, even
I don't paint my toenails! I'm not *that* low. [*Bitterly.*]
The mighty Lujans have gone to the dogs—you may as
well know now as later, Mrs. Crespo. Oh, when we had
money, they forgave us being a little unconventional! But
it's quite different now. The old dames don't visit us any
more—which I can tell you is a relief to me. The vicious old
gossip-mongers! We're beyond the tracks—as they say in the
States—and nobody—nobody who *is* anybody—would be
caught dead speaking to us. Now—there it is!
DOÑA CANDITA. I see. Your poor mother. And no friend to
comfort her. Tell her I'll come to see her—tomorrow.
NINON. They all say that—but they never come.
DOÑA CANDITA. [*Gently.*] Tomorrow at ten. Tell her.
NINON. [*After a moment—touched.*] I'll tell her, Doña Candita.
Thank you.
[*She goes out.*]
FERNANDO. Mother, can I ask Ninon and the *nana* to stay for
supper?
DOÑA CANDITA. If you like, Fernando.
FERNANDO. Mother! Isn't she the—! Isn't she the—! Oh, what the
hell!
[*He hurries after her.* DOÑA CANDITA *stands there, bent and
sorrowful. Then she goes quietly, and kneels before the Virgin. For a
moment, a moment only, it seems absurd and laughable. But in a
moment, she begins to speak.*]

DOÑA CANDITA. Mother of God. I am an old woman and my life is behind me. I ask nothing for myself anymore. God has showered infinite gifts upon me. But the others—the weary and struggling ones alive in the world, and crying out! Be gracious to them before it's too late. That little child, with her life hardly begun. The little Ninon. Hurt and bitter already, full of hate and anguish much too hard to bear. Help her to find happiness. She is too young to suffer . . . too young.

CURTAIN

Scene Four

A field of hemp stretching away, precise and green and regular. At one side, part of a limestone wall and a crumbling Mayan ruin. Close to this stands an easel with a partially completed painting on it. It is late afternoon—an hour later.

TRINO is sprawled on the ground. BETO *is standing a little apart, a* machete *in his belt.*

TRINO. [*Almost to himself.*] Chela is almost to Progreso by this time.
BETO. Yes.
TRINO. Tomorrow she'll be in Havana.
BETO. I know. [TRINO *sighs deeply. Then he gets up, goes over to the painting, and with a heavy brush smears it.* BETO *looks at him curiously.*] You've ruined it.
TRINO. [*His sharpness of mood subsiding.*] I don't feel that I belong here, Beto. Not at all.
BETO. How is that, Trino?
TRINO. I don't know.
BETO. Your grandfather belonged here.
TRINO. My grandfather was a strong man.
BETO. There is strong blood in your veins.
TRINO. No, Beto, not in mine. Listen, Beto, my grandfather was a tyrant, an oppressor. It's no wonder he was at home here. Slaves to command—to torture if it pleased him—forcing them to work like beasts to fill his own money-bags. Women slaves to enjoy at night. The rich gluttonous old Spanish bastard! It's no wonder he was just like that with that old despot, Don Porfirio Díaz. They were birds of a feather. You should hate them—hate us all—hate *me*.

BETO. We don't hate. We Mayans have never hated.

TRINO. It would be better if you had. Look at these ruins—at the ruins of Chichén Itzá,[1] Uxmal—a dozen cities, their walls down, their story dust. The Toltecs[2] crushed and buried your temples under their own. The Spaniards came, and put yokes around your necks, hating your freedom and your beauty. A little hate would have saved you. The *machete* was in your belt—and you wouldn't use it!

BETO. Hate kills the people it inhabits.

TRINO. And the people it's directed against, Beto?

BETO. No, we don't die. Trino. A horse, covered with iron to protect him, his feet sharp shod, his nostrils snorting, goes into battle. Against what? Nothing. No enemy. What happens? He sinks in the spongy grass, the marsh. The *cenote*[3] filled with reeds and rushes swallows him. Nothing has happened. All is as it was before.

TRINO. Do you like your lot, then?

BETO. We bear it. We are grass.

TRINO. Trampled underfoot, bruised and bleeding—you bear it!

BETO. Yes.

TRINO. And you—you personally, Beto—do you like your lot?

BETO. Who am I—personally?

TRINO. Flesh and bone! Hope in you—or not in you!

BETO. I don't know such words. I work. That's all I know.

TRINO. You should hope and struggle and fail—and rise up and fight and conquer!

BETO. What should I conquer?

TRINO. The earth.

BETO. [*With a mounting asperity.*] Like your ancestors. And what happens after they conquer? They decay. Look at those haughty ones and wonder. Look at yourself. Who are you to instruct me?

TRINO. Don't be offended, Beto. If you are not my friend, I have no friend.

[BETO *looks at him quietly a moment, then turns away.*]

BETO. [*Softly.*] We have no right to be friends.

TRINO. Why not?

BETO. I feel it.

---

1 Southeast of Mérida on the Yucatán Peninsula, an ancient Mayan city famous for the Pyramid of Kukulcan, also known as El Castillo, and for the largest ballcourt in Mesoamerica.

2 Influential precursors to the Aztecs in central Mexico.

3 Sinkholes filled with water that are common on the Yucatán Peninsula.

TRINO. I am white and you are Indian. And this is Mexico. Is that it?

BETO. Perhaps.

TRINO. But the land is yours—soon, Beto. The government is giving it back to you.[1] They have said so. [*Gently.*] I ask for your friendship. You are my superior.

BETO. You think of high and low. You are not to be trusted.

TRINO. Why do you say it?

BETO. You will betray me. And not know how you have done it.

TRINO. No, I won't, Beto.

BETO. To you some must be above, some below. It's in your blood.

TRINO. [*Narrowly—like an accusing challenge.*] We are not so different. The blood, I mean. You have white blood, Beto.

BETO. [*Deliberately—also knowing the secret.*] You should know that.

TRINO. Yes. I know.

BETO. [*In deep controlled protest.*] It doesn't make me white. I am Mayan! An Indian only!

TRINO. Yes, you are Indian—but—

[BETO *goes away, dark, troubled deeply.*]

BETO. [*After a moment—quiet again, measured.*] But I have half your sickness, Trino. Half. So I can understand you enough to be your friend. I will be your friend, Trino. I can't help it.

[PILAR *comes in. She stops, seeing that* TRINO *is not alone.*]

PILAR. Oh.

TRINO. What is it?

PILAR. I was looking for you. I thought you'd be alone.

TRINO. Beto is with me—as you can see.

BETO. I'll go.

TRINO. Stay.

BETO. There are rocks in the *milpa*[2] that must be cleared away before nightfall.

TRINO. But it's Sunday.

PILAR. Sunday is nothing to you, is it, Beto?

BETO. Nothing.

PILAR. [*To* TRINO.] You see? Let him do what he wants to.

TRINO. I want him to stay. Please stay, Beto.

BETO. As you like.

---

1 Trino refers to the land reform policies of President Lázaro Cárdenas, instituted from 1934 to 1940.

2 A field for crops as well as a common process in the Yucatán Peninsula that involves clearing an area for cultivation for a few years, then leaving it fallow.

TRINO. What do you want, Pilar?

PILAR. I can't speak before—before strangers.

TRINO. Beto and I are friends.

PILAR. What do you mean by friends?

TRINO. A thing you would never understand.

PILAR. [*In troubled protest.*] You shut me out, Trino. You're hostile to me. You've always been. What am I supposed to do!

TRINO. Leave me alone. Leave me alone!

PILAR. You needn't shout at me. I am your sister—even if I am not your friend. Even if your confidence, and your trust and love are given to others—to just anybody.

TRINO. [*With deadly quiet.*] Pilar—what kind of monster are you? A spider in the center of one of those webs. But not waiting. Spewing a poisonous vapor, involving every living thing within hearing, within sight. *You leave Beto out of this, do you hear?*

PILAR. [*In tears.*] What am I to do? Are you lovers already? Are you friends? What goes on between people? *But between me and people—only hate.* What's the matter with me!

TRINO. I don't believe even your tears.

PILAR. [*Choked.*] Someday you— Someday. . . .
[*She goes off. A pause.*]

BETO. [*Quietly.*] If you are white—someone must win. Who?
[TRINO *looks at him.*]

CURTAIN

Scene Five

The hemp mill, that night after supper. Moonlight. Under a shed, on a platform reached by steps, is the simple machine with its belt and claws and hopper, where the hemp is shredded before drying. Down front, at one side, a tiny car, on its tracks, is loaded with green hemp. Beyond the mill and the open shed can be seen the hemp fields in the moonlight. The reddish glow of an open fire is inside the shed.

Sitting or sprawling on the hemp mill and on the platform and floor are Indians, the machetes *in their belts. Two of them are twanging away at guitars. They are all singing a rousing song.*

BETO, TRINO *and* FERNANDO *are listening. The song finishes. Shouts of all. The mood is high and excited.*

BETO, TRINO, FERNANDO. [*During the hubbub.*] Hurray, hurray!

TRINO. Sing it again! Again!

FERNANDO. [*Who has been drinking.*] Yes, again! Or something else! The *Alma y Vida.*[1] I'll give you presents. I'll give you wine! ·

TRINO. It isn't yours to give.

FERNANDO. So?

TRINO. [*Sharply.*] No! Nor theirs to accept! They have better stuff to drink!

FERNANDO. What have they got?

TRINO. *Ron de caña.* Cane rum. Their own.

FERNANDO. [*Surly, looking for trouble.*] My God, cane rum—that sticky mess! Wine, I say! *Vino por los Indios!* I'll get it. I'm a generous man— I'll make them happy!

TRINO. Stop it, Fernando! You can't give them wine, you can't give them anything.

FERNANDO. [*Short and pugnacious.*] And why can't I?

TRINO. Because they have it already—the thing you ought to crawl on your knees to get!

FERNANDO. For God's sake—riddles!

[*He breaks away.*]

TRINO. [*Stopping him by force.*] Yes, riddles you used to understand. It was all talk. Shooting off your mouth!

FERNANDO. What the hell's the matter with you?

TRINO. *You* hear me!

FERNANDO. What's happening to you?

TRINO. I might ask what's happening to *you?* Good God, I used to respect you! Jesus, you and your paternalism! Your generous nature! You'll give them wine! The Good God Bountiful! The good god-damned *fool!*

FERNANDO. [*Turning on him with fury.*] Take it back, take it back!

TRINO. You're drunk.

BETO. [*Quickly interfering.*] Fernando! Trino! Play, Valdez! Play! *Viajera! Poemas de mi Patria!*[2] Anything!

[*The Indians begin to play loudly. The brothers subside.* PILAR *and* CUCO *hurry in gaily, followed by the breathless* JOSEFA.] ·

PILAR. *Fernando!*

FERNANDO. [*Sulkily.*] Well?

PILAR. The de la Sornas are giving a party at their *hacienda.* They

---

1 Spanish: "Soul and Life."
2 Spanish: "The Traveling Woman"; "Poems of My Fatherland."

have an orchestra from Cuba, *bals de carnets*,[1] punch and champagne, everything!

FERNANDO. Let them have it.

PILAR. [*Gaily.*] I wouldn't stop them! I can hear the music—the gaiety! Aren't you even interested?

FERNANDO. [*Snapping his fingers.*] Not that much.

PILAR. Oh, but you will be, when you hear! We're all invited. Josefa says so. Isn't it so, Josefa?

JOSEFA. They gave me the message. "Invite all the Crespos," they said. They're full of curiosity to see you.

FERNANDO. Let them die of it.

JOSEFA. What?

FERNANDO. Let them die of it. I'm not going.

PILAR. But Fernando. I can't go without you, without someone.

FERNANDO. What's the matter with Cuco?

PILAR. I have to have a chaperon. A brother, at least.

FERNANDO. Why?

PILAR. [*With good-natured raillery.*] It's the custom, silly. He thinks he's in the States.

FERNANDO. I know damn well I'm not in the States.

PILAR. [*At his angry manner.*] What is it, Fernando?

FERNANDO. [*And now it's out.*] Is Ninon invited? Is she? Is her mother, Amira Lujan, invited?

PILAR. I don't know. I'm sure, I—

JOSEFA. No, they're not, I can tell you!

FERNANDO. No, of course not. And why is that? Tell me why? The Lujans aren't good enough, is that it?

JOSEFA. Nobody invites the Lujans anymore. Those *awful* people! It isn't done. Good families wouldn't think of having them in their house.

FERNANDO. To hell with them, then! And you, too!

CUCO. Hey, now! [*Then genially and kiddingly.*] Oh, so there is the wind and where it blows! Ninon. I noticed you casting your eyes at the little Ninon all during supper. But of course you couldn't have known about her—or you'd have restrained your animal instincts.

FERNANDO. I know everything about her—everything.

CUCO. That I seriously doubt. My *innuendos* at supper ought to have informed you.

FERNANDO. You didn't have to be rude to her, my fine *Señor!* Nor you either, *Señorita* Saldívar! You humiliated her with your

---

1 French: i.e., *carnets de bal*, dance cards or dance programs.

remarks—you drove her home in tears by your rudeness. Be rude in your own house—not in ours!

JOSEFA. [*With quick anger.*] I'll be rude wherever I damn well please!

FERNANDO. Someday you'll get slapped.

JOSEFA. [*Unable to believe her ears.*] Slapped? *Me—slapped!*

CUCO. [*Angrily.*] See here—you young—!

PILAR. [*Quickly.*] No, no, Cuco! Let him alone.

JOSEFA. What kind of a family—!

PILAR. He doesn't know what he's saying, he's—he's been drinking.

FERNANDO. I know well enough.

PILAR. [*Embarrassed and ashamed.*] Really, he doesn't—he'll apologize tomorrow—he'll be ashamed of himself—he isn't like this, he—

FERNANDO. Lay on the plaster, whiten the sepulchre![1] Paint your pretty picture, and fall in a swoon of admiration! [*With cold emphasis.*] I know what I'm saying, my fine sister. I'm going to marry Ninon.

PILAR. [*Appalled.*] You *couldn't.*

FERNANDO. In spite of you!

PILAR. You can't— Father will prevent it.

FERNANDO. Instructed by you, his decision made for him? It'll do you no good. If she'll have me, I'll marry her.

PILAR. [*Her Tuero blood rising.*] "If she'll have you." Fernando, you can't do it!

FERNANDO. And why not? The Lujans aren't the right people anymore, is that it? "Good families don't have them in their house."

PILAR. What do I care about her family?

FERNANDO. [*Contemptuously.*] Everything!

PILAR. I don't know them. They're nothing to me. I'm talking about her—about Ninon.

FERNANDO. What about her?

PILAR. That cheap little girl!

FERNANDO. Cheap, is she?

PILAR. As dirt! God, the ones you had in New York were better— the gum-chewing floosies. Ninon, for God's sake! [*Letting him have it.*] A common vulgar little snatcher after whatever she

---

1 Tomb. See Matthew 23.27, in which Jesus likens Pharisees and other hypocrites to "whited sepulchres, which indeed appear beautiful outward, but are within full of dead men's bones, and of uncleanness."

can get. You must be blind, and out of your head completely. Slobbering around after little tarts you could pick up for a dime a dozen!

FERNANDO. I warn you!

PILAR. Oh, warn me—! Do you think I'm afraid of your threats? You're a cowardly drunken bum! Marry her—marry her for spite! Tear what little respectability we have left to shreds. Ruin your life if you like—it's yours—and live to curse yourself for your dereliction! You're no brother of mine!

FERNANDO. [*With mocking sardonic defiance.*] Disinherited, by God! Thrust from the splendor and the glory! No sister, no brother, no kin! Freedom triumphant. I embrace you for this deliverance!

JOSEFA. [*With crazy despair.*] Oh! That I'd ever find myself rolling, positively rolling in corruption! And all because he won't go to a party!

[*The mood is broken.* PILAR *seizes the moment to pull it back to normal.*]

PILAR. I'm sorry, Josefa. If he doesn't want to go—it doesn't matter, anyway. [*With hardly any hope.*] Trino won't go, I know. Will you, Trino?

TRINO. No.

PILAR. Cuco! I have it! Couldn't we just go without a chaperon?

CUCO. Would you dare? I would!

PILAR. Oh yes, Cuco. It can't be a crime exactly. Let's do it!

JOSEFA. [*This is too much.*] For heaven's sake, Cuco! Pilar, such a thing to say!

PILAR. Is it so bad?

JOSEFA. [*Quite overcome with amazed indignation.*] Cuco, how could you let her even consider it? It's indecent. Have you lost your mind completely? They'd never stop chattering. Such vile things they'd say!

PILAR. What could they say?

JOSEFA. They'd say you were one of those loose women from New York, that Cuco was running after you just to get what he wanted, and without any idea of marrying you—and—

CUCO. Josefa, for God's sake.

JOSEFA. [*Not stopping.*] —and they'd remember Uncle Bernardino, the way he carried on with just anybody who was female and—oh, the way they talk! It's disgraceful!

PILAR. Oh, Josefa—all of you! It doesn't matter at all. I thought it would be such fun—our first day at home—seeing the people—a typical Yucatecan party—it would be new. I remember hardly anything. I used to creep along the *corredor* when I was little—and try to hear what was going on, but I couldn't hear a thing but the noise, mostly the thump of the drum—and then someone always spotted me and shooed me off to bed again. [*Sitting down, run down by her efforts to shut* JOSEFA'S *mouth.*] We'll stay here. It's better anyway. The night's a dream. The music's lovely.

TRINO. You might listen to it, then.

PILAR. [*Subsiding.*] Oh.

[*They all listen a moment, as the music continues.*]

JOSEFA. [*After fidgeting in disdain a moment.*] The Indians don't know how to play. Such a banging.

PILAR. I'd rather be here. I would, really.

JOSEFA. *I* wouldn't. There's nothing to keep me here. Nor you either, Cuco. I'm going to the de la Sornos so you'll have to take me.

PILAR. Yes, Cuco. Josefa's bored. Please take her.

CUCO. I'd rather not, thank you very much.

PILAR. It must be dismal for you here.

CUCO. I'll make out.

JOSEFA. He won't go. I see it all. And I know why he won't. You don't have to be a mind reader, either. Men are *awful*.

CUCO. Shut up, Josefa!

JOSEFA. Such a lovely party it was going to be, too. The band is to play in the living room—refreshments in the new *jacal* they've built for a play room. Just like an Indian *jacal*, only not shabby, like an Indian one. A concrete floor painted vermilion, and gold chairs! Such a gold! And here we are— not even a chair to sit on—listening to Indians trying to entertain us. What a life it is!

[*The Indians have been getting up and leaving, the song gradually being dropped by one after the other.*]

PILAR. What are they doing?

TRINO. What would you do in their shoes?

JOSEFA. [*With a silly complaining wail.*] They're leaving! Just as we get settled. We weren't doing a thing, not a thing. Oh, the Indians—always insulting you without opening their mouths! It's disgusting!

TRINO. Can you blame them?

JOSEFA. Certainly, I can blame them! Who do they think they are, these days?

TRINO. Good God, these are men—with feelings—not inanimate objects, not so many picturesque Indians in a Rivera painting![1] They work like dogs, and live on a starvation diet of beans—and not enough of them—to put cake in your mouth and silk on your backs and gold chairs to sit on! [*The Indians are pausing, listening.*] They sit there on the hemp mill—the very symbol of their oppression and slavery—and make a song. And you can't even listen! Go to your stupid party, with your bands from Cuba, and guzzle champagne—you'll live to regret it! There are people, and I'm one of them— who'll never rest till you're all down, down in the dirt where you belong! Get out, get out—all of you—and leave a little privacy to your betters!

FERNANDO. [*Dangerously, approaching him.*] And what do you think you are now, my brother? Are the Indians yours? Do the down-trodden belong to you now that your brother has deserted? You were here. Have you a better right to be here than we have?

TRINO. [*Sickened by his defection.*] Fernando!

FERNANDO. Have you?

TRINO. [*His voice low.*] I was invited. Get out.

PILAR. [*Distressed and uncertain.*] Perhaps we'd better. Josefa. Cuco. I'm sorry this happened. It's my fault.

CUCO. He can't talk like that to us!

JOSEFA. He most assuredly cannot! It isn't done. See here—little Trino—we're your guests.

TRINO. You're my enemy.

FERNANDO. [*Facing him dangerously.*] *I* am your enemy, my brother.

TRINO. [*Slowly.*] I've found that out, Fernando. [*With deep hurt and growing anger.*] You used to talk about the servitude of the millions, the blind crawling in darkness who needed help, and I listened and learned. It was talk—it meant nothing to you—I see that now— But I listened. I used to pray to God to make me like you—in your image, your clear belief, your passion! Your words rang in my ears—"Give me a place," you said—"where the issues are clear. Then if you die, you'll know why your blood has been shed." Once you said that. Where have you gone, what hideous lechery of the blood has betrayed you? Here, the issues are clear—too clear!

FERNANDO. Yes, clear—crystal clear! In this country of darkness! This is a land of masters—don't you see it?—of right

---

1 Diego Rivera (1886–1957), a Mexican painter known especially for his murals, which often depicted the Indigenous peoples of Mexico.

and wrong, the washed and the filthy, the mighty and the diseased! Nothing between! And there are rules for everything. You've just listened to a few of them. Obey them and live. Violate them and die! Can't you see it yet! Is the fog and the dream still in your eyes to blind you? You were born one of the masters. So was I. And I keep what I've got, and get all I can the way everyone does in this benighted hell-hole! I'll show you who gives the orders—and who obeys! [*To one of the Indians, in a fury of drunken passion.*] Play, Chucho, play! Do you hear me?

CHUCHO. *Señor?*

FERNANDO. A song! Make it roar in our ears like doom—the kind you sing when you think no one can hear—a song to chill the blood—that blinding day that's to come—when you strike off the chains, and are free! Sing it!

TRINO. Fernando!

FERNANDO. I command you, you greasy bastard! Sing!

CHUCHO. As you say, *Señor* Fernando.

[*The Indian strums his guitar softly. He is lifting his voice, dim and troubled, when one of the Indians jerks out his* machete *like lightning, leaps upon the platform.*]

TRINO. Chucho!

VOICES. What's he doing! Stop him!

[*The* GIRLS *cry out. The* machete *crashes down, one swift brutal stroke, and the guitarist lies in a huddled heap of death.*]

VOICES. I couldn't stop him!

Why did he do it?

Holy Mother!

JOSEFA. Cuco!

[*She clings to him.*]

BETO. [Stoops over the body, straightens up.] He's dead.

TRINO. [*To* FERNANDO, *sickened.*] *You* did it—*you!*

[*He turns away, bent over.*]

PILAR. [*Her heart pounding with horror.*] A minute ago he—!

BETO. No matter who fights, what brother against what brother— it's the Indian who dies.

PILAR. A little while ago they were all singing. [*She looks fearfully at the night.*] I'm afraid. Afraid!

CURTAIN

INTERMISSION

Scene Six

The corredor *again, seven months later. October. Six o'clock in the morning. A little painted Yucatecan trunk stands by one of the pillars.*
Present are DOÑA CANDITA, DON SEVERO, PILAR, CUCO, JOSEFA, A PRIEST, A SACRISTAN, INDIAN WOMEN *beating chocolate,*[1] INDIAN MEN *of the* hacienda, *and* NINON *and* FERNANDO, *who are kneeling before the priest.*
Great masses of tuberoses[2] *are everywhere. The marriage ceremony is ending.*

PRIEST. . . . I pronounce you man and wife. Whom God hath joined together, let no man put asunder.
[*The* BRIDE *and* GROOM *rise. A stir as the spectators crowd around.* DOÑA CANDITA *embraces* FERNANDO, *and kisses* NINON.]
DOÑA CANDITA. My child. I prayed for your happiness long ago. My prayer was answered. Be happy.
NINON. Thank you, Mother Candita.
DOÑA CANDITA. I would have liked your marriage to be in the Cathedral. But Pilar said "no." I can't think why.
NINON. It doesn't matter. It's beautiful here—it's . . .
[*She holds her close.*]
DON SEVERO. My son.
[*He gives him an* abrazo.[3]]
FERNANDO. Father.
DON SEVERO. The first son of my house. [*To* NINON.] My child.
CUCO. [*Cordially, but a little embarrassed.*] Congratulations.
JOSEFA. Well, you are a fine-looking couple, I'll say that, at least! I have to wish you well.
[*Everyone laughs.*]
PILAR. [*Coming over to* FERNANDO.] Fernando. [*She embraces him—turns to* NINON.] Ninon—if I've spoken ill of you, forgive me now.
NINON. Yes, Pilar.
PILAR. [*Gently.*] Make him happy.
NINON. Yes.
PILAR. I know you will. And that will be the joy you're looking for, won't it?

---

1 Mesoamericans invented chocolate, from the Nahuatl *chocolatl*. Riggs refers to the traditional way of preparing hot chocolate in Mexico.
2 Flowering plants (genus *Agave*) native to Mexico.
3 Spanish: embrace, hug.

NINON. Yes, Pilar.

PILAR. [*With sincere wonder.*] You're not afraid to go into the *chicle*[1] jungles with him?

NINON. What is there to be afraid of?

PILAR. The loneliness—no friends.

NINON. I love Fernando.

PILAR. [*Troubled.*] The crawling jungles, the horrible stillness at night, the pests of the air—a miserable hut to live in—the heat—are you so brave?

NINON. I have my husband.

PILAR. [*Tenderly.*] And he has you. He's lucky, after all.

NINON. Thank you, Pilar.

[PILAR *embraces her.*]

THE PRIEST. The sun is rising, my children. His benediction will be added to our own. The day begins.

JOSEFA. [*Complaining.*] Six in the morning—what an hour for a wedding!

DOÑA CANDITA. [*Serenely.*] It's the classic hour for a Yucatecan wedding, Josefa.

JOSEFA. I suppose it's all right—but it's a nuisance, all the same. I'm perishing.

[*She yawns fearfully.*]

DOÑA CANDITA. And hungry, no doubt. There's breakfast in the dining room. [*As the Indian* WOMEN *approach with mugs of freshly-beaten individual chocolate.*] And see—the chocolate is ready. Smell the cinnamon! Bring it with you. Oh, such food—Maruca has been cooking for days! Father. Come in. All of you. [*They all go out, except* JOSEFA, *who calls* CUCO *as he is about to leave.*]

JOSEFA. Cuco! I never thought I'd live to see the day!

CUCO. [*Amused at her woeful appearance.*] Josefa, you look groggy! Such a face!

JOSEFA. Six in the morning! How could you ask me to get up so early? And for such a purpose. They say the wedding was here at the *hacienda*—for reasons.

CUCO. [*Bored with her.*] What reasons?

JOSEFA. The family is ashamed of the marriage. They were afraid to have it in town.

CUCO. What nonsense!

---

1 Gum, harvested from sapodilla/chicozapote trees in the forests of the Yucatán Peninsula.

JOSEFA. Oh, not nonsense at all! [*Lowering her voice.*] They say
  something else, too. He *had* to marry her.
CUCO. [*Not the least bit interested.*] Who says so? Come on, I'm
  starving.
JOSEFA. Everyone says so.
CUCO. Well, what of it?
JOSEFA. Oh, nothing now. It's all right now—they're married.
  Now there won't be a scandal. That's a comfort.
CUCO. [*Smiling.*] To you, Josefa?
JOSEFA. Of course to me! Cuco—such a thing I heard in town! It's
  said that as early as two months ago the little Ninon was—
  you know what! But Don Severo is a doctor—don't forget—
  he has all those diplomas—so the little matter was taken care
  of—and just in time!
CUCO. [*Disgusted with her.*] Josefa, you know that's a lie. How can
  you listen to such—!
JOSEFA. It was told me for true—yes, by a first cousin of the
  Tueros. Juanito—the one who put both his eyes out for
  spite—just so he wouldn't have to look at his wife anymore.
  And who could blame him? If there was ever a more horrible
  unsightly mass of . . .
CUCO. Josefa, I forbid you to gossip about the Crespos!
JOSEFA. Oh, protect them. It's well known why you hang
  around them all the time. [CUCO *turns away with despairing
  impatience.*] Fernando could have waited, it seems to me. It
  isn't as if he was getting a prize, either. That cheap little bag
  of flea-bitten nothing!
[NINON *comes out of the house.*]
NINON. Mother Candita says won't you please come in to
  breakfast.
JOSEFA. [*Going to her.*] Darling little Ninon! Did you ever think all
  this would come to pass—did you?
NINON. I hoped it would, *Señorita* Saldívar.
JOSEFA. Naturally you did, little lamb—naturally you did. Every
  girl does. What else is there for her to hope for? But you know
  how it happens too often in Yucatán—if a girl gives herself to
  her fiancé before they're safely married, the brute refuses to
  marry her at all!
NINON. Please, *Señorita*.
JOSEFA. Oh, my child, I don't mean you. Everybody knows about
  you, you dear thing. But it's been the fate of so many girls—
  girls who were unwise, I mean. Women are weak, yes, they are
  indeed! I wonder why it is men champ at the bit so! It gives

me the creeps. But you are a lucky little bride, and I hope such happiness for you. Here, do drink my chocolate. It's too rich for me. [*She puts the mug in her hands.* NINON *looks at her for a troubled violent moment, and slams it on the floor. She runs into the house.*] Well, for the love of the saints—I didn't open my head! Such impudence—it's insufferable! At six in the morning. You know what it does—it proves it—every word I said! Oh, a nest—veritably a nest! How can you want to marry into such pollution?

CUCO. [*Furiously.*] You ought to be shut up in a hole somewhere. You're a foul-mouthed slut, Josefa!

JOSEFA. Foul-mouthed, am I? I speak only the truth which everybody knows—but you can't hear it because you're mad for the precious Pilar! [*Cunningly.*] And where do you spend your evenings now—my little brother! Oh, I hear you creeping in at dawn!

CUCO. My business is my own!

JOSEFA. Night after night! Such behavior! But bad as you are, I condone everything, I bow my head, I . . .

CUCO. You're the bitch of the world, Josefa!

JOSEFA. Bitch, am I? And all because I want to save you from messing yourself up completely! Now I'll really tell you something. You noticed that Trino wasn't here at the wedding, didn't you? Well, where is he—what's become of him, would you like to know! I'll tell you! Your fine holy Crespos!

[PILAR *comes out of the house.*]

PILAR. Aren't you hungry, Josefa?

JOSEFA. Ravenous, ravenous!

PILAR. Please come in and eat.

JOSEFA. [*Going.*] I thought you were starving, Cuco.

CUCO. Go ahead.

JOSEFA. [*With her nasty meanings.*] Starving—and you can wait? It isn't like you, not at all. I never saw you wait before—for something you wanted.

[*She goes in.*]

CUCO. [*Bursting out.*] My sister's a witch! A venomous old witch! Like most of the high-born ladies of Mérida.

PILAR. I know. I suppose today gives them plenty to talk about.

CUCO. *Any* day! If nothing happens, they're very inventive.

PILAR. Why are they like that?

CUCO. Their world is here, this little peninsula. It's all they know. The big world doesn't intrude very much. And they have nothing else to do, so they talk, the bitches!

PILAR. [*Thoughtfully.*] The leisure and security their ancestors created for them—and this is the way we use it!

CUCO. Not you, Pilar. You're not like that.

PILAR. I'm not any better.

CUCO. You're a million times better! Pilar—listen to me. I won't let you talk against yourself.

PILAR. You can't stop me thinking. I'm sick of everything—myself most of all.

CUCO. What is it? You're troubled. Is it the wedding? You didn't want Fernando to marry her.

PILAR. It's what he wanted. She loves him deeply. I've accepted it—even his going away to the steaming jungle to work in the *chicle.*

CUCO. Then, what? [*Genuinely.*] You know I'm your friend. If you're unhappy, I'm miserable as hell, you know that. Can't you trust me?

PILAR. [*Harassed but kindly.*] I do trust you, Cuco. Only there's so much—why should you bother with the Crespo problems? That's what's on my mind most of the time now, why I seem so abstracted and dull—sometimes unkind to you, Cuco, whom I don't want ever to be unkind to.

CUCO. Thank you, Pilar. But why don't you think of yourself—not always of the Crespos?

PILAR. But I do.

CUCO. No, it's always the family, the family!

PILAR. I *must* think of them. [*With febrile distress.*] I can't forget that it was I who forced us all to come back here. I thought it would be better—it's got to be—even if—! [*Seeing it clearly.*] Cuco. That day in February—the sky was so blue and the air so amber. We drove from the docks of Progreso. Mérida was like the swept snug house of a rich peasant expecting a visit from the king. The open carriages and the hoofbeats of horses echoed in the still streets. The smell of flowers burst over their walls, drowning the senses. And the road here—like the first road of the world—not a cloud over it—the assured bell-song of birds startled by our passing—the lovely hemp—the miles of stone. And at last Techoh . . . I cried for joy! Then— [*Her face darkens.*]

CUCO. Then?

PILAR. Chela ruined that magic—oh, she couldn't help it, she had to! She went away. [*Seeing it darkly.*] And that night—our first night here—in the hemp mill there was sudden bloody death.

CUCO. Oh, Pilar, don't think of it!

PILAR. [*Unheeding.*] A sign.

CUCO. [*Impatiently.*] I thought you were above superstition!

PILAR. Not here. This isn't the city—that man made with his brain. Nature crowds the air with fore-knowledge in this land. Superstitions are wiser than the mind. [*Painfully.*] And I keep seeing Chela in Havana—the dim streets, her tawdry room—I see her bruised and hurt by the life she's chosen. My mind makes pictures of her shame.

CUCO. Pilar, don't, don't!

PILAR. And Trino—oh, he's here, he's all right, I'm behaving badly. . . . Don't listen!

[*She tries to throw it off.*]

CUCO. Pilar, why didn't Trino come to his brother's wedding?

PILAR. Trino isn't living in the house any more.

CUCO. Why not?

PILAR. I don't *know!*

CUCO. What's happened to him? Where is he?

PILAR. He's living in a *jacal* beyond the gates.

CUCO. An Indian *jacal?*

PILAR. Yes.

CUCO. Why?

PILAR. [*Restlessly.*] I don't know, Cuco, I don't know!

[*She goes and switches on the radio impatiently. A voice begins to come over, as it warms up.*]

CUCO. You never let me see you alone any more. What have I done? My God, I'm dying, can't you see it? I used to think oblation— true oblation—would melt a heart of stone. I was wrong.

PILAR. You aren't wrong, Cuco. Be patient. Please be patient.

CUCO. How can I be, how?

PILAR. [*As the voice begins to be clear.*] Listen!

[*They listen. It is unmistakably* CHELA *singing.*]

CUCO. Why, it's—

PILAR. [*Overjoyed.*] It's Chela! On the radio. She's done it!

CUCO. You see—?

PILAR. Yes, Cuco.

CUCO. Your foolish foolish fears.

PILAR. I'll get mother.

[*She hurries in the house to do so. The song goes on. It is a common song of the cheap cabarets of Havana.* CUCO *listens curiously.* DOÑA CANDITA *hurries out, her face radiant.* PILAR *follows.*]

DOÑA CANDITA. It is! Little Chelita! A miracle!

[*They listen. The joy in* DOÑA CANDITA'S *face slowly vanishes. She sits down in a chair. When the song ends, her handkerchief is at her eyes.*]

VOICE OF THE RADIO. You have just heard *Las Desgraciadas,*[1] sung by *Señorita* Chelita Crespo.

[*Other music begins to come over softly.* PILAR, *deeply troubled, goes to her mother.*]

DOÑA CANDITA. [*Lifting her head.*] The song . . . so strange . . . Is it a nice song, Pilar?

PILAR. Of course, mother. Of course. [*She lifts her up gently, takes her to the door of the house.* DOÑA CANDITA *goes in. Facing him.*] What do you think now?

CUCO. Well, I—very nice. She sings well.

PILAR. But—something—is it the kind of song—?

CUCO. It's the kind they all sing.

PILAR. All who, Cuco? [*No answer.*] Tell me.

CUCO. The whores of Havana.

PILAR. [*Sighs deeply.*] Yes.

CUCO. [*Protesting.*] What of it? The girls have to. People like it. What's the matter with it, anyway? She sings very well.

PILAR. Yes.

CUCO. Oh here, Pilar!—you ought to be celebrating! She's doing what she wants to—doing it damn well. She a singer—she's on the radio—you ought to be glad for her!

PILAR. [*Recovering—grateful for his help.*] I am. I'm glad, Cuco. I'll make myself be glad.

CUCO. [*Tenderly.*] Little Pilar. When you first came, you seemed hard and ruthless—but so desirable. [*His deep feeling surging up.*] I loved you then.

PILAR. [*Softly, touched.*] I know you did.

CUCO. I couldn't help myself, my eyes followed you everywhere, my thoughts—! You're different to me now. Not so cold to me—softer, more alluring than ever. I loved you then. I love you even more now. Don't keep me waiting, Pilar. [*With deep bitterness.*] It's hell. You don't know! [*Pleading and strong.*] You've been here since February. Seven months. Seven times I've asked you to marry me. What is it to be? You've said "No" so often.

PILAR. [*With a little smile.*] Four times, Cuco. The fifth was "perhaps."

CUCO. And the sixth, "maybe." [*Bitterly.*] What good is "maybe"!

PILAR. And the last time—I remember it well—we were under the almond tree and the leaves were falling all around us. I said, "Soon I'll decide, soon I'll tell you, Cuco. Don't be sad. I'm not worth it."

---

1 Spanish: "The Miserable Women."

CUCO. Pilar. [*With grave tension.*] Will you marry me?

PILAR. Yes.

CUCO. [*Overwhelmed.*] No!

PILAR. Yes, yes!

CUCO. Oh, my God!

[*He snatches her to him.*]

PILAR. [*Running it all together in her excitement that is close to tears.*] Oh, Cuco, I *do* love you! Thank you— God bless you for loving me—how could you!

CUCO. I was about to give up— I thought you hated me!

PILAR. How could I hate you?

CUCO. And now you—oh, the day, the day! When will you marry me, Pilar? Right away. Now! The priest is here, the sacristan.

PILAR. Oh, Cuco—you know we couldn't.

CUCO. Why not?

PILAR. Well, for one thing—the banns.[1]

CUCO. The banns—what good are they? Rules, rules!

PILAR. We didn't make them. It's the Church.

CUCO. Two weeks, then. Three.

PILAR. Very soon. I have to see—

CUCO. What is there to see? Pretty soon you're going to lose the *hacienda*—and damn quick, from all accounts. Then you'll have to marry me! What else can you do? If you've got a picture of Cárdenas, I'll kiss it, I swear I will!

PILAR. [*Thoughtfully.*] Lose the *hacienda?* It can't be true.

CUCO. Very soon, little baby. The government has already dismembered the estates in the Laguna district. They're beginning in Vera Cruz. Next Yucatán. It won't be long.

PILAR. It won't happen. It can't. Can't it be stopped?

CUCO. Not a chance. Cárdenas is a determined man, and the Indians are back of him. He's arming them, too—in case there's trouble.

PILAR. [*Quietly.*] I prayed for a year here—and the year is going— it's October already, and so many things have gone wrong . . .

CUCO. There you are—at it again! Worrying.

PILAR. Who will if I don't?

CUCO. I'll do it, little Pilar. For us both. From this time forth. You'll marry me—practically at once—we'll get the hell out of Yucatán—travel—Paris, London—!

PILAR. I couldn't—not right away.

---

1 Announcements of marriages, posted publicly in time to allow for objections to the union.

CUCO. You *will.*

PILAR. Desert them? Cuco, I got them into this. I have to see them out of it. You understood it before. Understand it now.

CUCO. [*Sulky and accusing.*] You don't love me at all.

PILAR. I *do.*

CUCO. How can I wait any longer? The agony goes on—only it's worse now.

PILAR. You're acting like a child.

CUCO. [*With feeling.*] I'm a man—with a man's natural appetites. I'm not made of clay. What am I supposed to do? You'll kill us both with your postponing.

PILAR. [*Lightly, trying to appease him.*] Cuco. Why, look—we're *engaged!* I'm yours. I'm promised.

CUCO. A word isn't the same as the fact. I've got to have you—*it must be—!* You say it will happen—then you condemn me to hell again. What's the use? I don't want you.

PILAR. [*Gently.*] Yes, you do, Cuco. Don't be angry. Wait a little while. Not long. [*Radiantly.*] I thought everything was lost— closing in—and now— Let me sample this bliss—! It's a new day. The mists are clearing. Hold me close!

CUCO. [*Seduced.*] You're trembling.

PILAR. I could sing!

CUCO. [*Dazzled—excited.*] Pilar—I forgot! I brought you a present.

PILAR. Where is it?

CUCO. [*Getting the tiny trunk.*] Here.

PILAR. A trunk. It's beautiful, Cuco!

CUCO. There's something inside.

PILAR. What is it? Open it. [CUCO *opens the little trunk—and lifts out a beautiful old dress.*] Cuco!

CUCO. Your wedding dress.

PILAR. [*Overcome.*] Oh!

[*She holds it close to her.* JOSEFA *comes out of the house.*]

JOSEFA. Pilar—in the name of all the saints—what are you doing with that dress, grandmother's wedding dress?

PILAR. [*Quite crazily.*] Josefa, Josefa! [*She seizes her, whirls her round.*] I'm to be married in it—to Cuco—darling Cuco, wonderful Cuco! I love Cuco, I love everybody!

[*She runs into the house.*]

JOSEFA. Merciful heavens—madness! It'll never fit her—never!

CURTAIN

Scene Seven

Inside BETO'S *jacal—two months later. December. The part we see is half of the perfectly oval jacal, the traditional hut of the Mayans, split down its length. The curving walls are of poles chinked with mud. The high sloping roof is made of over-lapping palmetto leaves. Through the open door at back, the hemp fields bake in the hot and humid air of noon. Two hammocks hang from their hooks.*

First TRINO, *then* BETO, *with a heaped bowl of food, come in from the outside where they have been preparing their noon meal. They are shirtless, having had their showers, and look cool and comfortable. Their trousers are rolled up sloppily, and they have on* alpargatas, *the Yucatecan sandal.*

TRINO. The shower does it, eh, Beto? Brrr! I'm cold now!

BETO. I'm hungry.

[*He starts to eat, having sat down on a hammock.*]

TRINO. [*Putting his bowl down, getting a shirt, a* guayabera,[1] *and struggling into it.*] Will we finish this afternoon, do you think?

BETO. Yes.

TRINO. With luck.

BETO. With work.

[TRINO *laughs.*]

TRINO. Yes. And sweat. Would you believe it—here it is December and baking. In New York the icicles hang from your ears.

BETO. New Yorkers must look very silly, then.

TRINO. You'd be surprised how silly.

[*He starts to eat.* PILAR *and* DOÑA CANDITA *appear at the door.*]

TRINO. [*Jumping up.*] Visitors! Come in.

[*They come in.* BETO *gets up.*]

DOÑA CANDITA. We're intruding.

TRINO. No, little *mamsie.*

DOÑA CANDITA. You're eating your dinner.

TRINO. And there's plenty for you. Will you? I'll get it. It's outside on the fire.

DOÑA CANDITA. We eat at one o'clock—as always. I'll wait.

TRINO. Well, sit down, anyway. Pilar?

[*He shows them places to sit. They sit down.*]

DOÑA CANDITA. Good day to you, Beto.

BETO. Good day, Doña Candita.

---

1 Short-sleeved shirt of light material, worn untucked.

DOÑA CANDITA. [*To* TRINO.] Are you comfortable here?

TRINO. In every way.

DOÑA CANDITA. What are you eating?

TRINO. *Posole.*[1]

DOÑA CANDITA. Holy Mother. Is that all?

TRINO. No, baby. We have *tortillas* of maize . . . And a melon—
fresh from the vine.

DOÑA CANDITA. But hot from the sun.

TRINO. Not a bit of it. See! [*He lifts it out of a tub of water.*]
Cooling.

DOÑA CANDITA. I've brought you some cakes, and a pudding. I
made them for you—for both of you. The pudding is a little
fallen, I don't know how it happened. I am disappointed in
that pudding. But the taste is there.

TRINO. Thank you, mother.

DOÑA CANDITA. I haven't been in an Indian *jacal* since I was a
girl. [*Looking about.*] It seems clean here.

TRINO. Of course it's clean. A broom in the morning—and much
scrubbing at night. It's easy. What did you expect?

DOÑA CANDITA. I don't know. Dirt—pigs all over the place.

[TRINO *laughs.* BETO *smiles.*]

TRINO. There is a pig—but he seems to be out. He hasn't smelled
the food yet.

PILAR. We've hardly seen you—for over a month, Trino. Since a
while before Fernando's wedding.

TRINO. I know.

PILAR. We see you only in the distance—or crossing the lawn at
nightfall.

TRINO. I've been busy.

PILAR. You look pale, Trino.

TRINO. [*Cheerfully.*] When you lift rocks all day in the broiling
sun—you're bound to show it a little.

DOÑA CANDITA. Lift rocks, Trino? Why is that?

TRINO. For a new *milpa.* Beto and I have cleared away a new piece
of the jungle. Now we're piling up the *mojoneras,*[2] laying out
the field. This month—a barren place. Next month—the
corn, green shoots. Eventually—harvest, food in the stomach,
happiness in the heart. That's the way it goes.

DOÑA CANDITA. Are there not Indians enough to do such work?

TRINO. Ah—and to spare. But they're busy in the hemp. They

---

1 A stew with pork and hominy, among other ingredients.

2 Spanish: boundary markers.

haven't any time to raise food for themselves. So *I* must work, too.

[*A pause.*]

DOÑA CANDITA. I'm troubled, son.

TRINO. What is it?

DOÑA CANDITA. Why did our forefathers toil so—if their descendants have to struggle like the beasts of the field?

TRINO. Our forefathers toil, *mama?* Cracking a whip all day long, till their fat right arms ached—was that work?

DOÑA CANDITA. I don't understand you.

TRINO. Don't try, little mother. Put me down for a fool.

DOÑA CANDITA. You aren't painting anymore.

TRINO. Painting? Rot! What good is it?

PILAR. I liked your painting, Trino.

TRINO. I don't remember it that way, Pilar.

DOÑA CANDITA. You painted so beautifully!

TRINO. Flowers in a vase—flowers alert—flowers dropping their petals—flowers dead on their stems!

DOÑA CANDITA. I have kept them all.

TRINO. [*With his first show of violence, but quiet and controlled.*] No, mother! Don't keep them! They're sickening and they're a lie! Burn them, *mamacita,* burn them! Don't have such lies about you. Open your eyes and see!

DOÑA CANDITA. [*Softly.*] My eyes are old—and tired of looking. What I see hurts me—like staring at the sun. Forgive me, son. I'll go now.

[*She gets up.*]

TRINO. [*Going to her, touched.*] Mother, sweet little mother.

DOÑA CANDITA. You love me, don't you, Trino?

TRINO. You know I do, mother.

DOÑA CANDITA. Come back to us.

TRINO. I'm here. I'm by your side.

DOÑA CANDITA. Come back to your old room—in the house of your people.

TRINO. No, mother.

DOÑA CANDITA. I beg you!

TRINO. [*Turning away, troubled by his inability to comply.*] I can't.

DOÑA CANDITA. Where are you going—what are you doing with the life I gave you from my body? What folly and madness possesses you? Come back.

TRINO. [*Quiet and sure.*] Death is in that house, Mother. The walls are cracking. In the darkness of night, haven't you heard the shifting of stone on stone?

DOÑA CANDITA. The house has stood this long. It will stand.

TRINO. Not long, Mother.

DOÑA CANDITA. It was built to last forever.

TRINO. So were the temples of Uxmal, the mighty pyramid of Chichén! But the jungle—the living vine—the crawling vital piercing tendrils creep at the base, at every crack—and make of their splendor a jumble of stones for lizards and vermin to breed in! Life is in the earth, mother—in the earth and the people of the earth—not in the arrogant stone!

PILAR. You're hurting her!

TRINO. I'm sorry. [*Fiercely.*] *You* put her up to it, Pilar!

DOÑA CANDITA. No, it is from me, your sorrowing mother.

TRINO. [*Tenderly.*] I do what I must do, little mother. You've borne a lot. Bear this.

DOÑA CANDITA. We've lost Chela—Fernando. Must we count you among the lost ones?

TRINO. I'm *here,* mother. And for the first time in my life—happy.

DOÑA CANDITA. [*Touched, bowing to her fate.*] I must content myself with that, then—if you are happy. I'll try, son, I'll try.

PILAR. Why must she be content with that? Why are the old asked to bend and bend, till they can bend no more? You're cruel, Trino.

TRINO. This is between me and mother.

PILAR. [*Accusingly.*] Will you kill her? She's with us for a little time only, you know that. What are you doing, in this wilful and selfish way, that's so important it can't wait?

TRINO. Wait!

PILAR. [*With contempt.*] Lifting stones, sweating in the fields like an ox—what good is it?

TRINO. [*Sharp and sultry.*] That isn't it! How little you understand! I'm allied with something at last—can't you see it?—allied with something—and it's no longer death. I'll help all I can to wipe out the stench of rottenness in this land—the stench our fathers left behind them!

PILAR. Fernando talked that way in New York. Thank God he got over it!

TRINO. And how did he get over it? Why? His own pollution—and a piece of flesh he wanted! And he's forgotten everything!

PILAR. [*With deadly emphasis.*] You'd do well to do the same.

TRINO. Is it on that side you bark now? I seem to remember you hated his marriage, you thought it beneath him.

PILAR. [*With sharp insistence.*] His marriage was a mistake! I say so still. But a natural one. *Not like you, my brother—not like you! Fernando's* mistake was a *natural* one! [*A horrible thing is happening. They both know it, the air is tense with it—but they are powerless to stop. The words pour out, swift and barbed.*]

TRINO. What do you mean?

PILAR. [*With heated contempt, her meaning still veiled.*] Can't you even talk to your own family any more without others present? Why is this? Are you a coward alone?

TRINO. Nearly all men are cowards alone.

PILAR. [*With cutting passion.*] There's reason for your bravery now, little brother! And I know what it is! I'm not blind—and I won't be silent. This sore will see the light, do you hear? You have Beto, that's what it is—you have Beto and you're not afraid! My brother's a *puto*, a stinking *puto!*[1]

TRINO. [*His voice husky with menace.*] Take it back!

PILAR. I won't! [TRINO slaps her. She stands unbending, in deadly defiance.] I say it again!

TRINO. [*Sickened.*] You make me sick at my stomach. [*With accusing power.*] Would I be having an affair with my brother? Would I? Not with my brother—or with any man!

PILAR. [*With superb contempt.*] Brother!

TRINO. *Yes, brother!* Beto is my brother—*your* brother.

PILAR. Recognized by whom?

TRINO. By me!

PILAR. That doesn't make it true!

TRINO. Close your eyes to the fact, if it pleases you. The fact is still there.

[DOÑA CANDITA, *unable to hear any more, goes out, her head bowed in shame and grief.*]

PILAR. [*Weakly.*] How can you say things like that in front of mother? Just the memory of father's unfaithfulness is enough to make her sick. You want to prove it, to put the living shame in front of her, to turn the knife blade in the wound. All afternoon now, all night, she'll be on her knees.

TRINO. [*In anguish.*] Praying for me. I know.

PILAR. [*Sick.*] For us all. Her children—who give her nothing but pain. [*They are sickened by the thing they have brought to pass. Hating herself.*] God—how could I let this happen? [*After a moment—her voice flat and dead.*] You were right, Trino. I put her up to it.

---

1 Spanish: an extremely offensive insult to gay men or men considered weak. Compare *puta* (feminine): prostitute.

TRINO. The cost, Pilar, the cost!

PILAR. [*In bitter despair.*] Yes, I know. I thought it was wrong for you to have left the house. I saw the family—the family I honor and believe in—one by one—falling away. I thought it my business to interfere—to try to stop the inevitable. I used mother—not for her good—to serve this passion in me. Why do I have to be like this? I could kill myself. Where will it end—where?

[DON SEVERO *comes in, a letter in his hand. They all look at him, with premonition, waiting his word. He seems older, tireder.*]

TRINO. Father!

DON SEVERO. Yes. It's happened. The Government's order of dispossession. The blow has fallen.

PILAR. [*To herself.*] At last. [*Lifting her head.*] When do we have to leave?

DON SEVERO. At once. This afternoon. Or tonight.

PILAR. [*Rising.*] So much to do. Does mother know?

DON SEVERO. Not yet. It's hard to—will you tell her, Pilar!

PILAR. [*After a moment, seeing how hard it will be.*] Yes. I'll tell her. Poor mother! This, too.

TRINO. I can't pretend to be sad about it. I thought it would never come!

DON SEVERO. [*Reminded.*] There's more, Trino . . . [*Looking at the letter.*] The government knows your interest and concern for the welfare of the Indians. "Your son, Trinidad," it says. "He will report at once to the office of Sr. del Rio in Mérida, to assist in the partitioning of all *haciendas* in eastern Yucatán."

TRINO. Father!

DON SEVERO. Also—"An Indian boy on the *hacienda* of *Techoh*,"— Beto, it means. "Will render aid and advice in the correct dismemberment and reapportionment of the lands of the *hacienda* of *Techoh*, where he now resides."

TRINO. But what—how did they know?

DON SEVERO. They asked me for suggestions.

TRINO. I could kiss you for this!

PILAR. [*Knowing the answer.*] You'll do what they tell you, Trino? You're on their side?

TRINO. Can you doubt it?

PILAR. No. [*Hunting something to cling to.*] Was there no other mail, father—word from Chela? Fernando?

DON SEVERO. Yes. A letter from Fernando.

PILAR. What does he say? Let me have it.

DON SEVERO. [*Reluctantly.*] Hardly anything.

PILAR. Is he doing well, is he all right?

DON SEVERO. [*Lifting the letter, skimming through it.*] "Bitten with flies, lice . . . the putrid food. . . . The steaming unbearable heat of the *chicle* jungle. . . . Ninon is pregnant. . . . I lie in my hammock at night, cursing . . ."

[*He stops.*]

PILAR. Yes.

DON SEVERO. "Cursing the blood that drove us to this . . . cursing myself for being so low as to blame anyone else for my weakness and my despair." [PILAR *bows her head, goes. A moment of a feeling silence. His voice low.*] Fernando—my first-born son. He was to be the solace and the comfort of my old age.

TRINO. [*Gently.*] I know, father.

[DON SEVERO *lifts his head, looks at* TRINO *and* BETO.]

DON SEVERO. [*Softly.*] My sons. [BETO *looks at him.*] You don't hate me, do you, Beto?

BETO. No.

DON SEVERO. I'm proud of you both. [*Quietly, simply, with deep feeling, but without self-pity.*] Being a father is a lonely thing. He is halfway between past and future. Weary of the past, and fearful of the future. And the present is empty.

[TRINO *comes over, puts his hand on his father's shoulder, in unspoken sympathy. After a moment,* BETO *does the same. Tears flood up into* DON SEVERO'S *eyes.* PILAR *comes in, quiet and gentle.*]

PILAR. I've come to apologize to Beto.

BETO. [*Sincerely.*] It doesn't matter. Don't think of it.

PILAR. [*Gratefully.*] Thank you, Beto. [*Turning to her father—gentle and compassionate.*] Father—your son.

DON SEVERO. Yes.

PILAR. My brother.

TRINO. You admit it?

PILAR. [*Her voice very low.*] Yes. What else can I do? [*She looks from one to the other. She feels the strong and poignant bond between the three, she feels her loneliness, her inability to enter into that magic. Like a little child—wistful and alone.*] I've interrupted! You don't want me. I'll go.

[*Her lips are trembling. Tears are welling up in her eyes. She goes. . . .*]

CURTAIN

Scene Eight

DOÑA CANDITA'S *bedroom again, that night. The room is stripped for departure, except for the altar, a chair, the pictures, some things piled on the rumpled great bed. The room is spottily lighted, with ominous shadows at the corners, and sudden splashes of light from the kerosene lamps. The radio is still there, and a voice is coming over it.*
DOÑA CANDITA *and* PILAR *are listening, breathless and tense.*
DOÑA CANDITA *is dressed for traveling.* PILAR'S *clothes are severe—worthy of tragedy.*

VOICE. [*Tense and dynamic.*] Attention, *señoras y señores!* News comes of a series of further tragedies in the state of Yucatán. The partitioning of the *haciendas* has begun there, as decreed by the federal government. On the *hacienda* of Don Ernesto Solis, the Indians, inflamed to passion against *Señor* Solis for his cruelties and abuses over the many years of their servitude, seized tonight the moment of their coming to power to raid the Solis house and to massacre all people within. The dead: Don Ernesto, his wife, his young daughter. The older son escaped with his life, but on the road to Mérida was ambushed and left in the road for dead. He will recover.
DOÑA CANDITA. Poor Doña María! In the old days, I knew her.
VOICE. Also at the *hacienda* of the Three Towers—the dead: all members of the family of Don Fausto Pavon. That is all. We take you now to our studios.
[*The radio switches to dim music.*]
DOÑA CANDITA. Pilar—we are to be murdered.
PILAR. No, no, *mamacita!* For cruelties and abuses, the radio says. We've not been cruel.
DOÑA CANDITA. [*With a touch of prescience.*] It's not what we've done—it's what we are. [*There is a burst of singing, loud and throbbing with triumph from the Indians outside, ending with crazy shouts.*] You hear? [*She hurries to a window, looks out.*] They are drinking the cane rum and shouting. From there it is but a step to— [*She closes the window, bolts it. The other remains open.*] We must fly, Pilar. I have left my room to the last. Do finish for me, Pilar. The pictures—there's a box there to put them in. The things on the bed.
PILAR. [*Quietly, absorbed.*] My heart's not in it. It's strange.
DOÑA CANDITA. Please, please, Pilar, stir yourself!
PILAR. Yes, mother.

DOÑA CANDITA. I must see what your father is doing. He is so slow. He must see that the carriage is ready. The cart is nearly full already. A thousand things to think of! [*There are shots off, more shouts.*] You hear—?

PILAR. They are only celebrating our dispossession. Don't be afraid, little *mamsie*.

[*But her face shows that she is beginning to be afraid herself. She goes quickly to begin packing the pictures.*]

DOÑA CANDITA. No. Perhaps you are right.

[*She hurries out.* PILAR *looks about anxiously with some fear showing in her face. Then she takes a picture from its hook.*]

VOICE. [*Radio.*] And now, ladies and gentlemen—our beloved songster from Yucatán— [PILAR *listens.*] La Señorita Chelita Crespo. A transcription.[1]

PILAR. Chela.

[*The song is in Spanish, common and haunting, such as* PILAR *heard earlier.* PILAR *turns to switch off the radio impatiently, but she can't. She throws the picture on the bed, and stands listening. The door opens before the song is finished and* CHELA *comes in. She has changed. Her eyes burn with a febrile fire. She has been hurt, and is hard with the hardness of the hurt. But there is a rude undespairing power in her. Her clothes are flamboyant.*]

PILAR. [*In astonishment.*] Chela! [*She looks from Chela to the radio just finishing Chela's song, in bewilderment.*] But Chela—

CHELA. I'm not a ghost. It's a recording. I made it a week ago.

PILAR. [*Going to her, her arms out.*] Chela, Chela, my darling Chela! [*She takes her in her arms.* CHELA *does not respond.*] What's the matter?

CHELA. Matter? Here I am at home, good God, all is love—what could be the matter? *Nada, nada*, little chicken! Where's *mama?*

PILAR. Somewhere—probably in father's room. Oh, Chela, we've lost the *hacienda!* We're running away.

CHELA. For your lives, I gather. Yes, I heard all about it. What a shame! [*But her tones have contempt in them.*] How can you stand it?

PILAR. I don't know. I don't know how I can. And what a home-coming for you.

CHELA. Homecoming! Home is where the *chapeau* is, where hangs the bright *sombrero!* And how do you like *mine?* [*She indicates her hat.* PILAR *is silent.*] You don't like it. [*Viciously.*]

---

1 An electrical transcription: a recording for radio broadcast.

What the hell do I care what you like!

PILAR. [*Quietly.*] You've changed.

CHELA. Thank God for that! Did you like the song? [*No answer.*] Did you?

PILAR. Yes.

CHELA. Hypocrite! No nice girl sings songs like that—and you say you like it—! You're a liar, Pilar.

PILAR. [*Staring at her.*] Your eyes are strange.

CHELA. [*Panicky, turning away.*] Leave me alone!

PILAR. Chela! Look at me.

CHELA. No, no!

PILAR. It's *marihuana!*

CHELA. It's not true!

PILAR. Your eyes show it!

CHELA. [*Giving in—her voice hard.*] So what?

PILAR. How could you?

CHELA. [*Flaring out.*] What do you expect? I'm a working girl, see. The hours face you—and the men clamor for you and paw at you as you pass. And fight over you! But you go home by yourself if you can. But you can't! You remember what you must do to get ahead in the chivalrous Latin world! And you go crazy, or you take to something. *Marihuana* for mine. Have one yourself! [*She shoots out a package.*] It'll solve your troubles, the stars will sing! [*At* PILAR'S *revulsion.*] Don't be so damned pure and mighty. You've got something—your family about you—Cuco—love—! What have I got?

PILAR. [*Touched.*] Poor Chela.

CHELA. [*Recovering.*] Don't worry about me. I'll get along. [*Conviction growing in her.*] It's life anyway—it's what I asked for. I'll get through this. I'll win out. I'll be happy someday. I know it, I know it deep!

[TRINO *comes in. He is dressed for going away, has come to his mother's room to say goodbye.*]

TRINO. Chela!

CHELA. Trino, Trino darling!

[*She runs to him, clings to him.*]

TRINO. I didn't know you were—

CHELA. [*Brokenly.*] Trino! Take me to mother.

TRINO. Yes, baby, yes. We'll find her.

[*He takes her out. As* PILAR *watches, a dark shape passes the window.*]

PILAR. [*With a start of fear.*] Who's there?

BETO. [*Appearing in the door.*] Beto, Pilar.

PILAR. What are you skulking about for?

BETO. Nothing.

PILAR. We've been thrown out—the land, everything is yours. Aren't you satisfied? Why do they send you here to spy on us, and gloat over us?

BETO. I am responsible for your safety, that's all.

PILAR. [*Her breath drawn in quickly.*] Safety? Are we in danger then?

BETO. I don't think so.

PILAR. [*Sharp with fear.*] You're lying! They intend to kill us! Why don't you say so! On the radio—we heard it—the butchery—! [*Her voice dim—and husky with panic.*] Trino, Trino!

BETO. [*Stopping her.*] Please, please, Pilar. Trino asked me to watch. That's all. Don't be frightened.

PILAR. [*Weakly, recovering.*] Beto, my nerves are on edge. Everything is— I'm all right now. I didn't mean to speak to you like that.

BETO. It doesn't matter.

[*Trino appears at the door, comes in.*]

TRINO. [*Puzzled.*] What is it?

BETO. Trino, I—

[*He goes out.*]

TRINO. Chela has changed.

PILAR. [*After a brief moment, struggling to sound calm.*] Yes.

TRINO. I never expected to see her again.

PILAR. Little Chela. Creeping home for comfort. We'll make it up to her.

TRINO. Didn't she tell you?

PILAR. What?

TRINO. She hasn't come creeping home. Not her! She was about to sail for New York. She only came to see us—Mother really—in case she never saw her again.

PILAR. Oh.

TRINO. She's to star in a music show on Broadway. Her name in lights! She's got what she wanted—most of it.

PILAR. [*Dimly, to herself, hurt.*] She didn't tell me.

TRINO. I've said goodbye to them. I must go now.

PILAR. Must you, Trino?

TRINO. I should have gone this afternoon. They're waiting for me.

PILAR. Yes. Trino—you wouldn't leave us here, if you thought we were in danger, would you?

TRINO. Of course not. What foolishness! [*Gently.*] Father's got a place for you in town. It's hard—I know—I'm sorry.

PILAR. [*Without acrimony.*] But you're glad too, Trino.

TRINO. Yes. It's right—what's happened. I know it is. The others are to have their chance now—as we had ours, without earning it.

PILAR. And what will they do with power, tell me that.

TRINO. The Mayans have always accepted authority from above, meekly. Now there's no authority above them—for the first time in centuries. There'll be abuses at first. It's inevitable. The *politico* crooks and dispossessed *hacendados*[1] will scheme their guts out to get back what they've lost to ignorant Indians, accustomed only to the labor of the body. But the idea of the right to power goes to starving cells quickly. And it won't die so easily in their veins. *They'll learn to fight.*

PILAR. And to win?

TRINO. And to win.

PILAR. You believe—and aren't troubled. I believe, too—they have no right to do this to us. But they do. Does it mean I'm wrong?

TRINO. *I* think so.

PILAR. What star were you born under that let you see what was to be?

TRINO. [*Offended, but quiet.*] Pilar. I didn't see what "was to be." I'm not on the right side for my own good.

PILAR. I'm sorry.

TRINO. It's all right.

PILAR. [*With wonder.*] You're gentle and kind now—even to me. Why?

TRINO. I don't feel sorry for myself anymore. The world moves somewhere—with pain for so many. I haven't time to think of myself—there's work to do.

PILAR. Would you have learned this in New York?

TRINO. Perhaps not. I'm grateful to you for bringing us here. [*Softly, with tenderness.*] Pilar. My good is your downfall—I see that.

PILAR. I can fall. I can die.

TRINO. [*With quiet strength.*] Don't die. *Live.* Goodbye, Pilar. [*He takes her in his arms.*]

PILAR. Goodbye.

[*He goes out.* PILAR *is deeply moved, thrust along a road she can't see the end of, and no help, and no guidance. A burst of shouting, more shots ring out from outside. Laughter, wild and high.* CUCO *comes in, haggard and quiet.* PILAR *goes quickly to him, into his arms.*]

---

1 Owners of large estates.

PILAR. Cuco, Cuco darling—hold me, hold me close! Something dreadful is coming—and I can't see what it is!

[*Something queerly unearthly, close to hysteria, is in her voice.*]

CUCO. Pilar.

PILAR. There's a mist around me, everywhere I look—shapes of horror thrusting up with menacing eyes. Chela's come back—she hates me still—she looks at me. Fernando's lost in the jungle, dying of bitterness—his pitiful pregnant wife—Trino's gone away forever to make our ruin complete—till the last of the Tueros and the Crespos and all such people are slaughtered—slung in the grave! What's to come now? I can't see, but I know it's there. What is it? I can't see, but I know it's there, I—

CUCO. Quiet, quiet!

PILAR. [*Going away, stumbling into the chair, her hand at her head, wearily, struggling for control.*] Oh—

CUCO. [*In a strange hard voice.*] Your mother told me to help you. Let's get at it.

PILAR. Yes, the pictures.

[*He goes toward them.*]

CUCO. Yes, the pictures. The pretty pictures.

[*He jerks one savagely from its hook.*]

PILAR. [*Noticing.*] What is it, Cuco?

CUCO. Nothing.

PILAR. Yes, tell me. Something.

[*She goes toward him, throwing off her dismay.*]

CUCO. Pilar, you'll marry me now, won't you? At once.

PILAR. As soon as we're settled in town.

CUCO. [*With savage insistence.*] "As soon, as soon!" I'm sick of it. I've heard it for the last time. It'll be now, I tell you—tonight. *I'm* giving the orders.

PILAR. You have no right to talk to—

CUCO. I have every right! For months I begged you to marry me—I pleaded with you on my knees. It took you months to say "Yes"—and then you began again with your god-damned "soon." Why was this, why?

PILAR. [*Alarmed at his mood.*] You know. You know!

CUCO. All the time you loved me, wanted me. You *did* love me, didn't you?

PILAR. Yes, I did. I have for a long time.

CUCO. But you kept putting me off.

PILAR. I was putting myself off, too. Don't you think I'm human?

CUCO. [*Agonized, the words pouring out in his desperation.*] I don't know. You don't know what it is to be a man. A man in love—tantalized with "soon, soon." Till his whole body's an aching torture, and there's no sleep for him, and no help for him from the one who ought to help him. Till he can't stand it, and he roams the streets, and meets in the dark places whatever fate lies in wait for him. Or he goes to the houses, with their hearty wenches shipped from Vera Cruz or worn-out mulattoes from the racket in Mexico. The promise of peace! It's me I'm talking about—me!

PILAR. No, no!

CUCO. Straight from the arms of my beloved—to women who can be paid—women glad of a little money to take away the fever that's destroying me!

PILAR. [Sick with revulsion.] No, no, Cuco, don't tell me!

CUCO. Ten long months you've done this to me, and you say "Don't tell me!"

PILAR. Please!

CUCO. How do you like it, eh? Sweet, isn't it? Well, have a little hell-fire yourself for a change. Stew in it—as I do! I ought to kill you!

[He throws himself into a chair, weak with fury at her and at himself.]

PILAR. [After a horrible moment.] Take me. If it means anything to you.

CUCO. Pilar—what're you—!

PILAR. Take me.

CUCO. You don't understand. I'm filthy. I've rolled in the mires of women—any woman—white, yellow, black, any woman I could find—night after night—!

PILAR. I don't care. Take me.

CUCO. Pilar! You don't know what you're saying!

PILAR. Yes, I know. What does it matter? Take me. I'm yours.

CUCO. You don't mean it, you can't!

PILAR. Yes. I didn't know, I didn't know.

[He runs to the door, bars it.]

PILAR. What're you—no, Cuco—not here—!

CUCO. Here! Now!

PILAR. The others! They'll come in!

CUCO. They've gone!

PILAR. Gone!

CUCO. Yes. I told them I'd bring you with me. They haven't waited. We're alone.

PILAR. No, Cuco, no! This room. This is mother's room. Her things are here. Her altar. Her pictures.

CUCO. Pictures!

[*He smashes one across the room.*]

PILAR. They're watching us!

CUCO. They don't see you. They don't know you—they're dead!

PILAR. Their eyes are on us—ashamed, accusing. I couldn't!

CUCO. They don't know you.

PILAR. They know me.

CUCO. [*With bitter contempt.*] And *I* know you. *Now* I know you! These—these are between us. Not only the living—the dead!

PILAR. Yes, yes!

CUCO. I might have known. It isn't to be. You're free—free to lick the feet of the dead—who don't give a damn! They *don't!* The dead have betrayed you! And the living don't want you. Your family doesn't. *Nor do I!* I wouldn't have you now.

PILAR. Cuco!

CUCO. I can see your fate. No one in Mérida will speak to you, you know that. They'll say I refused to marry you, because I had you before marriage. Josefa will see to that. You won't be able to stand it! Ninon and her mother couldn't—what the tongues did to them. You can't either. You'll have a walking death, whispers always in your ears! Your last chance is gone. Your grave is dug for you.

PILAR. [*Her voice dead.*] Yes. You've said it all. Get out.

CUCO. [*Weakening.*] Pilar!

PILAR. Get out!

[CUCO *goes to the door, unlocks it, opens it, turns.*]

CUCO. I can't leave you!

PILAR. You will leave me.

CUCO. [*Agonized.*] Say it—I'm a toad, a snake, the lowest— disgusting, crawling—!

PILAR. You're a Latin, Cuco. A high-born aristocratic Yucatecan— the privileged, the inheritor of all good—the ultimate dream, the triumph of the blood. [*Her voice shaken with realization.*] *Like me*—Cuco. Save yourself if you can. Get out before it's too late.

CUCO. What will you do?

[*He goes out. After a moment* PILAR *goes to the bed, crawls up in it, a tiny stricken figure on the great bed, shaken with sobs.* DON SEVERO *and* DOÑA CANDITA *come in.*]

DOÑA CANDITA. [*In alarm.*] Pilar. Cuco said he'd bring you. I was worried. Come, child. Hurry, hurry!

PILAR. [*Lifting herself up, wearily.*] I'm not going.

DOÑA CANDITA. Pilar.

PILAR. Leave me, mother.

DOÑA CANDITA. The saints in heaven—we can't leave you here!

[A desperate resolve is growing in PILAR. It is in her face clearly.]

PILAR. You must!

DON SEVERO. Pilar—what kind of insanity—!

DOÑA CANDITA. You poor baby, what is it?

PILAR. Father. Long ago in New York—I called you a failure. Have you ever forgiven me for that?

DON SEVERO. I haven't forgotten it.

PILAR. Then you can leave me. And never reproach yourself. Forget me. I don't exist.

DON SEVERO. I don't understand.

PILAR. Cuco will tell you. I can't go with you.

DOÑA CANDITA. [Seeing the firmness in PILAR.] I'll stay here with you. I won't leave you.

PILAR. [Tortured.] No, little mother—it's best, I know it's best!

DON SEVERO. Candita.

DOÑA CANDITA. Yes, Severo.

DON SEVERO. Come with me.

DOÑA CANDITA. How can I!

DON SEVERO. Leave her if she wants to stay. Come!

DOÑA CANDITA. No, no!

DON SEVERO. Candita!

DOÑA CANDITA. Don't make me.

DON SEVERO. Do as I tell you.

DOÑA CANDITA. [Weary and sad.] Yes, Severo. [Her old voice dim.] I've bent too long to the will of man. I'm too old to change . . . too old. [To PILAR.] Forgive me. [Her eyes go about the room—choked, almost inaudible.] The room. You were born here.

[They go out. The radio music, which has been playing all this time, comes surging up, crowded with despair—but with a desperate hope beating in it. There are scraps of singing from the Indians, and some shouts. BETO comes into the doorway, a lantern in his hand.]

BETO. I've come to light your way.

PILAR. [Like one drugged, the words meaningless to her.] Light my way?

BETO. The others have left you. I've saddled a horse for you. This lantern will show you the path.

PILAR. Beto. No, no, listen to me! [She runs to him.] Let them kill me.

BETO. They won't kill you, Pilar. They have the fields, the yielding earth. All life is before them. Why should they kill you?

PILAR. They will! They must! I don't want to live!

BETO. They're celebrating. They're happy. There's no hate in them.

PILAR. I've seen them turn from singing to murder. In a moment it happens! That night at the hemp mill! The *machete.* One clean stroke. Turn them against me. Let them kill me! Do this for me.

BETO. No.

PILAR. Please, Beto—I beg you. On my knees, I beg you!

BETO. No, Pilar.

PILAR. You're my brother. You've got to help me!

BETO. I can't.

PILAR. [*Desperately persuasive.*] Yes, Beto! You're gifted, you're wise. You see things the way they are. Understand this, then. Not till I die—not till all such people as myself are dead—we, the ones who've lorded it over the weak and lowly—not till all of us are in the grave can a stricken people sing again, be free again! *You must see this!*

BETO. [*Reluctantly.*] It may be so.

PILAR. It is so, it's the truth! I've looked too long at the past, tried to bring back the past, the way it was. That's *me.* I can't change. My way is death, not life. Make them see it! They can't allow me to live. I'm their enemy. Tell them!

BETO. [*Throwing off her persuasiveness.*] No! I will tell them nothing. Come, you must go! [*With a quick nervous glance round.*] At once! [*A wild and terrible cry bursts from the Indians, menacing and terrifying.*] I didn't want to tell you—it's dangerous!

PILAR. Ah.

BETO. There's drunkenness there, a fever—any moment something may happen, they may begin to—

[*He stops.*]

PILAR. [*In a thrumming excitement, knowing the answer.*] May what, Beto?

BETO. They may break loose—their passion, their anger, their lust! No one could protect you! Come with me, quickly—now!

PILAR. [*Sensing what to do now, controlled, hard, quiet, deliberate—her voice as of old low and imperious.*] Go to the rail where the horse is tied.

BETO. Pilar!

PILAR. Go! Wait for me there.

BETO. I don't dare leave you.

PILAR. [*Sharply authoritative.*] Do as I say! I am still your master.

Go. Wait for me. Do this.

BETO. [*After a moment of effort, in which her dominating will wins.*]
As you say, Pilar. I am accustomed to obey. It's too early yet
for me to change. [*Lifting the lantern.*] This lantern . . .

PILAR. [*Firmly, sensing the symbol, seeing what the end is to be.*] Keep
it. I shan't need it. There's light enough.

[*Quietly he goes, turns along the* corredor, *passing the open window,
disappears. The voices of the Indians surge up, loud again, uncontrolled.*
PILAR *watches* BETO'S *departure carefully, holding on to her high
and desperate courage. Turning, she notices a few pictures still on the
walls—those pictures that are her past, the past of her race—all she has
held dear. She moves to them, takes them down in a quick movement,
stares at them. Painfully, she drags herself away from their hypnotic
and weakening influence, and throws them crashing into the middle
of the room. Now she turns, faces straight back to where the firelight
is leaping, and the ghostly and menacing shadows move and cry out.
Quietly, she moves straight through the door, straight toward her fate,
her immolation. Angry voices accost her—jibing, earthy voices. More
shots. At the same moment, the muted music of the radio dims down,
and a voice is distinguishable.*]

RADIO VOICE. . . . *Buenos noches, señoras y señores.* You are listening
to the Voice of Mexico!

[*The music swells up, the triumphant concluding bars brassy and
stirring.*]

CURTAIN
THE END

THE CREAM IN THE WELL

People

MRS. SAWTERS
BINA
JULIE
MR. SAWTERS
OPAL DUNHAM
GARD DUNHAM
CLABE
BLOCKY LOCKHART

Scenes

Act One
SCENE 1. Living room of the Sawters farmhouse on the shores of Big Lake, near Verdigris Switch,[1] Indian Territory. Late afternoon of a Spring day in 1906.
SCENE 2. Clabe's bedroom. That night, about ten o'clock.
SCENE 3. The same. Near dawn the next day.

Act Two
SCENE 1. The living room again. Mid-afternoon. Thanksgiving day, the same year.
SCENE 2. The same. Later that night.

---

1 Verdigris, sometimes called Verdigris Switch, is a town in Rogers County, Oklahoma, less than 10 miles southwest of Riggs's hometown, Claremore. Several characters call it "the Switch" later in the play.

Act One

Scene 1

The living room of the Sawters farmhouse on the shores of Big Lake, near Verdigris Switch, Indian Territory, on a Spring afternoon in 1906. Sunset fades as the scene progresses and dark comes gradually over the land.

The room is typically comfortable, massive and ugly, crowded with the furnishings and feeling of the period. On the walls are framed enlargements of family portraits in color—especially one of Clabe, the son of the household, in the uniform of the U.S. Navy. The chairs are heavy and somber, most of the rugs are rag, the clock is ornate, the kerosene lamps are gaudily painted ones, the organ is complex and full of mirrors, the rock fireplace generous, the built-in cupboard roomy.

In one wall, a door goes to the dining room; opposite it are windows and a glass door which goes outside to the boat landing. At the back, double sliding doors are pushed aside, and a few steps of the stair that leads upward from the hall can be seen.

All the necessities of living are gathered together in this big, tall-ceilinged, well-built house, for the place is far from anything approaching civilization. The little general store and post-office at Verdigris Switch, two miles away, is only a slight contact, parsimonious and inelegant, with the great world.

BINA, *the younger daughter of the household, is playing something doleful on the organ. She is awkward and likeable, she is the ugly duckling. Her speech is loosely colloquial and ungrammatical, as is her father's. The other members of the family speak a more orthodox English, with practically no flavoring of the backwoods.*

MRS. SAWTERS *comes in from the hall. She is in appearance a gentle enough woman—but she is sardonic—and knowing. Her talk is apt to be barbed with puzzling inner meanings, with unpredictable and subtle ironies. Her face is flat and strong. She has long ears, pierced and ringed, a sharp and dominant nose.*

MRS. SAWTERS. Mercy, what a racket, Bina. Thought you were in the kitchen.

BINA. Everything's done, Maw. Jist about. The pig's in the oven and pretty as a picture.

MRS. SAWTERS. I can imagine.

BINA. And I already finished the pies—first thing this mornin'. Two kinds.

MRS. SAWTERS. Two?

BINA. Apple and cherry. Take your pick. Set down, for heaven's sake, Maw. You been at it since daylight.

MRS. SAWTERS. [*Sitting.*] There's a weariness in my bones. [*With a deep pleasant sigh.*] Ah me! Sunday's a lonesome day. Always hated it. [*Then noticing* BINA'S *noisy efforts.*] Gloomy piece you're playing.

BINA. [*Cheerfully.*] I feel so *gloomy!*

MRS. SAWTERS. Lands, when you've lived with gloom as long as *I* have—

BINA. You? Pshaw.

MRS. SAWTERS. Yes, me. You get used to it. [*With a cackle.*] Or you'd better.

BINA. You just have to keep busy or you— [*But she shuts this off, turning her mind away.*] What does Vox Humana mean?

MRS. SAWTERS. The human voice. It's Latin.

BINA. Imagine knowin' that!

MRS. SAWTERS. Oh, I went to school, child.

BINA. Ain't it funny, I never could learn?

MRS. SAWTERS. Every one has his own talents, I expect. Yours is cooking. Poor child, you never took the opportunity your sister and brother did for making your brain work. That is, by schooling, I mean.

BINA. [*Still cheerful.*] It wouldn't a-worked, nohow. Julie's got the brains around here. Julie—and you.

MRS. SAWTERS. Oh, don't count on me. I'm pretty rusty, I'm afraid. Way off here in the wilds. Brains rust, you know that?

BINA. You mean like a plough-share?[1]

MRS. SAWTERS. Like anything else you don't use. Use 'em and use 'em. Brains, I'm talking about. Till they sparkle. Till they shine. Yes, siree.

BINA. Uh-huh. [*Thoughtfully.*] I'd ruther be a rusty old plough-share for me.

MRS. SAWTERS. I think you would.

BINA. Settin' out in the rain. *Or* the *sun.* A plough-share don't worry—but takes the weather like it comes. [*This seems to remind her.*] Julie's so *nervous!* Always sump'n. She tires me out.

MRS. SAWTERS. You oughtn't to let her worry you.

BINA. Orten't to—but do.

---

1 The lower blade of a plow, for cutting the furrow, or depression, in a field.

MRS. SAWTERS. People walled up in a house together are bound to get on each other's nerves.

BINA. They don't get on yours.

MRS. SAWTERS. Laws, child—I haven't got a nerve in me. Except my teeth.

[JULIE, *eldest of the Sawters children, comes down the stairs, carrying a pitcher. She is in her late twenties. Striking and dark, she has inherited something from her mother. There is power here, a nervous but self-assured power and arrogance. But something is gnawing at her, something darkly troubling and dangerous. She, too, however, like her mother, is full of a deep, controlled cynicism; she usually means much more than she says. In one continuous motion, she has crossed the room while they watch, and gone out the door on to the boat landing. The gentle lapping of water can be heard while the door is open.*]

MRS. SAWTERS. [*Calling after her.*] Julie! [JULIE *appears.*] You want something?

JULIE. A pitcherful of lake water.

MRS. SAWTERS. [*Sardonically.*] Well, dip it up. Don't fall in.

JULIE. [*Coolly.*] I think I can manage.

[*She goes out again.*]

BINA. Ain't hardly a ripple on the lake today. Smooth as glass. [*Curiously.*] What does she want lake water for? [MRS. SAWTERS *shrugs expressively.*] What's she been doin' all afternoon?

MRS. SAWTERS. Oh, you know Julie. Her nose stuck in a book, I imagine. While we've been getting things ready for tonight.

BINA. She's been in her room doin' sump'n.

MRS. SAWTERS. Or nothing.

BINA. And Clabe's room, too. I heared her in there. Up and down. Talkin' to herself.

MRS. SAWTERS. Talking, anyway.

BINA. Talkin' to herself. Who else? Nobody's been there since Clabe went away. Except to clean.

MRS. SAWTERS. Julie goes there most every day of the week. Sundays, too. Didn't you know?

BINA. What on earth for?

MRS. SAWTERS. [*Who isn't telling all she knows.*] I wouldn't care to speculate on Julie and her goings-on.

BINA. [*Coming to her Mother.*] Maw. When is Clabe comin' home?

MRS. SAWTERS. Does any woman know what her children aim to do? I don't—and never did. I don't pretend to read the future. The past is deep enough for me, the Lord knows. Your brother'll come home when he gets ready, or he'll stay in the navy, and roust about till he's eighty-two and paralytic, I couldn't say. Anyway, it's immaterial to me.

BINA. I don't see how we'll ever—!

[*But she doesn't finish.*]

MRS. SAWTERS. Ever what?

BINA. [*Bursting out.*] They's jist too much to do around here for Paw! Why, with all us kids' Cherokee allotments,[1] and what land you and Paw own, this farm's might' nigh half a section. It's jist too much!

MRS. SAWTERS. [*With easy jocularity.*] I never heard any part-Indians[2] complain before about being given too much land.

BINA. Well, I wish the old gover'ment would jist take part of it back. Or I wish to goodness Clabe had his belly full of the navy by this time and would come on home and pitch in and help Paw out.

MRS. SAWTERS. [*With her light and maddening mockery.*] Why, Bina, I never saw you so intense.

BINA. Oh, it jist makes me mad! What'd he ever go away for in the first place!

[JULIE *has come in with her pitcher of water.*]

JULIE. [*Pausing.*] Who?

BINA. Clabe.

JULIE. [*With that slightly superior, but infinitely subtle and secret scorn.*] Maybe he had to.

BINA. You *know* he didn't have to!

JULIE. [*Smiling.*] Do I? It must be wonderful to read people's minds—to be able to tell them what they know and what they don't know!

[*She goes toward the stairs.*]

BINA. [*Controlling her annoyance.*] What you been doin' upstairs in your room so long?

JULIA. Primping.

BINA. Primping! I don't see why. Jist because Gard and Opal are comin' to six o'clock dinner! The Dunhams ain't nobody to primp for.

JULIE. I'm not primping for the Dunhams.

BINA. Who then?

JULIE. [*Cool and precise.*] Myself.

---

1 For allotment, see Preface, pp. 11, 14; Introduction, pp. 18, 26.
2 A person with Indigenous and other ancestry. The "jocular" Mrs. Sawters uses it to describe, not to demean, her family.

[*She disappears up the stairs.*]

MRS. SAWTERS. [*Slapping her thigh appreciatively.*] I'll bet she is, too!

BINA. Maw, you don't reckon she's sweet on Gard Dunham, do you?

MRS. SAWTERS. Sweet on a married man?

BINA. Oh no, she wouldn't be, him married and all.

MRS. SAWTERS. Wouldn't she, child?

BINA. Naw. But *he* could be sweet on *her*—like he used to be 'fore he married Opal.

MRS. SAWTERS. He could be, yes. That's possible.

BINA. Oh, he was sparkin'[1] her all right, all right. I heared him. He said she was the only woman for him, and how she stirred him all up, and tied him in hard knots and—What'd he mean by that?

MRS. SAWTERS. I wouldn't care to speculate.

BINA. I guess he didn't mean a thing, for right after that he up and married Opal 'fore you could say "Jack Robinson."[2] The whole thing jist puzzles me.

MRS. SAWTERS. I expect it does—and I expect it always will. You're a sweet child, Bina—your own mother admits it—but—

BINA. I ain't bright, is that it?

MRS. SAWTERS. Oh, you're bright enough—in your own way. But why don't you stick to what's easy—and keep the wrinkles out of your forehead? What *are* you scowling for, anyway?

BINA. Got up on the wrong side of the bed, I guess. [*Quietly, but with a rush of uncontrolled feeling.*] Maw, if I was to leave here and go off some'eres—what would you do?

MRS. SAWTERS. Go? Where?

BINA. Oh, Claremore, Chelsea, Tahlequah[3]—anywhere. I know I'm ignorant, and you're ashamed of me, and I ain't never had a feller, and I look like sump'n drug out from under a rock and—!

MRS. SAWTERS. Bina! For heaven's sake!

BINA. Won't you let me get up and get out of here? Get

---

1 Slang for courting, or pursuing someone romantically.

2 Very quickly. The idiom dates back to the eighteenth century in England.

3 Towns in Rogers County, Oklahoma. Chelsea is about 20 miles northeast of Claremore; Tahlequah, the capital of the Cherokee Nation in Cherokee County, is approximately 60 miles southeast of Claremore.

educated, see things. I don't want to be a disgrace to you all my life!

MRS. SAWTERS. Why, Bina, I thought you liked it here, your own home, your family. I thought you never wanted to leave. You could have, you know. Gone to the Seminary[1] when Julie did. We couldn't make you.

BINA. Oh, I don't know what's come over me! Shakin' aigers[2] or sump'n.

MRS. SAWTERS. [*Gently.*] Lonesome?

BINA. No, not lonesome. Afraid.

MRS. SAWTERS. Of what?

BINA. I don't wanta die an old maid! It don't make sense, it's jist crazy, it's—

MRS. SAWTERS. [*Amused, but sympathetic.*] It certainly is. Here, get hold of yourself! Would you want someone to see you like that? Julie'll be coming downstairs again any minute.

[*That will bring her to her senses, and* MRS. SAWTERS *knows it. It does.*]

BINA. I'm all right.

MRS. SAWTERS. You act plumb hysterical. I always thought you were the one I could count on.

BINA. You can count on me, Maw. Sure you can. A minute ago I didn't know how I could last out the summer. I could a-died dead and been happy. Stuck in my coffin with forget-me-nots in my hair. Lawsee! I better see to things in the kitchen.

MRS. SAWTERS. It's a good idea!

BINA. Drat the time! It oughta be basted—and here I set! The pig, I mean. [*At a noise at the front door.*] There must be Paw.

MRS. SAWTERS. I didn't hear him drive up.

BINA. I hope he remembered to get the sugar. Paw! For the cake icin'! [*She sticks her head round into the hall.*] Did you get the sugar?

MR. SAWTERS' VOICE. In the kitchen. A hundred pounds. That do you?

[*He can be heard coming along the hall.*]

BINA. [*Flying toward the dining room.*] That oughta be enough. [*She snickers.*] For a little *bitty* cake.

---

1 The Cherokee Nation built the Cherokee Female Seminary near Tahlequah in 1889. After statehood, it became Northeastern State Normal School, now Northeastern State University.
2 Presumably a corruption of ague, a fever characterized by chills and paroxysms, sometimes symptomatic of malaria.

[*She hurries out.* MR. SAWTERS *comes in, a Tulsa paper several days old under his arm, and makes for his accustomed chair. He is a big, kindly man, once gusty and powerful. But the years are getting him down, and he is a little bewildered by the change. He is abstracted now, brooding on something.*]

MRS. SAWTERS. What's new at the Switch, Dave?

MR. SAWTERS. Nuthin' much. Oh, yes. They're puttin' on another train on the Frisco.[1] Comes in at three in the mornin'.

MRS. SAWTERS. That's two trains a day now. Must be a boom on.

MR. SAWTERS. Country's openin' up fast. Gonna join the Union, they say. Paper says.

MRS. SAWTERS. That'll just ruin everything.

MR. SAWTERS. No, I don't reckon it'll do that. It's bound to come. Lot's of people rootin' for it. Jine up the two territories together is the idy. Only trouble is what to call it—Indianokla or Indiahoma.[2] Reg'lar knock-down drag-out about it.

MRS. SAWTERS. Well, there's lots of land out here.

MR. SAWTERS. And lots of people back east 'thout dirt enough to spit on.

MRS. SAWTERS. The march of progress, I guess you call it.

MR. SAWTERS. [*Abstractedly.*] Yeah. [*Then revealing what's really on his mind, handing her a letter.*] Here's a letter.

MRS. SAWTERS. From Clabe? [MR. SAWTERS *just nods.*] What's he say?

MR. SAWTERS. He ain't comin' home.

MRS. SAWTERS. [*Beginning to look at it.*] Oh. You mean this spring?

MR. SAWTERS. Nor this summer, nor never. He says it there.

MRS. SAWTERS. That's the way children are.

MR. SAWTERS. Yes. [*He sighs deeply.*] I'm kinda tired.

MRS. SAWTERS. He doesn't spare the language.

MR. SAWTERS. I didn't read it all. My eyes.

MRS. SAWTERS. Seems to know his mind. Seems to.

MR. SAWTERS. [*Slamming his paper to the floor.*] He's a God-damned chicken-hearted ungrateful bastard!

---

1 Like Vinita, Claremore, and Tulsa, Verdigris was on the line of the St. Louis-San Francisco Railway, or "Frisco."

2 Mrs. Sawters draws attention to the politics of Oklahoma statehood and suggests concerns about statehood's effect on Indigenous people. Mr. Sawters appears not to share her reservations. A proposal to create another state out of Indian Territory, called Sequoyah and governed by Indigenous people, was approved at the Sequoyah Constitutional Convention in 1905 and sent to the US Congress, which refused to consider it.

MRS. SAWTERS. [*After a moment to let her scorn for his vehemence sink in.*] You don't make much by questioning his paternity.

MR. SAWTERS. I'm sorry, Lou. But God damn it! I don't understand it. Used to be you couldn't get him off the place. Then he flew off and joined up with the navy like a boy gone out of his mind. He liked the farm. He liked the life. I give him a calf once when he was seven. You remember. He raised her and she had calves. Pigs galore, his own raisin'. Used to love growin' things, makin' 'em grow up and multiply. All that schoolin' we give him didn't seem to matter. Jist learned him what he really wanted to do. Loved to see the fields bearin', the grainary full to burstin'. [*Deeply troubled.*] Ah, I don't know what's goin' on, anymore—him or anything. I see only misery and trouble ahead, the poorhouse crackin' open its jaws. For me and mine.

MRS. SAWTERS. [*Smiling.*] It's not that bad.

MR. SAWTERS. [*Deeper into himself.*] And other things, too. In the night, I cain't sleep good. I lay there in the dark. And the dark ain't friendly like it used to be.

MRS. SAWTERS. [*Trying not to be reached.*] Don't.

MR. SAWTERS. I guess I'm gettin' old.

MRS. SAWTERS. [*Holding on to herself—quietly.*] Not yet. Not for a while.

MR. SAWTERS. You're stronger than I am.

MRS. SAWTERS. No. I feel things less. I *make* myself. Afraid not to. That's weakness.

MR. SAWTERS. Nuthin' strong about blurtin' out the way you feel.

MRS. SAWTERS. You feel what you can't help feeling, Dave—and you're not ashamed. That's good. That's right. You're a good man, Dave, and you'll last. Longer 'n anybody. I know you will.

MR. SAWTERS. [*Comforted.*] I feel better, anyway.

MRS. SAWTERS. Course you do. Come out in the kitchen and read your paper. It's cozy out there. Or better—you can make yourself useful. Beat up some egg whites for me if Bina hasn't beat you to it. [*Amused.*] I like to see a man in the kitchen. A bull in a china shop.

MR. SAWTERS. Well. Someway, I'll have to get help, though. Looks like no one wants to work for others in this country.

MRS. SAWTERS. You can't blame 'em for wanting to be their own boss.

MR. SAWTERS. No, but that don't help *me* none. Winter wheat's froze clear out. I took a good look on the way to Verdigris.

Have to plow up the whole west eighty and put 'er down in oats, I guess. When? Godamighty, I only got two hands.

MRS. SAWTERS. We'll find someone. What about Gard Dunham? He could pay some of his rent money in work instead of crop.

MR. SAWTERS. Could if he would.

MRS. SAWTERS. Have you asked him?

MR. SAWTERS. I don't like to do it.

MRS. SAWTERS. I don't see why. He's a good farmer. One of the best—and you know it.

MR. SAWTERS. A married man likes to keep to hisself—in his own home.

MRS. SAWTERS. He wouldn't have to *live* here.

MR. SAWTERS. I don't see him rowin' acrost the lake ever' day to work for me.

MRS. SAWTERS. Ask and find out.

MR. SAWTERS. I don't know.

MRS. SAWTERS. Well, come out in the kitchen while I see if everything's done. No good to mope. Maybe I could ask him tonight.

MR. SAWTERS. Would you, Lou?

MRS. SAWTERS. I'll see. Maybe.

MR. SAWTERS. It'd shore take a load off my mind if he would.

MRS. SAWTERS. [*Serenely.*] I asked them over just in case. [*She goes.*]

MR. SAWTERS. [*Following.*] I wondered why you was havin' 'em over to eat. Say—he might do it, at that!

[JULIE *comes down and into the room. She does a little picking up, retrieves her father's paper from the floor, straightens the room. She picks up one of two dining chairs and takes it out to the dining room. She comes back immediately for the other. Almost to the door, she meets* BINA *just coming through.*]

BINA. They comin'?

JULIE. I don't think yet. I didn't look.

[*She goes out.* BINA *goes and looks out toward the lake.* JULIE *comes back in.*]

BINA. I think I can jist see 'em startin' out. Looks like a boat, anyhow. Lands, they better hurry! It's cloudin' up.

JULIE. Is everything ready?

BINA. Jist icin' the cake. Maw's doin' it. She run me out and said to get dressed. Gollee, I'm dressed. As much as I ever am.

JULIE. You don't look very dressed up to me.

BINA. [*With a faint resentment.*] I ain't the dressy kind.

JULIE. I don't know that *I* qualify.

BINA. Oh, you do, though—and that's a fact.

JULIE. Just an old dress I can't seem to wear out.

BINA. You look mighty spick and span to me.

JULIE. I hope that's a compliment.

BINA. And you're wearin' the brooch Clabe sent you. From China, he said it come from.

[*She comes to admire it.*]

JULIE. Pretty, isn't it?

BINA. Must have cost a sight. Them rubies and silver and all. Don't know how he could afford it on sailor's pay.

JULIE. Saved his money.

BINA. Well, that's one thing to do with it.

JULIE. Are you mad because he didn't send you one?

BINA. He never sent me a thing, not a thing! Not even a post-card.

JULIE. I'll let you wear it sometime.

BINA. No, thanks. I like my own things.

JULIE. Suit yourself.

BINA. I cain't suit nobody else. Slave away—and who cares?

JULIE. Are you intimating that no one does any work but you, Bina?

BINA. You been primpin' all afternoon while Maw and me got things ready for tonight.

JULIE. [*Furiously.*] Oh! You silly creature! Who cleaned up upstairs? All the bedrooms? This room? For pity's sake, if you don't like the arrangement we agreed on, say so, and let's change it! The cellar's full of fruit and berries. I canned them. The backbone and sausage I put down in lard last winter we're still using. Who made all the new curtains, who keeps them in repair? If the truth were known, I do a lot more work around here than you do!

BINA. [*Retracting.*] Oh, I guess you do, Julie. I don't know what's the matter with me!

JULIE. If you want us to change, speak up. I hate cooking and the little drudgeries you're so fond of. But if you're going to be a baby, I'll change with you—and gladly. I can't bear people who're sloppy, and complaining and whining all the time!

BINA. I'm sorry, Julie.

JULIE. I should think you would be! Why do you try my patience like this? You know I've got a temper.

BINA. It's jist that I'm—I'm miserable.

JULIE. [*After a moment, dark and inward.*] Yes, I know. [*But she doesn't want to discuss things like this with* BINA. *She goes over, puts a match to the well-laid fire, watches the flames shoot up. In the darkening room, the firelight makes an eerie illumination that does not reach the gloom-shadowed corners.*] Take the chill off.

BINA. [*Watching her.*] You're so—so sure of yourself, Julie. You look at me like I was low or sump'n. Clabe's the same way.

JULIE. [*Sharply.*] Leave Clabe out of it!

BINA. Jist because he's had lots of schoolin', I guess.

JULIE. He's got nothing to do with it.

BINA. You both look down on me. You know you do. You had secrets together, too. You left me out, like I was poison!

JULIE. [*Getting control of herself—cold and sure.*] Listen, Bina! You and I aren't anything alike. Clabe and I are. Try to remember that. I don't think you're low—and I don't think I'm high. I have things on my mind, too, same as you. Things you don't even know about—and never will. But I don't ask for your sympathy—and I don't know why you require mine all the time.

BINA. I said I was sorry.

JULIE. I wonder if you are.

BINA. [*Flaring up again.*] Do you have to kick a body when he's down? Do you?

JULIE. [*Contemptuously.*] Why don't you learn to finish what you begin?

[MR. *and* MRS. SAWTERS *have come in from the dining room.* MRS. SAWTERS *has* CLABE'S *letter in her hand, as if she had just finished reading it, and had come out expressly to find* JULIE.]

MRS. SAWTERS. What's the matter?

JULIE. [*Coldly.*] Nothing that would interest anyone.

MRS. SAWTERS. [*Who sees more than one would guess.*] I see. Your father got a letter from Clabe.

JULIE. [*Holding out her hand at once.*] Clabe? What does he say?

MRS. SAWTERS. [*With determined malice, and a sardonic pleasure coloring her anger.*] I'll read it to you.

JULIE. I can read it.

MRS. SAWTERS. Bina hasn't heard it, either. I doubt if either of you could make it out. More of a scrawl than hand-writing. [*She begins to read:*] "Dear Dad and Maw—" It's from San Diego, California.[1] "I don't like to say this, knowing the way you feel—but I won't be able to get home this summer.

---

1 Clabe is stationed at Naval Base San Diego, from which the Pacific Fleet sailed until June 1940, when President Franklin Roosevelt (1882–1945) moved it to Pearl Harbor, Hawaii.

And, furthermore, I won't in the fall, either—nor next winter or the following spring—or, for that matter, *ever*. In two months I'll likely be half the world away again—South Seas, Singapore, God knows where—but far. If you want to know why, ask Julie. Your son, Clabe."

JULIE. [*Involuntarily.*] Not ever.

[*They look at her for explanation. She is silent.*]

MR. SAWTERS. [*Impatiently.*] Well? God damn it, Julie, what's behind it?

JULIE. I got him to go away—but I didn't mean forever.

MR. SAWTERS. You got him to?

JULIE. Yes, yes—I asked him to. I *made* him do it.

MR. SAWTERS. But why?

JULIE. His own good, of course.

MR. SAWTERS. How do you know what's his own good? He liked farmin'. He was cut out for it. So we've got you to thank for the hole we're in!

JULIE. What hole?

MR. SAWTERS. Do you think I can run a big farm like this single-handed?

JULIE. I don't know anything about that.

MR. SAWTERS. They's a lot of things that never come in to that head of your'n. Here I been blamin' Clabe for bein' the damn fool.

JULIE. I'll take whatever blame there is.

MR. SAWTERS. Blame! I ain't interested in blame. I'm interested in runnin' this farm and payin' my honest debts, like any man ort to. I'm interested in gettin' ahead—and seein' my kids get ahead. I don't know why you have to work against me!

JULIE. I've done nothing against you, that I can see.

MR. SAWTERS. You've done harm against Clabe, and harm against me. For that matter, against us all! I'd thank you to explain yourself.

JULIE. [*Calmly.*] I'll try to make you understand.

MR. SAWTERS. [*Infuriated.*] And none of that God-damned hoity-toityness, either! By God, we're all jist about as good as you air!

JULIE. [*Coolly.*] You're all perfect! You're the salt of the earth.

MR. SAWTERS. Listen to her!

MRS. SAWTERS. Yes, listen. I'm sure she can explain it all. Can't you, Julie?

[*It is hard to recognize the malice and scorn in* MRS. SAWTERS' *words, so artfully does she manage them. But* JULIE *knows her mother as no one else does.*]

JULIE. [*Evenly.*] Yes—and I fully intend to.

MRS. SAWTERS. There, Dave. Now listen! Listen to Julie.

JULIE. That spring, three years ago—just about this time, there was that big box-supper over at the Verdigris School House.[1] We all went.

BINA. Yes, in two buggies. You went in one with Clabe, I went with Paw and Maw. *You* remember, Maw.

MRS. SAWTERS. I'm not apt to forget it.

JULIE. Clabe was drinking. He was drinking a lot.

MRS. SAWTERS. And doing other things, too, it seems to me. He got engaged to Opal that night, out in a buggy somewhere.

JULIE. Yes. He did. And, afterwards he took her home. And I had to come home with Gard Dunham.

MR. SAWTERS. I don't see what all this has to do with—!

MRS. SAWTERS. Dave! Just be patient. Julie'll tell you. Go on, Julie!

JULIE. The next day was Sunday. In the afternoon, I went out for a walk, out through the orchard. There were wild flowers everywhere. You could smell the blooms of the fruit trees.

MRS. SAWTERS. Yes, they do smell.

[JULIE *just looks at her, till even* MRS. SAWTERS, *who is afraid of nothing, cannot stand it, and turns her eyes away.* JULIE *resumes. A new note is in her recital. A deep and troubling emotion grips her. She creates the scene so vividly that her family is spell-bound.*]

JULIE. Where the orchard drops down to the lake-side, there's a mossy bank.
The sun was on it.
The lake sparkled.
The water was lapping against the stones.
It was a day anyone ought to care about.
It was a day a young man ought to feel like singing—
Just for the day itself,
And for being alive—
And especially a man engaged to a girl he was mad to marry.

---

1 The *Claremore Messenger* for 14 February 1902 announced a "new building [that] will be known as the Verdigris School House." The school was operational by summer 1902 and used for community purposes until at least 1950.

But lying on the bank by the lake was Clabe—
And he wasn't singing.
He was crying.
I felt so sorry for him.

I tried to comfort him—but for a long time he wouldn't be
comforted.

It's not pleasant to see someone you care about, a grown man,
Your own brother
As sick in his soul as he was.

MRS. SAWTERS. [*Softly.*] And what did he say?

JULIE. He said that he hated Opal, he was drunk, he didn't know
what he was doing, he didn't know what in God's name he
was to do now that—! [*More quietly.*] More like that. Almost
out of his head. So I told him to go away.

MRS. SAWTERS. Without even saying Good-bye to us?

JULIE. Without seeing anyone, just to hop a freight train out of
Verdigris and stay away till everybody had forgotten. It was
the only thing to do. I drove him over.

BINA. [*Softly.*] Poor Opal cried her eyes out for weeks.

MR. SAWTERS. [*Heavily.*] So that's it.

JULIE. [*After a moment.*] That's part of it. [*Quickly, as if afraid to
stop.*] Here was his chance—forced on him, it's true—but he
was smart enough to take it! All his life he'd wanted to see the
world, to see what went on in towns and foreign lands, the
way the world was made.

MR. SAWTERS. He never wanted any such thing!

JULIE. [*Sharply, on the defensive.*] He did! You don't know him the
way I do. He didn't have any secrets from me. He was sick
to death of the smallness and lonesomeness, the killing work
that never let up, year in, year out, the hum-drum grind,
slaving away in the backwoods, while he was young and
adventurous and all life beckoned to him and—

MR. SAWTERS. Julie! [*Quiet and sure.*] He liked it here, his home.
He was meant for such a life, jist like I was. I know my boy.
He's worked beside me in the fields. I know him very well.

JULIE. You think I'd lie about it?

MR. SAWTERS. I think you're lyin'!

JULIE. Why would I! What reason would I have!

MR. SAWTERS. I don't know. They's sump'n here too deep for me.
All I know is, I wanted him to do what he was meant to do.

JULIE. He's doing it.

MR. SAWTERS. I say he ain't. I'm ashamed of him.

JULIE. I'm not. He had the courage not to marry a little nit-wit like Opal and tie himself down to a few miserable clods of earth, nothing but grime and sweat, and maybe a houseful of brats to feed. I'm not ashamed of what he's done. I'm proud of him!

MRS. SAWTERS. He's not so proud of you.

JULIE. What do you mean?

MRS. SAWTERS. [*Lifting the letter.*] There's a post-script.

JULIE. [*With premonition.*] Read it.

MRS. SAWTERS. I intend to. [*Reading.*] "P.S. I'm sorry if I've brought grief to you—for you always expected great things from me. But I have to write this, this is the way things are: my life is a complete mess, and the only course I see is to ruin what there is left of it. Everything I've done, Julie can have on her conscience, if she's got one. But I doubt if she has. I don't know why it is so—but there is something wrong, something awful and evil driving her. *Now I know it.* And you'll never see me again the way I am, for that would mean I'd have to look on her face again. And I pray God I'll never have to do that, never in this world."

JULIE. [*Stunned, hardly able to speak.*] He said that?

MRS. SAWTERS. [*Offering the letter.*] See for yourself!

JULIE. No. I don't want to see it.

MRS. SAWTERS. You may as well.

JULIE. [*Turning her hurt and anger on her mother.*] No! Leave me alone! [*Then her voice low and tortured.*] How could he say things like that?

BINA. [*With quick instinctive understanding sympathy.*] Oh, Julie.

JULIE. [*Cruel and hunted.*] Save your sympathy for people who need it.

BINA. I'm sorry.

JULIE. [*With calm, deliberate hate.*] Clabe hasn't heard the last of this. Not by a long shot!

[*She turns and goes up the stairs. No one speaks for a moment, each absorbed in his own private reactions to the scene.*]

BINA. [*After a moment.*] Clabe 'd orta be whipped.

MRS. SAWTERS. Hush, child!

BINA. Well, it's awful to say things like that!

MR. SAWTERS. [*Deeply troubled.*] It don't sound to me like Clabe.

BINA. Now Julie'll get one of her spells. Won't be able to live in the same house with her for weeks.

MRS. SAWTERS. [*With grim amusement.*] I wouldn't like to be the

Dunhams tonight—especially Opal. Julie can be mean as a copperhead.

MR. SAWTERS. I don't see much chance of gettin' Gard to— It wouldn't work.

MRS. SAWTERS. You want to give up asking Gard to come help you?

MR. SAWTERS. I don't know what to do. God damn it! Clabe didn't sound like hisself to me. Never comin' back . . .

MRS. SAWTERS. People change their minds.

MR. SAWTERS. Usually it's too late then to do any good.

GARD'S VOICE. [Outside.] Howdy, howdy? Anybody home?

BINA. [Scurrying to the door to the boat landing.] Lord, they're here! [Throwing open the door, calling out as she disappears.] Come in, come in! Jist tie 'er up, Gard. You don't have to take the oars in. We never do. How are you, Opal?

[The confused mumble of their greetings comes in, above the sound of the lapping waves. MR. and MRS. SAWTERS light the lamps. The room becomes more cheerful. OPAL and GARD DUNHAM come into the room with BINA. OPAL is a backwoods girl, vain and not very scrupulous. But she has been thwarted rather seriously; unstable and morbidly fearful, she is bitter and very close to hysteria. GARD is muscular and slow-moving, slow-speaking, full of a heavy and tenacious cruelty, as if he felt himself cheated—but had no intention of letting it be so forever.]

OPAL. Howdy do, Mrs. Sawters? Evenin', Mr. Sawters. 'D you see me rowin' the boat?

MR. SAWTERS. We wasn't noticin', Opal.

OPAL. I did, though—quite a piece. You'd think—to hear folks talk—they was some trick to it. Why, it's easy.

GARD. If you could call what you done, rowin'. Splashin' around, gettin' nowhere fast. Evenin' to you, ma'am. Hi, Dave! And she near turned the boat over, changin' places, to boot. Whatever you tell her not to do—that's what Opal does. Ever' time.

MR. SAWTERS. Lots of women like that.

MRS. SAWTERS. I wouldn't give a whoop for a woman that didn't have some gumption.

GARD. It's more'n gumption in Opal's case. Pure orneriness. Like a chicken its head cut off. You don't know where she's goin', but she's on 'er way.

OPAL. I don't know why you have to belittle me all the time!

MRS. SAWTERS. He doesn't mean it, Opal.

OPAL. Oh, he means it, all right. Jist because I made him row across the lake 'stid of us drivin' round in the buggy. He didn't want to come even, another thing. All he wants to do is set at home with his shoes off. Cain't even get him to go to church.

MR. SAWTERS. I know jist the way he feels.

OPAL. No, you don't. *You* wouldn't brood around and sulk and snap at a body for nuthin'. Why cain't he tell me what he's mad at, and get it over with, like I do—'stid of keepin' it in and holdin' it back, and jist pick at me and pick at me! I'm gettin' tired of it!

GARD. For the Lord's sake, Opal! Is this your comp'ny manners?

MRS. SAWTERS. [*Perversely amused by the unpleasantness.*] They say everything happens to you if you live long enough.

OPAL. I never can do nuthin' right!

GARD. [*Who's had enough of this.*] No, that's right—you cain't.

OPAL. [*With a silly wail.*] Oh! You see the way he does me? I won't stand for it—not another minute. I'm goin' home!

MRS. SAWTERS. Never mind, child. Men talk. Here, take a drink of this cider.

BINA. [*Pouring it.*] Do you good.

OPAL. [*Tasting it reluctantly—grimacing.*] It's hard. I cain't drink it hard!

MRS. SAWTERS. It won't hurt you a bit.

OPAL. [*Fluttering.*] Won't stay down, I know it won't! When people are mean to me—takes me a long time to get over it! I jist go to pieces!

GARD. I wouldn't a-brung you over if I knowed you was gonna act up.

BINA. Let her alone, Gard. She's nervous.

OPAL. I'm high-strung, that's what I am! You don't appreciate me!

GARD. [*With cold brutality.*] Oh, I know what's come over you, you cain't fool me. It's comin' to this house—where Clabe used to live.

OPAL. It ain't so! Jist listen to him!

GARD. You never got over him turnin' you down. Your pride jist couldn't stand it. I know all about you! Personal—I think it served you right.

[*There is an embarrassed silence.* BINA *comes to the rescue.*]

BINA. I better dish up the dinner. Wanta come out in the kitchen with me, Opal?

MRS. SAWTERS. Yes, you run along with Bina.

OPAL. [*Her mouth drawn into a stubborn hard line.*] No, I'll stay here. Less'n you need me to help, Bina.

BINA. Laws, no—not jist this minute, anyhow.

GARD. Where's Julie at?

OPAL. [*Who has paused on her way to the organ.*] Yes. Where is Julie?

BINA. Upstairs. She's not very well.

[*She goes out.*]

OPAL. Oh, that's too bad—about Julie bein' sick.

MRS. SAWTERS. Oh, she's not really sick. But I don't think she'll be down.

OPAL. [*Deliberately.*] Gard'll be sorry. We both will.

GARD. [*Dangerously.*] Now jist what do you mean by that, Miss Opal?

[*Pleased at her successful thrust,* OPAL *turns her back on him, goes to the organ and begins to thump out a tune and to sing it impudently.* JULIE *appears on the steps and comes into the room. She has changed to her best dress—and she is stunning. She is gracious, too—biding her time, dominant, calculating and driven.*]

JULIE. Music. How nice! Good evening, Opal!

OPAL. Oh, good evenin', Julie.

JULIE. You look so pretty, Opal. Doesn't she, Maw? Hello, Gard!

GARD. [*Taking her offered hand.*] Howdy, Julie!

JULIE. We hardly ever see you any more—either one of you. It's a shame, too—such close neighbors.

[*She releases her hand.*]

OPAL. [*Spitefully.*] There ain't much time for farm people to go callin'.

JULIE. Then we'll just have to make time. This may be the backwoods, but we're not animals exactly—we might make as decent a social life as we can, don't you think so? *I* have it! You and Gard spend the night here!

OPAL. [*Unable to believe she's heard correctly.*] What!

JULIE. Yes! Why not? And—well, see for yourself. It's begun to rain, and the wind's whipping the lake pretty bad. It wouldn't be pleasant to row back. It mightn't even be safe. Besides—I insist.

OPAL. Oh, we couldn't think of doin' that. Thanks so much. Could we, Gard?

GARD. Why couldn't we?

OPAL. Put people out? Oh, no, it wouldn't do a-tall! We'll have to get on home, Julie. Mr. Sawters'll lend us a buggy and team 'f we need it. Won't you, Mr. Sawters?

GARD. Good God, that *would* put 'em out, Opal! Come to your senses!

MR. SAWTERS. [*Smiling.*] You'd better stay. You'd be welcome, and no bother.

MRS. SAWTERS. Opal, you seem to be over-ruled.

GARD. We'll be right proud to stay, won't we, Opal? Tell 'em so.

OPAL. [*After a moment.*] We'll be glad to. Thank you.
[*But a deep premonition has struck her.*]

JULIE. There, it's all settled. [*Deliberately.*] I've decided to put you in Clabe's room.

OPAL. [*Strangely stirred.*] Clabe's room?

JULIE. It's the nicest room in the house. And it's right next door to mine. Maybe we could have a little talk. I've been promising myself to try to get really acquainted with you for a long time.

BINA. [*Sticking her head through the door.*] You folks might jist as well set down and— [*Then, noticing* JULIE.] For land's sake— Julie! And she's went and changed her dress!

JULIE. Well, what of it? We don't see the Dunhams every day. It's an event. They're going to stay the night, too. Aren't you, Opal?

OPAL. It looks that-a-way.

BINA. [*Flabbergasted.*] Well, I never! [*Then.*] You can all go in and set down. Pig's on the table 'th an apple in his mouth. Paw can start carvin'!

JULIE. Oh, Bina—here's something for you.
[*She holds out* CLABE'S *brooch, which she has been carrying in her hand.*]

BINA. Clabe's brooch!

JULIE. It's yours if you want it.

BINA. You mean I can have it for keeps?

JULIE. Yes, of course.

BINA. Julie! [*Then suspiciously.*] You think I won't wear it, but I will.

JULIE. Of course wear it! Put it on right this minute.

BINA. Pin seems to be bent. It won't fasten.

JULIE. Easy enough to straighten.

BINA. [*Who has been struggling with it.*] Yep, now it's comin'. Looks like it had been banged up hard against sump'n. [*She puts it on.*] Or more like you took it off and throwed it on the floor.

JULIE. I wouldn't do anything so childish. What an idea! [*Putting her arm about* OPAL.] Come on, Opal! You poor thing, you must be starved.
[*She goes out with* OPAL; MR. SAWTERS *and* GARD *follow;* BINA *puts out a restraining hand to her mother.*]

BINA. [*In open-eyed puzzlement.*] What's come over her? Why, she was even nice to Opal—nice as pie!

MRS. SAWTERS. [*With her quiet mockery.*] You said there were two kinds of pie. Which?

BINA. [*Completely puzzled.*] What?

MRS. SAWTERS. I mean—the evening's just started, child.

CURTAIN

END OF SCENE I

Act One

Scene 2

CLABE'S bedroom. 10 o'clock that night. A beautiful room, but shadowy and mysterious.

It is not very large, but it is not crowded with junk, and so looks roomier.

At one side, two windows jut out toward the lake, from a mansard roof.[1] A bed stands between the two windows, projecting into the room. It is large and high, and has a draped mosquito netting attached to a frame over it.[2]

At the back is a fireplace, and a door, partly ajar, into JULIE'S room. A roomy armoire is at the other wall, and the door into the upstairs hall. A lighted lamp is on a table.

MR. SAWTERS, a pipe clenched in his teeth, is laying a fire.

MRS. SAWTERS comes in from the hall. Music—the organ—and voices come faintly from below, from the four younger people. During the scene someone begins playing a piece on the organ, haunting and minor and strange, the very mood of the room.

It is BINA playing—and she keeps it up intermittently through much of the scene.

MRS. SAWTERS. I'll just turn the bed down.

MR. SAWTERS. Ummm.

MRS. SAWTERS. [*At the bed.*] Why, it's already done! Neat as a pin.

MR. SAWTERS. Julie, I guess.

MRS. SAWTERS. [*Thoughtfully.*] Yes. Julie. That's funny.

---

1   A roof with four sides, each with an initially gentle slope that steepens to accommodate dormer windows.

2   Malaria, transmitted by mosquitos, was a common and serious health concern in the United States, especially in warm regions, into the early twentieth century.

MR. SAWTERS. [*Soberly, troubled.*] I guess it is, at that.

MRS. SAWTERS. [*Indicating.*] Flowers on the mantel, too.

MR. SAWTERS. More Julie.

MRS. SAWTERS. Must have brought them in from *her* room. *Why,* I wonder?

MR. SAWTERS. I don't like it.

MRS. SAWTERS. What's she up to?

MR. SAWTERS. No good is my guess.

MRS. SAWTERS. Pshaw! I wouldn't take Clabe's letter too seriously.

MR. SAWTERS. It ain't that. It ain't *only* that. Givin' 'em Clabe's room to sleep in. Why'd she do that? Always seemed to me like Julie wanted to keep ever'body out of here. [*Softly.*] I tried the hall door here only two days ago—wanted one of them pipes Clabe used to have so many of. The door was locked. [*Sardonically.*] I got in, though. Through Julie's room.

MRS. SAWTERS. 'D you find the pipe?

MR. SAWTERS. This is it.

MRS. SAWTERS. A man can smoke a pipe when he's dying. Listen to that wind!

MR. SAWTERS. Many a wind has blowed around this house, Lou. It's still standing, though.

MRS. SAWTERS. Hmmmm. A house either stands up or falls down according to what goes on inside of it.

MR. SAWTERS. I don't see that.

MRS. SAWTERS. Your planning, your work, the thoughts you've thought day after day—that's what makes a house last. That's the fire that takes the chill off in winter, the damp off when it's raining. When that fire dies down, the walls cave in. You lit a fire in this house, Dave.

MR. SAWTERS. What about you?

MRS. SAWTERS. [*Gently, softly.*] You *know* about me, Dave.

MR. SAWTERS. [*Looking around, deeply aware.*] Lots of things happened to us, Lou.

MRS. SAWTERS. We were young married folks here in this house. I remember they thought we were crazy to build right on the lake. The damp, they said, would mould everything, make it rot away. They were wrong.

MR. SAWTERS. It seems so long ago.

MRS. SAWTERS. The children born here. Your Maw died. Edward died. [*Quietly.*] It's hard to lose your first-born. The others never seem the same.

MR. SAWTERS. [*Heavily.*] Yeah. The next to die'll be us, I reckon.

MRS. SAWTERS. Not yet awhile. [*Trying to rouse him out of his mood.*] You're certainly all on the down side these days. Why, only back a year or two ago, you wouldn't have said a thing like that.

MR. SAWTERS. If we only had Clabe back, I could rest easier.

MRS. SAWTERS. We haven't got him back, though.

MR. SAWTERS. [*Softly.*] No. In a way, though, seems like he's close.

MRS. SAWTERS. [*Almost whispering.*] It's the room. Clabe's room.

MR. SAWTERS. Yeah. Almost see him.

MRS. SAWTERS. Uhummm.

[*The wind swirls up.*]

MR. SAWTERS. The way he touched things, throwed his belongings on the floor.

MRS. SAWTERS. Yes. I never could get him not to.

[*They consider this a moment. His presence is very real.*]

MR. SAWTERS. [*To throw off the mood.*] I better light the fire.

MRS. SAWTERS. Might as well. Make it more cheerful. [*He does.*] You ought to get on to bed, Dave. You're tired. The Dunhams won't mind.

MR. SAWTERS. I still got to put the mules out in the corral.

MRS. SAWTERS. Let 'em stay in the barn one night. Won't hurt 'em!

MR. SAWTERS. They tromp and rear so. And chew the troughs to pieces. You'd think they'd ruther eat wood than oats, the way they carry on.

MRS. SAWTERS. Well. You know best. If Gard went with you— maybe you'd get a chance to sound him out.

MR. SAWTERS. Ummmm.

MRS. SAWTERS. [*Becoming conscious that there are footsteps approaching, the sound of a door opening.*] I guess they're going to bed. Here's someone. It's Julie.

[JULIE *comes in from her room. She looks at them sharply, not liking their being there.*]

JULIE. Everything was ready. I got it ready right after dinner.

MRS. SAWTERS. Your Paw lit a fire.

JULIE. Oh. I forgot that.

MR. SAWTERS. You need a fire, a night like this.

[*He goes out into the hall.*]

MRS. SAWTERS. I'd like to ask you something, Julie.

JULIE. Some other time. It's late.

MRS. SAWTERS. Not some other time. It's got to be now.

JULIE. What is it, then?

MRS. SAWTERS. What is it you're planning?

JULIE. Planning?

MRS. SAWTERS. I know you very well, Julie. No use lying to *me*.

JULIE. I haven't got any plan.

MRS. SAWTERS. Listen, Julie—for your own good. Once when you were about ten, you had a kitten scratch you one day you were playing with it. You didn't say anything, you didn't even cry. Later on, we found that little kitten hung up in the barn loft by a piece of binder twine. I never told anybody what I thought.

JULIE. You're out of your mind, you think I—!

MRS. SAWTERS. Yes! I guessed then it was no accident—and I kept my mouth shut. To other folks you may be a mystery. But to me, you're a looking glass—a younger, handsomer looking glass—yes—but *when I look at you I see myself.*

JULIE. I'm not like you, I'm not!

MRS. SAWTERS. You either will be in time, or you won't be. I'd be careful. [*With deep comprehension.*] Be careful, Julie. I'm warning you. You don't know what blackness can rise up in you and strike you blind! [*Deeply reminded.*] If I hadn't married your Paw, I don't know. [*Gently.*] Hate's no good. It'll kill you if you let it. There's another side of any coin. Turn it over some time.

JULIE. Leave me alone! I can't bear to be looked through, and questioned and accused!

MRS. SAWTERS. And understood, eh, Julie? You can't bear that, can you?

JULIE. You don't know a thing about me!

MRS. SAWTERS. [*With aloof sincerity.*] I know a lot about myself. Some day, maybe I'll tell you. I'm not what you'd call a good woman, especially. But there are things in me that make me respect good. That's why I have to make a stand against what I think is bad. [*Satirizing herself.*] It's called character.

JULIE. [*Jeering, impatient.*] Yes, of course! Character! I know!

MRS. SAWTERS. [*Heatedly.*] It's called something else, too! It's called being a man—or a woman—a member of the human race. [*Quieter.*] Anyway, I've warned you. [*Pointedly.*] And you understand. [*She is going. She pauses.*] Why did you want lake water this afternoon?

JULIE. [*Reluctantly.*] I— For the flowers. They keep better in lake water.

MRS. SAWTERS. Maybe so. Time will tell.

[*She goes out.* JULIE'S *hands clench with impatience and annoyance. She turns quickly, goes into her own room, comes out again at once with a small colored picture. She hangs it on a convenient nail by the fireplace.* OPAL *comes in from the hall.*]

OPAL. Oh.

JULIE. [*Turns about quickly, sees who it is, gracious, full of guile.*] Just putting this up. It's a miniature of Clabe. Have you ever seen it?

OPAL. [*Wondering what is up.*] I don't think so. [*She comes over slowly to look.*] No. I never have.

JULIE. I had it made in Tulsa. It's like him, isn't it? I thought you'd like to see it.

OPAL. [*Suspiciously.*] What made you think so?

JULIE. You and Clabe were so—well, I naturally thought that . . .

OPAL. It don't interest me the least little bit.

JULIE. I'm sorry. I made a mistake. [*She moves to go, her dress rustling.*] You—perhaps you'd like me to go? You must be tired.

OPAL. I feel fine. Only there's— [*Something is on her mind; she goes restlessly to the window.*] This wind gets me jumpy.

JULIE. Does it?

OPAL. It always has. Sometimes it 'pears to me it lives out there on the lake.

JULIE. What?

OPAL. The wind. Its home is there. It never goes anywheres else, it seems like. But at night it comes clawin' and scratchin' at the winders.

JULIE. It doesn't seem that way to me. If you said lake—I could agree with you. It must be cold at the bottom of the lake. Cold as death. I think about that sometimes.

OPAL. I wish you wouldn't talk that-a-way!

JULIE. Goodness, don't be afraid, Opal! Nothing's going to hurt you.

OPAL. [*Too emphatically.*] I'm *not* afraid!

JULIE. Well, I've often thought—in spite of the chill and how lonely a way to die—if things ever got too bad, you could easily row out in the middle and jump out of the boat.

OPAL. [*On edge.*] Don't say that! Please, Julie!

JULIE. Why, Opal. I'm not talking about you. I'm talking about myself.

[OPAL'S *thin, little mouth is getting under control. Her really savage will comes to her rescue in time.*]

OPAL. I think you mean me.

JULIE. You think I—?

OPAL. And why *shouldn't* you mean me? If ever anybody had

a cause to hate another'n—I guess you got it, far's I'm concerned. *I got even with you, Julie.* And they's few that has.

JULIE. Of course you realize I don't know what you mean. It sounds crazy to me.

OPAL. [*Who can't stand the word.*] It's *not* crazy! I'm the only one. You can't do *me* a dirty trick and expect me to jist lay down and let you. I'll bet you feel sick ever' time you think of it. And I bet you think of it often, too. [*Maddeningly, childishly triumphant, she sits.*] Yes, we're even now. So it's your next move. If you can think of one.

JULIE. If this is a game, I think I ought to know the name of it. And what you get if you win.

OPAL. Oh, for God's sake! Listen, Julie. I know you kept Clabe from marryin' me.

JULIE. Mercy, Opal, is that it? Why, he'd have been lucky to get you.

OPAL. I know you did, no matter what you say.

JULIE. If you're so sure, then, I may as well admit it.

OPAL. You might as well. You might as well admit *why* you done it, too!

JULIE. [*Coolly.*] If you must know, you weren't good enough for him.

OPAL. [*Contemptuously.*] Where I come from, my family wouldn't have even spoke to the likes of you, Julie. Virginia people have their pride you wouldn't know about.

JULIE. Really?

OPAL. Maw liked to died when I told her about Clabe and me. You should've saw her face! She thinks to be part Cherokee Indian is the same as bein' part nigger.[1]

JULIE. I think I'd be careful, Opal!

OPAL. I'm not afraid of you.

JULIE. No. Why should you be? There's nothing to be afraid of.

OPAL. I know it. Because I know what the real reason is you wouldn't let Clabe marry me.

JULIE. [*With quick troubled outrage.*] You were a stupid little nobody who did nothing but giggle and air your superiority. A fine wife you'd have made!

OPAL. As good as you'd make any time. But I notice you're *not*. Not *anyone's* wife. Oh, I got even with *you,* all right!

---

1 A deeply offensive, racist slur used in various ways but primarily, then and now, to demean and dehumanize people of the African diaspora in the United States.

JULIE. How did you do that?

OPAL. How did I do that! I guess you felt pretty silly when I snatched Gard away from you, right out from under your nose!

JULIE. [*Laughs with relief.*] Snatched! That's wonderful! [*Then with smiling superiority.*] You vain little beast. I turned Gard down, do you hear? I told him to get out of my sight, and stay out, I never wanted to lay eyes on him again. Snatched, indeed!

OPAL. It ain't so!

JULIE. I suppose he's wild about you? I can see how he pampers you, won't let you lift one of your dainty little fingers. He's put you on a pedestal where he can fall down and worship. Yes, I've heard him talk to you. He despises the ground you walk on.

OPAL. He don't!

JULIE. He told me so.

OPAL. He never! You ain't saw him since we was married. So how could he tell you anything?

JULIE. He told me tonight while you were entertaining us so beautifully at the organ. And what do you say to that?

OPAL. [*After a moment, feeling her defeat, but gathering her powers.*] This is what I say. Gard may hate me like you say. I reckon he does. I reckon no one could treat another'n the way he does me—unless he hated me. I don't keer. I've took so much off of life I don't expect much anymore. I never got what I wanted the most—hardly ever. A rubber-tired buggy and a team of bays. Humm! Onct I'd a-give my soul for such things. Taffeta[1] dresses, and jewels to sparkle on my hands from sunup to sundown. They wasn't for me. I had to do without. [*Triumphantly.*] But one thing I got, people'd give their lives to get. And it's mine. Mine! *Clabe loves me.* Try and take that away from me!

JULIE. [*With light scorn.*] I wouldn't lift a hand.

OPAL. You would, though! You done it once—and you will again! When you find out! [*Spitefully.*] Quit smilin' to yourself, and purring like a cat that's ate his belly full—and look at the truth! You won out once. You had to cheat and lie and deal 'em out from the bottom—but you won. *Only you didn't. I did.* [*She thrusts two or three letters which she has pulled from her*

---

1 Smooth, shiny fabric made from silk until the twentieth century, now manufactured from synthetic fibers.

dress, in front of JULIE.] See there! Letters from Clabe. From all over . . . wherever he went. Eatin' his heart out!

JULIE. [*Perturbed, but outwardly calm.*] You wouldn't be getting letters from Clabe. Gard wouldn't allow it.

OPAL. But what if Gard wouldn't know it?

JULIE. He'd have found out.

OPAL. You see 'em, don't you? Mr. Vance at the Post Office at the Switch hands 'em out to me on the sly. Gard don't know.

JULIE. I don't believe it. It's a lie. They aren't from Clabe.

OPAL. You know his handwriting, don't you?

JULIE. It's a little bit like it.

OPAL. Maybe you'd like to read one? [*As* JULIE *lifts her hand.*] I'll read it to you.

JULIE. No. Don't.

OPAL. I won't give it to you in your hand. I know you too well!

JULIE. I don't care to see other people's mail, thank you. [*She moves as if to go.*]

OPAL. [*Triumphantly.*] You know they're from him! You needn't run away, Julie. I've got something else to tell you. Some day he'll come back. And it's *me* he'll come back to—understand?

JULIE. He'll never come back. He said so.

OPAL. But he will, just the same! I *know* he will. And I'll leave Gard then so quick he won't know what struck him!

JULIE. You wouldn't do that. You're married to him.

OPAL. Do you think that'd stop me? Not on your life! Now I know the way Clabe feels about me. And he'll take me away from here—and just try to stop it this time. *And this time he won't come back.* Neither one of us will!

JULIE. You've got it all figured out, haven't you? You know exactly what you want and how to get it, don't you?

OPAL. You bet I do!

JULIE. *Don't be too sure.*

OPAL. If you think you're gonna tell Gard, don't waste your time. It won't make no difference.

JULIE. [*Thinking it out, planning quietly, but desperately.*] I won't tell Gard. It's none of my affair. I could make it mine, though. I could stop your jeering mouth once and for all. It's a fight you want, is it? Over what? A bunch of silly letters. From one cheap vicious little good-for-nothing to another, just like him. Well, I promise you. I'll get those letters. I'll burn them to ashes. And you'll not have anything to gloat over any more.

OPAL. And how do you think you'll do that?

JULIE. There are ways.

OPAL. What ways?

JULIE. [*Her distress showing through her violence.*] Ways you wouldn't know about! I won't let you do this to me! Never! Never! [*Then drooping.*] Don't listen to what I say.

OPAL. [*With cool triumph.*] You know when you're licked, don't you?

JULIE. [*Dimly.*] Yes. I know.

OPAL. It's time you realized it.

JULIE. I have to learn how to lose.

OPAL. Sure! You'd better!

JULIE. And how to win, too. Even a small victory. [*She pauses, briefly.*] Even a big defeat.

OPAL. [*Almost touched.*] I could purt' near feel sorry for you.

JULIE. I'd rather you wouldn't. [*With what looks like sincerity.*] We might have been friends.

OPAL. I'm willin' to let bygones be bygones—if you are.

JULIE. Thank you, Opal.

OPAL. What's the dif? Life's too short.

JULIE. [*Low and broodingly.*] Short, yes? And not very pleasant for any of us. When I was younger, I thought it could be. Why don't they tell you the truth?

OPAL. It's funny—I don't mind you so much now I see you're kinda human.

JULIE. I must be that. Maybe that's been the trouble, all along. You couldn't understand that. You never had a brother that you were devoted to.

OPAL. No. I never had no one.

JULIE. When your mother died, I almost came to you—and explained things, told you how sorry I was. I don't know what held me back. Unless—unless it was that I felt guilty—as if I'd done things against you.

OPAL. You *had.* You know you had.

JULIE. It wasn't *against you,* what I did. It was *for Clabe. For myself.* But I couldn't face you. Not then. When you needed a friend—badly, I guess. It was sad losing your mother the way you did.

OPAL. [*With strained guarded suspicion.*] What do you mean?

JULIE. Lingering that way. So much fever and pain. Out of her head. It must have been a great trial to you.

OPAL. Who said she was out of her head?

JULIE. Why, Opal, everyone said that.

OPAL. It ain't so! I'd thank you not to talk that way, you hear!

JULIE. Opal! What have I said?

OPAL. Oh, what's the use? It's silly to be so secret about it! Didn't you ever hear anything else? You must have.

JULIE. Just that she was sent back east to be buried.

OPAL. [*No longer able to restrain it.*] Buried! She's not even dead, so how could she be buried! She's alive—alive as you are!

JULIE. It isn't possible!

OPAL. It's *so!* I wish to God it *wasn't* so!

JULIE. But where is she, then? Did she go away?

OPAL. [*Close to hysteria.*] She went away, all right. And she won't come back, either. I can't keep it back any longer. At night, I wake up in a cold sweat. Seems like someone's in the room, callin' to me. It's her!

JULIE. Tell me.

OPAL. Why don't she leave me alone! [*Then a little quieter.*] Something preyed on her mind. For years it went on. We had to keep people away from the house, it got so bad. I told everybody how sick she was, how she couldn't see anyone. She was sick, yes—sick in her mind, that's where. They took her to Vinita.[1] They shut her up.

JULIE. Opal.

OPAL. Now you know. I can't go on, keepin' it to myself. It's most drove me out of my mind!

JULIE. Of course!

OPAL. I couldn't stand it, people knowin', and pointin', and gabbin' about it the way they would if they knowed!

[*A tremendous and excited certainty is taking control of* JULIE. *The weapon of disaster is being placed in her hands.*]

JULIE. And you were right—the way people talk. Yes, you did well to keep it a secret. It's not the kind of thing you want everyone to know. Opal. Opal. I see how it must be. I don't know how you stand it. Ah, so this is what he—!

[*She stops, looks at* OPAL *piercingly, unbelievingly, as if she saw her for the first time.*]

OPAL. What? Why do you look at me like that? What is it you're thinking?

JULIE. Something I heard. At the Seminary, a new professor. He's been in Europe somewhere, studying. He told us things they never heard of down there at Tahlequah.

OPAL. [*Gripped by* JULIE'S *intensity.*] What things?

JULIE. You take a room—any room. Like this one. It has things in

---

1 Vinita, home of the Eastern Oklahoma Hospital for the Insane, is in the Cherokee Nation, approximately 40 miles northeast of Claremore.

it you can't see. Things in the air. In the walls. The dead come back, yes—but I don't mean that. This man says *not only the dead.* The *living* come back. Their thoughts carry them places. They move among things they knew in happier times. [*Her eyes probing the mysterious shadows.*] This room . . . Someone here—besides *us.* Can you feel it? Do you know who it is?

OPAL. [*Almost whispering.*] It's Clabe.

JULIE. Clabe, yes. He's always here. Like you could see him. *If you knew how to look.* [*Turning back to* OPAL.] And this you tell me—about your mother. You say she calls you?

OPAL. In the night. I wake up and hear her.

JULIE. [*With dark prescience.*] I believe you. You must have heard her—*for she was there.* Close as your breath. Those things are true. They know now.

OPAL. Julie . . . !

JULIE. Yes! Case after case. They've proved it. *And other* things too. About people whose minds get filled with one thing— and only that one thing. Insanity. *You can inherit such things.* The way you inherit looks, or the shape of your hands. Your mother knows.

OPAL. No, Julie, no!

JULIE. She must. Why do you think she calls you? You're close to her. Those with diseased minds are so alone—so lonely. They have to hang on to what's theirs. They know what it's taken us years to find out: the truth—and the danger. *The sickness is in the blood—and it doesn't end when your own life ends.* Your mother wants to warn you.

OPAL. I won't listen to you!

JULIE. The fear you have, that's eating you up. So that's what it is! It must be hell. Always there. Never asleep. *You're afraid you, too*—like your mother . . . ! Sleeping or waking—that fear in front of you—when?—when will the same thing strike? My poor Opal . . .

OPAL. Oh, please! Let me go!

JULIE. Go? Where do you want to go?

OPAL. You're puttin' things in my mind!

JULIE. They're already there! I can see it in your eyes! You're scared to death!

OPAL. Gard! Gard!

JULIE. [*With infinite scorn.*] Why do you call on a man who hates you? Why don't you call for Clabe? Clabe—who worships the ground you walk on! Let Clabe save you!

OPAL. I won't stay in this house!

JULIE. You wouldn't dare leave. Where would you go? There's a
storm out there on the lake! Where do you think you'd get to?
OPAL. [*Violent and crazed.*] Home! Home! Let me go, let me
go! . . .
[*She runs out of the room.*]
JULIE. Stupid, stupid . . . !
[*Grim and triumphant, she walks once swiftly across the room. She
stops, listening to invisible sounds, from below. She goes to the window,
looks out. She backs into the room, having seen something that tightens
her with apprehension and triumph. Sounds are heard on the stair, and*
BINA *bounds in at the open door.*]
BINA. Gard! Gard!
JULIE. [*With superhuman calm.*] Well, what?
BINA. Where's Gard at?
JULIE. How should I know?
BINA. I got to find him!
[*She turns to go.* MRS. SAWTERS *comes in.*]
MRS. SAWTERS. What's the matter?
BINA. That crazy Opal! She tore out on to the boat landing, right
in the storm! What's come over her, anyway?
MRS. SAWTERS. Find Gard. Hurry!
BINA. Where is he?
MRS. SAWTERS. He went out to the barn with your father, I think.
[*There are sounds below, consternation and calls of the two men.*]
BINA. [*Flying out.*] There he is! He musta stopped her! I never saw
the like!
MRS. SAWTERS. [*Sternly.*] What happened here, Julie?
JULIE. I was talking to her. She must have gone crazy. Said she
was going home, she wouldn't stay here in this house.
MRS. SAWTERS. What did you say to her?
JULIE. I said she was a fool to go out in such a storm!
MRS. SAWTERS. Before that, *before!*
JULIE. Nothing. Nothing!
MRS. SAWTERS. Julie! Look at me! I warned you!
JULIE. I know what I'm doing.
MRS. SAWTERS. No! *No, you don't.* But some day you will. And
God help you! [*With dark certainty.*] *Only He won't. No one will.*
[BINA *hurries in, near collapse. She clings to her mother.*]
BINA. Maw!
MRS. SAWTERS. Child. Baby.
BINA. O Maw, I seen her!
MRS. SAWTERS. What is it?
BINA. She tried to jump in the boat. Some way, she must have

fell and hit her head on the oarlock. She fell off in the water.
Gard got her. He's bringin' her up.

MRS. SAWTERS. Is she hurt bad?

BINA. They think she— Oh.

[*She sobs quietly, unable to speak.*]

MRS. SAWTERS. We better try to help.

[*She leads her out.* JULIE *stands a moment. Her face is filled with
animal triumph, but with something else, too—as if there were dread at
having succeeded so well. She goes up to* CLABE'S *picture.*]

JULIE. [*Low and tense.*] Is this what you wanted? How do you like
    it!

[BINA *and* MRS. SAWTERS *come in, go over to the bed, one on each
side, and pull down the linens. It is solemn, dream-like, ritualistic.*
GARD *comes in carrying* OPAL, *dripping. He carries her over and
lays her down.* MR. SAWTERS *comes in, pausing by the door.* MRS.
SAWTERS *with a cloth wipes the face. Then she and* BINA *pull up the
sheet higher and higher—till it covers her entirely. They release the
mosquito netting. Its white folds envelop the bed.* JULIE *stands by the
fireplace, watching, rigid and silent. She sees that the sheet is a shroud.*]

CURTAIN

END OF SCENE 2

Act One

Scene 3

CLABE'S *bedroom, toward morning. The light has been dimmed down.
Sitting in the semi-gloom, in the firelight, are* MR. *and* MRS.
SAWTERS *and* GARD.

*They speak in the quiet voices people use at night, or in the presence
of the dead.*

MR. SAWTERS. We'll jist have to get along the best we can then, I
    guess.

GARD. Any time I c'n get away from my own work though, I'll be
    glad to lend a hand. But it wouldn't suit me to be bounden to
    another man. I cain't do 'er, Dave. Never could.

MR. SAWTERS. I never could myself.

MRS. SAWTERS. But with no one to look out for you now—

GARD. I c'n get along without a made bed. And I c'n cook up my
    own grub as well as—better, if I told the fact.

MRS. SAWTERS. You'll be mighty lonely over there by yourself.

GARD. Oh, I might plan to take keer of that before long. You never can tell. A feller don't always do a good job of pickin' the first time.

[*They consider this a moment, his meaning.*]

MR. SAWTERS. No. People make mistakes.

MRS. SAWTERS. Yes, and have to try again—and keep on trying. I guess we understand that.

MR. SAWTERS. [*Quietly, almost to himself.*] In ever' kind of thing it's the same. When we first come here to Verdigris, this was long before the gover'ment allotted us Indian land—we was all set to buy the old Lowry Place we had rented. It suited us ever' way—'cept one. They had a well there—a big ole stone well with the clearest coldest water in the section. It was shore a treat to dip 'er up on a hot day and guzzle 'er down. But we'd hang the milk and butter and things down in it—the way you do to keep it cool—and ever' time the blame stuff 'd spoil. I couldn't figger it out. Why, the butter 'd get so rancid you couldn't stay in the same room with it. Good fresh cream and eggs we'd put down there—and ever'time the same dadburned thing. We never knowed what could be the cause. A funny thing. We shore let that place go like a hot potato, and found us another'n. [*Gravely.*] Yeah, more things in this life you have to watch out for. So many things—*and most of 'em you cain't even see.* It's too much for me.

MRS. SAWTERS. You better get on to bed, Dave.

GARD. You both had.

MRS. SAWTERS. Someone ought to wait up with you, Gard.

GARD. I wouldn't mind bein' by myself a while, ma'am. Won't be long till daylight now.

[MRS. SAWTERS *and* MR. SAWTERS *move to go.*]

MRS. SAWTERS. Well. [*She pauses.*] The girls made up a room for you across the hall. If you get too tired, you better turn in a little while.

GARD. Thank you, ma'am.

MRS. SAWTERS. [*After a brief compassionate look at* OPAL.] Good night then!

GARD. Good-night.

[MR. *and* MRS. SAWTERS *go out.* GARD *remains in his chair, barely visible in the gloom. After a moment,* JULIE'S *door opens, and* JULIE *stands there, in her nightgown, a wrapper thrown about her. She moves softly in, looks at the still figure of the dead girl. She goes over, lifts the end of the netting, hooking it up, and stares at the corpse. Then she goes to the mantel, takes out the flowers and going over again lays them on the foot of the bed.*]

JULIE. [*Softly.*] I wish I could take it back. [*Quiet and anguished.*] Why did you have to fight me? It wasn't *you* I was fighting. Won't you try to know that? I'll never rest if you don't.

[*She pauses, and after a moment, lets down the swathing netting.*]

GARD. [*Leaning forward into visibility.*] Julie.

[*She turns, startled. After a moment to gain her control, she tries to explain.*]

JULIE. Just putting some flowers here. I thought you'd all gone.

GARD. Somebody's got to watch with the dead.

JULIE. I'll stay now. You go to bed.

GARD. A husband's got his duties; they tell me. I reckon this is one of 'em.

JULIE. All right.

[*She moves to go.*]

GARD. Cain't you keep me comp'ny?

JULIE. Well, I—

GARD. A little while. [*After a moment, she acquiesces, sits down, near the firelight. He moves his chair a little closer.*] A man gets to thinkin' . . .

JULIE. Death makes you do that.

GARD. A man don't get much out of life, when you look at it.

JULIE. Some men get a lot.

GARD. A lot, maybe. But not what he wants. I never did. What I wanted the most. And still want. And still aim to get.

JULIE. [*Getting up, knowing his meaning.*] I'll go now.

GARD. [*Rising to prevent her.*] Not for a minute. [*It comes close to being a command, instead of a plea.*] I want to talk to you.

JULIE. [*Impatient, nettled.*] Tomorrow. Not now.

GARD. You've kep' outa my way for a year.

JULIE. I don't have to see people I don't want to.

GARD. You're in the same room with me now—and you'll hear what I got to say.

JULIE. You're a guest in this house! Try to behave like one.

GARD. I'll behave the way I am. I never laid claim to bein' a parlor man.[1]

JULIE. You're disgusting.

GARD. I'm a man and you're a woman. What's disgusting about it? It's you I want, and you know it!

JULIE. Your wife is lying there dead!

---

1 A man with polished manners.

GARD. Yes! I know that. I'm damn glad of it—and so are you!

JULIE. It's not true! I wish it hadn't happened.

GARD. Then why was it she told me what she did?

JULIE. What?

GARD. Just as I picked her up. With her dyin' breath. "Julie drove me to it. Julie."

JULIE. [*Appalled.*] No! She couldn't have said that!

GARD. I couldn't make it up. I heard it. [*With grim satisfaction.*] How much'll you give if I keep my mouth shut?

JULIE. I don't make bargains.

GARD. You'll have to.

JULIE. No one could believe such a lie!

GARD. You know it's the truth—that's the important thing.

JULIE. What do I care if—! [*Struck by his truth, sickened.*] Oh. [*She turns to look at the dead girl, with bitter contempt.*] You had to accuse me like that when you were dying! And I was feeling sorry for you! [*To* GARD, *almost tearfully, with angry despair.*] You may have hated her, your precious wife! But you don't know what a sneaking little cheat she was. She's got letters— from another man. She showed them to me. I told her I'd burn them up. I can still do it. I ought to! Even if she's dead, she'll know I kept my word.

GARD. [*Taking the letters from his pocket.*] Are these the ones?

JULIE. Where did you—?

GARD. Your Maw found 'em.

JULIE. You know who they—?

GARD. I read 'em. I had a right to!

JULIE. [*Weakly, trapped.*] All of them?

GARD. Ever'one. Here. Burn 'em up. [*As* JULIE *stands tranced, unable to move.*] Do as I tell you! You said you'd burn 'em. Do it!

[*She takes them, puts them on the fire.*]

JULIE. [*In weak horror.*] They're still wet! They won't burn!

GARD. Give 'em time.

JULIE. It's no use! They won't!

GARD. [*As the letters begin to flame up.*] There. That'll be the end of 'em. Forget 'em. You kep' your word. Now I'll make you a promise. I won't tell no one—nuthin'. And I'll keep *my* word—like you kep' *yourn.*

JULIE. [*After a moment—steeling herself, with forced hard poise— seeing what she has done, all of it.*] What do you want?

GARD. You know what I want. [*Close to her, roused, seeing that he is to win.*] It wouldn't cost you! You needn't let on like it would!

You're not the icicle you act like. You're burnin' up inside. It shows on you. It's in your eyes, your mouth. You cain't deny yourself all your life. Who do you think you're savin' yourself for! One man's as good as another'n. I'm good enough for you!

JULIE. All right, then.

GARD. Julie, Julie!

JULIE. [*Febrile, desperate, but resolved.*] Yes! Not because you threaten me. Not because I'm afraid of what I've done. Another reason! Because I don't care what I do now, do you understand? *Just so it's filthy and disgusting.*

GARD. Don't talk that-a-way. I'll be good to you. I'll treat you right. It's drove me crazy not havin' you! [*He takes her in his arms, fierce and passionate, kisses her hungrily.*] You'll marry me and come away from here, won't you?

JULIE. Whenever you say. The quicker, the better. Now! I'll lie in your bed, yes! Why not!? The slops they throw out to the pigs . . . the muck of the barnyard! Any place! *It's where I belong. . . . I know what I am.* [*Breaking.*] Oh, God! Take me away from here! . . . Take me. . . .

[*She slumps, fainting, against him.*]

CURTAIN
END OF ACT ONE

Act Two

Scene 1

The living room again. Mid-afternoon of Thanksgiving Day, the same year. The sliding doors are closed now. A huge stove has been set up in the room, the fireplace being inadequate in keeping out the cold. The organ is wheezing out a sprightly old-fashioned piece. Surprisingly it is not BINA *this time, but* MR. SAWTERS, *pumping away, and nodding his head in time to the music. Now he bursts into cracked and not very tuneful song.*

BINA, *flushed from the stove, hurries in from the direction of the kitchen and stops dead when she sees who is responsible for the uproar.*

BINA. [*Flabbergasted.*] For heaven's above! Paw!
MR. SAWTERS. Didn't think I could do it, did you?
BINA. Land of livin'! [*Overcome, she wipes her steaming forehead with her apron.*] You ain't tetched that organ since Heck was a pup.
MR. SAWTERS. When I was younger I sung like a meaderlark.
[*He tries another not very accurate phrase.* MRS. SAWTERS *comes in, and stands looking on, amused.*]
BINA. [*To her mother.*] Did you ever see the beat? Oh, I know *why.* Jist because Clabe's comin' home. You don't see *me* havin' fits about it.
MRS. SAWTERS. No, but I notice you made three kinds of pie and two kinds of cake.
BINA. [*Abashed.*] Well, what of it? I *like* to cook. Besides he's got that Blocky Lockhart bringin' him out. We cain't *starve* a stranger.
MR. SAWTERS. Blocky Lockhart ain't no stranger. Used to come out here purt' near every Sunday when he was a kid. Why, you've played Anty-Over[1] and Black Man[2] with him.
BINA. I wouldn't know him from Adam. He's a stranger to me.
MR. SAWTERS. Used to tease the livin' daylights out of you, too.
BINA. He better not try it now. I'll take a flat-iron to him.
MRS. SAWTERS. Hadn't they ought to be here by now? It doesn't take all day to drive from Claremore.[3]
MR. SAWTERS. [*Consulting his impressive turnip watch*[4]] 'Tain't but three.

---

1 A child's ball game, known by many other names.
2 Perhaps Black Peter, an antecedent of the child's card game Old Maid.
3 Claremore is 7 miles northeast of Verdigris.
4 A large pocket watch.

BINA. He said *before* three. The turkey's gonna dry up and blow away, they don't get here soon.

MR. SAWTERS. [*Teasing her.*] Maybe the buggy broke down. Maybe they froze to death. They's a half inch of ice on the lake and the wind cuts you like a knife. Or maybe Clabe jist forgot the way.

BINA. Paw! You reckon?

MR. SAWTERS. Or maybe they ain't comin'. I bet that's it.

BINA. [*In dismay.*] You think they ain't!

MRS. SAWTERS. Don't be a goose. Your Paw's funning you.

BINA. [*Bewildered by such actions from* MR. SAWTERS.] Well, I never! Actin' like a loon! [*He spanks her, and she flies out of the room. Then she flies right back in.*] What on earth 'd you reckon's happened to Julie and Gard?

MRS. SAWTERS. [*Her old sardonic self.*] They'll be here if they have to walk. Julie will.

BINA. [*Puzzled.*] Julie never was late for nuthin' in her life.

MR. SAWTERS. I never seen such a worrier. [*To* MRS. SAWTERS.] Lou—if I had some of that good port wine left, I'd have me a glass.

MRS. SAWTERS. [*Pleased, on her way to the cupboard.*] It wouldn't do a mite of harm.

[*She gets it out, with some glasses.*]

MR. SAWTERS. Why, you musta been hidin' it on me!

MRS. SAWTERS. You never notice a thing anymore. It's been right there all the time. [*She pours out a glass for them both.*] Bina?

BINA. [*Coming out of her puzzled concern, noticing.*] And gettin' drunk on wine, too! Well, I never!

[*She goes out toward the kitchen.*]

MR. SAWTERS. [*Holding his glass up, soberly.*] Thanksgiving Day.

MRS. SAWTERS. Something to be thankful for.

MR. SAWTERS. Yes, siree. [*They drink.*] I was wonderin'—

[*He stops.*]

MRS. SAWTERS. [*Nodding, smiling indulgently.*] Dave, you're as easy to read as a book with big printing. You're wondering if Clabe's coming home to stay.

MR. SAWTERS. Well, ain't you?

MRS. SAWTERS. Certainly. But I'm not pulling a long face about it.

MR. SAWTERS. Ahn, it's borryin' trouble to worry, I reckon. He'll do what he wants to, I guess.

MRS. SAWTERS. [*With a significance even* MR. SAWTERS *can't miss.*] Maybe so. Maybe not. He hasn't always done it, I notice.

MR. SAWTERS. No. But this time he—shorely by this time he must be growed up and in his right mind. [*With enthusiasm.*] Why, if he stays—we could break out that bottom land next year. We still could get into them stumps and burn 'em all out now 'fore winter sets in. And next spring Clabe 'd have him the richest cornland you ever laid eyes on!

MRS. SAWTERS. *Clabe* would?

MR. SAWTERS. Sure. It's most of it his Indian allotment, anyway. And it's never been tetched.

MRS. SAWTERS. More land, more work.

MR. SAWTERS. Who's afraid of a little work? By God, you're gonna see some changes around here!

MRS. SAWTERS. [*Pleased at his tone, but unable to refrain from chiding him a little.*] You're singing a brand new song this fall, it looks like. I can remember back—oh, not so long ago—not even a month ago, you—

MR. SAWTERS. I don't wanta hear about it. I'm gonna quit lookin' back. From now on. *Jesus!* The time a man can waste in regret or feelin' sorry for hisself!

MRS. SAWTERS. [*Smiling.*] You know what I think I'll do? I think I'll kiss you.

[*She does so.*]

MR. SAWTERS. Now what in hell 've I said to bring *that* on! [*A door slams.*] I guess it's them. I think I'll jist kiss you back. [*He does.*] Now we're even.

BINA. [*Bounding in.*] Here's someone! [*She hurries to open the sliding door.*] Oh. It's Julie. Howdy, Julie.

[JULIE *comes in, dressed against the cold. She is paler, the planes in her face stand out sharply.*]

JULIE. Has he come?

BINA. Not yet. We're waitin' for him.

[*She closes the doors.*]

MR. SAWTERS *and* MRS. SAWTERS. Howdy, Julie.

MR. SAWTERS. Welcome home.

JULIE. Happy Thanksgiving.

BINA. [*Accusingly.*] Julie, we ain't laid eyes on you in I don't know how long.

JULIE. I've been busy.

BINA. Not that busy. If Paw hadn't run onto you and Gard at the Switch, you wouldn'ta knowed about Clabe comin'—and serve you right, too!

JULIE. [*Nervous and haunted.*] I've been thinking that—maybe I shouldn't have come.

MRS. SAWTERS. Why not?

BINA. *Now,* what's eatin' her!

JULIE. Maybe Clabe won't even speak to me.

MRS. SAWTERS. Of course he will.

JULIE. After what he said, I don't know. For a whole week now,
I thought about it and thought about it. But I had to come,
anyway!

BINA. Well, if you hadn't, *I* wouldn't speak to *you,* so there! Of all
the craziness!

JULIE. [*Absorbed.*] I hope I did right to come. Something
happened to make me think so. Just as we started out the
gate, Smoky's colt came running up and before I could stop
it it ran out the gate. I couldn't get the wild little thing back.
But I thought maybe he'd follow, all right. But he didn't
follow, at all. *He led the way.* That colt was born here—but
we took it away, you remember, right after. And it's never
been back. I kept wondering how it knew the way—every
turn, every cross-road, around the lake and to the left. It even
dodged the barbed wire coiled up there in the dried grass
where the old fence used to be. I had to drive fast to keep
up with it. It was like something you read about, the way it
snorted and pranced, and kept far ahead. I couldn't take my
eyes off it all the way. [*With a wry laugh, becoming conscious
of her curious excitement.*] I don't mean I felt like that colt
exactly, but I suddenly found myself glad to be coming home.
Knowing it was the right thing to do. Wondering why I'd put
it off so long.

MR. SAWTERS. [*Genially, heartily.*] Well, you're here and you're
gonna spend the night, like you said. Put that in your pipe
and smoke it! [*Then puzzled.*] You mean to tell me Gard set
there and let you drive all the way—lickety split for election?

JULIE. Yes.

MR. SAWTERS. Well, where's he at?

JULIE. [*Reminded—after a moment, hesitantly.*] He had to hitch the
team.

MR. SAWTERS. Them horses ort to be put in the barn this kind of
weather! He ort to know that.

JULIE. Somebody else'll have to do it, then.

MRS. SAWTERS. Why, what's the matter?

JULIE. Gard's drunk—that's what the matter is.

MR. SAWTERS. [*Puzzled.*] Drunk? I never knowed Gard was a
drinkin' man.

JULIE. You know it now.

BINA. Is *that* why you was so late?

JULIE. I couldn't get him started. I've been after him since before noon. At first, he wasn't coming at all. Then he wasn't going to let *me* come. Finally, I threatened to walk across the lake.

MRS. SAWTERS. [*Sardonically.*] You wouldn't have got far.

JULIE. It brought him to his senses—what little he's got left.

MR. SAWTERS. I better go see.

JULIE. You'd better stay out of his way.

MR. SAWTERS. I never seen a drunk yet I couldn't handle.

MRS. SAWTERS. Dave, you stay right here out of the cold. I guess he can get to the house without falling down.

JULIE. No telling what he's liable to—! [*Sick at heart.*] Oh. [*A door slams. They all listen.*]

MRS. SAWTERS. It's all right, Julie. Take your things off. [*She helps her out of her coat.*] Sit down here by the stove. You must be cold.

JULIE. Cold, yes.

[*She sits.* GARD *pushes the sliding doors open. He is in an ugly mood, but now and then his subconscious hurt and bitterness break through his sullenness.*]

MR. SAWTERS. Happy Thanksgiving, Gard.

GARD. [*Eyeing the room—deliberately.*] The same to you. [*To the others.*] And you too. All of you. Includin' Julie.

MR. SAWTERS. Come on in.

GARD. Where's Clabe? Trot him out.

MR. SAWTERS. He ain't come yet.

GARD. I wanta see what he looks like. I wanta see the color of his hair.

MR. SAWTERS. Take off your coat and make yourself at home. It's Thanksgiving Day, you know. I was gonna offer you some port wine, but I reckon you don't need it.

GARD. No, and I don't want it, neither. I brung my own. [*He pulls a jug out from under his coat.*] And it ain't port wine.

JULIE. Gard!

GARD. [*Staring at her, his eyes half-closed.*] Mrs. Gard Dunham, my lovin' wife. My fine high-toned woman. None like her on land or sea. She knows the right fork to use—for she learned it at the Seminary. She knows how to treat a man when she's tied up to him legal. Yeah, you ort to know her, folks—the way I know her.

[*Sick with annoyance and disgust,* JULIE *rises, goes quietly out of the room, through the sliding doors. After a second,* GARD *goes over, finds a glass, pours out a big drink.*]

BINA. Paw, you orten't to let him have any more.

MR. SAWTERS. Let him have all he wants. 'S good for him.

BINA. [*Appalled.*] I never saw the beat and equal!
[*She goes out.*]

GARD. They say 'f you drink enough of this, ever'thing goes black
on you.
[*He pours down half the glass.*]

MRS. SAWTERS. [*With grim amusement.*] I don't think he'll have to
wait long.

MR. SAWTERS. That's the idy. [*He has got* GARD'S *coat off by this
time and helps him into a chair.*] We looked for you over here at
thrashin' time, Gard. We could shore a-used you. [*No answer.*]
I had a hard time gettin' fall plowing done, and winter wheat
in, too.

GARD. I got eighty acres over there to take keer of. They need all
the attention they can get.

MR. SAWTERS. Yeah, *need* it, all right.

GARD. [*After a moment.*] If you mean they need it and don't get it,
it's my business. I ain't beholden to nobody.

MR. SAWTERS. [*Gently.*] Now look, Gard, I don't want no quarrel
with you.

GARD. Keep out of my affairs, then.

MR. SAWTERS. [*Gently.*] Part of it's my affair, I guess. The crop
rent you turned over this year is the poorest that place has
made in many a day.

GARD. I cain't help that.

MR. SAWTERS. A farmer that don't farm is like a hen that don't lay
eggs. I ain't blamin' you, Gard. All I wanta know is *why?*

GARD. [*Dark, inward.*] Yeah, why. [*He looks at his glass.*] This is
why. [*He drains it down.*] Let it go at that.

MRS. SAWTERS. Yes, but why this? Why whiskey?

GARD. I don't wanta talk about it.

MR. SAWTERS. That's right, Gard—you just set there and forget it,
whatever it is. How about another'n?

GARD. Don't mind if I do. [MR. SAWTERS *pours him another glass.*]
Have one yourself.

MR. SAWTERS. No, thank you jist the same. That stuff 'd have me
talkin' Chinee[1] in two shakes![2]

[BINA *flies in and hurries to open the sliding doors.*]

BINA. Now *this is* them!

---

1 An offensive term for a Chinese person or person of Chinese descent.
2 Quickly. From the expression "two shakes of a lamb's tail."

[*She disappears, and we can hear the door open and her excited greetings to* CLABE *and* BLOCKY. MRS. SAWTERS *and* MR. SAWTERS *stand rigid, suspended,* MRS. SAWTERS *not far from the sliding door which* BINA *has left open. Even* GARD *puts down his drink and stands heavily, waiting.* BLOCKY LOCKHART'S *loud and happy voice can be heard, and in a moment* BINA, CLABE *and* BLOCKY *come into sight.*]

BLOCKY'S VOICE. Yep, if you ain't growed clear out of recollection! I never would a-knowed you from a stray heifer 'f Clabe hadn't told me—

[*They are in the door now, and he becomes conscious of the room, with people in it—and conscious too that this is* CLABE'S *moment, not his.*]

BLOCKY. [*Hurriedly, quietly, to* BINA.] Got a *lot* of things to say to *you,* Miss Bina.

[CLABE *is dark and hefty, and used to facing tough situations. But there is more to him than male arrogance; he is haunted and bitter, his mind is complicated by dark passions and an almost-violent necessity to survive. In this, his kinship to* JULIE *is very apparent. He is dressed in ordinary civilian clothes of the period.* BLOCKY *is young, big, red-faced, and hearty. He is almost bursting out of his clothes with too much fat and awkwardness and muscle and his overwhelming animal good spirits.*]

CLABE. Maw.

MRS. SAWTERS. Howdy, Clabe. I never expected to see it.

[*He comes over, takes her offered hand. Then they embrace. In a moment, he goes over to* MR. SAWTERS.]

CLABE. Paw.

[*They shake hands.* MR. SAWTERS *is speechless, moved.*]

MRS. SAWTERS. Cat's got your Paw's tongue, I reckon. Clabe, that's Gard Dunham over there. Julie's husband.

CLABE. Howdy, Gard. Been a long time.

GARD. Howdy.

MRS. SAWTERS. You know Julie was married, didn't you?

CLABE. Blocky told me. This is Blocky. Blocky Lockhart. You ought to remember him.

MRS. SAWTERS. [*Smiling.*] I remember a loud-mouthed little boy used to go swimming with you.

BLOCKY. [*With loud amusement.*] Ho! And still loud-mouthed, they tell me! How'd do, Mrs. Sawters. That's what it takes to be a rising young lawyer in this country. A good loud voice and a set of law books. I got both of 'em! Gonna run for state Senate on the strength of one of 'em. I ain't figgered out *which!* Howdy, Mr. Sawters.

MR. SAWTERS. Howdy, Blocky. Any friend of Clabe's is always welcome.

MRS. SAWTERS. Gard Dunham.

BLOCKY. Howdy, Gard. Used to have a brother name' Gar. Without the D. Short for Edgar. Went off to the war in Cuba,[1] and never amounted to a damn from then on. Yes, sir! [*They have taken off their coats by this time, and* BINA *has disposed of them in the hall, leaving the sliding doors open.*] Funny thing about my brother Gar. I used to ask him to tell me all about it and he— [*Breaking off.*] Whoa, whoa back! Shut my mouth, cain't you, someone? I guess it's Clabe you wanta hear from—and here I go shootin' my head off, as usual!

[CLABE *is looking at the room. They watch him hopefully, stifling their nervousness.*]

MRS. SAWTERS. What is it, Clabe?

MR. SAWTERS. Glad to be home, son?

CLABE. [*After a moment.*] Everything looks just about the same.

MR. SAWTERS. Things move slow in the country.

CLABE. That glass door to the boat landing is new. And that stove didn't used to be there. What's the matter with the fireplace? Doesn't it heat enough any more?

MR. SAWTERS. Winters seem to be gettin' colder. Or maybe *we* are, I don't know.

MRS. SAWTERS. There's a new enlargement of you over the mantel. Don't miss that.

CLABE. I was coming to that.

MR. SAWTERS. You must have pictured the way ever'thing was in your mind all these years, didn't you?

CLABE. I thought about it some.

BINA. Don't look to me like you wanted to get here! Why was you all so long drivin' from Claremore? I orten't to give you any dinner!

BLOCKY. It was all Clabe's fault. Now don't look at me, Miss Bina!

CLABE. We drove around the lake. Then we looked at the pasture over toward Verdigris. Your barbed wire is down over there.

---

1 During the Spanish-American War in Cuba (1898), Theodore "Teddy" Roosevelt (1858–1919), the future twenty-sixth president of the United States, led the First US Volunteer Cavalry, or "Rough Riders." Indigenous people from Indian Territory served in that unit. The play coincides with Roosevelt's term (1901–09).

The fence all along needs a lot of fixing. There was a bunch of stray cattle with a 2K brand all over the cornfield.

MR. SAWTERS. [*Amused.*] Corn's laid by long ago. They're welcome to what they can find. Nuthin' there but cuckleburrs.

CLABE. You ought to get a silo and save all that fodder. It's just going to waste.

MR. SAWTERS. I expect you're right.

CLABE. And whatever's happened to the orchard? I counted five apple trees blasted.

MR. SAWTERS. Wind tore 'em to pieces last year.

CLABE. You could have had them trimmed.

MR. SAWTERS. I been meanin' to do that.

MRS. SAWTERS. [*Coming to the rescue.*] Well, your Paw puts things off and puts things off. He's been a changed man now for quite a while.

CLABE. [*Low and troubled.*] I can understand that. A man starts out with something and he thinks he's got it for keeps. Only it doesn't work out that way. Some little maggot of a nerve turns this way instead of that—and he finds himself doing things that aren't like him, things he lives to regret. Then he wonders how it ever happened.

MRS. SAWTERS. [*Gently.*] Is anything wrong?

CLABE. [*Brassy and harsh.*] Wrong? In this best of possible worlds, what could be? Haven't you heard it yet—it's the Millennium? The country's on fire with progress. Indian Territory's on the high road to statehood. Everybody's going to be rich and the old U.S.A.'s about to become heaven on earth. It must be so—because T. R.[1] says it's so.

BLOCKY. That's the way this mutt's been talkin' to me ever since he got back. I don't know what's got into him!

CLABE. I'm a citizen of my time. You'll have to get used to it.

BINA. You ain't well, Clabe.

CLABE. I'm as sound as a drum. The medical inspector will vouch for it. I've got a long life ahead of me to dedicate to good works.

MRS. SAWTERS. [*Troubled.*] Clabe . . . Clabe . . .

CLABE. I'm sorry. I'm just tired, I guess.

MRS. SAWTERS. You'd better have your dinner and go right to bed.

CLABE. I'm all right.

BLOCKY. [*Taking a hand.*] Well, there he is, folks—the prodigal

---

1 Theodore Roosevelt.

son. I plumb expected him to get off the train in one of them middie blouses.[1] But the son of a gun claims he's got his *Dis*charge. [*He snickers.*] A Dishonorable *Dis*charge, too, I bet you—if they *is* such a thing!

BINA. Now you let him alone! I've heard about enough out of you!

BLOCKY. Now that's where you're wrong, Miss Bina. Yes, sir—I shore come to the right place, I guess! You couldn't a-stopped me with a six mule team when I remembered you got eighty acres of land in your own name.

BINA. Oh, foot!

BLOCKY. Who'd a-thought it? Why, I remember you when you was freckle-nosed and four foot tall.

BINA. [*Absurdly, striking at him.*] I never was! Maw, make him le' me alone!

[JULIE *has come down the steps. She pauses uncertainly at the foot of the stairs. She has put on the brooch* CLABE *gave her, and which she had given* BINA.]

MRS. SAWTERS. [Softly.] Clabe. Here's Julie. [He turns, looks at her, a suspended moment. Then he goes over, takes her in his arms, hungrily.]

JULIE. [*Overwhelmed with relief, dim and touched.*] Clabe. . . . Clabe. . . .

[*Her head is buried against him. He kisses her. Then he withdraws, his eyes on her.*]

CLABE. [*Huskily, moved.*] I didn't know if you were here.

JULIE. I didn't know if you'd speak to me. [*With nervous forced gaiety.*] My, you look so well! The navy seems to have done you good. Isn't it nice to have him back? I can hardly realize it.

BINA. [*In astonished annoyance.*] Julie! Who said you could wear that brooch? You give it to *me*.

BLOCKY. Here, here!

BINA. Why, she went and stole it out of my room. Of all the Indian givers![2]

BLOCKY. Aw, I'll give you a brooch. I'll give you one of them heart-shaped doodads with pink smellamagoody perfume inside of it. Next time I come out to see you.

---

1 A loose-fitting shirt with a sailor collar, first worn by a "middie" (midshipman).

2 Offensive term, with origins in the eighteenth-century term "Indian gift," for someone who gives a gift and expects it to be returned.

BINA. I ain't invited you, I hope you notice.

BLOCKY. I won't wait for no invite. I might be too old to enjoy it!

MRS. SAWTERS. Julie, this is Blocky Lockhart. Remember him?

BLOCKY. Howdy, Miss Julie. You're the gal I never could tease.
Used to jist walk out on me ever' time!

JULIE. I'm glad to see you again. But Clabe! You're not in
uniform. I thought you would be.

CLABE. I've been discharged.

JULIE. You have?

CLABE. The navy'll have to get along without me. They can sail
their gun-boats into whatever harbor they like. They can take
over the little yellow people or the little brown people for the
good of their heathen souls—but they can do it without me.
I've seen too much. I've had enough.

JULIE. Then that means you—you've come home to stay.

CLABE. I don't know.

JULIE. You don't know?

CLABE. Blocky here has got some kind of crazy notion.

BLOCKY. Nothin' crazy about it! He can do jist like I done. And
go a long ways fu'ther than I'll ever go, too. I want him to
come into my law office at Claremore and read up on the law.
He's smart as a whip, and always has been. Ain't no tellin'
what'll come of it. Why, this is brand new country out here
with opportunity knockin' so loud it'd raise the dead! Why,
even a old country boy like me expects to run for senator
soon's as the state comes in. And Clabe here might even get
to be the governor 'fore long—if he knows a good thing when
he sees it.

MRS. SAWTERS. What does Clabe say about it?

BLOCKY. [*Disgusted.*] Claims he don't know yet what he wants to
do. Claims he has to rest up and think it over. And chances
jist slippin' out of his hands!

CLABE. If I miss this one, there'll be another.

BLOCKY. You're only young once.

CLABE. When I was young, I didn't have sense enough to do what
I wanted. Now I've got on to a few things. I've had a look at
the world—and a good one at myself. This time I'll make up
my own mind.

MR. SAWTERS. You do that, son. I guess that's right.

JULIE. But if the opportunity is so good, as Blocky says—you
wouldn't want to throw it away. We wouldn't want you to.

CLABE. [*Looking at her—levelly.*] Why is it, the minute I get home
again, you want me to leave?

JULIE. I don't, Clabe. Why, I'm not even used to your *being* here yet.

CLABE. [*Strange, withdrawn.*] Will you ever get used to it, I wonder? I don't think so. Not in a million years.

JULIE. [*Almost in tears.*] Clabe! What have I done?

[GARD *has risen to his feet, and stands unsteadily, staring at* CLABE.]

GARD. Yes. What has she done? Tell her, Clabe. She asked for it. You're the bright boy can tell her. We're countin' on you.

MR. SAWTERS. Now, Gard.

MRS. SAWTERS. Here, Gard, none of that.

GARD. I can take keer of myself. Jist keep outa this. [*He moves closer to* CLABE.] Why'd you come here? What'd you want here?

MR. SAWTERS. Now see here, Gard.

GARD. [*Harsh and ugly.*] Answer me! What's so all-fired great about you they all go down on their hands and knees? I want a few answers out of you!

CLABE. [*With dangerous calm.*] Why do you talk like that to me? I'd rather you didn't.

GARD. [*With drunken, helpless fury.*] God damn you, anyway!

CLABE. [*Sharply.*] Shut up! You're drunk!

GARD. Yeah . . . drunk. . . . [*Deeply withdrawn.*] I don't understand it. Cold . . . cold as ice . . . I knowed she hated me from the very first. I thought she'd change. But I can see the way she looks at me . . . even in the dark . . . Jesus, I—

[*He relaxes weakly.*]

MR. SAWTERS. [*Taking his arm quickly.*] Get him upstairs. Help me, Bina.

[*Between* BINA *and her father, they help him toward the door.*]

MRS. SAWTERS. Put him in Julie's room.

JULIE. [*Involuntarily.*] No, no . . . !

MRS. SAWTERS. It's the only place. We've put Blocky in the spare room.

[BINA *and* MR. SAWTERS *have got him out, and they disappear up the stairs.*]

CLABE. I should have hit the son of a bitch—drunk or not!
    [*Wryly.*] Getting soft in my old age.

MRS. SAWTERS. Don't mind him.

CLABE. [*Sardonically.*] This country air. Peace on earth, good will to men.

[*He turns thoughtfully, figuring out something.*]

JULIE. [*Almost in tears—stricken.*] I'm so ashamed. . . .

CLABE. [*Tranced.*] Do you know what it means?

JULIE. [*Spellbound, not moving.*] He wanted to humiliate me.

CLABE. He must care about you an awful lot.

JULIE. He hates me.

CLABE. Yes, that must be part of it.

JULIE. [*With quiet desperation.*] Clabe, I've needed you badly. I
have to talk to you. There's no one else to talk to.

MRS. SAWTERS. Then you'll have to wait a bit, I'm afraid. Bina's in
a big enough stew, as it is.

[BINA *flies down the stairs, headed for the kitchen.*]

BINA. Lawsee! As if I didn't have enough on my mind!

BLOCKY. Want some help?

BINA. If you can jist keep from teasin' me for five minutes, you
can make yourself useful.

BLOCKY. [*Hurrying after her.*] I can lay off for jist four—and not
one second longer! Say, you don't know how you plague a
feller!

[*They disappear.* MR. SAWTERS *comes down.*]

MRS. SAWTERS. Is he all right?

MR. SAWTERS. Well, he fell on the bed like he aimed to stay there
the rest of his life. Don't worry about him. Let him sleep it
off. I better see to the teams, I guess.

CLABE. I'll come with you.

JULIE. No, please, Clabe. Not yet.

MRS. SAWTERS. He may as well start making himself at home
around here. Go on, son. [*Putting her hand on his arm, gently.*]
Your Paw's missed you, Clabe. We all have.

[*He looks at her a moment, moved. Then he turns and follows his father
out, closing the sliding doors.* JULIE *moves toward the doors.*]

MRS. SAWTERS. Julie. Gard 'll be all right.

JULIE. I don't care whether he is or not.

MRS. SAWTERS. I think you ought to.

JULIE. Do you have to torture me, too? Haven't I stood enough?

MRS. SAWTERS. Julie, come here. I'm your mother, but I wish I
could be your friend.

JULIE. [*Quietly, without self-pity.*] I haven't any friends. Not one.

MRS. SAWTERS. [*Compassionately.*] Julie, I wanted them all to go.
I want to tell you something. I'm not going to pretend it's for
your own good. It's not. It's for good, though, I think. And I
hope you'll be able to see it.

JULIE. What do you want to tell me?

MRS. SAWTERS. [*Touched by her lack of defenses.*] I don't want to
hurt you any more than I can help. Please believe that. But
the time has come when I have to take a hand.

JULIE. I'll listen to you. What is it?

MRS. SAWTERS. You're very unhappy, aren't you?

JULIE. I never expected to be happy.

MRS. SAWTERS. I wish you had. A human being has a right to expect happiness—even if he knows how hard it is to find. I'm sorry for you.

JULIE. Don't be. I don't want that.

MRS. SAWTERS. If you were defiant and angry, it would be easier. [*With deep sincerity.*] It's Thanksgiving and I ought to be full of good will. And I would be. But I know it's times like these, when you're afraid of causing pain, that the wrongs pile up till you can't see over them, and dark comes, and night overwhelms you. Over and over, you put off making a stand, and think it'll be all right. No. *It won't ever be. Till you oppose the thing that threatens you and the folks you love.*

JULIE. [*Dim, with breathless alarm.*] What are you trying to tell me?

MRS. SAWTERS. I love my son. I love your father. I've seen him just now, under my eyes, change from a broken-down old man to a man again. *I won't let you take that away from him.*

JULIE. What're you accusing me of?

MRS. SAWTERS. You want Clabe to go away again.

JULIE. No, it's not true.

MRS. SAWTERS. Yes! Even Clabe knows it. You're glad to see him, yes. You've thought about nothing else for weeks, months. But now he's here—you want him to go away again. Why is this, Julie? Tell me why.

JULIE. You're making it up. Just because I suggested—

MRS. SAWTERS. [*Low and sure.*] No. It's there. Too strange for me to understand. But that's the way it is. And you'll succeed in this, as you've always had your way in everything. You'll succeed—if I let you. And I won't *let* you.

JULIE. [*Deeply troubled.*] You think I'm full of plans of some kind! You've always seen me as I've never been. That's not the way it is—can't you understand? I'm tortured in ways no one can see. If I were stretched out on a rack, it couldn't be worse. Surely you can see by looking at me that I'm telling the truth. Please. Why can't you? I need someone to know. You see me as something—a snake coiled up, waiting a chance to strike. *It's myself the poison reaches.* [*Pleading—with quiet agony.*] Mother. I need help, not to be accused. I can't see farther ahead than my hand. And where it leads me, I don't know. I don't.

MRS. SAWTERS. To something horrible beyond knowing, I think. Julie, you didn't have any plan the night poor Opal died. But she's a forgotten thing in the grave, with no one to weep for her. You tied yourself up to Gard and you hated him. Now look at him. I don't hold any brief for Gard. He wasn't much of a man when you married him. But he was a worker and a good one. What is he now? What made him like that? [*Deeply aware.*] I know so much about things you wouldn't believe. You've turned the hate you've got for yourself against Gard now. I know how a cold scheming woman can do these things to a man. Because I did the same. Yes. When I was young and didn't know any better. But your father came along and saved me. He didn't understand any of it—but he was good, and he loved me. His love saved me. Who will save you?

JULIE. What is it you intend to do?

MRS. SAWTERS. To tell Clabe everything I know.

JULIE. [*Stunned.*] No!

MRS. SAWTERS. Yes! I will! I've got to!

JULIE. What will you say?

MRS. SAWTERS. Just what I've told you.

JULIE. No, mother, no! You're my mother. You can't do this to me.

MRS. SAWTERS. I brought you into the world. But even so—you have to earn affection, you have to deserve love. What have you done to earn it?

JULIE. I've behaved as I had to.

MRS. SAWTERS. And I must do the same.

JULIE. [*Cornered, desperate.*] Let *me*, then! Let *me* tell him!

MRS. SAWTERS. No. I don't trust you to do it.

JULIE. [*Choked with fear.*] I'll die. You know I'll die.

MRS. SAWTERS. The strong never die by wishing they were dead.

JULIE. They can do more than wish! They can have a hand in their death.

MRS. SAWTERS. I haven't any control over death. Only a little bit over life. It's life I'm serving now. I know what I have to do.

JULIE. No, mother, no!

MRS. SAWTERS. [*Spent, almost broken, tearful, but having to go on.*] Yes . . . yes, Julie.

JULIE. [*Her head bowed, dazed, fateful.*] I know now who my enemy is. It's not you.

[*But she doesn't say who it is—for it is not her mother—it is life itself.*

BINA *flies in from the dining room.*]

BINA. Maw, Julie. Please come. The others are all sittin' down. Paw and Clabe came in the back.

BLOCKY. [*Sticking his head in.*] For the love of God, ain't nobody

starved but *me?* [*Then remembering his manners.*] 'Scuse *me!* I
shore have made myself at home!
[*Quietly,* JULIE *and* MRS. SAWTERS *go into the dining room. They are
bruised and empty and alone—like people walking in sleep.*]

CURTAIN
END OF SCENE I

Act Two

Scene 2

The living room.
    Later that night. About 10 o'clock.
    JULIE *is in the room. It is apparent that she has been under a terrific
strain.* BINA *is close to the stairs on her way up to bed.*

BINA. Now you *will* blow out the lights—and you *will* go to bed
    pretty soon, won't you, Julie?
JULIE. Yes. Of course I will.
BINA. Well, I don't know. You act awful funny.
JULIE. I'm just worried.
BINA. Oh, I should think you would be! About Gard and all.
    Look, Julie, you can come sleep in my room 'f you want to.
JULIE. Maybe I will. Thank you, Bina.
BINA. [*Absurdly.*] I don't think I snore. And, anyway, 'twouldn't
    be no worse than a drunk man. [*Frowning.*] What do you
    think Maw's been gabbin' with Clabe about so long?
JULIE. [*Almost unable to find her voice.*] I don't know. . . .
BINA. I wish they'd go on to bed. If *you* don't come up 'fore long
    I'll be after you with a hickory switch—so watch out! Here it
    is after ten o'clock . . . !
JULIE. Bina—when you go up—if Maw's not in Clabe's room—
    ask him to come down here. I want to see him.
BINA. Talk, talk, talk! Well, I'll tell him. But I don't know why it
    won't wait till mornin'.
[*She disappears up the stairs.* JULIE *goes restlessly to the glass door,
stares out at the lake. Once she hears voices faintly from above, and
listens, straining to hear. After a moment, she hears steps on the stairs,
and turns to face them, her head up, stifling the sick terror she feels.*
CLABE *appears, and comes into the room. They look at each other a
brief moment.*]

JULIE. [*Quietly.*] She told you?

CLABE. Yes.

JULIE. There's nothing for me to say, then.

CLABE. No. Nothing. [*Pause.*] There's something I'd like to say, though—that might interest you. I told Paw he could count on me to stay here—from now on. I know where I belong. Any objections?

JULIE. No. No objections.

CLABE. Good night, then.

[*He turns to go.*]

JULIE. [*A desperate plea in her voice.*] Clabe! . . . [*He comes back.*] We used to be friends. We used to think we were different from everybody else—and that drew us together. Why did you write that letter last spring? It was cruel.

CLABE. It was meant to be.

JULIE. You couldn't have meant all you said about me. Most of it hadn't even happened then. Why did you have to do it?

CLABE. I was bitter. I hated you.

JULIE. And now?

CLABE. The blaming you part of it, I take back. I was weak and a coward—and you were strong, you knew what you wanted. I didn't know then why you were so bent on my going away. Now I know.

JULIE. [*Quickly.*] For your own good, Clabe. It was best, I was thinking of you all the time, I—

CLABE. Let's not have any more lies. It's late for that. You didn't want me to marry Opal.

JULIE. [*After a pause.*] No.

CLABE. Why?

JULIE. I couldn't bear to see you tie yourself down to a foolish, stupid little nobody who'd shatter every hope you had in life to be happy.

CLABE. That wasn't it.

JULIE. It *was,* I tell you.

CLABE. Shall I tell you the real reason?

JULIE. [*Involuntarily, unable to face it.*] No.

CLABE. You were afraid then. You're scared to death now.

JULIE. Oh, please! There were lots of reasons. The world. You needed it, to travel, everyone wants all the experience he can have, the broadening . . .

CLABE. It was *you* put those thoughts in my head.

JULIE. But it's done you no harm. Look—you speak differently even, you're smarter, you're better off in every way. You've had a fine life, better than most—and you have such memories, of places, people.

CLABE. [*Grimly.*] Yes. Memories.

JULIE. You've served your country honorably, and have your honorable discharge. Isn't that something worthwhile?

CLABE. My name's not exactly white in the navy records, Julie. You can't find any way to be proud of it, no matter how hard you try. My discharge is a Bad Conduct Discharge.

JULIE. Bad Conduct?

CLABE. Yes.

JULIE. But it couldn't be for anything serious. It must have been something that happened accidentally, not your fault. It *was* like that, wasn't it?

CLABE. My conduct was deliberate. There wasn't any accident to it. Once I deserted.

JULIE. That isn't so bad.

CLABE. [*Impatiently.*] O God, Julie! Can't you realize I tried every way I could think of to blacken my name, and ruin my character! There are plenty of reasons for my disgrace. All good ones! That brooch you're wearing, for instance . . .

JULIE. It's beautiful. Until . . . your letter that time—I always wore it to remind me of you.

CLABE. I sent it to you out of pure malicious contempt.

JULIE. Clabe!

CLABE. Wouldn't you like to know where I got it? You must have guessed it cost a pretty penny. A lot more than you can save out of a sailor's pay.

JULIE. You stole it?

CLABE. No.

JULIE. [*Numb with foreknowledge.*] Where, then?

CLABE. Oh, I bought it, all right. [*With significant but understated emphasis.*] There are ways open to the young.

JULIE. You—made money off of women?

CLABE. No. Not women. All sorts of creatures hang around the ports on the look-out for whatever they can find. They're lonesome and they're desperate. But some of them have money—and are glad to pay for their pleasures. [*As* JULIE *turns away, sickened.*] I didn't care one way or the other. When you're bent on destroying yourself—you'll do anything—and gladly—just so it fills you with disgust. [JULIE *takes off the brooch, in revulsion, drops it on the table.*]

JULIE. How can you bear to look at yourself? How can you bear to remember such things!

CLABE. I *don't* remember them—hardly ever. I've learned a little
secret. Even to think about evil is death. I've learned that.
JULIE. Then why do you remember now? [*Anguished.*] Why do
you have to tell me?
CLABE. [*With fire.*] I want you to know the worst, the way I do!
There must be something we can learn out of it. We were
born, surely we were, Julie!—with some good in us, the power
to do good in the world. And instead, we've been killing each
other, killing ourselves. The record piles up—viciousness
multiplied and multiplied—till no good is left in either of
us—nothing but hate and death and disgust and more hate.
The way to fight destruction is not with destruction—don't
you see it yet? If you don't believe it, look what wars have
done to the world already. It's the same thing—bigger and
more deadly. [*Gently.*] I have no war with you. *What there is
between us is not war—and you know it.* And it never has been.
JULIE. [*Stricken.*] You must be right. It must be so—everything
you say. Oh, Clabe . . . [*She bows her head, blind with tears.
After a moment, she can speak again.*]
When we were young, everything was so clear and bright.
We were happy.
[*Simple and moving, without self-pity.*]
If you could see my real self now—
My soul
If there is such a thing.
It's a field that wagons have been driven over, over and over again
in the rains.
The wheels have cut the juicy earth to pieces.
It's packed solid underneath the ruts—
Solid—like rock.
And no seed will ever grow there any more.
Never.
It's me that drove those wagons up and down,
Me that wanted the field to be different,
The crop that grew to be another kind of grain.

I can't lick what I am.
I see it now.
CLABE. [*Softly.*] Quit trying.
JULIE. But you have to try. Everybody does.
CLABE. That's what causes so much misery in the world—people
trying to defeat what they are! Miserable people—pathetic
from the first.

JULIE. I'll never be that. It's not in me to be pitiful.

CLABE. You're close to it.

JULIE. No! If I can just get rid of what I've done, the thoughts I've had, the needs!

CLABE. The needs—yes! There's only one way to wipe it all out— make it like it didn't ever happen, any of what's happened. *Give in to what you are.*

JULIE. [*Breathless, knowing the answer.*] What do you mean?

CLABE. The thoughts you've thought, the needs that are killing you! Give in to them.

JULIE. [*Appalled—low and tortured.*] You're my brother. Don't say such a thing to me!

CLABE. I'm saying it.

JULIE. No. I can't! It's more evil . . . sin that could never be wiped out.

CLABE. How do you know?

JULIE. It's in the mind, it's in the blood. The whole race of man is against it.

CLABE. Not all. Let's say it out plain, and see if it can hurt us. We're in love with each other. We always have been. It's taboo, they say. Who says so? It's happened like that. We fought it, both of us, fought each other, turned our sickness and disgust at ourselves toward others. Look at Opal, Gard, Paw and Maw. Look at us! Jesus! We were wrong . . . and ignorant. But now we know. *All there is to know.*

JULIE. [*In quiet agony.*] Horrible. . . . Maw told me once—hate on one side of a coin. Turn it over. On the other side, love. But *this—this*—love. No, it can't be!

CLABE. [*With tense conviction, pleading.*] Yes! It *can* be. *Any* love ever offered to you has things against it. Sometimes things that frighten you to look at. But at least it's something positive. It declares you on the side of life, instead of the side of violence and death.

JULIE. [*Tortured.*] I can't see it.

CLABE. [*His eyes on her, unbelievingly, but fearfully, aware of the answer.*] Are you so committed to darkness you can't make one step against it? Julie! Can't you cross a border that has no existence, none whatever? Are you lost that far!

JULIE. Lost, yes! Of course I am.

CLABE. [*Pleading against all hope.*] Don't be, Julie! Save yourself. You must. It's not too late. One step. One. [*As she hesitates, torn.*] There's no other way.

JULIE. [*Breathless with discovery.*] I know a way.

CLABE. What?

JULIE. Another way! Yes. I know. It'll save us—save us both.

CLABE. How? What is it?

JULIE. I can walk out a little way! Not far. The ice is thin.

CLABE. Julie! No! Come away from there!

JULIE. You're to sit there calmly—calmly, do you hear me? I'm going out that door.

CLABE. You mustn't, Julie. No!

JULIE. Yes! I must. You're not to come after me, not to tell anyone. Fifteen minutes. Give me time. Do that for me.

CLABE. [*Crying out.*] Father!

JULIE. Clabe, quiet! Don't do this to me.

CLABE. It's cowardice and you know it!

JULIE. I call it courage. I can hardly do it. And I've got to.

CLABE. I'll go with you, then.

JULIE. [*Pleading.*] No. You have something to do. You're needed. You can bring life, hope to this house again. Work will save you. To work, to *make* something—it's the only way to fight destruction. You must see it. *You gave your word to stay.*

CLABE. What good is my word? It's never been worth a damn!

JULIE. [*Pleading, desperately.*] Change that. Yes! As you love me—I can say it now—as you love me, change. You're young. You can do it. *You can look at yourself without shame.* I can't. I know I can't. I'm tired and old, sick. Let me go. *Let me do one good thing.* Please let me.

CLABE. I can't stop you. [*In quiet horror at himself.*] I don't want to stop you. God help me.

JULIE. [*Almost overcome.*] Sweet— [*But this is weakness. She steels herself, but it is hard to speak now that she is inescapably alone, and there is still a thing, the most difficult of all to do.*] You'll— you'll remember me sometimes, won't you?

CLABE. Yes, Julie.

JULIE. Clabe. You *mustn't* remember me. Ever! From this moment.

CLABE. How can I help it?

JULIE. Listen to me. Forget me. *I never existed.* It's best.

CLABE. Best?

JULIE. Yes! Even to think about evil is death. You said so. Hang on to that. Forget everything—you—me—my life—the rottenness—everything horrible.

CLABE. Yes. [*Spent with the effort, relieved and wan,* JULIE *slowly and deliberately goes to pick up the brooch and fasten it to her dress.*] What're you doing?

JULIE. This goes with me.

CLABE. You can't wear it now—that—that *thing!*

JULIE. I will, though. Like a badge. Like a banner. Where I go, it must go too. There'll be nothing left to remind you—of it or of me. *Even the memory of evil is death.* We both know it now. [*She pauses by the door, looks down at the brooch.*] See— It weighs nothing at all—such thin silver, a thimbleful of stones. [*She envisions it clearly, dragging her to the muddy depths. After a moment—she is not afraid.*] But it's heavy enough. Like a weight. [*She goes out.* CLABE *remains staring before him. The tick of the clock seems to grow louder and louder. His ears are strained toward the lake. All at once* BINA *bounds down the steps and into the room.*]

BINA. Julie! Julie!

[CLABE *springs toward her quickly. Takes her arm.*]

CLABE. Be quiet!

BINA. Where's Julie?

CLABE. She's gone to bed.

BINA. It ain't true. I looked in her room. Just Gard is in there— dead drunk. She must be somewhere. Julie!

CLABE. [*Desperately, putting his hand over her mouth.*] No, Bina. She's all right. You can't do anything for her. Wait till morning. The night will pass. A few hours. It's best. She said so. [*He lets her go, sits heavily in a chair.* BINA *stares at him.*] I don't feel guilty. Not yet. I don't think I ever will.

BINA. I don't know why you act so funny. [*No answer.*] But I think there must be a good reason. [*Puzzled at the thought.*] I feel somehow *you're* good, too, Clabe—not mean like you used to be. Do you mind my sayin' so?

CLABE. No.

BINA. I've noticed it ever' since you come home. [*Softly, secretively.*] I don't know where Julie's gone—and I don't care. I don't. And I think it's good I don't care. *Good*—not bad. Do you think I'm awful?

CLABE. No.

BINA. [*Like a care-free child.*] Oh, I feel so good tonight—like a load was lifted off of my shoulders! [*She goes toward the organ.*] I don't know—maybe it's the weather.

CLABE. [*Remembering* JULIE'S *words—softly.*] Tomorrow will be clear and bright.

BINA. [*Gaily.*] Uh huh. Bright as a daisy. I bet it will. [*Then, slightly abashed.*] Blocky's nice, ain't he? [CLABE *nods.*] I hope he comes to see us, like he said he would. [*Then, quite crazily, at that dizzying prospect.*] Oh! For once in my life, I jist don't care a hoot if I wake up the whole blame house! I feel so *good!* [*She hammers out some gay runs and chords.*]

CURTAIN
THE END

Appendix A: Lynn Riggs on the Performing Arts

1. "When People Say 'Folk Drama,'" *Carolina Playbook*, vol. 4, June 1931, pp. 39–41

[The success of *Green Grow the Lilacs*, which opened on Broadway in January 1931, raised Riggs's professional profile. "Folk drama"—a theatre of rustic settings, characters, and speech—was already in vogue, thanks in part to diverse playwrights such as Eugene O'Neill (1888–1953; *Desire Under the Elms* [1924]), Sidney Howard (1891–1939; *They Knew What They Wanted* [1924]), and Riggs's friend Paul Green (1894–1981; e.g., *The Last of the Lowries, In Abraham's Bosom* [both 1926]). The *Carolina Playbook* was produced by the University of North Carolina's Carolina Playmakers, with which Green was affiliated.]

When people say "folk drama" to me, which they do very often, I don't know what they're talking about. What's important to me in drama is what happens between people, or between a man and his inner glowing core. I don't care whether it's happening in Texas or Connecticut. It ought to be telling something about the human heart. If it doesn't do that, there's no wisdom in it, and there's not apt to be much drama. That's my feeling, anyhow.

I suppose, however, there are several good reasons for my continuing to write about Oklahoma. In the first place, I was born there and I know it rather better than any other section. Perhaps I wasn't very wise or very seeing when I lived there. But there's something about the impact of life on young people which is more astonishing and more rememberable than things that happen afterwards. This was my case, I think.

Also, when I was a child there, the country and the people were very dramatic. A primitive violence was always close to the surface, always apt to break out at any moment. It was all about me. Under a sometimes casual exterior, there was a fever and a thrumming. Just by an accident of nerves, I suppose, I was always conscious of this hidden excitement.

Most people think of small towns and of backwoods life as drab and uneventful. It isn't true at all. They're practically exploding with life. I tried to prove it once in a play. I tried to show an entire small town, its great range, its complex social structure, its vivid strange secret life. It's been lately attempted also, and very successfully, in a book called *Oklahoma Town* by a new young writer, George Milburn.[1]

Outsiders never seem to see it. But I was born in it. It conditioned me, it was my earliest experience. So far, I can't get away from it. I don't want to get away from it.

Then, too, the Oklahoma speech of earlier days was a rich poetry. The people had little education, so they used the imagery at hand. Things out of their lives. It was a fine and ringing speech—better speech than we have today in America. And the really stirring thing about the use of it was that they often did it self-consciously. They knew they spoke well . . . like the Irish.[2] They gloried in it a little. They sharpened it up. They enlarged their lives by using with delight the visible and known thing. A chair was not a chair, but a presence. A plough was an appendage of the hand. An old dress, handed down, was a walking demonstration of the unimportance of death. The things in their lives were touched, handled, loved, glorified in their language. If I could even approximate the imagery and the speech rhythms of my own aunts and uncles, for example, I'd be very happy.

But a complete and undeviating respect for character and speech rhythms, I am aware, is a dangerous devotion. It seems to me that too much realism gets in the way of a play. That is, too much photographic realism. Nearly all my plays, by intention, have a slight edge beyond realism. In other words, the little lying thing beyond realism makes them important to me. Perhaps that's what Art is—a subtle lie, for the sake of telling the truth.

Realistic truth is not real enough, certainly not good enough. A realer truth has to be uncovered. I don't think I should like a play if at some time the drama didn't just walk right out of realism on to a more illuminating and wiser plane.

In spite of everything I've said, I haven't any theories about playwrighting. Every play to me is a new problem. But there are some general things I believe about the drama.

---

1 Like Riggs, Milburn (1906–66) was born in Indian Territory and attended the University of Oklahoma. His short-story collection *Oklahoma Town* was published in January 1931. He and Riggs knew each other and were often mentioned together as regionalist writers.

2 Likely referencing the early-twentieth-century Irish Literary Revival, specifically the "peasant drama" of William Butler Yeats (1865–1939), Lady Augusta Gregory (1852–1932), and, in its apotheosis, John Millington Synge (1871–1909).

In the first place, I believe in the symphonic nature of a play. Chekhov[1] must have believed some such thing because his plays, with all their subtle complications, move quietly toward a symphonic finish where the people are revealed and the theme known. Second, I believe that what a dramatist is—the curious cellular synthesis that is the man—determines nearly everything about his work: the locale, the point of view, the tone, the comment it has to make, the characters it has to explore, and the luminosity by which it dazzles or offends. There on the lighted boards or on the open page is the man—his dark and shambling and monstrous essence. For his mortal satisfaction, the man who is dramatist too may hope to make the revealment less dark, less monstrous, more like a radiance in which a few lambent realities may cluster. It's a decent ambition, it seems to me. And that's the reason I go on writing plays, call them "folk" or whatever you will.

2. "High, Wide, and Handsome," Review of *Singing Cowboy: A Book of Western Songs*, collected and edited by Margaret Larkin, piano arrangements by Helen Black (Knopf, 1931), *The Nation*, vol. 133, no. 3467, 16 December 1931

[As a musician and a music lover with an abiding interest in the region of his birth, Riggs was the perfect reviewer for this collection. His visibility after the success of *Green Grow the Lilacs* made him the obvious one, too. Folk music—specifically "western" or "cowboy" music—was always central to his conception of that play, which he had formerly subtitled "A Folk Play in Six Scenes, with Songs and Ballads of the Period." In 1932, the publisher Samuel French would highlight Riggs's musicological interests, and his new-found commercial status, by publishing *Cowboy Songs, Folk Songs and Ballads from Green Grow the Lilacs*. Riggs, Margaret Larkin,[2] and Helen Black[3] knew one another

---

1 Anton Chekhov (1860–1904), the revered Russian playwright.
2 Larkin (1899–1967), aka Margaret Maltz, was a guitarist, singer, activist, and writer; she is best remembered for *The Hand of Mordechai* (Hebrew, 1966; English, 1968), a response to the Arab-Israeli War (1947–49). In a forthcoming book on Helen Black, Kristy Ironside asserts that "Larkin toured with the first performances of [*Green Grow the Lilacs*] and played selections from *Singing Cowboy* on stage." We thank Professor Ironside for sharing her work in progress. Riggs acknowledges Larkin in *Cowboy Songs* for "much advice during rehearsal and for generous permission to use some of her little-known ballads" (4).
3 Larkin's friend and collaborator Helen Black (1890–1951) *(continued)*

from Santa Fe, where, for example, they served together on a 1924 committee, chaired by Witter Bynner (1881–1968), to plan a highly theatrical "Pasatiempo" parade for the annual civic fiesta; and, along with Bynner, Spud Johnson (1897–1968), and others, on a committee to support Robert "Fightin' Bob" La Follette's (1855–1925) third-party presidential campaign against Calvin Coolidge (1872–1933) that same year.]

Miss Larkin's introduction to her collection of cowboy songs is the best possible evaluation of her book. Therein she defines the limitations of her material: ". . . the basis of choice was that they be worth singing over and over. . . . Although 'Singing Cowboy' is not an exhaustive collection, it is a representative one. It contains work songs, love songs, dance tunes, dirges, sentimental ditties, hymns, and narratives of daring deeds." This basis of selection and this range seem to me admirably justified. And being a poet herself, Miss Larkin has had an eye and an ear for aptness of rhythm and phrasing. None of the songs—the traditional ones—could, of course, be called literary. But many of them have fresh earthy imagery packed into their singsong and artless meters.

However, the collection is an especially happy one for this reason: Miss Larkin knows the cowboy. That he is vainglorious, simple, mildly passionate, chivalrous, whimsical, gay, sentimental, unafraid; that he is about one-half actor; that his emotional fluctuation, though "high, wide, and handsome," is not deep—these are things the cowboy himself will never know. But the book understands and exhibits him: indeed, the cowboy could learn from it, if he cared to, how to express himself more completely.

With these songs, with Miss Black's simply contrived piano arrangements, with some quaint and vivid steel engravings of sky and herd, of broncos and slaughter-houses and wide prairies, this book does a gay and valuable thing: it holds the West.

I have one complaint—the kind of complaint singers and collectors of ballads are heir to. Surely both Miss Larkin and Mr. Carl Sandburg[1] err in setting down: "I ride an old paint and I lead

---

was a pacifist, a Communist, and, from 1931 to 1951, a Soviet agent working in the United States; see Horbal. Like Black and Riggs, Larkin was a musician. Riggs acknowledges her in *Cowboy Songs* for "[having] set down and arranged the music which makes this pamphlet possible" (4).

1   Carl Sandburg (1878–1967), poet and compiler.

an old dam . . ." instead of the colloquial "A-ridin' old Paint and a-leadin' old Dan . . . ."[1]

3. **"Poetry—And Poetry in the Theatre," 16 November 1932, Lynn Riggs Papers, Yale Collection of American Literature, Beinecke Rare Book and Manuscript Library, Yale University, YCAL MSS 61, Box 23, Folder 379**

[In October 1932, Riggs arrived in Iowa City, preparatory to his directing of *The Cherokee Night* at the University of Iowa early in December. A heading in his typescript establishes the date of this "radio talk" and its delivery over WSUI, Iowa City. After sharing general thoughts on poetry and reading selections from *The Iron Dish* (1930), Riggs surveys the state of modern drama in the United States and elsewhere and expresses his own interest in a "poetic theatre."]

It is with real reluctance that I read poetry over the radio, or for that matter any place. Not that I consider it unimportant or too precious or too unrelated to the present world, nor that I imagine it to be a recluse art, one for the study only, nor that I think its special qualities are too delicate to compete with the sizzling violences of our time.

On the contrary, I consider poetry to be completely important, more immediately related to the modern world than any of the arts -- not recluse at all, but a thing for the communication of man with man.

But people in general in America are apt to be suspicious of it and rather justly. It is usually taught to them as something highly moral, something to become bettered by. "Listen my children--" and "So live that that when thy summons comes--" etc. Or it is taught to them as something cloying sweet, sticky and soft, like the incredible and endless, sunny, vapid smile of southern California, for example. Unless he's luckier than most of us, anyone who has

---

1   Sandburg in fact prefers "I ride an old Paint, I lead an old Dan" (12) [cf. Larkin: "I lead an old dam" (18)]. Riggs's phrasing also appears in Act 1 of *Green Grow the Lilacs*. His source is evidently Woodward "Tex" Ritter (1905–74), who played Cord Elam in the Broadway production and whom Riggs listed in *Cowboy Songs* among those whose "versions of songs" he had incorporated into that production (4). Sandburg's or Larkin's preferred phrasing appears in recordings by Woody Guthrie (1912–67), Pete Seeger (1919–2014), Johnny Cash (1932–2003), Loudon Wainwright III (b. 1946), Linda Ronstadt (b. 1946), and no doubt others.

been through school can hardly help feeling that poetry is sweet or pretentious, or childish and overstrained, or sentimental, hysterical, bombastic, or soft and vaporous -- and that it's made by a rather ineffectual man, one who doesn't seem to function very well in the rough outside world, of course, but nice, oh, very nice.

The poets I know are not like that -- and I know a great many. And, more important, poetry is none of those things.

Few people have bothered to say -- and fewer have bothered to hear that poetry is hard, not soft, exact not diffuse, clear and sharp and crystal and not muddy. That poetry is a real exploration into the psychical and physical mystery of what life is about. That it's an attempt to know -- beyond confusion, beyond acridity and despair -- the truth, however sharp and terrible it may be to hear. That poetry is the final and correct means of communication between spirit and spirit. That poetry is full of whatever bravery man can summon and whatever courage is left him to state and define the possible grandeur left to him. It is made very simply of sounds, words, which at their best intend, not to say for the poet "I this" or "I that", but seek to communicate and change as by chemical explosion the very cellular body of their listeners.

Poetry makes demands on the attention, most of us are not willing to accede to. It's something like work to listen and to see -- <u>visually</u> -- image after image which the poet piles up to create an emotional effect. It's not easy to attend the subtle relation of sound and sound. The effort is rewarding perhaps. But it's simpler to turn a switch -- to hear the moon come over the celebrated mountain again,[1] and the suave voice of the Old Maestro.[2] But when all marshmallow moons are in eclipse and the intricate seduction of jazz is dead, poetry will still say its important say. For the word -- as the Elizabethans knew and as the early Jewish prophets knew -- the word is God.[3] No man is exactly a fool who bows before something really majestic and austere.

But I am not the one to make a brief or plea for poetry. Being a poet is a state of being; whether people write poetry or not, they

---

1 "When the Moon Comes Over the Mountain" was a hit for Kate Smith (1907–86) in 1931.
2 Ben Bernie (1891–1943), bandleader and a popular radio personality in the 1930s.
3 Referencing John 1.1 ("In the beginning was the Word, and the Word was with God, and the Word was God") but apparently noticing Shakespeare, whom Riggs references momentarily, and certainly acknowledging the Old Testament tradition of Jewish prophecy initiated by Abraham.

are poets or they aren't. Their every sense is constituted to transmit to the brain a correct sensuous impression, whether it's beautiful or not -- correct. Or their senses are locked forever against assault by anything as intangible as words, which are nothing but air.

It is because then I believe poetry to be the final and exact expression of what man is that I am reluctant not only to talk about poetry but to read my own work which so faultily and so meagerly illustrates what I mean. I could read Shakespeare or the King James version to better purpose.

My poetry is only an attempt to chart a little of what I have felt and tried to communicate. Most of it is simple. Hardly any of it will be radiant enough to change your life in any way. Your cellular activity will remain just where it is -- or it might decrease. I hope not. But since I have agreed to read from my book of poems "The Iron Dish", I'll go ahead and do it.[1] Afterwards for a moment, I am going to say a few words on poetry in the Theatre.

Spring Morning - Santa Fe
Wonder
The Slight Voyagers
The Intimate Cleavage
Advice to a Mendicant
Morning Walk – Santa Fe
For a Silent Poet
Moon
The Corrosive Season
Footprints
Before a Departure
Portrait Of a Peer
Still Season

The American Stage has come to a strange place. There was a time when every stage in the land was full of romantic fables, sugary versions of man and woman who, darkly, through treachery and vicissitudes of every description, found each other at last and sank into their haven of delight, living happily ever after. The man was strong and brave. The woman was sweet and given to fainting spells. Both were excessively pure. These plays, having little -- practically nothing -- to do with life, vanished from the boards.[2]

---

1 Riggs identifies, below, the poems he would read on this occasion.
2 Riggs alludes to melodrama that flourished on US stages after the Civil War period, the residue of which he will acknowledge below.

Then the problem play[1] arrived. A practically insoluble personal or social predicament was settled in Act III, judicially and with thumping climaxes by a playwright who, acting the part of God, pulled the right strings.

Next we came to an age of experiment in which, as in poetry, other fields of life were studied for a while in the name of experiment, in the name of pushing out the boundaries. New people walked on the stage. The man of the docks, of the fields, clerks in offices, mad-men, quaint characters and frivolous women, etc.[2] After a while, they not only walked, they ran up ramps, waved their arms from curious structures symbolizing hopelessness or fell before purely symbolic machines.[3] In other words, the American stage began to experiment not only in realism but in the "beyond realism" theatre imported from Russia through Germany -- Impressionism, Expressionism.[4]

Then came a lull, and in the lull the slick photographic, swift moving realism of the American stage came to the front. It was mostly melo-drama, though sometimes it was a tear-jerker, like "Coquette". Or it had a social base, a critical point of view.

---

1 The social problem play, as distinct from the Shakespearean problem play, is a subset of realism associated with Henrik Ibsen (1828–1906), Bernard Shaw (1856–1950), and American followers such as James A. Herne (1839–1901) and Clyde Fitch (1865–1909), both of whose mature work melds melodrama and realism.

2 "Man of the docks" presumably references Eugene O'Neill's *S.S. Glencairn* plays of the 1910s and perhaps his *Beyond the Horizon* (1920); "[man of] the fields" suggests *Beyond the Horizon* and O'Neill's *Desire Under the Elms* (1924). "Clerks in offices" nods at Sophie Treadwell's (1885–1970) *Machinal* (1928), perhaps also at Elmer Rice's (1892–1967) *The Adding Machine* (1923). "Mad-men" and "frivolous women" are common in the drama of this period.

3 In the penultimate scene of O'Neill's *Dynamo* (1929), Ruben Fife kneels before the symbolic dynamo, "his arms stretched out to it supplicatingly" (876); at play's end, he "throws his arms out over" the generator and dies on an elevated platform (884). Designer Robert Edmond Jones's scenic sketch for the Young Woman's march to death in *Machinal* calls for angular lighting, suggestive of a ramp.

4 The most prominent exemplars of German theatrical expressionism were playwrights Georg Kaiser (1878–1945) and Ernst Toller (1893–1939). O'Neill (e.g., *The Emperor Jones* [1922]), Rice (*The Adding Machine*), and George Kaufman (1889–1961) and Marc Connelly (1890–1980) (*Beggar on Horseback* [1924]) were among the form's American proponents. The Russian director and theoretician Konstantin Stanislavsky (1863–1938) had recently credited his Moscow Art Theatre's First Studio with having "introduce[d] impressionism in the theatre" (434).

These were the days of "What Price Glory", "Broadway", "Processional", "The Show-Off", "The Royal Family", etc.[1]

As we came to about the year 1930, the talkies[2] began to supplant the stage in what it was doing best. In other words, it was easier to do on the screen the plays which were the very flower of the American Theatre, so the American stage began to look around for other things to do. It is still looking.

The American Stage looks at the Russian Theatre, with its thundering mass work, its vivid blood and thunder of Soviet propaganda. The theatre whose dramas are played by the audience as well as by the actors; not always literally, in the sense that they use the whole theatre, which often they do, but in the complete unity between what is going on on the stage and what is going on in the audience. This drama is about a burning conviction in the heart of every Communist, or so we are told, so that the Theatre is a directed exciting sharing in a political experiment.[3]

The American Stage looks at the French Theatre. But in the main the French Theatre is a classic, poetic morgue, with no life but the rustling evocation of dead Racines and Victor Hugos.[4] Even its modern plays are built for French acting which is a quaint

---

1 Most of these shows fared well on Broadway but have not endured: *Coquette* (1927–28) by George Abbott (1887–1995) and Ann Preston Bridgers (1891–1967); *What Price Glory* (1924–25) by Maxwell Anderson (1888–1959) and Laurence Stallings (1894–1968); *Broadway* (1926–28) by Philip Dunning (1889–1968) and Abbott; *Processional* (1925) by John Howard Lawson (1894–1977); *The Show Off* (1924–25) by George Kelly (1887–1974); and *The Royal Family* (1927–28) by Kaufman and Edna Ferber (1885–1968), which Riggs had co-directed in 1931, in Santa Fe.

2 Talkies, or "talking movies," debuted in 1927.

3 Pre–World War II Soviet theatre was abundant and well funded. The Kamerny Theatre continued after the Bolshevik Revolution (1917) under the directorship of Aleksandr Tairov (1885–1950) and Alisa Koonen (1889–1974); the renowned Moscow Art Theatre, co-founded by Stanislavsky in 1897, moved into the new era as well. New theatres included the First Workers Theatre and the Red Army Theatre. Other influential Soviet practitioners include director Vsevolod Meyerhold (1874–1940); playwrights Sergei Tretyakov (1892–1937), Konstantin Trenyov (1876–1945), and Mikhail Bulgakov (1891–1940); and theorist/playwright Vyacheslav Ivanovich Ivanov (1866–1949).

4 The neo-classical playwright Jean Racine (1639–99) is best remembered for his verse-tragedy *Phèdre* (1677); the Romantic writer Victor Hugo (1802–85), durably popular for his fiction and poetry, wrote the dramaturgically forbidding plays *Cromwell* (1827) and *Hernani* (1830), also in verse.

and finished elaboration for the vanity of actors. O[r] it is polished and witty, and sets out on the Boulevards again and again, the play about Him and Her -- and another Him -- or another Her. The triangle. Connubial lack of bliss. Naughty intrigue. Elegant dereliction.[1]

The American stage looks at the German Theatre,[2] but though the German has its highly trained audiences, its state theatre, its city theatre, its freedom from censorship, the American Theatre, for all its vitality and real attempt to confront life can only hope for a future when enough theatrical guile has passed under its own bridges before it can so completely dictate the terms under which it will operate.

Its next step, it seems to me, has to be in the direction of the poetic theatre.[3] It has gone through everything else, or at least found it impossible for our brand of being.

When I say the poetic theatre, or more accurately the poetic drama, I want to stipulate that poetry is exact, not diffuse, hard not soft, clear and sharp and crystal and not muddy. The American stage, it seems to me, must become a platform for fervor, for eloquence, for a blinding revelation of man. It must be hard and delicate and precise and lyric and exalted. It must be more than entertainment, more than life, more than ritual, more than color and glamour. It must touch and illumine the spirit of striving man. It must believe in the word -- which is God. That's the Theatre I believe in. That's the Theatre I intend to spend my life in. There are signs that I am not alone.

---

1 Perhaps decorously, Riggs overlooks the French avant-garde theatre that flourished in the late 1920s and criticizes the commercial "Boulevard plays" that enjoyed a short revival in the 1920s, and the backward-looking programs of the Comédie-Française and the Théâtre national populaire. Riggs's implicit dismissal of Jean Giraudoux (1882–1944) is noteworthy; Jean Anouilh (1910–87) was not an established playwright at the time of Riggs's broadcast.

2 Germany has a long history of affordable and innovative government-sponsored theatre. Bertolt Brecht (1898–1956) and the Austrian Franz Werfel (1890–1945) were prominent among dramatists working in Germany during the 1920s. In 1926, the Theatre Guild produced Werfel's *Boksgesang* on Broadway, as *The Goat Song*. A great era in theatre history ended with the Nazis' ascent to power in 1933.

3 Riggs's commitment to "poetic theatre" perhaps accounts for his positive response to *The Glass Menagerie* (1944); see Carroll. See also "Vine Theatre Letter" (Appendix A4).

4. Letter to Paul Green ("Vine Theatre Letter"), 5 March 1939, Paul Green Papers, 3693

[By 1939, Riggs felt stymied, professionally. During one of his many trips to Santa Fe, he wrote to fellow playwright Paul Green, reporting on recent conversations with Enrique Gasque-Molina (Ramón Naya),[1] his partner at the time. The letter is of the moment in its enthusiasm for the contributions of recent Russian émigré theatre practitioners and its dissatisfaction with Broadway theatre: in 1938, similar concerns had prompted the establishment of the Playwrights' Company by Maxwell Anderson, Elmer Rice, and others. Nothing concrete came of Riggs's proposal. Riggs, who owned a home in Santa Fe at this time, would again list photographer Ernest Knee's P.O. box as a return address later in March, presumably against a looming departure.]

Care of Ernest Knee, / Box 801, / Santa Fe, N. M.

Dear Paul:

I am sorry I couldn't come down and help with the production of The Year of Pilar. Too many complications prevented it for the present. Now I have come out here where I hope to remain as long as I can, still anxious to keep out of Hollywood if possible.

I am writing you now on a matter of great moment and importance to me -- and I feel it may possibly be so to you, too.

Ramon and I have had a great many discussions of the drama this winter and had reached, about a month ago, a few conclusions as to the nature of a theatre we could respect and belong to, and had begun to formulate -- purely, as if there were no obstacles -- such a theatre.

The poet in the theatre of today, we discovered, is bound to have a disgruntlement with the way things are. He has no home, no place to operate from, no platform from which to be eloquent, no audience to stir and change by truths he has found and the burning compulsion he is under to give his discoveries form and to make them heard.

You yourself -- your vigorous and lyric talent -- have no continuous life in the theatre. It's a disgrace and a loss. It's true that you've had productions, it's true that your name is respected. But you have never been truly seen or even moderately realized.

---

1 Naya (1912–80), whose relationship with Riggs began in 1937 and had ended by early 1941, was an accomplished painter and a fledgling playwright.

They begin, those little people, to chip you down, blur your edges, resolve your dissonances, re-channel your extravagances, confine your song -- even before they deign to put your work in rehearsal. This should not be. They have the effrontery to think you have much to learn. In all justice, however, those uncreative souls have most to learn from you.

Not only you, Paul -- not only the poets -- but the director, the actor, the designer, the musician, the dancer, the stage hand -- all these are slowly being conditioned to be less than they are; their talents, once lucid and pure, are wasted and at last destroyed before our eyes.

This must not be allowed to go on. A theatre must be created to use people, not to maim them.

One day we were talking to Mary Hunter[1] and she got so excited about not only the idea but the practicality of such a theatre that, knowing our feeling for Andrius Jilinsky,[2] she quickly arranged a meeting for the four of us. During that meeting (and subsequent meetings) we agreed on a great many points (as well as the ones covered in this preliminary note). We want you to know what they are -- because we unite in a common love for Paul Green; you are the only other American playwright we feel could possibly belong to such an enterprise. It is not only your plays, but your almost single-handed attempt to re-evaluate the theatre and the drama, not by what you have seen before your eyes but by what you have learned of the past and dreamed of for the future and for our time.

For a long time I have felt, and I believe you must have felt, that the theatre which you call "the theatre of the imagination" would come into being, of itself -- because there is a deep need for it. Now I know, and the others know, that such a theatre is not to be created by wishing. It must be built solidly by creators who have the capacity to make the vision real. And the first step, we feel, in making such a theatre a living actuality, is to produce a clear and exact body of theory -- in the way revolutions are made.

Here, then -- and numbered for your convenience -- are some of the things we agreed on. They are not listed in order of importance.

1.

The theatre we could work in should have, first of all, a program, not just a vague, idealistic desire to produce plays. That program

---

1 Mary Hunter, aka Mary Hunter Wolf (1904–2000).
2 Andrius Jilinsky (c. 1892–1948); born Andrius Matveyevich Oleka.

must be very clear, very precise, -- and no secret. We should know, before we begin, why the theatre is to exist, and what its intentions are.

2.

It must change the cells of the people who come within its doors. The theatre of entertainment can pass the idle time for the people who want to be amused. The person who goes away from a play of ours should not be the same person who came in. He must have had as vital an experience as life itself can give to him. Or rather -- it should give him <u>more</u> than a life experience, exhibiting with magic and eloquence the truth underneath experience.

3.

People are not to be lured into our theatre to be educated. They have come to share.

4.

This place is to be a place of creation, not of destruction. The way to combat destructive forces is not by destruction. Rather our accent will be always on creation. In the world today, forces in opposition to the triumphant, arrogant state are demolished by pogrom, by discriminatory laws -- and the other tools of inhumanity and cruelty. We do not believe that those forces really achieve their ends. We believe that the way to destroy is not to destroy. The way to change the world is to offer such a living and singing force that all people in whom the germ of truth resides, however deeply, will be drawn and changed by an instinctive need to ally themselves with life instead of death. Our theatre will attack nothing. It will expose the state of the world, of course, but it will lean, by its very nature, to the affirmative principles of goodness and truth. It will be aggressive in the way an oak is aggressive; not as the cannon is.

5.

We must re-evaluate the meaning of the word "theatre." Now it is a racket. We shall remind people that it is an art.

6.

We will maintain a continuous alliance with life-giving forces. We will look at the world -- our world just outside the door -- and speak of it from the beginning.

7.

This is not to be an "ivory tower" theatre.[1] We shall not aim just to produce good plays. Having looked at the world, we shall aim our

---

1 The "little theatre" movement at which Riggs gestures, and the "folk drama" with which he was often associated, had an academic (*continued*)

attempt to fix and comprehend that world right back at the forces that brought it into being.

8.

Our theatre, by its very nature, will produce new forms. We are not going to say right this minute what that form shall be. How can we know yet? We do know, however, that we shall try to use all the exciting manifestations of theatre art now current in theatrical usage. We shall certainly use the modern dance, which almost alone in New York at present is trying to do something about the world. We shall use music, new music, music that comes out of contemporary life. We shall use all the exciting mechanistic perfections of light and form and color and setting.

9.

This theatre is to be non-photographic and non-journalistic.[1] It is not enough to reproduce the color and smell of life. Let the movies do that. (A duty, by the way, which they are equipped to do but almost completely neglect). Or let the Broadway stage do it. It is not good enough for us. Slick representation will have no validity and wisdom for us or for the audiences we expect to reach.

10.

The dance groups -- Martha Graham, Humphrey and Weidman, Hanya Holm, etc.[2] -- have, either by accident, intention or necessity, gone out of New York into small towns; some even make transcontinental tours, playing not only in the big cities but in small towns and colleges. We shall eventually do the same. And we must keep that intention clearly before us, because our theatre will derive its new life from a continuous give and take with ever-widening circles of people. We are not going to sit in one place, closed

---

component, illustrated most pertinently by Harvard alum Frederick H. Koch's professorships of dramatic literature at the University of North Dakota, where Koch (1877–1944) founded the Dakota Players, and the University of North Carolina in Chapel Hill, where he founded the Carolina Playmakers. Riggs knew Koch from his own time in North Carolina, as did Green, a North Carolinian and affiliate of the Playmakers. Riggs's mid-period agent, Garrett Leverton (1896–1949), formerly professor of dramatic production at Northwestern University, is also apposite.

1 Presumably referencing the Federal Theatre Project's highly topical "Living Newspaper" productions. The FTP would be defunded later in 1939.

2 The "Big Four" choreographers of modern dance: Graham (1883–1991); collaborators (at the time) Doris Humphrey (1885–1958) and Charles Weidman (1901–75); and Holm (1893–1992).

in our four walls and ignore the dominant, joyous creative spirit of a wide land. We are going out to it, and give it something in return for something. This new blood, this new striving, this abundant precious vitality we shall always be on the lookout for, helping to keep it alive and helping to keep ourselves alive by this mutual contact. We shall find audiences, over a period of years and in widely separated places, so that it will not be possible for us to stultify and to die. We are going to say something about the world and, since we live in the United States, how can we possibly know the truth about it unless we go and look at it? We shall bring a certain amount of experience -- all of us -- to the theatre at first, but we shall never consider it enough. We must have ever more and more life.

11.

The world is full of sick people. Where are they to go for help? Religion and its solace has faltered for most of them. The political struggle of our time exhausts and defeats them. They achieve their small victories, and struggle, sometimes without hope, on toward new battle. It is very hard to live in our world. We want to make it not only easier; we want always to stimulate the impulse to veracity and the aspiration toward a new and better world. We want to stand like a rock in the midst of a world which fluctuates and staggers and doesn't know what to do or where to go. We need not be self-conscious or feel foolish at such an ambitious desire.

12.

We were discussing Christ. It is true he drove the money-changers from the temple with whips.[1] It is true that he sometimes denounced a man in his sins. However, the great contribution of Christ was the, to his enemies, dismaying habit of non-opposition. We can learn a great deal from this. We are opposing nothing. We are engaged in no battle. We have energy enough only to be constantly creative, constantly refilling the spring from which we drink. When we were discussing Christ, Jilinsky suddenly remembered a poem of Pushkin's.[2] We read it. Here it is:

---

1 Jesus' cleansing of the temple of Jerusalem is described in all four Gospels: Matthew 21.12–13, Mark 11.15–17, Luke 19.45–46, and John 2.13–16.
2 Alexander Pushkin's (1799–1837) poetic response to the Decembrist Revolt in Russia (1825) was published in 1826.

THE PROPHET
(Translated by Babette Deutsch)[1]
Athirst in spirit, through the gloom
Of an unpeopled waste I blundered,
And saw a six-winged seraph loom
Where the two pathways met and sundered.
He laid his fingers on my eyes:
His touch lay soft as slumber lies, –
And like an eagle's, his crag shaken,
Did my prophetic eyes awaken.
Upon my ears his fingers fell
And sound rose – stormy swell on swell:
I heard the spheres revolving, chiming,
The angels in their soaring sweep,
The monsters moving in the deep,
The green vine in the valley climbing.
And from my mouth the seraph wrung
Forth by its roots my sinful tongue;
The evil things and vain it babbled
His hand drew forth and so effaced,
And the wise serpent's tongue he placed
Between my lips with hand blood-dabbled;
And with a sword he clove my breast,
Plucked out the heart he made beat higher,
And in my stricken bosom pressed
Instead a coal of living fire.
Upon the wastes, a lifeless clod,
I lay, and heard the voice of God:
"Arise, oh, prophet, watch and hearken,
And with my Will thy soul engird,
Roam the gray seas, the roads that darken,
And burn men's hearts with this, my Word."
(1826)

These words are for us. We recognized what Pushkin meant -- and
how it related to us.
　　　　　"The green vine in the valley climbing"
Now we knew what the name of our theatre should be, "The Vine
Theatre"; for in the poet's concept it seemed as if he stood on a
great height out in space viewing the world and seeing the strong,

---

1　Babette Deutsch (1895–1982) and Avram Yarmolinsky's (1890–1975)
　translation of Pushkin's poem was published in 1921.

yielding, but always upward, always affirmative, and always green impulse toward the sun. Our theatre, green and resilient as a vine, must also thrust toward the sun.

13.

Ramon told a story:

"Suppose your father has just died. He was very close to you and you are overwhelmed at the loss, sick with dismay and the inability to make an adjustment. A friend comes to see you. He sees your pitiable state. He decides to divert your mind from your grief. He tells stories, makes jokes, gives you the latest gossip. Pretty soon you have forgotten your father. You feel better. Then your friend goes away again. Now you feel worse than you did before.

"A second friend comes to see you. He sees the state you are in. He is a wise friend. He makes no attempt to distract you. Instead, he talks to you about your father, remembers incidents of his life, reconstructs that vivid, dear, and inspiring presence. You see your father very clearly. The loss of his authority and love over-powers you. You feel very badly, worse than you felt before. Your friend helps you see that to be worthy of such a father you have certain things to do in yourself. You know it is so. Your friend goes away. Now you feel better, stronger; you have faced the fact of grief and you see that your life has to go on. You feel better able to cope with the world and your own difficult problems.

"In our theatre we shall be that second friend -- we shall speak of your dead father."

14.

The theatre has often been a place for small egos with their machinations and their duplicities. Our theatre is not to be such a place. Perhaps we shall put up a sign by the entrance door: "Check your intrigues here."

15.

We shall not set out to startle people.

16.

We shall start with a small nucleus -- a few actors -- perhaps selected for a particular play. We shall expect to reach only a very small group at first, but we intend to keep in mind the farthest corners of the country and we shall go there, as soon as we can, from our central plant. We are not going to harden into an esoteric admiration society. If we arouse any enthusiasm and loyalty, we are not going to stay stuck in that mud. We shall forever challenge ourselves by confronting people who have to be won.

17.

It is obvious that we shall need backing. We should like to get backing from one person. It will cost a lot of money and might prove impossible (that is, backing from one person). But we are agreed on this: We are going to have very clearly stated, and in black and white, our intentions -- before we even broach the subject to anybody. It is a psychic and physical fact that our program will displace by its vigor a certain amount of space. And we have no doubt of our ability to attract the necessary money to such a vital concept.

18.

We want, in the Vine Theatre, only people who have a life awareness. We don't want dilettantes, or people who might be better off in films or on Broadway. We want only those who are equipped by their senses to share what we consider a major adventure. It is not enough just to want to be in the theatre. We shall have only people who can not only endorse the essential nature of the Vine, but pour into it a fertile and continuously growing life spirit.

19.

This is not to be a theatre of ideas[1] but a theatre of feeling. If it doesn't awaken the sensibilities of man, it is a failure from the first.

20.

In the theatre as it is now constituted, an actor can stand in the wings at the moment before going on and say to himself, "Soon I go out on that stage and shine. Soon now I will show what I can do." In the Vine Theatre, our actor will stand in the wings trembling for fear he cannot live up to the ideal of the Vine. He will not be thinking of the presentation of his own small ego. In all humility he will feel the obligation laid upon him not to let the theatre down; and though he tremble with fear he will derive a courage from the fact that he is not alone in his pure and humble intention.

---

1 "Theatre of ideas" most likely indicates the anti-sentimental and explosively intellectual Bernard Shaw, a Nobel Prize winner for 1925 (awarded in 1926). Editions of Shaw's *Complete Plays* appeared in 1931 and, serially augmented, 1934 and 1937. A typed catalogue of Riggs's library includes entries for Shaw's *Caesar and Cleopatra* (1898) and three recent plays—*Too True to Be Good, Village Wooing,* and *On the Rocks*— that were published in one volume in 1934. See "Bibliography of Lynn Riggs' library" (1936–41), Riggs Papers, Beinecke, box 25, folder 428.

21.

The Vine Theatre, among other things, will remind human beings of the dignity of man.

22.

In all people who wish to ally themselves with the Vine, we shall look for an initial spiritual stature and possibility as a human being. This quality is absolutely necessary to our theatre. Without it, our theatre cannot exist.

23.

We shall make a home for ourselves in the Theatre. Our hearth shall be there. It must become that, too, to its audiences: as friends, though having their own home, go from time to [time] to the hospitality and warmth of another, which is a home for them also.

24.

Nobody in our theatre -- no playwright, no actor, no scene designer, no director, no stage hand, no dancer, no musician -- is to be whittled down from his initial stature as an artist or a craftsman. Whatever he has to start with will be used. And we shall develop playwrights, directors, actors -- and find new channels for all of us. It will be our constant purpose to enlarge and to help to seemingly-impossible achievement all those with whom we deal. It is obvious that the theatre must be a place for constant growth in all of us.

25.

We must be so clear that we will not ever be in the position of fighting anything. We cannot too much repeat: we have no worldly battle to fight.

26.

We must be ego-centric in this way: there being no standards, no law, and little precedent for this venture -- we shall have to be the law, we shall have to set the standards, we shall have to become the precedent. We cannot ever hark back (in our nature) to the Moscow Art Theatre,[1] for example, because we must be completely contemporary, meeting the conditions of our time and the needs of the present.

27.

This is to be a lyric theatre. And if we make it so truly, the stage hands will know it as well as the rest of us.

---

1   The renowned Moscow Art Theatre was founded in 1897 by Konstantin
    Stanislavsky and Vladimir Nemirovich-Danchenko (1858–1943). Stan-
    islavsky remained active in the company until 1928.

28.

We must never think of Broadway at all. This theatre has nothing to do with Broadway. The institution of Broadway exists and is a fact. It is a direction the New York theatre has taken. The Vine Theatre is not actually to be in the same field; so obviously there can be no competition and no comparison.

29.

Our goal and our audience is the <u>country</u>. Never forget that.

30.

We are to be, after a fashion, Messianic in our approach and our projection.

31.

Lenin[1] believed in the perfection of the spirit in the right kind of state.[2] We must keep our eyes on, and believe in, the perfection of the spirit in the Theatre State.

32.

Our audience is to be the young, not entirely in years but almost completely so.

33.

Jilinsky believes that all public utterances about the theatre are to come from the playwrights.[3] This is because they are supposed to be poets, with the habit of eloquence.

34.

We have discussed tentatively where the theatre is to operate, that is, where the physical plant is to be. Since it is to be a progressive theatre and the field being clear there, we thought of Washington. We have also considered Brooklyn, since it is out of the Broadway section. But, as yet, we have arrived at no conclusions.

35.

The Vine Theatre must constantly be both visionary and practical.

★★★

We discussed, Paul, a great deal more than this, (executive problems, financial considerations, questions of self-government,

---

1 Vladimir Lenin (1870–1924), political theorist and leader of Russia and the Soviet Union (1917–1924).

2 "Spirit" seems a stretch for Lenin, whose influential treatise *The State and Revolution* (1917) nonetheless argues for the creation of a radical proletarian state, as distinct from both the retention of a bourgeois state and the prompt demolition of a state apparatus, per se, as advocated by anarchists.

3 The sentiment is compatible with Jilinsky's written comments to Riggs about the responsibilities of playwrights, actors, and directors. See Jilinsky's posthumously published *The Joy of Acting* 3–10.

rehearsal plans, etc. etc.). But I am so impatient to get this word off to you, I don't want to go into everything at once; nor do I want to take time to write these notes as well as they should be written.

What we all need to know now is this: would you be interested in such a theatre? Will you help us to create it? Are there any points you'd like to discuss? We feel that the "body of theory" I mentioned can be built eventually from our correspondence while we are all so widely separated -- our Russian and our Irish-American being in New York, our Mexican in Mexico, our white man in the south, and our red Cherokee in New Mexico. We await your answer most anxiously and most hopefully.

As to the people involved, let me tell you briefly: Andrius Jilinsky.[1] He was with the Moscow Art Theatre and, along with Boleslawski and Vakhtangov, left to form the First Studio. After a time there he went to Lithuania as director of the State Theatre. Eventually he came to New York with Michael Chekhov and made a brief tour acting and being more or less second in command to Chekhov. He now teaches -- as does his wife, a brilliant actress[2] -- at Mme. Daykarhanova's School of the Theatre.[3] He has had in rehearsal for the American Actors' Company my play Sump'n Like Wings.[4] I have seen it run through several times and I have never had such a thrilling experience since I went into the theatre. The play is completely and faultlessly realized; its flow is so musical and so subtle and so moving that I found myself experiencing a play in production which had no previous relation to me. As Jilinsky pointed out, at one of our discussions -- at a certain place

1 Jilinsky's enthusiasm for the Vine proposal is evident throughout his uncollected correspondence with Riggs. See, e.g., Jilinsky to Riggs, c. 22 March 1939, praising the Vine letter and declaring himself "proud" to have been mentioned in it (Riggs Papers, Beinecke, box 3, folder 62).
2 Vera Soloviova (1891–1986).
3 The Lithuanian Jilinsky evidently joined Stanislavsky's Moscow Art Theatre in the 1910s. We find no support for Riggs's claim that Jilinsky had "form[ed]" the MAT-affiliated First Studio, which was founded in 1912 and included Richard Boleslawski (or Boleslavski, 1889–1937) and Yevgeny Vakhtangov (1883–1922) among its early participants and, perhaps, its cofounders. Jilinsky assumed the managership of the State Theatre in Lithuania in 1929. With MAT's brilliant director Michael Chekhov (1891–1955), he toured the United States in 1935; in 1936, he and Soloviova began their affiliation with Tamara Daykarhanova's (1889–1980) School for the Stage (not "School for the Theatre"). See Dobujinsky, in Jilinsky 147–57; and Wolf 130.
4 We find no evidence that the production was staged publicly.

in a play's progress toward production, the playwright vanishes, the director steps aside. I can't too strongly extol his comprehension and his artistry.

Mary Hunter. I knew her first in Santa Fe years ago. Two years ago, with some others, she organized The American Actors' Company, a small group of professional people who wanted to learn more about acting by working together.[1] She herself acts in Sump'n Like Wings, and gives a most moving and distinguished performance. In addition to her clear, artistic talents she has a great interest in the problems of the world, and such a warmth and sense of justice as one seldom encounters. She is, besides, extremely practical and has great executive ability.

Ramon Naya. His talent you know already. Lately other people besides ourselves have begun to recognize it. The Group has become more excited about him than any playwright in years. He is working with me now, as I told you, on a new kind of music play which is almost finished. In all fairness I must tell you that because of his fertility and purity and real taste, most of the ideas on which the Vine has begun owe their inception to him.[2]

Myself you know. What will be news to you is that since we have begun to see the Vine Theatre as possible, I begin to see a way of being really good -- and more, of doing good.

May we hear from you soon?

With affection, as ever,

Lynn Riggs

---

1 Hunter studied with Jilinsky at Daykarhanova's School for the Stage in 1936. A biographical sketch in the finding aid for the Mary Hunter Wolf Papers identifies Jilinsky as cofounder of the American Actors Company. In her "Reminiscences," Wolf describes the AAC as "an organization which grew out of the work done by a particular group of actors from Tamara Daykarhanova's and Vera Soloviova's scenes class and Jilinsky's technique classes" (137).

2 Naya was an accomplished painter and co-author with Riggs of the play *A Cow in a Trailer* (1939). A notice in the New York *Daily News* for 22 March 1939 reported that Naya "has won the Group Theatre's $500 play contest award with a drama called 'Mexican Mural'"; an addendum reads: "A special prize of $100 was awarded to Tennessee Williams for his 'American Blues,' a group of three sketches" ("Group's Play Award"). Riggs's letter to Green suggests that Riggs and Naya had been notified of this honor by 5 March. Jilinsky spoke well of Naya's playwrighting around that time. *Mexican Mural* ran in New York late in April 1942, with a cast that included Montgomery Clift (1920–66). Several 1942 newspaper entries reference Naya's receipt of "prizes."

5. "Some Notes on the Theatre," 19 February 1940, Lynn
   Riggs Papers, Yale Collection of American Literature,
   Beinecke Rare Book and Manuscript Library, Yale
   University, YCAL MSS 61, Box 23, Folder 381

[In February, March, and April 1940, Riggs stayed in La Jolla,
California, and worked on the San Diego Community Theatre's
premiere production of *A World Elsewhere*. The production ran for
five nights in April at the newly renovated Globe Theatre, with
Riggs co-directing. Per a dated note on the copy-text, the playwright presented this address to "the San Diego Community
Theatre, at the Globe Theatre." Riggs would have appreciated the
aptness of staging a play titled after Shakespeare (see *Coriolanus*
3.3) at a theatre modelled after Shakespeare's.]

Most people, it seems to me, are too casual about the theatre --
as perhaps most people are too casual about everything. I realize
that workers in a little theatre of this nature are here for various
reasons:
   it's fun to do plays -
   it's pleasant to work with people in a medium that gives an
      extra color and warmth to life -
   it's a way of killing an evening (and sometimes a morning and
      afternoon, too) -
   it's a fascinating world, magic, stimulating -
   it's a good place for self-expression -
   it enlarges your social life -
   it acquaints you with plays, dramatic literature you wouldn't
      perhaps otherwise encounter -
   it makes you more and more competent in one of the various
      arts and crafts of the theatre - acting, designing, directing,
      etc. -
   it's something that got wished on you and you can't get out of
      it -
   it's a deeply interesting and rewarding way of spending your
      spare time -
   it's something you intend to make your life work - you're going
      to be a professional (some of you of course are, or have
      been) -
   it's your training ground for learning your future calling.
And so, naturally, with this wide divergence of reasons for being
connected with a theatre like this, there's plenty of leeway for
casualness about it.

If your bread and butter doesn't come from it, if your future is not dependent on it, if you're not all on the board of directors - as I assume you're not - and thus can't dictate policy or pick plays - then if you don't take drama seriously, it's understandable.

However, I don't believe anyone should be casual about the theatre - no matter how minor his interest in it is. I feel so strongly that you've got something on your hands - and in your hands here -- and I'd hate to see it slip through your fingers before you've realized how precious it is, and, as an organism, how important and how profound.

Please don't get the idea that I think you should be religious about the theatre - that you should come in on tiptoe, with bated breath, full of awe and mysticism. Not at all. You should have some fun out of it. You shouldn't, I think, touch any aspect of the theatre without joy, honest-to-God delight. For it's platitudinous that joy is the very stuff of the creative instinct -- and so what I'm saying is, "Give that creative impulse a chance." And if you do, with gusto and joy, it will reward you greatly. And as it rewards you - it will reward the audiences who come to see your plays.

You certainly have no right to ask anyone to sit through one of your productions and to go out without being in some way changed. I don't mean completely made over, converted, changed in a moment to something new and strange and unrecognizable (like the villain in the last act of East Lynne,[1] or changed as I understand some people are by the ministrations of evangelists or a good woman). I mean only - an evening in the theatre should somehow, somewhere, change the cells a little. Or change one cell, even.

But you've got to give the spectator that little, or you're falling down on the job. (I realize that Broadway hardly ever does that. But in essence you can be superior to Broadway - in fact you are superior to Broadway in this respect: Broadway, even at its best, is a commercial enterprise - in fact, it's very largely solely a real-estate enterprise. "Rents. Terrible. How much do we have to take

---

1   Ellen Wood (1814–87) published her sentimental novel of the same title in 1861, under the name Mrs. Henry Wood. It was quickly adapted to the stage and would be a staple of US drama throughout the century. A Broadway revival failed in 1926; a 1931 film version was nominated for an Academy Award (Best Picture). In his designation of the play's "villain," Riggs evidently confounds the wronged, forgiving husband Archibald Carlyle and the intractable murderer and seducer Sir Francis Levison, but the famously tortuous plot encourages misprision.

in in order to keep open?" Of course, you have the problem, too
- but it's not the major one, nor on such a grandiose scale.)

This change then. To explain. You know how in life, more so
when you're young, and you haven't dulled your senses completely by indulgence, and stupidity, and all the horrible things
we do to ourselves to make us worthy of the grave before we're
really dead -- in life, you know, if your senses work at all properly,
how magical things sometimes happen to us. We see a lifted hand,
or a pattern of light and shade, or arrangement of color, or hear a
thrilling cascade or manipulation of sound, or see some physical
motion of a landscape or a crowd of people -- when something
stands out arrested, fixed in time, immortal -- and we are overcome with a pleasure beyond the personal, an aesthetic one, a tin-
gling of the spine, and perhaps a few tears -- tears not for anything
so suspect as sentimentality, but the natural animal response to
what we have had to call abstractly, beauty. And after this has happened to us, we are - even if minutely -- someone different, a little
different. We have had an experience that has reached us, and we
are never quite the same again.

Even more so - and more often, we should see those moments
on the stage. We - as theatre people - should make those moments
happen, or consider ourselves failing in our craft.

The stage is a platform for eloquence. Eloquence of word, of
light, of physical presence, of movement, of color, of sound. And
we are duty bound, with all these eloquences at our command, to
make those moments when the spine tingles, or the mind flares
with a new light, or the tears rise. This is the theatre - not life. It
is larger and more significant than life. It is a compression and
yet a heightening of life. It is a revelation of the symbolic and
overwhelming beauty and mystery of moments caught and held
and illumined. It is a rocket that flares and sparkles and bursts, its
tentacles streaming down grandly for a moment against darkness.
Well, the revealing thrilling moments happen in life. They must
happen more often and more grandly in the theatre.

Don't let anyone come in and go out unchanged. Reach them,
speak to them, make them hear, make them notice, feed and sustain them, change them. Don't maintain the status quo, never the
status quo - for the status quo is death.

I suppose most people don't realize that they're looking for
food and drink and light - looking for help - when they go to the
theatre. But I firmly believe they are. Oh, they've come to be
entertained, yes, but they want pathetically something to make
them more able to face life and the complexities of living. The

motion pictures, in the main, don't know this. And you notice how tired people have become of the endless repetition of a ridiculous picture world bearing no relation to life. And how people, by the millions, are staying away - in spite of double features, Banko, Screeno, Bunko, or what-have-you-O.[1]

Yes, people, even if they don't know it, want something. They want the illumined moment. And so you have a great instrument in your hands here. The living theatre. A place to enlarge and illumine life.

Now before we can enlarge and illumine life - we have to look at life. We have to inhabit this world crowding around us, not the world of the neighbor next door, and the friend down the block - that world, too, of course - but not that world only. The world of sections, of city, of state, of farm and crossroads, of America, of Peru, Patagonia - in short the entire globe. For we're tied together and we can't escape. And we know now we can't quite escape. We must constantly seek to comprehend, as well as the flow of tides, the flow of the tides of man in the aggregate, his needs, his impulses, and his right to dignity. It's a large order to be alive in the world today. It's strenuous and often demoralizing. But the more we seek to know and to comprehend, and <u>to add what we can to make it bearable for ourselves and others to live</u> - the more revelation we stumble on, and the more we have in our hands the power to change the world. (Even a cell at a time.)

As revelation comes to us - and it does a little at a time if we allow our God-given senses to function - we find we have something to say. As individuals we begin to have a special and unique wisdom. Thus it's time to ask ourselves, what do we know? What have we got to say? And how are we going to say it in the theatre? And I believe that you ought to be pretty clear about what you want, as an individual, to say about life - and what, as an organized theatre, you want to say.

In fact, I believe you ought to have a very clear program -- not a program merely of what plays you intend to do - but a program of your policy, of your aims and your goal. And I think this of the greatest possible importance.

Nothing on this green earth survives without an idea behind

---

1 Double features became popular in the 1930s; data assembled by Michelle C. Pautz show that movie-attendance diminished considerably from the early to the late 1930s. Banko is a board game; "Screeno" is presumably a jokey reference to the commercial cinema; Bunko is played with dice.

it, a burning abstract compunction, a pure concept, a central notion and aim. Look at our country itself. We'd be - right now - right this minute - completely disorganized and probably in ruins - certainly at war - we'd be many bickering states and tongues - if it hadn't been for some very fine ideas by such people as Mr. Thomas Jefferson.[1] Ideas - it's true - almost impossible of realization - such as "All men are created equal", etc. But without some such rigid and strong ideal concept, the practical forces toward such an end would never have got into our operation at all. We now largely believe that every man has a right to live and a right to work - and we stagger forward, and back a little, forward again a little farther, trying to achieve a torturing and difficult ideal: a government truly of the people, by the people, and for the people. But we wouldn't have been going anywhere - even staggering - unless we'd heard of that imposing ideal. You can't handle it, you can't see it with your eyes - and yet it's stronger than your flesh and blood, and it outlasts them both.

An ideal, a goal, an intention, an aim. Without it, there's no core to an undertaking. It's like a body without a heart to pump food to the farthermost cell. And without that core, that beating heart, you know what happens. The cells collapse, the body dies.

I realize that a theatre, your theatre, can stand for a time without any hard and fast intentions. (Perhaps you have them. I haven't asked.) All I want to tell you is that I believe they must not only be practical ones, they must be visionary ones, too.

I realize, too, that even if you haven't got them, they exist. Formless and chaotic - but real enough. For the composite need in all of you in this group is a driving force, and though inexact and not very clear, it directs what the nature of your enterprise is. (You know baking powder has a certain property, and when combined with other chemicals finds itself, say, in a biscuit. Combined with some other things (exactly what I wouldn't know) its original nature bends and contorts, is impinged upon (it goes through a kind of hell, I suppose), and it finds itself at last, instead of being in a biscuit, in an angel food cake. It has fulfilled its need, its function, to the letter - but the results are quite different).

What are you making here then - bread or angel food cake? Your cells are determining it. The thoughts you think and the deeds you do. You see, there's no accident about it. Every time we

---

1 Thomas Jefferson (1743–1826), one of the principal authors of the Declaration of Independence and the third president of the United States.

cut a piece of goods to make costumes, or dab paint on a flat, or walk across the stage, or pull a curtain, or put a word on paper - we reveal ourselves, what our nature is, who we are, what we think. What a betrayal it is!

I should think that if nothing else would, our vanity at least would make us stop and consider what trivialities of soul we are revealing. I should think we'd try to find out what we're doing, I should think we'd use our talents truly and deeply, to reveal the exact and the timeless, the important, the life-giving truth. I should think we'd take the theatre seriously. I should think we'd take life seriously. Which has been the burden of these few notes on the theatre. Thank you for hearing them.

6. "A Credo for the Tributary Theatre" (1940), *Theatre Arts*, vol. 25, no. 2, February 1941, p. 167

[This distillation of "Some Notes on the Theatre," reprinted above, appeared in *Theatre Arts* prefaced by the following "Editor's Note": *Because of its timeliness and eloquence,* THEATRE ARTS *publishes, in condensed form, this statement of faith delivered by Lynn Riggs in an address to the San Diego Community Theatre at the Globe Theatre early last year.*]

Casual as the personal reasons may be which bring the workers in a little theatre together, one dare not be casual about theatre itself. No one should touch any aspect of the theatre without joy, honest-to-God delight. For joy is the very stuff of the creative impulse, and this impulse must be given a chance if the worker and the audience which comes to see his work are to be rewarded.

Certainly no drama group has the right to ask anyone to sit through a production without being in some way changed; not necessarily made over, converted in a moment to something new and strange and unrecognizable, but somehow, somewhere, in at least one cell, different because for a moment something in experience has been made to stand out arrested, fixed in time, made immortal. Theatre people should make these moments happen, or consider themselves failing in their craft.

The stage is a platform for eloquence, on which life is compressed and heightened, made larger and more significant. It is a rocket that flares and sparkles and bursts, its tentacles streaming down grandly for a moment against darkness. Such revealing, thrilling moments happen in life, but they must be made to happen more often and more grandly in the theatre. The theatre is the place in which to enlarge and illumine life.

But in order that this may be done, life must be looked at: the world crowding around, of sections, of city, of state, of farm and crossroads, of our own country, of the entire globe. One must constantly seek to comprehend the flow of the tides of man in the aggregate, his needs, his impulses and his right to dignity. It's a large order to be alive in the world today. It's strenuous and often demoralizing. But the more we seek to know and to comprehend, and to add what we can to make it bearable for ourselves and others to live, the more revelation we stumble on, and the more we possess the power to change that world.

As revelation comes, we find that we have something to say. As individuals we begin to have a special and unique wisdom. If we are to draw on this, it's time to ask ourselves: what do we know? what have we got to say? how are we going to say it in the theatre? This means a very clear program, not merely of schedule and plays but of policy, of aims and goal. Nothing on this green earth survives without an idea behind it, a burning abstract compulsion, a pure concept, a central motion and aim. This country would be completely disorganized and probably in ruins — certainly at war — we would be many bickering states and tongues — if it had not been for some common ideas and ideals. We now largely believe that every man has a right to live and a right to work; true, we have staggered forward, and back a little, then forward again a little farther, trying to achieve a government truly of the people, by the people and for the people. But the point is that we would not be going anywhere — even staggering — unless we had that imposing ideal. One can't handle it; it can't be seen, and yet it is stronger than flesh and blood, and it outlasts them both.

An ideal, a goal, an intention, an aim — without it, there is no core to an undertaking. It is like a body without a heart to pump food to the farthermost cell. A theatre can stand for a time without any hard and fast intentions, but in the long run, if it is to live, it must have visionary as well as practical goals. Actually, these visionary ideals exist in every theatre group, often formless and chaotic but nonetheless real. The composite need that has brought the group together is a driving force; however inexact and unclear it may be, it directs the whole enterprise. There is no accident about it. Every time we cut a piece of goods to make costumes, or dab paint on a flat, or walk across the stage, or pull a curtain, or put a word on paper, we reveal ourselves, what our nature is, who we are, what we think, what we intend to do.

What a betrayal that can be. I should think that, if nothing else would, vanity at least might make us stop to consider what trivialities of soul we are revealing. I should think we would try to find out what we are doing, that we would wait to use our talents truly and deeply, in order to reveal the exact and the timeless, the important, the life-giving truth. I should think we would take the theatre seriously. I should think we would take life seriously.

7. "What the Theatre Can Mean to All of Us," 27 March 1940, Lynn Riggs Papers, Yale Collection of American Literature, Beinecke Rare Book and Manuscript Library, Yale University, YCAL MSS 61, Box 23, Folder 382

[Autograph addenda to our copy-text identify the occasion as a "Wednesday Club Luncheon[,] San Diego" and correct the typed date of "March 26." See also headnote to Appendix A5, above.]

Before I suggest to you what the theatre can mean to all of us - I'd like to tell you first what it means to me personally. There's a reason for this. If I can communicate a little of my own point of view as a playwright, a little of my own enthusiasm for a great and noble art - (an enthusiasm which actually absorbs me pretty much - beyond my will, my intention - and probably my health, certainly my peace of mind!) -- if I can give you a little hint of the fever that eats me, I have an idea it will tell you something about yourself, too.

In a lyric poem, you know how the poet - overwhelmed with an emotion, and the necessity to communicate it to paper and to us before it destroys him - you know how he finds the image and the music to do it with - And he pours it out, in his own person - (the "I" working overtime) - seemingly dismayed by his own egotistic response to the universe, dazzled by his own immortal soul.

But what happens? If what he feels is true and just and important and stirring and deeply human -- we find he's not only speaking for himself - he's speaking for us. We see his images, we inhabit the mood he's created - the mood of night, or wind, or love, or terror - we share his emotions, we respond to his truth - because his truth is our truth, too, and we have been reminded. This is the way we feel, the way we think, the way our pulses beat and our senses sing.

So let me tell you about myself. Maybe some of it is about you, too. (Anyway, here I am trying not to be charged with Narcissism. Maybe I'm going to. We'll find out in a minute.)

The playwright then. Myself. What does the theatre mean to me?

1. It gives me a chance to say what I feel about life.

(You might with some justice ask me why it's so important for me to say what I feel about life. You might say: "What makes you think you've got something to say that anyone wants to hear?!"

(My answer to that has to be: "I don't know whether anyone wants to hear it or not - but I can't keep my mouth shut.")

I tried it once for a year and it nearly killed me.

Like anyone who lives in relation to an art -- I have to keep on endlessly giving some form to life, I have to try to fix moments, moods, people, relationships -- so that I understand them, give them order, and, as nearly as I'm able, the great precision and dignity of an art form. The accident of my sensory equipment makes me do this in plays.

And I fail all the time. It's never quite satisfactory to me. (I wish you could see me rehearsing at the Globe - cutting lines, adding them, tearing things to pieces -- trying to get closer all the time to what I meant to say!)

But the important point is: I can't stop trying to find out what life is about, and I can't stop trying to say some of it in the form of a play.

Doesn't my predicament relate to you also? Don't you -- in your various occupations and duties -- try to give life order and distinction and grace and beauty and color and meaning? Of course you do. Whoever you are and whatever you occupy your time with. You paint, perhaps - or write, or play the piano, or run a house with finesse and cunning and care. You try to make the life around you bend more and more toward your concept of the good life. Better schools, decenter civil administration, good music, etc. (Lord, you even vote - for congressmen you think will pass laws that will make a better shape for the country we live in!)

You can't stop. Don't stop. Make. Create. You'll die if you don't do what's in you to do.

2. The theatre enlarges my life.

Here we're in the same boat exactly. It enlarges yours too.

Think - just as a matter of pure information - how much for instance we know about Ibsen's Norway from his plays. The provincial, clacking, hide-bound, smoldering, ruthless lives. The chicanery. The idle, bored and dangerous venom of the intellectual woman with no work to give meaning to her existence - Hedda Gabler.[1]

Think too, of the emotion we experience when, as in A Doll's House,[2] a woman dares to slam out of her husband's house for the first time in artistic history -- thereby declaring a woman's right to freedom and a soul.

Remember Shakespeare and Shakespeare's young England. Brawling, high-sounding, vital, self-conscious, bombastic, bear-baiting England -- with tyrannical old war horse, Elizabeth on the throne[3] -- and all life opening to a rude and shattering force among nations.

(Statecraft, cunning, and perhaps lack of conscience in the modern sense, and a staggering courage - built England. But I say - Shakespeare built England. He exposed the heights, and tragic depths, the complexity, and the lyrical and infinite reaches of what the Elizabethan only crudely felt -- he gave him meaning and direction - he composed the units of human impulse into a version of all it was possible for a man to be -- and thus we behold England, that warring, self-confident, dynamic thrust into the world -- and into the mind - that has colored and conditioned them and us ever since.

(Perhaps some of you think it's a shame -- if it's true - that Shakespeare made the British Empire. But that's beside the point. No politics today.)

And look how our life expands with a play of Chekhov - reading it - or better - seeing it in the theatre. The Cherry Orchard, say.[4]

In that terrible intimacy of looking across footlights through a

---

1 *Hedda Gabler*, by Henrik Ibsen, premiered in Germany in 1891, was translated into English that year, and first played in the United States in 1898, with Elizabeth Robins (1862–1952) reprising her Hedda from the 1891 London production. The significance of the play's eponymous character in shaping modern dramatic representations of women, like that of Nora Helmer in Ibsen's *A Doll's House* (see below), cannot be overstated. Hedda remains a prized role for enterprising actresses.

2 *A Doll's House* premiered in Denmark in 1879, was translated into English in 1882 (as *Nora*), and first played in the United States in 1883, with Helena Modjeska (1840–1909) as Nora Helmer.

3 Queen Elizabeth I reigned from 1533 to 1603.

4 Chekhov's *The Cherry Orchard* premiered at the Moscow Art Theatre in 1904 and was translated into English in 1908. The MAT's legendary director, Konstantin Stanislavsky, brought the play to New York in 1923.

wall that's no longer there - the pathetic, the poignant, well-meaning, but <u>actionless</u>, <u>will-less</u> people, seeing the vigorous new world creeping up on them, fraying their nerves, taking their money.[1] And at last we hear the axe slashing down the cherry orchard - the symbol of their by now useless lives (but so lovely, so pitiable!) a good dozen years before the axe actually fell on that bleak October, 1917.[2]

Now the theatre really means a great deal more to all of us than I have time to tell you. You know that. But I hope I have reminded you a little, which is all I can expect to do.

Now that I've mentioned some of the great ones - there's just time to read part of a scene from one not so great. I'd like to explain that high comedy seems to me the hardest kind of play to write. You have to be serious, and you have to appear not so. And yet every once in a while, like a small fountain spearing up, the hard clear water of truth must arise.

All I can give you in this beginning of my comedy, <u>Russet Mantle</u>,
   is the flavor of the place it's set in
   intimations of character - with
     very minor suggestions of their
      deeper impulses
     and some fun - I hope![3]

---

1 See also Riggs's teaching notes from October 1941, when he was on the faculty of Baylor University, under "Chekhov": "The aloneness of each one, talking to himself, repeating his theme" (Riggs Papers, Beinecke, box 9, folder 168, p. F-4).
2 Riggs likens Vladimir Lenin's October Revolution (aka the Bolshevik Revolution) in St. Petersburg, Russia, to the destruction of Mme. Lyubov Ranevsky's orchard in *The Cherry Orchard*.
3 An autograph addendum on the copy-text reads: "Read to Kay's entrance in <u>Russet Mantle</u>. (Club - staid mostly - Felt some consternation at what they must have considered risque [sic])." See Riggs, "Russet Mantle" 5–25.

8. "We Speak for Ourselves: A Dance Poem," *Theatre Arts*,
   vol. 27, no. 12, December 1943, pp. 752–57

[Riggs's collaboration with the innovative and influential dancer
and choreographer José Limón (1908–72) was performed on 5
September 1943, during World War II, as part of a miscellaneous
program entitled "Fun for the Birds." Admission was "free with
the purchase of a War Bond or Stamps," reported the *Richmond
News Leader* for 3 September ("Intermission Entertainment").
That paper puffed the event in an impressively democratic fashion. Although an entry for 31 August focused on "We Speak for
Ourselves," columns on 2 and 3 September ignored it and led,
respectively, with "Gerard and Carol, acrobatic dance team"
and "Private Veto [i.e., Vito] Mariani, accordionist, and Private
Abrasha Robofsky, operatic and concert singer" ("Lee's Show";
"Intermission Entertainment"). These performers, too, were
known before the war, if not as widely as Riggs and Limón. The
following prefatory note from the *Theatre Arts* text introduces the
creative team: "*The Special Service Office at Camp Lee, Virginia,
opened the War Bond Drive in Richmond this fall with a soldier revue,*
Fun for the Birds, *produced, directed and managed by Capt. Bruce
Conning, Sgt. Don Stevens and Pfc. Ray E. Hinkley. The feature of
the show was Lynn Riggs' dance poem, composed and danced by Pvt.
José Limon, long an outstanding member of the Humphrey-Weidman
company, with Pvt. Diane Roberts of the WACS (a dancer in her own
right) for partner, and a dance chorus of twelve infantrymen. The words
of the poem were spoken by Cpl. Richard Kendricks, a pre-war New
York actor.*"[1]]

SOLDIER NARRATOR
I am a soldier (*with quiet simplicity, with held-in authority*)
Like yourselves
And I tell you quite frankly I haven't got used to it yet,
Haven't got used to this uniform, these shoes. . . .

---

1 Don Stevens had worked at the William Morris Agency, as the *News
   Leader* for 4 September proudly declared. Limón studied with innova-
   tors Doris Humphrey and Charles Weidman; the studio they founded in
   1946 remains active and important today. Diane Roberts studied with
   the "Big Four" choreographer Hanya Holm and the dancer/choreogra-
   pher Ted Shawn, both of whom were also highly influential in the field
   of modern dance (see Prickett 183). Conning, Hinkley, and Kendricks
   ("Kendrick" at Appendix A9, p. 317, below) remain mysterious.

(Deeper inside the self, quiet and strong as if thrust up out of the subconscious)
Haven't got used to taking orders, obeying without question,
Haven't got used to hiking and marching and bayonet drill
    and latrine details and KP and choking in gas masks and
    having to live so close to others—in sweat and vulgarity and
    confusion.
Sometimes I hate the whole damn works and everyone in sight
    —and I'd give anything—*anything in the world*—to be alone
    again—a person again—a living walking breathing person
    again—back in the life I came from before I became a soldier.
But I am a soldier
Like yourselves,
Not much different from any of you.
And all the time, out in the company street—or scrubbing the
    floors or drilling or lying in my bunk at night—I keep asking
    myself Why?
Why is it like this?
What am I doing here?
Why? Why? *(pause)*
I wonder if you ask that too.

DANCE
Soloist and chorus: a dance based on close order drill, fatigue detail, police-up and so forth.

NARRATOR
And there's something else —
Another thing I do:
When I'm not asking myself Why? I'm remembering —
Remembering my former life,
What was good about it,
Remembering the street in my home town—my house there was
    two stories high, there was a maple tree and grass and kids
    playing hop-scotch and an old dog named Flip that didn't
    belong to anyone —
Remembering my father and mother—good people—my mother
    fussed over everybody, she liked to make people eat —
Remembering I had a girl, too, who liked me a lot. I even used to
    go to church with her. I'm not very religious, but Ann liked to
    go. We were together, that was the important thing.
She looked so fresh and beautiful always, but especially so on
    Sunday,

And like all girls she wore those silly hats that make you laugh—
    and she loved me. . . .
Remembering such little things about my life,
Little unimportant things,
I guess other people do that, too.
They don't remember the same things I do —
But they're not so very different:
The little unimportant things.
Where are they now? (*with involuntary deep quiet passion*)
Why do I have to give them up?
Why do they come to haunt me in the midst of being a soldier?
Why are they so far away now, why are they nothing anymore,
    nothing I can see with my eyes, nothing I can hold in my
    hand, nothing but a memory in the brain and a terrible
    anguish and loss in my heart?
Why? Why?

DANCE
Memories bring the soldier the image of his beloved. The NARRATOR
continues to speak.
The rain
The rain is falling on the leaves of the maple tree!
Get up, son, it's time for breakfast. Hot cakes today!
Go on looking the way you're looking. It's a dream!
The rain
The rain . . . !
Is falling on my heart!

NARRATOR
I know the answer —
Oh yes, I know it well enough!
The answer is there somewhere in the little unimportant things.
Those are the things I want to keep.
Those are the things I have lived for—that all of us have lived
    for —
Not just the large great words:
Peace and liberty and freedom —
It's the simple realities we live for:
Kids playing hop-scotch, their voices sounding under the maple,
    shrill and alert and lively,
And church bells,
And food on the table,

And the beauty of evening,
And someone to love again.

But our enemies oppose us with their own desires —
In the Solomons they oppose us, in the bloody reaches of Italy,[1]
    on land and sea—all over the world they oppose us —
And they have their wants, too, these enemies of ours, they have
    their gods —
And this is the look on their faces—the structure of their hearts:
Suppression,
Slavery,
Cruelty,
Starvation,
Rape and destruction and abiding hatred and murder.

If a man breaks down the door of your home—you will fight:
The door has been broken down.
We are not to have—ever again—the simple realities that give life
    dignity and meaning.
This is what they say.

Hear our answer to that, you men of evil and death!
Hear the answer of the United Nations![2]
Hear the cry of our men in the foxholes, and in the tanks, and in
    the plunging submarines, and high flying bombers:
These men are speaking now, they have a right to speak, this is
    what they say:

"We want to walk in decency and friendliness in a good world,
We want the rain in the trees, and happy faces around us,
Yes, even old friendly dogs that belong to nobody and to
    everybody,
And we want honorable work and the warmth of love for our
    bodies —
And all these things we shall have —
And people of good will everywhere in the world shall have them!
Though we walk through pain and blood and boredom and

---

1 Allied forces had been engaging with Japanese forces in the Solomon
   Islands since August 1942; the Italian campaign had begun in
   September 1943.
2 Riggs evidently refers to the Allied powers; the United Nations, per se,
   would be founded after the war.

hunger and shrieking agony and destruction and torture and
dismay—the good things shall live again, and we shall live
with them again.
And that's the reason we do our best —
Less than that is less than a man —
And we are men.
Bataan speaks for us —
And Midway and Stalingrad and Palermo and Tunisia speak for
us —[1]
And we speak for ourselves.
We are speaking now.
Listen to us and know the answer!"

DANCE
*Challenge and affirmation: soloist and chorus in fatigue and battle
dress, with movements of attack and the forward surge of battle.*

9. "A Note on 'We Speak for Ourselves,'" *Dance Observer*,
   November 1943, p. 103

[Riggs's comments on "We Speak for Ourselves" were published
before the text of the "dance poem" itself. We have altered the
sequencing, thus allowing "We Speak for Ourselves" to speak for
itself, first. By September 1943, Riggs had been discharged from
the Army but was working for the United States Office of War
Information. See Appendix A8.]

When José Limón and I first projected a dance poem for soldiers,
he was at Camp Upton and we could confer every week. Ideally,
we had intended a very careful collaboration of narrative, dance,
music and sound—each element making its statement when it
seemed most useful or more eloquent. But he was transferred to
Camp Lee, Virginia—and I feel that the project suffered some
from not being a closely inter-related thing, it being impossible
(except in one lyric interlude) to do otherwise than have sections
of narration followed by sections of dance, with drums and music
doing their best to maintain a unity that could best have been
achieved in a more artful way.

---

1 Bataan (1942), Midway (1942), Stalingrad (1942–43), and Tunisia
   (1942–43) were sites of significant World War II battles or campaigns;
   the United States and Britain bombed Palermo periodically from 1940
   to 1943.

The dance was impressive enough anyway. But it was actually, to us, a first draft of something whose unique importance we felt deeply: a dance poem conceived by soldiers (I have been one, too, for the preceding eleven months), danced by soldiers, and *for* them—indeed directed straight at them and intended to express the permanent complexity and drive of their actual feelings, their dismay, their disturbances, their searing memories, their faith arrived at through dark boredom and fire, through questioning and anguish. The soldiers who danced it (fourteen of them, including Mr. Limón and Miss Roberts, a WAC[1]) and the narrator, Richard Kendrick—felt it deeply, I was glad to note; and this visible ardor and sincerity communicated itself in large measure to a huge audience in Richmond where it was first performed.

Due also to the haste with which Mr. Limón had to prepare the dance—and training inexperienced soldiers quickly was time-killing!—he seldom was able to make his own work what he wanted it to be. It had his familiar power and thrust, his slumbrous subterranean flow, his spiritual elevation and warmth—and it had the distinction and clarity of movement for which Mr. Limón is admired. But these good things had to be often a decorative value placed around and through the pounding attack of the other dancers, and not something thrown out, violent and rude, from the explosive force of their passion demanding a further height and a more conclusive eloquence.

Sometime in the future, I feel sure, Mr. Limón and I will make this venture what it was meant to be. Meanwhile, I for one am very happy at the results of my first excursion into an art I have admired since the days when it alone of the theatre arts looked at life, and made its sometimes stirring comment and illumination.

---

1   The Women's Army Corps, a branch of the US Army, had been founded in 1942.

Appendix B: Productions of Plays by Lynn Riggs

[Information is drawn primarily from newspapers, via newspapers.com, but also from Newspaper Archive, biographies by Aughtry and Braunlich (*Haunted*), and Samuel French royalty statements (Riggs Papers, Beinecke, box 5, ff. 108–14). Readings, and television, radio, and stage adaptations, are excluded. So are high-school productions, notwithstanding the popularity of *Knives from Syria* and *Green Grow the Lilacs* in mid-century high-school drama programs. Unverified entries from Aughtry, Braunlich, and the royalty statements have generally been omitted, under the presumption that they indicate high-school productions. Cast lists are reproduced selectively and often compromised by their partial representation in the press. Directors are listed only when our sources allow for certainty. We do not pretend that this document is exhaustive or free of error, given, for example, inconsistencies of reporting among newspapers.]

Cuckoo

18 May 1922, Sooner Players, University Auditorium, University of Oklahoma, Norman, OK. Directed by Joe Graham. Cast: Ethel A. Beckstrom (Maw Hillbank), Robert E. Dobbins (Pa Hillbank), Thelma Wildrose (Josie), Ervis Lester (Doc Helm), Jay Mason (Joe Graham).
11 July 1922, Drama League, University of Oklahoma, Norman, OK. Directed by Veroqua Petty.

Knives from Syria

12 May 1925, Santa Fe Players, Rialto Theatre, Santa Fe, NM. Produced by Christine Hughes; directed by Ida Rauh. Cast: Norman McGee (Syrian Peddler), Margaret Larkin (Mrs. Buster), Rhodie (Elizabeth Holloman), Charley (Lynn Riggs). With *The Little King*, by Witter Bynner, and *Suppressed Desires*, by Susan Glaspell and George Cram Cook. Also 27 May.
6 October 1928, Dramatic Club of Ft. Benning, Main Theatre, Ft. Benning, GA. Directed by Captain E.M.S. Steward.

18 July 1930, San Buenaventura Community Players, Little Theatre, Ventura, CA. Directed by T.A. Proctor.

12 May 1931, Assembly Hall, Ball State Teachers College, Muncie, IN. Directed by Jewel Standerford.

16 December 1931, Blue Masquers, Edmund Hayes Hall, University of Buffalo, Buffalo, NY. Directed by Stanley D. Travis.

13 April 1932, Lathrop Auditorium, University of Missouri, Columbia, MO. Directed by Donovan Rhynsburger. Workshop presentation.

29 April 1932, Proscenium Players, St. Andrews Parish House, Bridgewater, NJ. Directed by Harriet Van Ollefen.

21 March 1935, EEP Drama Group, Lorimer Baptist Church, Chicago, IL. Directed by Charles H. Good.

27 May 1937, Montana Masquers, Student Union, Montana State University, Missoula, MT. Directed by Bob Gail.

c. 21 March 1938, Little Theatre Group, Willimantic State Teachers College, Willimantic, CT. Rehearsals directed by Ruth J. Bradley.

1 December 1939, Little Theatre [company], Sidonian Hall, Kane, PA. Directed by Mrs. Jarvis Rockwell.

24 July 1941, Oklahoma A&M University, Stillwater, OK. Directed by Geneva Walker. Class project. Martyne Woods, who played Rhodie, was a Choctaw actress.

17 January 1946, University of South Dakota, Vermillion, SD. Directed by Frances Wessleman. Performed by students at convocation.

12 November 1946, Studio Theater, University of Oklahoma, Norman, OK. Directed by Bill Skillman.

13 January 1950, Auditorium, Nebraska State Teachers College, Kearney, NE. Directed by Nellie Schnoor. Class project.

9 March 1950, Alexandria Little Theater [company], Roosevelt High School Auditorium, Washington, DC. Sponsored by the District Recreation Department.

16 February 1951, Mask and Mantle, Goddard Auditorium, Earlham College, Richmond, IN. Directed by Forrest Altman.

3 December 1953, Au-Ger-Du-Lo Players, Little Auditorium, Northeastern State College, Tahlequah, Oklahoma. Directed by Garry Sims. "Au-Ger-Du-Lo" is Cherokee for "maskers" ("masquers").

27–28 July 1954, American College Players, Barn Theatre, Dartington Hall, Dartington, Devon, UK. Directed by George Brendan Dowell. Also 9–13 August, Torquay Open

Air Theatre, Torquay, Devon, UK; 18–21 August, Hall Green Little Theatre, Birmingham, UK; c. 25–c. 28, Grange Theatre, Walsall, West Midlands, UK; 4 September, Questors Theatre, London, UK. Reported performances in Northampton, UK and on US Air Force bases in Gloucestershire have not been confirmed.

13 October 1955, Au-Ger-Du-Lo Players, Northeastern State College, Tahlequah, OK. Directed by Nancy Duke.

c. 10 May 1958, Lewis and Clark College Drama Department, Lewis and Clark College, Portland, OR.

3–4, 10–11, 17–18 November 1961, Waco Civic Theater, Waco, TX. Directed by Lyle Burt.

12–13 November 1976, Renegade Theatre, Norman, OK. Directed by Frank Parman and Jimmy Costello.

8–9 May 1993, Oklahoma Indian Theater and Dance Company, American Indian One-Act Festival, Chapel, Bacone College, Muskogee, OK.

Big Lake

8–c. 30 April 1927, American Laboratory Theatre (Broadway). Directed by George Auerbach. Cast: Stella Adler (Elly), Grover Burgess (Butch), Frank Burk (Lloyd), John S. Clarke Jr. (Plank), Helen Coburn (Betty), Francis Fergusson (Joe), Sam Hartman (Bud Bickel), Harold Hecht (The Davis Boy), Louis V. Quince (Sheriff), Francis Williams (Miss Meredith). Eleven performances in repertory.

29–31 March 1928, Tulsa Little Theatre, Alhambra Theatre, Tulsa, OK. Directed by Richard M. Dickinson.

23 March 1931, Dallas Little Theatre, Dallas, TX. Directed by Elroy Fulmer. Workshop presentation.

27–28 March 1931, Boar's Head Dramatic Society, Syracuse University, Syracuse, NY. Directed by Sawyer Falk.

29 June 1931, Pasadena Playhouse School of Theatre Arts, Pasadena, CA. Commencement performance.

3 March 1941, Actor's Workshop, New York, NY.

6, 11–12 March 1949, Little Playhouse, Schuster-Martin School of Drama, Cincinnati, OH. Directed by Norma Gerdsen.

19–c. 23 April 1949, Pasadena Playhouse School of the Theater, Pasadena, CA. Directed by Daniel Linnard.

The Domino Parlor

18–23 June 1928, Broad Theatre, Newark, NJ. Produced by
the Shubert Organization; directed by Edward Massey and
Zoe Akins. Cast: Irene Fenwick (Toni Devereau), Warren
William (Jude), Dodson Mitchell (Doc Beeman), Zelma
Tilden (Flossie), Arthur R. Vinton, Frank Conlan, Marius
Rogati, Henry Clarens, Pacie Ripple, Harry Ford, Jean
Sidney, Maurice Summers, Lizzie Cubitt, J.W. Guy, Frank
De Silva, Bernard Dirkes, Alan Goode, Don Beddoe, Ross
Matthews, Charles T. Lewis, William Watkins, Charles P.
Thompson, Edith Arnold, Teddy Jones, E. Conway Washburn,
Charles Udell, Henry Hoppe, John Brawn. Tryouts: 15 June,
Springdale, CT; 16 June, Playhouse, Great Neck, NY.

Rancor (aka *Rancour*)

12 July 1928, Hedgerow Theatre, Rose Valley, PA.
20 August 1931, Hedgerow Theatre, Rose Valley, PA. Also 27
October.
29 July 1931, Summer School Players, Syracuse University,
Syracuse, NY. Directed by Sawyer Falk.
16 December 1931, Santa Fe Players, Rialto Theatre, Santa Fe,
NM. Directed by Riggs and Anna V. Huey. Cast: Mildred
Maxey (Dorie Bickle), George Gormly (Ned Bickle),
Raymond Otis (Hez Breeden), Katherine Harvey, Hubert P.
Jeffus (Julius Bickle), Edwin Brooks (C. Guy Jones).
1932, University of Denver, Denver, CO. See Braunlich, *Haunted*
203. Production not verified.
2–3 August 1933, Summer School Players, Slocum Hall Theater,
Syracuse University, Syracuse, NY. Directed by Sawyer Falk.
10 October 1933, Kendall Hall, University of Tulsa, Tulsa, OK.
Directed by Margaret Wyndham and Mildred Maxey.
12 December 1933, University Players, Valparaiso University,
Valparaiso, IN.
16 August 1935, Hedgerow Theatre, Rose Valley, PA. Directed by
Jasper Deeter. Also 19 September; 1 October.
25 October 1935, Macbride Auditorium, University of Iowa,
Iowa City, IA. Produced by Hedgerow Theatre; directed
by Jasper Deeter. Also 2 November 1935, Nebraska State
Teachers College, Kearney, NE. These are the only confirmed
dates on which Riggs's play was offered during the Hedgerow's
repertory tour of the Midwest and Southeast, which began in

early October 1935 and ended in mid-February 1936.

28 February 1936, Hedgerow Theatre, Rose Valley, PA.

19–20 January 1938, Poet Theater, Founder's Hall, Whittier College, Whittier, CA. Directed by Winn Zeller.

30 June 1944, Hedgerow Theatre, Rose Valley, PA. Also 15 July, 5 August, 1 September.

20 June 1945, Hedgerow Theatre, Rose Valley, PA. Also 14 July, 22 September, 5 October.

Roadside

26 September–4 October 1930, Longacre Theatre (Broadway). Produced by Arthur Hopkins. Cast: Roderick Baybee (Town Marshall), Ralph Bellamy (Texas), Frederick Burton (Pap Rader), Jack Byrne (Buzzey Hale), Kendall Foster (Black Ike), Frank I. Frayne (Neb), Harry Hermsen (Judge Snodgrass), Gilbert Squarey (Red Ike), Ruthelma Stevens (Hannie Rader), Anne Tonetti (Mrs. Foster). Tryout: 22–24 September, Shubert Theatre, New Haven, CT.

17, 23 May 1931, Hedgerow Theatre, Rose Valley, PA. Also 2, 24 June; 4, 17 July; 4 August; 14, 29 September; 11 November.

18 March 1932, Hedgerow Theatre, Rose Valley, PA. Also 10, 16 April; 10 May; 11 June; 5 July.

11 August 1933, Hedgerow Theatre, Rose Valley, PA.

7–8 January 1935, Sacramento Community Players, California Junior High School, Sacramento, CA. Directed by Frank Blanchard.

29 May–8 June 1935, Pasadena Playhouse, Pasadena, CA.

3 July 1936, Green Mansions Summer Theatre, Warrensburg, NY.

6–8 November 1936, Dramatic Council, Associated Students of Stanford, Assembly Hall, Stanford University, Stanford, CA. Directed by Gordon C. Lange.

25–26 February 1938, Pueblo Players, Lobero Little Theatre, Santa Barbara, CA. Directed by A. Douglas Harmer.

8 April–1 May 1938, Musart Theatre, Los Angeles, CA. Produced by the Federal Theatre Project; directed by Mary Virginia Farmer.

27–29 October 1938, Ithaca College, Ithaca, NY. Directed by Winn. F. Zeller.

6–12 February 1939, Brattleboro Theatre, Brooklyn, NY. Directed by Harold Johnsrud.

5–8, 10–12 December 1940, Play Box Theater, Springfield, OH.

Directed by Ward Mendenhall.

28–30 August 1941, Blue Ridge Players, Lake Summit, NC. Directed by Arthur Coe Gray.

30–31 October 1941, University of Tulsa Experimental Theatre [company], Kendall Hall, University of Tulsa, Tulsa, OK. Directed by Ben Henneke. Reprised for homecoming weekend, 15 November.

5–6 December 1941, Blue Masquers, University of Buffalo, Buffalo, NY. Directed by Stanley D. Travis.

18 February–March 9, 1947, Masque Theatre, Los Angeles, CA. Directed by Michael Mark.

June 1947, Culver Military Academy, Culver, IN. Directed by Capt. Gerald Markley. Commencement play.

3–12 June 1947, Actors Theatre, Provincetown Playhouse, NY.

24–29 June 1947, Maverick Players, Maverick Theatre, Woodstock, NY. Directed by Paul Morrison.

5–10 May 1952, Mayde Mack Mummers of Oklahoma City, El Reno, OK. Directed by Mack Jones.

c. 3–c. 11 July 1953, Bam-a-Rama Summer Theatre, Morgan Hall, University of Alabama, Tuscaloosa, AL. Directed by Marion Gallaway.

4, 6 August 1954, Oak Grove Players, Oak Grove Theatre, Staunton, VA. Directed by Fletcher Collins.

17–19, 24–26 September, 8–10 October 1954, Barn Theatre, Porterville, CA.

22 October–12 December 1954, San Francisco Playhouse Repertory, San Francisco, CA.

12–19 February 1955, Geller Theatre, Los Angeles, CA.

28 November–3 December 1955, Princeton Community Players, Murray Theater, Princeton, NJ. Directed by Alan S. Downer.

4–8 May 1956, Amherst College Masquers, Amherst College, Amherst, MA. Directed by Edwin B. Pettet. Reprised for commencement, 8–9 June.

21–30 June 1956, Repertory Theatre, Santa Barbara, CA. Directed by Charles Metten.

2–6 July 1957, Theatre South, Barn Theatre, Nashville, TN.

19 November–8 December 1957, Margo Jones Theatre, Dallas, TX. Directed by Ramsey Burch.

25–26 July 1958, Vancouver Civic Theater, Kiggins Bowl, Vancouver, WA. Directed by Arthur Grey.

19–23 August 1958, Vagabond Players, Flat Rock Playhouse, Flat Rock, NC. Directed by Robroy Farquhar.

c. 12–16 May 1959, Palomar College, San Marcos, CA.

9–13 December 1959, Patio Theater, Pasadena Playhouse. Directed by Barbara Brown.

3–5, 10–12 May 1962, Cap and Dagger, Bucknell University, Lewisburg, PA. Directed by Harvey M. Powers. Reprised for Alumni Day, 2 June.

March 1963, Patrician Playhouse, Los Angeles, CA. Directed by Patricia Levin.

20 March 1965, Plymouth College Players, Charleston High School, Charleston, VT. Produced by Charleston Rotary Club.

28–31 May 1965, Barstow College, Barstow, CA. Directed by Bill Pullen.

5–9 December 1967, Kendall Hall, University of Tulsa, Tulsa, OK. Directed by Harold H. Barrows.

1–4 May 1974, Theatre ISU, Frazier Hall, Idaho State University, Pocatello, ID. Directed by Robert Chase.

17–19 October 1974, Theatre UMF, Alumni Gym Theatre, University of Maine at Farmington, Farmington, ME. Directed by Hershel Bricker. Also 28 February, 7 March, University of Maine at Augusta, Augusta, ME; 1 March, Westbrook High School, Westbrook, ME; c. 12 April, Alumni Gym Theatre, University of Maine at Farmington.

13–14 June 1975, Roadside Theatre [company], Clinch Valley College Summer Theatre Program, Clinch Valley College picnic grounds, Wise, VA. Directed by Jeffrey Hooper.

10, 11, 14, 18 July 1975, University of Idaho Summer Repertory Theatre, Performing Arts Center, University of Idaho, Moscow, IA. Directed by Edgar Reynolds.

4 July–9 August 1980, Oklahoma Theatrical Company, Tulsa Zoo, Tulsa, OK.

26 February–6 March 1982, Chapman Theatre, Kendall Hall, University of Tulsa, Tulsa, OK.

2 June–2 July 1983, Hedgerow Theatre, Moylan, PA. Directed by John Barrett and Janey Kelsey.

6–25 December 1983, Nassau Repertory Theatre [company], Hayes Theatre, Malloy College, Rockville Centre, NY. Directed by Clinton J. Atkinson.

13 August–5 September 1992, Lime Kiln Arts, Lexington, VA. Directed by Don Baker.

9–11 September 1993, Theatre Norman [company], Sooner Theatre, Norman, OK. Directed by Larry Nye.

12–15 October 1995, Tulsa Junior College, Southeast Campus, Tulsa, OK. Directed by Ted Kachel.

Green Grow the Lilacs

NB: In February 1943, the Theatre Guild briefly publicized a March Boston tryout of Rodgers and Hammerstein's unnamed *Oklahoma!* as the "musical version" of *Green Grow the Lilacs*.

26 January–21 March 1931, Guild Theatre (Broadway). Produced by the Theatre Guild; directed by Herbert J. Biberman. Cast: Franchot Tone (Curly McClain), Helen Westley (Aunt Eller Murphy), June Walker (Laurey Williams), Richard Hale (Jeeter Fry), Ruth Chorpenning (Ado Annie Carnes), Lee Strasberg (Peddler), Tex Cooper (Old Man Peck), Woodward Ritter (cowboy), Paul Ravell (another cowboy), William T. Hays (old farmer), A.L. Bartolot (young farmer), Jane Alden (Marthy), William Chosnyk (fiddler), Everett Cheetham (banjo player, farmer); Cowboys (chorus): Slim Cavanaugh, Chick Hannan, John Hibbard, Jack Miller, Pete Schwartz, Norton Worden; Farmers (chorus): Carl Beasley, Gordon Bryant, Elmo Carr, Roy Ketcham, Tommy Pladget, Paul Ravell, Joe Wilson; Girls (chorus): Alice Frost, Peggy Hannan, Faith Hope, Orlando Lee, Lois Lindon, Eleanor Powers, Jean Wood. Tryouts: 8–20 December 1930, Tremont Theater, Boston, MA; 29 December 1930–10 January 1931, Garrick Theatre, Philadelphia; 12–17 January, Ford's Grand Opera House, Baltimore, MD; 19–24 January, National Theater, Washington, DC. Tour: 23–28 March, Public Auditorium, Cleveland, OH; 30 March–4 April, Nixon Theatre, Pittsburgh, PA; 6–11 April, American Theatre, St. Louis, MO; 13–18 April, Pabst Theater, Milwaukee, WI; 20–25 April, Lyceum Theatre, Minneapolis, MN; 27 April–16 May, Illinois Theater, Chicago, IL; 18–23 May, Wilson Theatre, Detroit, MI.

27–29 October 1931, University Theatre, University of Iowa, Iowa City, IA. Directed by Vance Morton.

21 March 1932, Dallas Little Theatre, CIA Auditorium, Denton, TX.

28 June–10 July 1932, Pasadena Playhouse, Pasadena, CA. Directed by Gilmore Brown and Morris Ankrum.

18–22 July 1932, Northwestern University, Evanston, IL. Directed by Riggs.

2–4 September 1932, Carmel Community Players, Carmel Community Playhouse, Carmel, CA. Directed by Galt Bell.

6–7 October 1932, Berkeley Playhouse Association, Berkeley, CA.

3–5 November 1932, Venturans [company], Lobero Theatre, Santa Barbara, CA. Directed by Paul Whitney.

22–23 November 1932, Little Theater Players, Tootle Theater, St. Joseph, MO.

11–13, 19–20 May 1933, Illini Theater Guild, Mask and Bauble, Little Theater, University of Illinois, Champaign, IL. Directed by Wesley Swanson.

20–21 April 1934, Tucson Little Theatre, Tucson, AZ. Directed by Edward Freis.

23–24 November 1934, Santa Ana Community Players, Ebell Auditorium, Santa Ana, CA. Directed by Gladys Simpson Shafer.

11–14 December 1934, Fort Worth Little Theater, Fort Worth, TX. Directed by Robert Nail.

10 May 1935, Festival of Southwestern Plays, Southern Methodist University, Dallas, TX. Directed by David Russell.

28 October–2 November 1935, Manchester Repertory Co., Rusholme Theatre, Manchester, UK.

13 February 1936, Theater Workshop, Los Angeles, CA. Directed by Jean Muir.

5–6 March 1936, Bellingham Normal School, Bellingham, WA. Directed by V.H. Hoppe.

7–24 January 1937, Mayan Theatre, Los Angeles. Produced by the Federal Theatre Project; directed by Robert Henderson.

12–13 February 1937, Hull House Actors' Guild, Hull House, Chicago, IL.

16–18 March 1937, Curtain Club, Hogg Auditorium, University of Texas, Austin, TX. Directed by Tony Thomason.

2 June 1937, Eastern State Normal School, Madison, SD. Commencement play. Directed by Dr. Lena J. Myers.

30–31 July 1937, Studio of Acting [company], John Drew Memorial Theater, East Hampton, NY.

4–9 October 1937, Emery Auditorium, Cincinnati, OH. Produced by the Federal Theatre Project; directed by Franklin Raymond.

25–26 February 1938, Cranford Dramatic Club, Cranford High School Auditorium, Cranford, NJ.

23, 25 March 1938, Mummers, Washington University, Wednesday Club Auditorium, St. Louis, MO. Directed by Willard Holland.

5–14 May 1938, Studio Theater Players, Studio Theater School, Buffalo, NY. Directed by Jane Keeler.

16–21 August 1938, Washington Irving Theatre, Tarrytown, NY.

1–2 December 1938, La Crosse State Teachers College, La Crosse, WI. Directed by Marie Park.

20–22 November 1939, Las Mascaras Speech and Drama Club, Little Theatre, Tyler Junior College, Tyler, TX.

8–10 February, 1940, University of Tulsa Experimental Theater, Kendall Hall, University of Tulsa, Tulsa, OK. Directed by Ben G. Henneke.

15–20 July 1940, Westport Country Playhouse, Westport, CT. Directed by John Ford. Also 22–27 July, McCarter Theatre, Princeton, NJ.

7 February 1941, Fullerton Junior College, Fullerton, CA. Directed by Esther C. Litchfield.

30–31 October 1941, Little Theater, Texas State College for Women, Denton, TX. Directed by Emory G. Horger.

7–11 July 1942, Civic Summer Players, Syracuse University, Syracuse, NY. Directed by Sawyer Falk.

2–7 February 1942, Community Playhouse, Omaha, NE. Directed by Gordon Giffen.

24 February–14 March 1942, Pittsburgh Playhouse, Pittsburgh, PA. Directed by Frederick Burleigh.

11–12 December 1942, University of Idaho, Moscow, ID. Directed by Jean Collette.

15–20, 22 November 1943, Little Theatre of Shreveport, Margaret Place Playhouse, Shreveport, LA. Directed by John Wray Young. Also 21 November, Barksdale Field, Bossier Parish, LA.

7–12 February 1944, Town Theater, Columbia, SC. Directed by Frederick Coe. Purchase of a US War Bond was required for admission to the 7 February performance.

10–11 February 1944, Masquers of Friendly House, Friendly House, Davenport, IA. Directed by Mary Eleanor Fluhrer.

29 March, 1 April 1944, Pit and Balcony, Masonic Temple Auditorium, Saginaw, MI.

19–20 November 1945, University Players, Hardin-Simmons University, Abilene, TX. Directed by Katherine Boyd.

20 November 1946, East Central College, Ada, OK. Directed by D.J. Nabors.

9–10 December 1946, College Auditorium, Oklahoma A&M College, Stillwater, OK. Directed by James G. Barton.

11–15, 18–22 March 1947, Missouri Workshop [company], Jesse Auditorium, University of Missouri, Columbia, MO. Directed by Donovan Rhynsburger.

10–12 July 1947, University Players, University of Colorado, Boulder, CO.

16–20 July 1947, Yellow Springs Summer Theater, Yellow Springs, OH. Directed by Mack M. Greene.

12–16 August 1947, Tufts Summer Theatre, College Theatre, Tufts College, Bedford, MA.

13–16 August 1947, Village Players, Richland, MI. Directed by Jack Ragotzy.

14–16, 18–19, 21–23 August 1947, Southwest Summer Theatre, Baylor Theatre, Baylor University, Waco, TX. Directed by Paul Baker.

2 September 1947, Sterling Group, Caravan Theater, Pittsburgh, PA.

3–4, 10–11 October 1947, Baylor Theatre, Baylor University, Waco, TX. Directed by Paul Baker.

20–23 October 1947, Little Theater Company, Playhouse, University of Louisville, Louisville, KY. Directed by Boyd Martin.

29 October–1 November 1947, Hogg Auditorium, University of Texas, Austin, TX. Directed by Gordon Minter.

13–15 December 1947, Playhouse Club, St. Louis University, St. Louis, MO.

17–22 May 1948, Kendall Hall, University of Tulsa, OK. Directed by Rodman Jones. Also 29 May, for the university's "roundup" celebration of alumni/alumnae and others.

2–7 May 1949, University Street Playhouse, Fresno State University, Fresno, CA. Directed by George Nichols III.

12–14 May 1949, Riviera Auditorium, Santa Barbara College, Santa Barbara, CA. Directed by Theodore Hatlen.

23–25 June 1949, Three Theaters, Patchwork Theatre, Newnan, GA. Produced by the Shorter Players.

1–6 August 1949, Holiday Stage, Tustin, CA. Directed by E. Alyn Warren.

15–17 March 1950, Colorado Civic Theatre, Pioneer Theatre [company], Orchard Avenue School Auditorium, Grand Junction, CO.

23–25 March 1950, Maine Masque Theater [company], Little Theater, University of Maine, Orono, ME. Directed by Herschel Bricker.

4–6 May 1950, Masque and Wig, Bearcat Gymnasium, Lon Morris College, Jacksonville, TX.

18–28 October 1950, University of Iowa, Iowa City, IA.

20 October 1950, Little Theatre, Southwest Texas State College, San Marcos, TX. Directed by James G. Barton. Homecoming celebration.

26–28 October 1950, Rotunda Stagers, Rotunda, University of Virginia, Charlottesville, VA. Directed by Harold T. Jordan and James D. Helms.

1–2 December 1950, Mummers Guild, Wilson Auditorium, University of Cincinnati, Cincinnati, OH. Directed by Paul Rutledge.

29–30 June 1951, Theater Workshop, Los Gatos Adult School, Los Gatos High School auditorium, Los Gatos, CA. Directed by Lilian Fontaine.

3–14 July 1951, Totem Pole Playhouse, Fayetteville, PA. Directed by Karl Genus.

4–7 July 1951, Lydia Mendelssohn Theater, University of Michigan, Ann Arbor, MI. Directed by Claribel Baird.

17 July 1951, Camden Hills Players, Camden, ME.

14–15 December 1951, George Washington Players, Lisner Auditorium, Washington, DC.

7–8 March 1952, Masque and Dagger Club, Phoenix College Auditorium, Phoenix, AZ. Directed by John Paul.

8–10 May 1952, Baylor Little Theatre, Baylor University, Waco, TX. Directed by Mary Sue Birkhead. Also 21–24 July, Théâtre de Babylone, Paris, France.

14–17 May 1952, Fairchild Theatre, MSC Fine Arts Festival, Michigan State College, Lansing, MI. Directed by John Jennings.

21–24 May 1952, Sacramento Civic Repertory Theater, Eaglet Theater, Sacramento, CA. Directed by Lillian Allen.

18–21 November 1952, Troubadour Players, Troubadour Theater, Washington and Lee University, Lexington, VA. Directed by Carlson Thomas.

26–28 March 1953, Dramatics Club and Variety Show, College Theatre, Brockport State Teachers College, Brockport, NY. Directed by Louis Hetler.

5–9 August 1953, Huron Playhouse, Huron, ON. Directed by Donald C. Kleckner.

15–16 October 1953, Catholic Theater Guild, Woman's Club, Richmond, VA. Directed by Jay Lundy.

28–30 October 1953, TWC College Players, Magoffin Auditorium, Texas Western College, El Paso, TX. Directed by Milton Leech.

19, 21 November 1953, Powder and Wig, Women's Union, Colby College, Waterville, ME. Directed by Gene Jellison.

12–14, 15 February 1954, Clarksville Little Theatre, Clarksville, IN. Directed by C. Douglas Ramey.

23–24 April 1954, Oakland Drama Workshop, Community Building, Oakland, NJ. Directed by Beatrice King Stodola.

10–15 May 1954, The University Playhouse, University of Kansas City, Kansas City, MO. Directed by Lowell Matson.

24–29 August 1954, Grand Teton National Theatre, Jackson, WY.

17 September–2 October 1954, Glendale Regional Playhouse, Glendale, CA. Produced by John Calvin Brown; directed by Hap Graham.

5–6 November 1954, Kansas State Players, College Auditorium, Kansas State College, Manhattan, KS. Directed by Earl G. Hoover.

15–18, 20 November 1954, Texas Technical College, Lubbock, TX. Directed by Cecilia Thompson.

12–16 April 1955, Windsor Jesters, Loomis Theater, Windsor, CT. Directed by Philip Isaacs.

31 March–2 April, 8–9 April 1955, Convair Wing and Masque Playhouse, Fort Worth, TX. Directed by Perry Ratliff.

1–4 July 1955, Manistee Summer Theater, Manistee, MI.

October or November 1955, Masquers, Ranger Junior College, Ranger, TX. Directed by Mrs. David L. Norton.

7–8 November 1955, Lawton Little Theater, Auditorium, Cameron College, Lawton, OK. Directed by John Denney.

10–14 July 1956, Raleigh Summer Theater, Raleigh, NC. Directed by Dick Snavely.

20 August 1956, Roanoke Island School of Fine Arts, Waterside Theatre, Manteo, NC. Directed by James Byrd.

c. 6–22 September 1956, Santa Monica Theater Guild, Morgan Theater, Santa Monica, CA. Produced by Robert Connor; directed by James Brittain.

13–14 December 1956, San Angelo College Theatre Group, San Angelo, TX. Directed by Don Irwin.

13–16 February 1957, Curtaineers, Theresa Kaufmann Theater, Anna B. Heldman Community Center, Pittsburgh, PA. Directed by C. Edwin Shade.

22–23 February 1957, Hiram Hills Players, Hiram College, Hiram, OH.

3–11 May 1957, Little Theater, San José State College, San José, CA.

26–28 June 1957, Palo Duro Players, Branding Iron Theatre, West Texas State College, Canyon, TX. Directed by Lowell Matson.

2–3 August 1957, Stover Theater, Stetson University, DeLand, FL.

21–22 November 1957, Wilkin Auditorium, Northern Oklahoma Junior College, Tonkawa, OK. Directed by Ken Robinson.

6–8 March 1958, Purdue Playshop, Edward C. Elliott Hall of Music, Purdue University, West Lafayette, IN. Directed by H. Winn Park.

5–9 August 1958, Tufts Arena Theater, Tufts College, Medford, MA.

5–10 August 1958, Phoenicia Playhouse, Phoenicia, NY.

14–16 May 1959, Kenosha Little Theatre, Lincoln Jr. High Auditorium, Kenosha, WI. Directed by Thom Feuerstein.

31 July–2 August 1959, College Drama Department, Auditorium Building, Immaculate Heart College, Los Angeles, CA. Directed by Patricia Madsen.

11–15 August 1959, Barnard Summer Theatre, Minor Latham Playhouse, New York, NY.

31 March–2 April 1960, College Players, Santa Ana College, Santa Ana, CA. Directed by Robert Blaustone.

7–9 April 1960, American River Junior College, North Highlands, CA. Directed by Carl White.

6–7 May 1960, Curtain Club, Lee College, Baytown, TX. Directed by Jim Smith.

8–c. 23 July 1960, Corrales Community Theater, Albuquerque, NM. Directed by Doug Koss.

27–c. 30 July 1960, Mountain Theater, Braddock Heights, MD.

15, 17–19 November 1960, La Crosse State College Players, Campus School Little Theatre, La Crosse State College, La Crosse, WI. Directed by Marie Toland.

9–18 March 1961, Phoenix Little Theater, Phoenix, AZ. Directed by Charles Shorr.

5–8 July 1961, Playhouse Eagles Mere, Danville, PA. Directed by Alvina Krause.

6–10 August 1963, Denison Summer Theater, Granville, OH. Directed by Tom Calkins.

13–17 March 1964, Brownsville Community Players, Brownsville, TX. Also 27–c. 31 March.

3–8 May 1964, University Players, Fairleigh Dickinson University, Teaneck, NJ. Production not verified.

28 July–2 August 1964, Millbrook Playhouse, Mill Hill, PA.

7 August–12 September 1964, Long Beach Community Playhouse, Long Beach, CA. Directed by R.W. Royce.

15–24 October 1964, Little Theatre, Shreveport, LA. Directed by John Wray Young.

18–19 December 1964, Clarksville Little Theatre, Indiana University Southeast, Jeffersonville, IN. Directed by William Harbin.

7–9, 14–15 May 1965, Trail of Six Flags Theatre, Victoria, TX. Directed by Charles McCally.

30 June–3 July 1965, Summer Theater Guild, Theater-by-the-Grove, Indiana State College, Indiana, PA. Directed by Robert Ensley.

19–20, 27–30 January 1966, Amarillo Little Theatre, Amarillo, TX. Directed by Neil Hess.

6–8, 11–15 May 1966, Theater of Western Springs, Western Springs, IL.

1 July–c. 6 August 1966, Santa Monica Guild, Morgan Theater, Santa Monica, CA. Directed by Theodore Hatlen.

4–13 August 1966, Belfry Players, Williams Bay, WI. Directed by David Molthen.

1–3, 7–10 December 1966, New Theater, University of California, Santa Barbara, Santa Barbara, CA. Directed by Theodore Hatlen.

19–21 January 1967, Civic Theater of Gladstone, Oak Park High School, Kansas City, MO. Directed by Etta Marie Carlisle.

7–9 November 1968, San Antonio College Theatre, San Antonio, TX. Directed by Ron Lucke.

22–24 October 1969, Overstreet Auditorium, Southern State College, Magnolia, AR. Directed by Jake Whitehead.

29–31 July, 7, 12, 21 August 1976, Windham Summer Repertory Theatre, Windham College Fine Arts Building, Putney, VT.

4 July 1981, PCPA Theaterfest, Festival Theater, Solvang, CA. Directed by Michael Leibert. Also 8 July, Marian Theater, Santa Maria, CA. Performances alternated between venues until 19 September.

21–23, 28–30 October 1982, Canada College, Redwood City, CA. Directed by Bob Curtis.

12–15, 19–21 March 1992, Tulsa Junior College Community Theater, Tulsa Performing Arts Studio 1, Tulsa, OK. Directed by Ted Kachel.

19–20, 26, 28 April 2002, Public Square, Atlanta, GA.

3, 4, 10, 11, 17, 18 September 2004, Stage Door Theatre, Yukon Museum and Arts Center, Yukon, OK.

16–17 February 2007, Wesley United Methodist Church, Oklahoma City, OK.

17–18 November 2010, United States Naval Academy Masqueraders, Rasmuson Theater, National Museum of the American Indian, New York, NY. Directed by Christy Stanlake.

11–26 July 2015, Will Geer's Theatricum Botanicum, Topanga, CA.

Sump'n Like Wings

27 November 1931, Detroit Playhouse, Detroit Institute of Arts, Detroit, MI. Directed by Jada Leland.

13 January 1932, Théâtre Royal Flamand (Vlaamsche Schouborg), Brussels, Belgium. Translated by Omer Haeck as *Quelque chose comme des Ailes.*

A Lantern to See By

25 September 1930, Detroit Playhouse, Detroit Institute of Arts, Detroit, MI. Cast: Ervin Raymond (John Harmon), Jaddah Leeland (Thursey Harmon), Louise Altshuler (Jodie Harmon), Peggy White (Annie Marble).

11 July 1931, Hedgerow Theatre, Rose Valley, PA. Directed by Jasper Deeter. Also 5, 11, 18 July; 6 August; 1, 28 October; 1 September; 14 November.

7 January 1932, Hedgerow Theatre, Rose Valley, PA. Also 31 March, 8 April.

11 September 1933, Hedgerow Theatre, Rose Valley, PA.

The Cherokee Night

18, 20, 21 June 1932, Hedgerow Theatre, Rose Valley, PA. Directed by Jasper Deeter and Riggs. Also 8 July; 12, 21, 23 August; 20 September; 24 October.

7–9 December 1932, University Theater, University of Iowa, Iowa City, IA. Directed by Riggs.

6 January 1933, Hedgerow Theatre, Rose Valley, PA. Also 11 February.

12 February 1933, Public Hall, Little Theater, Cleveland, OH.

9–10 February 1934, Boar's Head Dramatic Society, Syracuse University, Syracuse, NY. Directed by Sawyer Falk.
20 July–1 August 1936, Provincetown Playhouse, New York, NY. Produced by Works Progress Administration.

The Son of Perdition (adapted from the novel of James Gould Cozzens)

25 February 1933, Hedgerow Theatre, Rose Valley, PA. Also 3, 9, 24 March; 1, 13 April.

More Sky

24–27 July 1934, Northwestern University, Evanston, IL. Directed by Riggs. Cast: Robert Breen and Winston O'Keefe (Critias and Mestor, twin kings of Atlantis), Earl Wynn (Glaucus, third king of Atlantis), Janet Macheimer (Hera), Ortha Smith (Callista), Dick Hadley, Marden McBroom, Ed Avison, Jerry Factor, Almon B. Ives, Juanita Rucker, C.E. Schneider, Royal Rompel, Thornton Shively; Chorus of Women: Elizabeth Campbell, Marjorie Roney, Doris Baddely, Lucille Benson, Halicia Naugle, Juanita Rucker, Margery Crampton, Clarice Matthews, Eulalie Burrus, Hilda Taylor, Martha Sievers, Margaret Rankin; Royal Guard: William Kauffman, Harry Carter, Fay K. Green, Will Potter, Everett Brown, Elmer Chlert, Ramon W. Kessler, P. Merville Larsen, Carl Ritzman, William Bellare, McCrae Hazlett, Fred P. Barnes, Gustav A. Carlson, Richard Martin, Albert Haughton, Frank Davis.

Russet Mantle

16 January–25 April 1936, Theatre Masque (Broadway). Produced by Jerome Mayer and Murray Jay Queen; directed by Robert Ross. Cast: Jay Fassett (Horace Kincaid), Harry Bellaver (Pablo), Evelyn Varden (Susanna Kincaid), Margaret Douglass (Effie Rowley), Helen Craig (Manuelita), Martha Sleeper (Kay Rowley), James Larmore (Scoot), John Beal (John Galt), Clare Woodbury (Mrs. Fawcett), Chief Bear (Salvador), Frederick Barton (Dr. Brown). Evelyn Varden was a Cherokee actress.
26–30 May 1936, Point Pleasant Playshop Theatre, Point Pleasant Beach, NJ. Directed by S. Iden Thompson.

13–19 July 1936, South Shore Players, Cohasset Town Hall, Cohasset, MA. Directed by Alexander Dean.

13–25 July 1936, Geary Theater, San Francisco, CA. Directed by Jerome Mayer. Also Belasco Theatre, Los Angeles, CA, 27 July–1 August 1936.

20–? July 1936, Ogunquit Players, Ogunquit Playhouse, Ogunquit, ME. Produced by the Manhattan Repertory Theatre Company; directed by Walter Hartwig.

5–7 August 1936, Northwestern University, Evanston, IL. Directed by John Baird.

c. 18 August–c. 22 August 1936, Westport Country Playhouse, Westport, CT.

August 1936, Colorado Springs Fine Arts Center, Colorado Springs, CO. Directed by Arthur Strickland.

9–11 September 1936, Mountain Park Casino, Holyoke, MA.

10–28 November 1936, Pittsburgh Playhouse, Pittsburgh, PA. Directed by Herbert V. Gellendre.

16–21 November 1936, Shubert Theatre, Newark, NJ.

17–21 November 1936, Brighton Theater, Brooklyn, NY. Directed by Jack Linder.

25–26 November 1936, Community Playhouse, Albuquerque, NM.

30 November–c. 9 December 1936, Resident Theatre, Kansas City, MO. Directed by W. Zolley Lerner.

2–6 February 1937, Music Auditorium, University of Minnesota, Minneapolis, MN. Directed by Albert Lovejoy.

23 February 1938, Habima Guild, Roosevelt Junior High School, New Brunswick, NJ. Directed by Selma Spielberger.

31 March–1 April 1938, School of Acting Stock Company, Guild Theater, Baltimore, MD.

20–23 July 1938, Civic Theater, St. Louis, MO. Directed by Gordon Carter. Reprised 24 August.

14–19 August 1939, Keene Summer Theatre, Keene, NH. Directed by Freeman Hammond.

13, 15–16 December 1939, McGill Players' Club, Moyse Hall, McGill University, Montréal, QC. Produced by Leslie Johnston; directed by John Melior.

14–16 March 1940, Little Theater of Hartford [company], Avery Memorial, Hartford, CT. Directed by G. Lester Paul.

20–21 November 1940, Pueblo Players, Alhecama Theatre, Santa Barbara, CA. Directed by Douglas Harmer.

3–16 November 1947, Spotlight Players, Spotlight Theater, Akron, OH. Produced and directed by Billie Lahrmer.
24 March–4 April 1948, Pasadena Playhouse, Pasadena, CA. Directed by Samuel R. Herrick.
c. 24 May 1957, East Balcony Theater, Pasadena Playhouse, Pasadena, CA. Directed by Charles Lucas.

The Lonesome West

29–30 June 1936, Hedgerow Theatre, Rose Valley, PA. Cast: Adrienne Bancker, Jay Davis, Happy Sheppard, Jasper Deeter, Cele McLaughlin. Also 7, 13, 24 August; 8 September.

A World Elsewhere

8–13 April 1940, Globe Theater, San Diego, CA. Directed by Riggs. Cast: Alberta Dewhurst (Lupita), Beni Vincent Marquez (Clemente), James Gavin (first mozo), Elsie Jumper (Señora Ortega), Elizabeth Martin (Sarah Jane Elliot), Frances Hervey (Jabby Nash), Eugene Michael (Ramon Chavez), Margaret Woodall (Hedda Chavez), Louis Welk (second mozo), Helen Butler (Claire Bodine), James Holloway (James Bodine III), Gilbert Warner (third mozo), Dan Bowers (Stuart Nash), Melanie Romera (Gardenia Seller), Cliff Robertson (fourth mozo).
5–6 February 1948, Master Institute Theatre, New York, NY. Directed by Joseph Anthony.
23–24 April, 26 April–1 May 1948, University Theater, University of Iowa. Directed by E.C. Mabie.

Hang On to Love (revision of The Domino Parlor)

19–c. 25 August 1940, Red Barn Theatre, Locust Valley, NY. Directed by Arthur Hopkins.
1946, Newark, NJ. See Braunlich, Haunted 201. Production not verified.
30 March 1946, Playbox Theatre, Pasadena Playhouse, Pasadena, CA. Directed by Gilmore Brown.

The Cream in the Well

20 January–8 February 1941, Booth Theatre (Broadway). Produced by Carly Wharton and Martin Gabel; directed by

Martin Gabel. Cast: Martha Sleeper (Julie), Leif Erickson (Clabe), Harry Bratsburg (Blocky Lockhart), Virginia Campbell (Bina), Myron McCormick (Gard Dunham), Mary Morris (Mrs. Sawters), Ralph Theadore (Mr. Sawters), Perry Wilson (Opal Dunham). Tryout: 14–18 January 1941, National Theater, Washington, DC. First Lady Eleanor Roosevelt attended the 18 January tryout performance.
23–24 May 1958, Theatre XIV [company], St. Andrews Auditorium, Philadelphia, PA.
3–7 December 1980, Communication Arts Studio Theater, University of Wisconsin–Parkside, Kenosha, WI. Directed by Norman Gano.

Borned in Texas (revision of Roadside)

NB: A production was widely reported for 9–20 December 1941 at Baylor University, Waco, TX, directed by Riggs. The absence of follow-up is presumably explained by the attack on Pearl Harbor on 7 December and the US's declaration of war on Japan the next day.

30 April 1942, Baylor University Spring Troupers, USO Club, Fort Sill, OK. Directed by Paul Baker. From a 12-week repertory tour, with performances of Borned at six Army bases in Texas and Oklahoma.
4–10 June 1945, Stamford Associates, Strand Theatre, Stamford, NY. Produced by Gus Schirmer Jr.; directed by Victor Jory. Cast: Victor Jory (Texas), Celeste Holm (Hannie Rader).
21–26 August 1950, Fulton Theatre (Broadway). Produced by Festival Theatre, Sam Wanamaker and Terese Hayden; directed by Wanamaker. Cast: Anthony Quinn (Texas), Marsha Hunt (Hannie Rader), Frank Twedell (Pop Rader), Clifford Carpenter (Buzzy Hale), Joseph Boland (Marshall), Dudley Sadler (Neb), Daniel Reed (Judge), Martin Newman (Red Ike), Wright King (Black Ike), Jane Hoffman (Mrs. Foster). Tryout: 14–19 August, Newport Casino, Newport, RI.

Laughter from a Cloud

15–20 July 1947, Woodstock Playhouse, Woodstock, NY. Produced by Jerome Mayer and Milton Baron; directed by Mayer. Cast: Ilka Chase (Lisa Walker), Edmon Ryan (Cleve Walker), Susan Douglas (Ann Ellison), Donald MacDonald

(Dr. Hank Burbage), Peter Harris (Dick Burbage), Ralph Longley (Mason Venn), Cynthia Latham (Addie Hall), Polly Rowles (Fanny Derr), Gene Byron (Crusita), John Heller (Tranquilino). Later tryouts: 21–26 July, John Drew Theatre, East Hampton, NY; 28 July–2 August, Cape Theater, Cape May, NJ; 11–16 August, New England Mutual Hall, Boston, MA; 25–30 August, Brattleboro Summer Theater, Town Hall, Brattleboro, VT; 2–6 September, Olney Theater, Olney, MD. Also August 1947, Tanglewood Theatre, Falmouth, MA (see Braunlich, *Haunted* 205; production not verified). The cast changed considerably during the tryouts.
21 December 1949, New Horizons Theatre, Los Angeles, CA.

All the Way Home

3–7 August 1948, Ridgefield, CT. Produced by Alexander Kirkland; directed by Mary Hunter. Cast: Bambi Lynn (Winnie Mayes), Leona Powers (Mary Mayes), Will Hare (Hugh Blakelee), Helen Kingstead, Lucille Fenton, Crahan Denton, Cliff Sales, Jared Reed. Later tryout: August 10–14, Hunterdon Hills Playhouse, Jutland, NJ.

Out of Dust

8–13 August 1949, Westport County Playhouse, Westport, CT. Produced by the Theatre Guild; directed by Mary Hunter. Cast: Helen Craig, Berry Kroeger, Joan Lorring, Billy (William) Redfield, Edwin Jerome, Hugh Reilly, Robert Foster, Everett Gammon, Crahan Denton, Carleton Carpenter.

Toward the Western Sky

11–13 June 1951, Cain Park Theatre, Cleveland Heights, OH. Staged by Nadine Miles. Original music by Nathan Kroll. Cast: William Evans (Thaddeus Eaton), Barbara Chandler (Abigail Eaton), Eugenie Miller (Louisa Eaton), Shirley Pleshinger (Tabitha Gun), William Jones (Ned Webster), Tony Riendeau (Eben Porter), Donald Holman (Beriah Stow), Jack Eykyn (Amasa Tinker), Ronnie Snyder (Birdsey), Clara Phister (Mrs. Bishop), Angela Romeo (Golda Parmelee), Donald Weightman (John Moses Spafford), Hal Synder ('Lije Clay), Harvey Levin (Anderson Stripwine), Leon Lee (Mr.

Herndon), Jack Held (Aaron Webster), Florence McGlenn (Lydia Addams), Larry Kuhl (Lacy Addams), Ellie Cate (Maisie Mills), Patricia Leatham (Honey Callahan), William McCollom (Professor X), Gene Dingenary (Kurt), Charles King (Jethro), Sterrett Neal (Mr. Clyde).

The Year of Pilar

5–20 January 1952, Amato Opera House, New York, NY. Directed by David Longstreet. Cast: Doris Jordan (Pilar Crespo), Sylvia Meredith (Doña Candita Crespo), Byrne Piven (Trino Crespo), Jack Cannon (Cuco Saldívar).

Textual Apparatus

Sigla

CN-TS1:The Cherokee Night (Lynn Riggs Papers, Department of Special Collections and University Archives, McFarlin Library, University of Tulsa, box 1, folder 9)

CN-TS2:The Cherokee Night (Lynn Riggs Papers, Department of Special Collections and University Archives, McFarlin Library, University of Tulsa, box 2, folder 3)

CN-TS3:The Cherokee Night (Performing Arts Research Collection, New York Public Library, LCOF+ Riggs, L. Cherokee night)

CN-SF: The Cherokee Night, in Riggs, *The Cherokee Night and Russet Mantle* (Samuel French, 1936)

YP-TS1:TheYear of Pilar (Lynn Riggs Papers, Department of Special Collections and University Archives, McFarlin Library, University of Tulsa, box 5, folder 9)

YP-TS2:TheYear of Pilar (Lynn Riggs Papers,Yale Collection of American Literature, Beinecke Rare Book and Manuscript Library,Yale University,YCAL MSS 61, box 21, folder 336)

YP-TS3:TheYear of Pilar (Leverton Theatre Collection Series, Lake Forest College Archives and Special Collections, Lake Forest College, box 2, folder 39)

YP-TS4:TheYear of Pilar (Lucy Kroll Papers, Library of Congress, box 575, folder 4)

YP-SF:TheYear of Pilar, in Riggs, *Four Plays* (Samuel French, 1947)

CW-TS1:The Cream in theWell (Lynn Riggs Papers, Department of Special Collections and University Archives, McFarlin Library, University of Tulsa, box 2, folder 4)

CW-TS2: The Cream in theWell (Lynn Riggs Papers,Yale Collection of American Literature, Beinecke Rare Book and Manuscript Library,Yale University,YCAL MSS 61, box 12, folder 215)

CW-TS3:The Cream in theWell (Lucy Kroll Papers, Library of Congress, box 572, folder 7)

CW-SF:The Cream in theWell, in Riggs, *Four Plays* (Samuel French, 1947)

1. Emendations

Broadview readings appear to the left of the square bracket, followed, when textual precedent is available, by the siglum that identifies the text in which the reading originates. Entries conclude with the rejected reading from the copy-text and, when such readings are extant, from other texts. Crossed-out elements and elements set between arrows indicate, respectively, autograph deletions and additions. The inferior carat (∧) indicates the absence of punctuation; "*om.*" indicates the absence of a word or passage.

The Cherokee Night

83.20 jist like this] j⟨u⟩↑i↑st like this (*CN-TS3*); just like that (*CN-TSS1–2, CN-SF*)

107.13 might' nigh] *CN-TS1*; might 'nigh (*CN-TSS2–3, CN-SF*)

111.19 *(part of which is left out)*; [*part of which is left out*] (*CN-SF*); (part of which is left out) (*CN-TS3*); *om.* (*CN-TSS1–2*)

113.34 Jonas'd] *CN-TSS1–3*; Jonas (*CN-SF*)

117.33 houn' dogs] *CN-TSS1–3*; houn'-|dogs (*CN-SF*)

122.13 any more] *CN-TSS1–3*; anymore (*CN-SF*)

128.28 hifalutin'] *CN-TSS1–2*; hifalutin (*CN-TS–3, CN-SF*)

134.12 waterbucket] *CN-TSS1–2*; water-|bucket (*CN-TS3*); water-bucket (*CN-SF*)

The Year of Pilar

151.21 *la niña Pilar,* Señora] la nina Pilar, Senora (*YP-TSS1–4*); *la niña* Pilar, *Señora* (*YP-SF*)

173.24 gossip-mongers] *YP-TSS1–3*; gossipmongers (*YP-SF*)

174.2 anymore] *YP-TSS1–3*; any more (*YP-TS4,YP-SF*)

178.11 *Ron de caña*] Ron de cana (*YP-TSS1–4*)

179.28 anymore] *YP-TSS1–3*; any more (*YP-SF*)

179.38 *innuendos*] innuendos *YP-TSS1–4*; innuendoes (*YP-SF*)

180.28 anymore] *YP-TSS2–3*; any-|more (*YP-TS1*); any more (*YP-TS4,YP-SF*)

191.2 *Señorita*] Señorita (*YP-TSS1–4, YP-SF*)

196.12 anymore] *TSS1–3*; any more (*YP-TS4,YP-SF*)

222.11 *With easy jocularity*] *CW-TSS1–3*; *Wih easy jocularity*
(*CW-SF*)
224.33 MR. SAWTERS' VOICE] *CW-TS1*; MR. SAWTER'S VOICE
(*CW-TS2–3, CW-SF*)
231.11 MRS. SAWTERS' *words*] *CW-TSS1–2*; MRS. SAWTER'S
words (*CW-TS3, CW-SF*)
234.11 GARD'S VOICE.] Gard's Voice: (*CW-TS1, CW-TS3*);
Gard's Voiceʌ (*CW-TS2*); GARD'S VOICE: (*CW-SF*)
238.13 *lake*] *CW-TS1–2*; *Lake* (*CW-TS3, CW-SF*)
244.26 anymore] *CW-TSS1–2*; any more (*CW-TS3, CW-SF*)
255.3 *Mid-afternoon*] Mid-afternoon (*CW-TSS1–2*);
Mid- | afternoon (*CW-TS3*); *Midafternoon* (*CW-SF*)

2. Textual Notes

The Cherokee Night

84.24 meant to be."] We have added the closing quotation in the
interest of clarity. See next entry.
84.27 "In the gray night] We have added the opening quotation
marks in the interest of clarity. See previous entry.
85.9–10 are you sunk already . . . ?] An immediately preceding
passage in *CN-TS1* is marked for deletion in the stage manager's hand in *CN-TS2*: "Where's the pride in us you had when
you was a boy / on the banks of Panther Crick? / Cherokee
you was then—and proud of it! / What happened to make you
forget? // The long arrow and its song, the scalpin' knife— /
you've spit on, and hid away. / Where have you hid 'em? /
What is your blood—water?" The passage had drawn particular commendation in the *Des Moines Register*'s review of 8
December 1932. Riggs, however, either requested or approved
its deletion, which is honored in *CN-TS3* and *CN-SF*.
105.21–24 GAR *shoots out a hand* . . . . HUTCH'S *voice flounders,
stops.*] On no textual authority, *CN-SF* merges the split stage
direction and introduces the closing sentence with a colon. We
have restored Riggs's setting from *CN-TS2* and *CN-TS3*. The
passage does not appear in *CN-TS1*.
110.30–111.4 *The three back away* . . . . *All below becomes dark.*]
CN-SF again merges two paragraphs, contrary to Riggs's settings in *CN-TSS1–3*. We have again restored Riggs's setting.

147.4 (and following) Yucatán.] See A Note on the Texts, above (p. 61), for our emendations of copy-text readings ("Yucatan," "Senora," etc.) that indicate the compositors' failure to meet Riggs's expectations for typesetting.

159.3 (and following) *Indians*] In *YP-TSS2–4*, Riggs followed his usual practice of uppercasing names of individual and corporate characters in stage directions and at-rise descriptions. This, he knew, would initiate house-styling: "BETO" would become "BETO" and so forth. With one exception in *YP-TS3*, typescripts of *Pilar* style this corporate character "Indians," not "INDIANS." The compositor(s), however, preferred "INDIANS" throughout the first half of the French edition but *"Indians"* thereafter. We have consistently favored *"Indians,"* per Riggs's tendency in his typescripts. We have followed copy-text, and Riggs's cues, by preferring "INDIAN WOMEN" (for "INDIAN WOMEN"), *"Indian* WOMEN" (for "Indian WOMEN"), and "INDIAN MEN" (for "INDIAN MEN") in Scene 6.

175.3 Chichén (and 195.5] The Mayan word is unaccented in the typescripts as in the copy-text; we have preferred the correct form, as Riggs did in his autograph manuscripts.

178.11 *Ron de caña*] The copy-text reading, *ron de cana*, appears in all typescripts, but the locution is absent from the autograph manuscripts to which we have ceded authority at such times. Our emendation fulfills Riggs's implicit expectations. See A Note on the Texts, above (p. 61).

The Cream in the Well

234.12–13 *Scurrying .... she disappears.*] *CW-SF* follows *CW-TS3* in bifurcating Bina's speech and introducing both sections with her name. In *CW-TS3*, the passage extends across a page-break; the repetition of the name was presumably meant to guide French's compositor through the tangle of speech and stage directions that coincided with the break. The compositor reproduced the cue, thus, eccentrically, letting stand consecutive speeches by one character. We follow *CW-TS1* and *CW-TS2* in setting Bina's speech as a single unit.

3. Word-Division

All compounds hyphenated at the end of a line in the Broadview texts are hyphenated in the copy-texts.

Broadview forms of compounds hyphenated at line-end in the copy-texts have been determined by the following hierarchy: 1) manuscriptal forms of the same passage or a clear antecedent; 2) settings elsewhere in the copy-text; 3) settings in other works published in the same volume as the copy-text; and 4) settings in other works by Riggs published by Samuel French.

The following list records our decisions in these instances. Compounds hyphenated at line-end in both the Broadview edition and the copy-text are indicated with an asterisk and have been set per the hierarchy enumerated above.

The Cherokee Night

73.25 *limestone*
78.32 *flashlight*
80.3 goddamned
82.25 half-witted
93.19 bloodshot
94.29 dictaphone
111.24 *bell-tower*
111.35 *bell-rope*
113.1 *sun-bonnets*
114.3 toad-frog
117.33 houn' dogs
120.40 *upstage*
123.38 madmen
126.15 *outskirts*
127.19 Whiteturkey
128.24 Whiteturkey
139.1 GRAY-WOLF'S
139.4 GRAY-WOLF
141.8 GRAY-WOLF
141.12 Gray-Wolf

The Year of Pilar

153.3 whore-house
160.36–37 buck-toothed*
160.38 seaweed

177.31 moonlight
187.27 flea-bitten
200.11–12 first-born*

The Cream in the Well

225.33–34 God-damned*
228.15 post-card
228.28 backbone
244.30 sundown
261.38 loud-mouthed
262.21 fireplace

Works Cited and Select Bibliography

Manuscript Collections

Alice Corbin Henderson Collection. Harry Ransom Center, University of Texas at Austin.

Barrett H. Clark Papers. Yale Collection of American Literature, Beinecke Rare Book and Manuscript Library, Yale University, New Haven, CT.

Betty Kirk Collection. Western History Collections, University of Oklahoma Libraries, Norman.

Horton Foote Papers. DeGolyer Library, Southern Methodist University, Dallas, TX.

Joseph Vann Riggs Collection. Claremore Museum of History, Claremore, OK.

Leo Cundiff Collection. Claremore Museum of History, Claremore, OK.

Leverton Theatre Collection Series, Lake Forest College Archives and Special Collections, Lake Forest College, Lake Forest, IL.

Lucy Kroll Papers. Library of Congress, Washington, DC.

Lucy Kroll Papers Relating to Lynn Riggs. Yale Collection of American Literature, Beinecke Rare Book and Manuscript Library, Yale University, New Haven, CT.

Lynn Riggs Collection. Western History Collections, University of Oklahoma Library, University of Oklahoma, Norman.

Lynn Riggs Family Collection. Claremore Museum of History, Claremore, OK.

Lynn Riggs Papers. Department of Special Collections and University Archives, McFarlin Library, University of Tulsa, Tulsa, OK.

Lynn Riggs Papers. Yale Collection of American Literature, Beinecke Rare Book and Manuscript Library, Yale University, New Haven, CT.

Paul Green Papers. Southern Historical Collection, Louis Round Wilson Special Collections Library, University of North Carolina at Chapel Hill.

Performing Arts Research Collection. New York Public Library, New York, NY.

Walter Stanley Campbell Papers. Western History Collections, University of Oklahoma Library, University of Oklahoma, Norman.

Walter Willard "Spud" Johnson Collection. Harry Ransom Center, University of Texas at Austin.

Witter Bynner Papers. Houghton Library, Harvard University, Cambridge, MA.

Published Plays by Lynn Riggs

Big Lake. Samuel French, 1927.

——— (selection). *Scenes for Student Actors: Dramatic Selections from New Plays,* vol. 2, edited by Frances Cosgrove, Samuel French, 1935, pp. 44–47.

The Cherokee Night. The Cherokee Night and Other Plays, edited by Jace Weaver, U of Oklahoma P, 2003, pp. 109–211.

———. *Russet Mantle and The Cherokee Night,* Samuel French, 1936, pp. 125–262.

——— (selection). *Scenes for Student Actors: Dramatic Selections from New Plays,* vol. 1, edited by Frances Cosgrove, Samuel French, 1934, pp. 20–22.

The Cream in the Well. Four Plays, Samuel French, 1947, pp. 155–222.

——— (selection). *Scenes for Student Actors: Dramatic Selections from New Plays,* vol. 5, edited by Frances Cosgrove, Samuel French, 1942, p. 25.

Dark Encounter. Four Plays, Samuel French, 1947, pp. 223–90.

Green Grow the Lilacs. Samuel French, 1931.

———. *Best American Plays: Supplementary Volume, 1918–1958,* edited by John Gassner, Crown, 1961, pp. 129–68.

———. *Best Plays of 1930–1931,* edited by Burns Mantle, Dodd, Mead, 1931, pp. 147–85.

———. *The Cherokee Night and Other Plays,* edited by Jace Weaver, U of Oklahoma P, 2003, pp. 6–105.

———. Limited edition, illustrated by Thomas Hart Benton, U of Oklahoma P, 1954.

———. *Nine Modern American Plays,* edited by Barrett H. Clark and William H. Davenport, Appleton-Century-Crofts, 1951, pp. 88–135.

———. *Plays for the College Theater,* edited by Garrett H. Leverton, Samuel French, 1934, pp. 513–46.

——— (selection). *Dramatic Scenes from Athens to Broadway,* edited by James B. Lowther, Longmans, 1937, pp. 231–33.

Hang On to Love. Samuel French, 1948.

The Hunger I Got. One-Act Plays for Stage and Study, Samuel French, 1949, 10th series, pp. 117–32.

Knives from Syria. Samuel French, 1928.

———. *One-Act Plays for Stage and Study,* Samuel French, 1927, 3rd series, pp. 191–207.

A Lantern to See By. Sump'n Like Wings and A Lantern to See By: Two Oklahoma Plays, Samuel French, 1928, pp. 99–186.

Out of Dust. The Cherokee Night and Other Plays, edited by Jace Weaver, U of Oklahoma P, 2003, pp. 215–339.

Reckless. The American Scene, compiled by Barrett H. Clark and Kenyon Nicholson, D. Appleton, 1930, pp. 553–66.

———. *One-Act Plays for Stage and Study,* Samuel French, 1928, 4th series, pp. 103–15.

———. *Representative One-Act Plays by American Authors,* rev. ed., edited by Margaret Mayorga, Little, Brown, 1937, pp. 447–62.

Roadside. Samuel French, 1930.

———. *Twenty-Five Modern Plays,* edited by S. Marion Tucker and Alan S. Downer, Harper, 1953, pp. 801–38.

——— (selection). *Play-Readings for School, Radio and Screen Tests,* edited by Louise M. Frankenstein, Samuel French, 1933, pp. 129–57.

——— (selection). *Scenes for Student Actors: Dramatic Selections from New Plays,* vol. 3, edited by Frances Cosgrove, Samuel French, 1937, pp. 105–06.

Russet Mantle. Russet Mantle and The Cherokee Night, Samuel French, 1936, pp. 1–121.

——— (selection). *Scenes for Student Actors: Dramatic Selections from New Plays,* vol. 3, edited by Frances Cosgrove, Samuel French, 1937, pp. 37–38.

——— (selection). *Scenes for Student Actors: Dramatic Selections from New Plays,* vol. 4, edited by Frances Cosgrove, Samuel French, 1939, pp. 114–17.

Sump'n Like Wings. Sump'n Like Wings and A Lantern to See By: Two Oklahoma Plays, Samuel French, 1928, pp. 1–97.

Toward the Western Sky: A Music Play. P of Western Reserve U, 1951.

A World Elsewhere. One-act version, *The Best One-Act Plays of 1939,* edited by Margaret Mayorga, Dodd, Mead, 1940, pp. 31–73.

A World Elsewhere. Two-act version. Samuel French, 1941.

———. *Four Plays,* Samuel French, 1947, pp. 73–154.

The Year of Pilar. Four Plays, Samuel French, 1947, pp. 1–72.

Works Cited

"And Now Lynn Riggs: After Several Ventures in the Theatre, He Arrives With 'Green Grow the Lilacs.'" *New York Times*, 1 February 1931.

Atkinson, Brooks. Review of *The Cherokee Night*, by Lynn Riggs, directed by Jasper Deeter, Hedgerow Theatre (Rose Valley, PA). *New York Times*, 26 June 1932.

——. Review of *The Cream in the Well*, by Lynn Riggs, directed by Martin Gabel, Booth Theatre (New York). *New York Times*, 21 January 1941.

Aughtry, Charles. *Lynn Riggs, Dramatist: A Critical Biography.* 1959. Brown U, PhD dissertation.

Borowitz, Albert. "'Pore Jud is Daid': Violence and Lawlessness in the Plays of Lynn Riggs." *Legal Studies Forum*, vol. 27, no. 1, 2003, pp. 157–84.

Braunlich, Phyllis Cole. *Haunted by Home: The Life and Letters of Lynn Riggs.* U of Oklahoma P, 1988.

Carroll, Walter. "'I Refuse to Care.'" *Durham* [North Carolina] *Herald-Sun*, 4 March 1951.

The Catalog of Copyright Entries. United States Copyright Office. https://onlinebooks.library.upenn.edu/cce/

Chansky, Dorothy. *Composing Ourselves: The Little Theatre Movement and the American Audience.* Southern Illinois UP, 2004.

Clark, Barrett H. *An Hour of American Drama.* Lippincott, 1930.

——. "Our New American Folk Drama." *English Journal*, vol. 16, no. 10, December 1927, pp. 759–70.

Conley, Robert J. *The Cherokee Nation: A History.* U of New Mexico P, 2005.

Cox, James H. "'Saw E. O'Neill ... Yes!': Lynn Riggs to Barrett H. Clark, August 14[, 1928]." *Eugene O'Neill Review*, vol. 44, no. 1, 2023, pp. 1–5.

Deloria, Philip J. *Indians in Unexpected Places.* UP of Kansas, 2006.

Denson, Andrew. *Demanding the Cherokee Nation: Indian Autonomy and American Culture, 1830–1900.* U of Nebraska P, 2004.

Dobie, J. Frank. *Guide to Life and Literature of the Southwest.* U of Texas P, 1931.

——. *Guide to Life and Literature of the Southwest.* Rev. ed., Southern Methodist UP, 1952.

Dobujinsky, Mstislav. "Jilinsky—and Soloviova—Remembered."

Andrius Jilinsky, *The Joy of Acting: A Primer for Actors*, edited by Helen C. Bragdon, Peter Lang, 1990, pp. 147–57.

Erhard, Thomas. *Lynn Riggs: Southwest Playwright*. Steck-Vaughn, 1970.

Ezell, Brice. E-mail to the editors. 14 December 2022.

Fallaw, Ben. *Cárdenas Compromised: The Failure of Reform in Postrevolutionary Yucatán*. Duke UP, 2001.

Garroutte, Eva Marie. *Real Indians: Identity and the Survival of Native America*. U of California P, 2003.

Green, Paul. *A Southern Life: Letters of Paul Green, 1916–1981*. Edited by Laurence G. Avery, U of North Carolina P, 1994.

"Group's Play Award." [New York] *Daily News*, 22 March 1939.

Hammerstein, Oscar. Letter to the drama editor. *New York Times*, 5 September 1943.

Horbal, Bodgan. "NYPL Researcher Spotlight: Kristy Ironside." New York Public Library, 2 November 2022, https://www.nypl. org/blog/2022/11/02/nypl-researcher-spotlight-kristy-ironside

"Intermission Entertainment Will Feature Army Show." *Richmond News Leader*, 3 September 1943.

Jilinsky, Andrius. *The Joy of Acting: A Primer for Actors*. Edited by Helen C. Bragdon, Peter Lang, 1990.

Larkin, Margaret, editor, and Helen Black, arranger. *Singing Cowboy: A Book of Western Songs*. Knopf, 1931.

"Lee's Show to Feature Dance Team." *Richmond News Leader*, 2 September 1943.

Little Thunder, Julie. "Mixedbloods and Bloodlust in *Cherokee Night*." *The Midwest Quarterly: A Journal of Contemporary Thought*, vol. 43, no. 4, Summer 2002, pp. 355–65.

Mantle, Burns. Review of *Big Lake*, by Lynn Riggs, directed by George Auerbach, American Laboratory Theatre (New York). [New York] *Daily News*, 9 April 1927.

———. Review of *The Cream in the Well*, by Lynn Riggs, directed by Martin Gabel, Booth Theatre (New York). [New York] *Daily News*, 21 January 1941.

Mathews, John Joseph. *The Osages: Children of the Middle Waters*. U of Oklahoma P, 1961.

McDermott, William F. Review of *The Cherokee Night*, by Lynn Riggs, directed by Clancy Douglas Cooper, Little Theater of Public Hall (Cleveland, OH). *Cleveland Plain Dealer*, 13 February 1933.

Miles, Tiya. *Ties That Bind: The Story of an Afro-Cherokee Family in Slavery and Freedom*. U of California P, 2005.

"News of the Stage." *New York Times*, 2 January 1941.

O'Brien, Jack. "SUI Theater Holds Pre-Broadway Hearing of Riggs' Play." Review of *A World Elsewhere*, by Lynn Riggs. *Daily Iowan*, 23 April 1948.

O'Neill, Eugene. *Dynamo*. *Complete Plays, 1920–1931*, edited by Travis Bogard, Library of America, 1988, pp. 819–85.

———. Letter to George Jean Nathan, 3 September 1927. *"As Ever, Gene": The Letters of Eugene O'Neill to George Jean Nathan*, edited by Nancy L. Roberts and Arthur W. Roberts, Fairleigh Dickinson UP, 1987, pp. 73–74.

Pautz, Michelle C. "The Decline in Average Weekly Cinema Attendance, 1930–2000." https://ecommons.udayton.edu/cgi/viewcontent.cgi?article=1023&context=pol_fac_pub

Peery, William. "American Folk Drama Comes of Age." *American Scholar*, vol. 11, no. 2, 1942, pp. 149–57.

Pollack, Arthur. Review of *The Cream in the Well*, by Lynn Riggs, directed by Martin Gabel, Booth Theatre (New York). *Brooklyn Daily Eagle*, 26 January 1941.

Prickett, Stacey. "Dancing the American Dream During World War II." *Dance and Politics*, edited by Alexandra Kolb, Peter Lang, 2011, pp. 167–92.

"Proof that Persistence Wins." *University of Oklahoma Magazine*, vol. 10, no. 2, February 1922, p. 5.

Rauh, Ida. Letter to the drama editor. *New York Times*, 2 February 1941.

"Rialto Rambling." *Brooklyn Citizen*, 28 October 1938.

Riggs, Lynn. *Cowboy Songs, Folk Songs and Ballads from "Green Grow the Lilacs."* Samuel French, 1932.

———. "High, Wide, and Handsome." Review of *Singing Cowboy: A Book of Western Songs*, collected and edited by Margaret Larkin, piano arrangements by Helen Black. *The Nation*, vol. 133, no. 3467, 16 December 1931, p. 674.

———. Letter to Barrett H. Clark, 26 June 1931. Private collection, www.carpelibrumbooks.com/lynn-riggs-tls-to-barrett-clark-1931.

———. "We Speak for Ourselves: A Dance Poem." *Theatre Arts*, vol. 27, no. 12, December 1943, pp. 752–57.

Sandburg, Carl. *The American Songbag*. Harcourt, Brace, 1927.

Shanley, John P. "Trouble in Yucatan." *New York Times*, 7 January 1952.

Stanislavsky, Konstantin. *My Life in Art*. Translated by J.J. Robbins, Little, Brown, 1924.

Sturm, Circe. *Blood Politics: Race, Culture, and Identity in the Cherokee Nation of Oklahoma*. U of California P, 2002.

Vestal, Stanley [Walter Stanley Campbell]. "Lynn Riggs: Poet and Dramatist." *Southwest Review*, vol. 15, no. 1, Autumn 1929, pp. 64–71.

Weaver, Jace. Foreword. *The Cherokee Night and Other Plays*, by Lynn Riggs, edited by Jace Weaver, U of Oklahoma P, 2003, pp. ix–xv.

———. *That the People Might Live: Native American Literatures and Native American Communities*. Oxford UP, 1997.

Webster, Ann. Letter to the drama editor. *New York Times*, 9 March 1941.

Weitzencamp, Mark Philip. "The Influence of Barrett H. Clark on American Theatre." 2003. U of Wyoming, PhD dissertation.

Wilson, Eloise. "Lynn Riggs, Oklahoma Dramatist." 1957. U of Pennsylvania, PhD dissertation.

Wolf, Mary Hunter. "Reminiscences of Andrius Jilinsky and His Teaching." *Wandering Stars: Russian Emigré Theatre, 1905–1940*, edited by Laurence Senelick, U of Iowa P, 1992, pp. 129–39.

Further Reading

Allen, Chadwick. "When a Mound Isn't a Mound, But Is: Figuring (and Fissuring) Earthworks in Lynn Riggs's *The Cherokee Night*." *The Routledge Handbook of North American Indigenous Modernisms*, edited by Kirby Brown et al., Routledge, 2023, pp. 17–28.

Braunlich, Phyllis Cole. "*The Cherokee Night* of R. Lynn Riggs." *The Midwest Quarterly: A Journal of Contemporary Thought*, vol. 30, no. 1, Autumn 1988, pp. 45–59.

Brown, Kirby. *Stoking the Fire: Nationhood in Cherokee Writing, 1907–1970*. U of Oklahoma P, 2018.

Conley, Robert J. *A Cherokee Encyclopedia*. U of New Mexico P, 2007.

Cox, James H. *The Political Arrays of American Indian Literary History*. U of Minnesota P, 2019.

———. *The Red Land to the South: American Indian Writers and Indigenous Mexico*. U of Minnesota P, 2012.

Cox, James H., and Alexander Pettit. "Fugitive Indigeneity in Paul Green's *The Last of the Lowries* and Lynn Riggs's *The Cherokee Night*." *The Routledge Handbook of North American Indigenous Modernisms*, edited by Kirby Brown et al., Routledge, 2023, pp. 182–90.

Darby, Jaye. "Broadway (Un)Bound: Lynn Riggs's *The Cherokee Night*." *Baylor Journal of Theater and Performance*, vol. 4, no. 1, Spring 2007, pp. 7–23.

A Day in Santa Fe. Directed by Lynn Riggs and James Hughes, 1931. *Unseen Cinema: Early American Avant-Garde Film 1894–1941*, curated by Bruce Posner, Anthology Film Archives, 2005, vol. 6.

Driskill, Qwo-Li. "Ha'nts: The Booger Dance Rhetorics of Lynn Riggs's *The Cherokee Night*." *American Indian Performing Arts: Critical Directions*, edited by Hanay Geiogamah and Jaye Darby, UCLA American Indian Studies Center, 2009, pp. 179–96.

Eaton, Rachel Caroline. "The Legend of the Battle of Claremore Mound." *Chronicles of Oklahoma*, vol. 8, no. 4, December 1930, pp. 369–76.

Goins, Charles Robert, et al. *Historical Atlas of Oklahoma*. 4th ed., U of Oklahoma P, 2006.

Justice, Daniel Heath. *Our Fire Survives the Storm: A Cherokee Literary History*. U of Minnesota P, 2006.

Knight, Alan. "Racism, Revolution, and Indigenismo: Mexico, 1910–1940." *The Idea of Race in Latin America, 1870–1940*, edited by Richard Graham, U of Texas P, 1990, pp. 71–113.

Kraft, James. *Who is Witter Bynner? A Biography*. U of New Mexico P, 1995.

Lowe, Robert Liddell. "The Lyrics of Lynn Riggs." *Poetry*, March 1931, pp. 347–49.

Mihesuah, Devon A. *Cultivating the Rosebuds: The Education of Women at the Cherokee Female Seminary, 1851–1909*. U of Illinois P, 1993.

Mooney, James. *Myths of the Cherokees*. Government Printing Office, 1900.

Reed, Nelson. *The Caste War of Yucatán*. Rev. ed., Stanford UP, 2001.

Starr, Emmet. *History of the Cherokee Indians and Their Legends and Folk Lore*. Warden, 1921.

Ware, Amy M. *The Cherokee Kid: Will Rogers, Tribal Identity, and the Making of an American Icon*. UP of Kansas, 2015.

Weaver, Jace. *That the People Might Live: Native American Literatures and Native American Communities*. Oxford UP, 1997.

Womack, Craig S. *Red on Red: Native American Literary Separatism*. U of Minnesota P, 1999.

Permissions Acknowledgements

The following material by Lynn Riggs is published by permission of the Estate of Lynn Riggs. All rights reserved.

The Cherokee Night (1932)
The Year of Pilar (1938)
The Cream in the Well (1941)
"A Credo for the Tributary Theatre" (1940)
"We Speak for Ourselves" (1943)
"High, Wide, and Handsome" (1931)
"When People Say 'Folk Drama'" (1931)
"A Note on 'We Speak for Ourselves'" (1943)
"Poetry—And Poetry in the Theatre" (1932)
Letter to Paul Green ("Vine Theatre Letter") (1939)
"Some Notes on the Theatre" (1940)
"What the Theatre Can Mean" (1940)

Image credit: Postcard with photograph of Claremore Mound and text to Barrett Clark (1931). Image courtesy of the Beinecke Rare Book and Manuscript Library, Barrett H. Clark papers. Text on reverse published by permission of the Estate of Lynn Riggs.

Index

Page numbers in italics denote illustrations, footnotes are indicated by "n" followed by the note number, and unnumbered locators indicate notes continued on the subsequent page.

French theatre, 287–88, 287n4, 288n1
Frost, Robert, 19, 51
Fulton Theatre (Broadway), 50

Gabel, Martin, 64
Gasque-Molina, Enrique. *See* Naya, Ramón
Geddes, Virgil, 31
General Allotment Act (1887). *See* Dawes Act (1887)
German theatre, 286, 286n4, 288, 288n2
Gershwin, George, 35, 47
Glaspell, Susan, 31, 44
The Glass Menagerie (Williams), 37
Globe Theatre (The Old Globe), 23, 48, 301
Goldwyn, Samuel, 46
Graham, Martha, 292, 292n2
Green, Paul
  and *The Cherokee Night*, 26, 45
  correspondence with Riggs, 58, 59–60
  as folk dramatist, 31, 33, 279
  friendship with Riggs, 17
  The Lost Colony, 33, 50–51
  and "Vine Theatre Letter," 33, 47, 289–300
Green Grow the Lilacs (Riggs)
  adaptation as *Oklahoma!*, 22–23, 24, 39, 49, 60
  composition of, 43–44
  limited edition published, 38
  movie rights, 46
  productions of, 22, 45–46, 326–34
  reading of, 45
  success of, 21–22, 45–46
Greenwich Village Players, 32
Guide to Life and Literature of the Southwest (Dobie), 33, 39
Guild Theatre (Broadway), 45

Hammerstein, Oscar II, 22–23, 49, 60, 326

Hardré, Jacques, 51
Haunted by Home (Braunlich), 39, 41, 53
Hedda Gabler (Ibsen), 310, 310n1
Hedgerow Theatre, Moylan, Pennsylvania, 20, 27, 31, 45, 55
Helburn, Theresa, 49
Hinkley, Ray E., 312, 312n1
Hollywood, California, 18, 34–35, 42, 44, 46, 47, 289
Holm, Hanya, 292, 292n2, 312n1
Hopkins, Arthur, 21
Howard, Sidney, 279
Huey, Anna V., 45
Hughes, Hatcher, 43
Hughes, Jim, 45
Humphrey, Doris, 292, 292n2, 312, 312n1
Hunnef, Jenna, 40
Hunter, Mary. *See* Wolf, Mary Hunter

Ibsen, Henrik, 310nn1–2
Indian Territory
  geography of, 11–12, 71n2
  in Riggs's work, 13, 14, 17, 20, 21, 22–23, 25, 25n1, 29–30, 33
  loss of land and autonomy, 13–14, 18, 18n2, 25–26, 30, 121n2, 225n2
  Riggs family allotments, 10, 11, 18, 18n3, 41
  Riggs's youth in, 18, 20n2, 41
  See also Cherokee Nation, Oklahoma; Oklahoma
Inge, William, 37
Iowa City, 46, 283

Jesus Christ, 293
Jilinsky, Andrius
  and American Actors Company, 299, 300n1
  life and career, 290n2, 299n3, 300n1
  on Ramón Naya, 300n2

About the Publisher

The word "broadview" expresses a good deal of the
philosophy behind our company. Our focus is very
much on the humanities and social sciences—especially
literature, writing, and philosophy—but within these fields
we are open to a broad range of academic approaches
and political viewpoints. We strive in particular to
produce high-quality, pedagogically useful books for
higher education classrooms—anthologies, editions,
sourcebooks, surveys of particular academic fields and
sub-fields, and also course texts for subjects such as
composition, business communication, and critical
thinking. We welcome the perspectives of authors from
marginalized and underrepresented groups, and we have
a strong commitment to the environment. We publish
English-language works and translations from many parts
of the world, and our books are available world-wide;
we also publish a select list of titles with a specifically
Canadian emphasis.

broadview press